A HISTORY OF CATHOLIC THEOLOGICAL ETHICS

James F. Keenan, SJ

Paulist Press
New York / Mahwah, NJ

Cover image by Sunset And Sea Design / Shutterstock.com
Cover and book design by Lynn Else

Library of Congress Cataloging-in-Publication Data
Names: Keenan, James F., author.
Title: A history of Catholic theological ethics / James Keenan, SJ.
Description: New York ; Mahwah : Paulist Press, [2022] | Includes index. | Summary: "An introduction to Catholic theological ethics through the lens of its historical development from the beginning of the church until today"—Provided by publisher.
Identifiers: LCCN 2021048890 (print) | LCCN 2021048891 (ebook) | ISBN 9780809155446 (paperback) | ISBN 9781587689420 (ebook)
Subjects: LCSH: Christian ethics—Catholic authors—History.
Classification: LCC BJ1249 .K3769 2022 (print) | LCC BJ1249 (ebook) | DDC 241—dc23/eng/20211115
LC record available at https://lccn.loc.gov/2021048890
LC ebook record available at https://lccn.loc.gov/2021048891

ISBN 978-0-8091-5544-6 (paperback)
ISBN 978-1-58768-942-0 (e-book)

Published by Paulist Press
997 Macarthur Boulevard
Mahwah, New Jersey 07430
www.paulistpress.com

Printed and bound in the
United States of America

To my colleagues in
Catholic Theological Ethics in the World Church
We have an extraordinary vocation
and are blessed in our calling.
I love working with you.

Contents

Preface

True story.

In late March 1981, a year before I would be ordained a priest, I was living in Cambridge, Massachusetts, studying theology at what was then called Weston Jesuit School of Theology. The phone in the hallway rang and I answered it. The caller asked, "Can I speak to Jim Keenan?" "Speaking." "Jim, it's Al. I'd like to see you." "Al? Al, who?" "Al Bartlett, your vice provincial for formation." "Oh, hi, Al. You want to see me? When?" "Today or tomorrow if necessary." "But I'm in Cambridge and you are in New York." "No, I'm in Cambridge." "Why?" "To see you." "But, Al, everybody else from the province is away." "No matter, I only came to see you."

In the history of religious life, unannounced visits by religious superiors are rarely a cause for joy.

"Where are you?" "Across the street, at the superior's office." My anxiety surged. "I will be right there."

When I met with Al Bartlett, he told me he had come because the previous day the provincial consultors met and, during the meeting, the provincial made the decision I was to do doctoral studies. "Since we made the decision yesterday, we thought you should be the first to know."

In 1981 I had been a Jesuit for eleven years, facing one more year before ordination. This was the first time I had ever considered doctoral studies. "In what?" I asked. "We thought maybe urban studies, maybe political science. Does not matter. We want you to a get doctorate and you and I are meeting tomorrow right here at the same time, and you are going to tell me what you will study."

Ignatian discernment for Jesuits is a lot more rushed than when it is offered to our lay colleagues.

I decided I would wait until dinner to ask my community members what they thought. I need to mention that among the dozen community members were two superb theologians: Brian Daley and John O'Malley. In my years at Weston Jesuit, I effectively became John's disciple. I took several courses with him, but it was by living with him that I learned what living scholarship was like. His influence on my way of articulating and pursuing both pedagogical and research goals, as a theologian, is without parallel.

When I told my community about my day, to my astonishment, there was an immediate consensus on two points: thank God somebody told me to do a doctorate (O'Malley was the loudest on this point), and that I should study moral theology. Why? According to them, whenever I spoke up in class on any matter related to moral theology, I was insightful and interesting.

I never had such validation in one day.

The next day, I went to see Al. Moral theology, I told him.

"Where?" he asked. I said, "Probably the Gregorian University in Rome, I want to study the tradition and I want to study with Josef Fuchs."

And so I did.

I went to study in Rome because I believed that the Catholic moral tradition was richer and more complex and less repressive and more responsive than most thought it was. In 1981, in the United States, I believed progressives were not much interested in the tradition, while conservatives were very interested in keeping it tethered to the past. I believed only by going to Rome could I learn the tradition well.

In hindsight, I do not know if the Gregorian University was the best place to learn the tradition, but I got what I wanted. I studied especially with two exceptional moralists, Klaus Demmer, MSC (1931–2014)[1] and Josef Fuchs, SJ (1912–2005).[2] I did my licentiate with Demmer and my doctorate with Fuchs, being the last student who enrolled with him. Besides their direction, I studied several courses with wonderful teachers like Louis Vereecke, CSsR (1920–2012), Edouard Hamel, SJ (1920–2008), Wilhelm Ernst (1927–2001), Francis A. Sullivan, SJ (1922–2019), Jared Wicks, SJ (1929–), and Jean Zizioulas (1931–). Every one of these faculty members was interested in an understanding of theology as rooted in a living and ongoing tradition.

Preface

In my years of teaching since starting in 1987, I have been trying to share with my students an appreciation for the humane complexity and giftedness of the tradition. Therein along the way I have been trying to put together a narrative of that tradition.

To fashion that narrative, I have developed over the past thirty-three years a repertoire of graduate courses that might give you an idea of how I have worked to write these pages that you have now in your hand. One was a reading of the *Pars Secunda* of Thomas Aquinas's *Summa Theologiae*. This course covers the entire middle part of the *Summa*, which singularly focuses on moral theology: the 114 questions of the first section, which provides the foundations, and 189 questions of the second section, which covers the specifics of morals according to the seven virtues. I enjoy watching graduate students eventually engage scholastic language as they grow in familiarity with it and then begin to appreciate the development of Aquinas's theology, to say nothing of the breadth, depth, and nuance of it.

I have also developed a course entitled "Catholic Theological Ethics: 1300–1900." Here I taught basically a major text each class: Peter Abelard's *Ethics*, Peter Lombard's *Fourth Book of the Sentences*, major questions from Thomas's *Summa*, disputation texts of Duns Scotus and William of Ockham, Erasmus's *Enchiridion* and *The Complaint of Peace*, Francisco de Vitoria's *Political Writings*, Bartolomé de las Casas's *In Defense of the Indians*, *The Catechism of the Council of Trent*, Francisco Suárez's *A Treatise on Laws and God the Lawgiver*, a number of texts on Jesuit casuistry such as Friederich Spee's *Cautio Criminalis*, and Alphonsus Liguori's *On Conscience*.

I have also taught a history of the twentieth century, studying how a century that so definitively began with little inclination for any kind of change became a century not unlike the sixteenth century, a time of enormous challenge and accompanying innovation. This allowed me to get a sense of what it was like to slow down the narrative and descend into the particular.

My favorite graduate course has remained the same for these thirty-three years, "An Introduction to Fundamental Morals," in which I take fundamental concepts like sin, conscience, intentionality, and virtue and try to show the historical/traditional claims they have on us. This book is born out of that course.

In the middle of offering these courses, around 1994, Daniel

Harrington invited me to team-teach a course on the New Testament and ethics. Dan and I taught together for more than twenty years, first teaching the Synoptic Gospels, then Paul, and finally the Gospel of John. That experience with Dan convinced me that this history needed to start with the New Testament.

Now, at this point, I offer you a brief history of Catholic theological ethics and I need to conclude with three points of explanation. First, let me say a word about the difference between moral theology and theological ethics. Until the end of the last century, moral theology was about the formation of judgment for one's personal and interpersonal conduct. As such, basic courses on moral theology have been taught from the time seminaries were designed, that is, in the wake of the Council of Trent. At the start, this area was quite comprehensive. In time, other separate fields of investigation arose, notably sexual ethics, in part because the hierarchy dedicated so much time to this topic, and then in the late nineteenth century, social ethics, which effectively developed when Pope Leo XIII (1810–1903) promulgated the first social encyclical, *Rerum Novarum* (1891). Later, another field developed in the 1950s known as medical ethics. Later, after Vatican II, questions were raised about how moral theology taught its foundational anthropology or vision about the person. Rather than emphasizing the person's uniqueness, a significant turn developed about the person as constitutively relational or social. In time, moral theology needed to be integrated not only with sexual and medical ethics but also with social ethics. This more comprehensive, inclusive view, which in fact is how the field started in the beginning of the seventeenth century, is what we now call theological ethics.

Second, though this work is called a history, I am not a historian and in fact most of those who have already tried to offer a history were, like me, theological ethicists. Here I think of John Mahoney's *The Making of Moral Theology: A Study of the Roman Catholic Tradition,*[3] John Gallagher's *Time Past, Time Future: An Historical Study of Catholic Moral Theology,*[4] and Renzo Gerardi's *Storia della Morale: Interpretazioni teologiche dell'esperienza Cristiana.*[5] My attempt is different from theirs. Gallagher was very much focused on the *proprium* of moral theology. As we will see in the fifth chapter, moral theology does not become an actual field of inquiry until the Council of Trent and its subsequent formation of seminary education. Gallagher superbly took us through the accomplishment of Trent and its legacy from the so-called moral manuals, or textbooks. Rather than Gallagher's explication of these texts, Mahoney's interests were to name and study some of the sources of the moral tradition that may have compromised a more Spirit-based moral theology that could more faithfully serve the people of God. His was a work aiming at reform. Gerardi framed a variety of theological interpretations of Christian experience and presented them in a historico-encyclopedic fashion. His was a foundational resource for teachers in the field.

I take from Mahoney and Gerardi the belief that moral theology is more than the moral manuals, but unlike Mahoney I believe that the tradition was founded on the pursuit of holiness and not, as he believed, on the confession of sin. Unlike Gerardi's more episodic focus, I attempt more of a narrative.

Moreover, in crafting a narrative, I am less interested in the historical development of particular moral concepts like sin, conscience, authority, or the virtues, nor in particular teachings on divorce, marriage, abortion, and the like. These later topics have been done already by, among others, John T. Noonan Jr. I am trying, instead, to make sense out of why at different times particular ways of thinking about the moral life arose, crested, and ebbed, and why other topics, stances, and methods subsequently replaced them.

I develop this narrative aware of you the reader. I am welcoming you into my classroom. Here as a teacher, I am not only presenting why these historical cultures happened, but I am giving my particular read on them. In a word, I am trying to teach you the moral tradition as I understand it, and I believe that you the reader come to this text with a set of presuppositions that I very much am interested in engaging. Hopefully what I offer takes you beyond your present understanding of the tradition. Still, the narrative that I offer is neither seamless nor complete. Rather it's fragmentary, as Mahoney's and Gerardi's were as well.

While studying at Weston Jesuit, I learned that the work of theology is to bring the tradition forward so that the people of God have the resources to respond and to anticipate the challenges that they encounter. There, I learned that bringing the tradition forward made sense; the very word *tradition* comes from the Latin *tradere*, "to deliver, hand over, or bring forth." In a word, the tradition is something that you pass on, but as you do, it has to be adaptable, able to address what it will encounter in the future. There I learned that the tradition has to develop and adjust if it is going to help us live out our connection not only to the past but to the future.

When I studied theology in Rome, I learned that working with the tradition was fundamentally a progressive work; progress is constitutive of the tradition. From Demmer and Fuchs I learned that while history narrates the development of the tradition, theological ethics must occasion such a development.

This book is about those who occasioned such developments; it is about those responsible for the progress of theological ethics. That is how I teach theological ethics, as an enterprise that literally responds ethically to the emerging signs of the times.

Many histories about the development of thought highlight the masterpieces within a tradition. We will do that, certainly by looking at Augustine and Thomas Aquinas, but more than the magnificent achievements within the tradition, I want to introduce you to the innovators. I want you to meet those who took the long view of the future, proposing a new approach, method, insight, or strategy to go forward.

I want to introduce you to those who have been long overlooked because they did not do a masterpiece like the *Confessions* or the *Summa Theologiae*. Yet until you understand the innovators, you will not understand how theological ethicists really think, and if you do not know how they think, you will not learn the history of moral theology.

I believe, as you will see, that the history was formed not by the grand achievers but more by the innovators: they took the first step; the achievers perfected those steps.

Take, for instance, Abelard's *Sic et Non*. Probably most of you do not *yet* know it, but once you understand what Abelard did there, you will realize how Aquinas and others conceptualized a *Summa*. Abelard's text was the first blueprint for Aquinas's. Similarly, the casuistry of the mid-sixteenth century was ignited when John Mair, years before anyone else, argued through the case method in his *Commentary on the Fourth Book of the Sentences*. And, although everyone knows the achievement of Jesuit Francisco Suárez, the canvas on international law was well developed by Francisco de Vitoria, seventy years earlier.

In the last chapter that leads us to the incredible transitional period of the twentieth century, we will see one innovator after the other. We start with Alphonsus Liguori who brought advocacy, pastoral care, and moral theology together in a way that no one in theological ethics did before and conclude the book with two other innovators, William Spohn and Yiu Sing Lúcás Chan, who chartered the field of biblical ethics, which, thanks to them, is just now emerging.

My narrative is then a corrective, by finally recognizing the oft-overlooked innovators who had the imagination, vision, diligence, and fortitude to carry the tradition forward. I am interested in you learning about these innovators; learning from innovators, we learn too to anticipate tomorrow by reading the indicators today.

Finally, forty years after Al's surprise visit, I am ready to share this first attempt of my understanding of the tradition that I have been so interested in knowing. It is very much a first attempt. I hope that it generates others to try to do similar projects, that by offering my reflections, others will subsequently want to develop theirs, by correcting, negating, expanding, or critiquing what I have done here. I hope that this project empowers others who want to give a more global approach or a less Eurocentric one than what I provided here, though I hope they find in this offering a worthy cornerstone, or better, a foundational slab.

Indeed, hopefully this will yield other histories of theological ethics that highlight more effectively the voices and arguments of women or the thoughts and practices of particularly inspired movements. These are all much needed.

I close noting that a colleague and friend of mine in Vienna, Sigrid Müller, is working now on a similar history that likewise begins with the Bible and ends with Pope Francis.[6] Hers, I suspect, will be more "academic" than mine. Still, we both believe that such works are needed now, believing that we can be assisted in living the moral life as Roman Catholics by appreciating the developments of the tradition. And therein hopefully by understanding the rich and complex ways that our predecessors pursued and lived the moral life, we might also, like them, understand the call to "Go and do likewise."

Acknowledgments

In 1979 I had my first course in theology at Weston Jesuit School of Theology. It was with John O'Malley, the church historian, and it was unforgettable. I was assigned to live in the same small Jesuit community with him. During my three years as a student there he became my mentor and friend and, happily, remains so to this day.

At Weston I learned that the Roman Catholic tradition needed to be received and developed in every generation if it was to be carried forward into the next generation. That appropriation and participation in the active shaping of the tradition was the work of all of my teachers at Weston, from our canon law professor, Jack Finnegan, who repeatedly told us that the tradition was "not the dead faith of the living, but the living faith of the dead," to Francine Cardman, Peter Fink, Daniel Harrington, and Stanley Marrow, among others.

There too I became introduced to moral theology and studied with Lisa Sowle Cahill, David Hollenbach, and Edward Vacek. Above all, Sr. Mary Emil Penet, IHM, who had been mentored by Josef Fuchs before arriving at Weston, incited in me the call to moral theology.

In 1982 I went to the Gregorian University in Rome to study the tradition of moral theology. Josef Fuchs and Klaus Demmer became my mentors, and I am proud to say that I was the last student to come under Fuchs's tutelage, writing for him my dissertation on Thomas Aquinas.

There, I also studied with Francis Sullivan and the Redemptorist Louis Vereecke who taught us our history of moral theology courses. I also read nearly all the accounts of the development of moral theology by John T. Noonan Jr. Later, I studied the works by the historian of bioethics and casuistry, Albert Jonsen, with whom I enjoyed many wonderful conversations when I was the Lane Center Summer Scholar in Residence at the University of San Francisco.

Finally, Jack Mahoney, in his ground-breaking and magisterial *The Making of Moral Theology: A Study of the Roman Catholic Tradition,* provided me with the terrain and pathway for doing my own version of this history. I applaud him for his recent *The Holy Spirit and Moral Action in Thomas Aquinas.*

In 1987 I began teaching and since then I have tried to cultivate among my students, whether at Fordham University, Weston Jesuit School of Theology, John Carroll University, Loyola School of Theology in Manila, Dharmaram in Bangalore, Jnana Deepa in Pune, the Gregorian University, or Boston College, an appreciation for the call to understand, receive, shape, and advance the moral tradition. At Boston College, for nearly twenty years now, I do this work with a wonderful cohort of friends: Lisa Sowle Cahill, Daniel Daly, Kristin Heyer, Kenneth Himes, OFM, Mary Jo Iozzio, M. Cathleen Kaveny, Stephen Pope, and Andrea Vicini.

All these people influenced me in writing this book, and I am grateful for what I learned from them.

A few others have more directly shepherded this text from me to you and they are notably the people at Paulist Press. Among these is Mark-David Janus, who welcomed the project, encouraged me throughout the years, and assigned in 2013 Christopher Bellitto to be my editor. For these eight years, Chris has exceptionally accompanied me, generously and wisely advising me every step of the way. Thank you, Chris, for your patience with me but even more for your keen eye, prudential judgment, and unflagging encouragement. Finally, Donna Crilly has seen this project through from submission to publication with her characteristically warm and engaging professionalism.

Over the years I have had several wonderful Boston College undergraduate and graduate research fellows assisting me whom I want to thank here: Daniel Cattolica, Connor Murphy, Luke Murphy, Jacob McErlean, Liam Haffey, Sara Samir, Charles Powers, Aidan O'Neill, Grace Christenson, Emma McDonald, and the indefatigable Lindsay Marcellus.

Finally, I have the real pleasure through Catholic Theological Ethics in the World Church to work with my colleagues in theological ethics all around the world. I love our work together serving the church and the world. I pray in thanksgiving for you and for all who have prompted in me the common call to act justly, love with mercy, and walk humbly with our God.

Chapter One

Jesus in the New Testament

The Inspiration and Foundation of Catholic Theological Ethics

I. PRELIMINARIES

Why Start with the New Testament?

The New Testament is the necessary place to start a brief history of Catholic theological ethics. Other authors have begun their histories by looking at early Christian texts, at sociological claims about the lifestyles of early Christians, or at the lives of early charismatic figures who influenced others to emulate them. In a way, we will do that in chapter 2 when we study the early life of the church. From there on, we will look at how the church taught what today we call theological ethics.

We start with the Scriptures because we cannot simply recount our history as a narrative of what was taught from one generation to another. A history of Catholic theological ethics can never be simply a descriptive account, like the history of a war, of the development of a nation, or of the discovery of a new drug. Those histories have their standards of evaluation answering the question: But did it happen that way?

A history of Catholic theological ethics must certainly be measured by that same standard, but it is simultaneously a history of what we claim to be moral truth and, therefore, it claims to be instructing us in what ought to happen and what ought not to happen. It makes these claims precisely because we share the same faith in Jesus Christ. Therefore, we cannot simply ask, were these the teachings that were taught? We also have to ask, but were those teachings true to the faith in Jesus Christ?

Because our teachings claim to be moral, we as members of the church must in conscience ask the question about their truthfulness. This question arises not from doubt or suspicion, but from faith and trust. We must read our history of moral teaching against the Christ event, for the truthfulness of the teachings depends on that. Are our teachings on abortion, divorce, capital punishment, money lending, slavery, war, and so on, true to the message that Christ brought to us?

Of course, these teachings develop and/or are changed and articulated differently as the years advance, as circumstances shift, and as insight grows or diminishes. We will not be able to stop at any one moment and say, "Hold that historical frame: this is the most correct expression of the moral truth that we can have." Neither history nor our humanity affords us these moments of freezing, for forever, moral truth. Moral truth does not escape history.

Nevertheless, as we read this history, we need to have a basic guide or set of claims that prompt in us a *critical read* of our history. We need to have, if you will, in the back of our minds, the blueprint of the Christ event, so that we can read this history as Catholics in faith looking for moral truth.

Moreover, our teachings are called Catholic not simply because popes, bishops, or theologians actually taught them as such, but rather as a response to what we as a community of believers understand to be God's will. As we will see shortly, the New Testament presents to us how we are to receive the message of Jesus Christ and how we are to witness to that message, and therein it provides that fundamental background against which we proffer all subsequent Catholic moral teachings.

In fact, the Scriptures invariably animate and serve as the foundation for all subsequent practical Catholic teaching. As such, the Scriptures are always prompting us to follow Christ and look for the kingdom of God. Effectively they urge us to move forward and guide us as we pass our moral tradition ahead from one generation into the next. Inevitably, moral progress depends on it.

John T. Noonan Jr., who has written histories of church teaching on divorce, abortion, contraception, and usury, recently wrote a book about change in Catholic moral teaching. As he noted, inevitably, the truthfulness of a teaching needs to be tested against the faith, hope, and love that animate the Catholic community. Change happens when we hear more clearly or acutely the call to faith, hope, and love. Noonan gives us the case of slavery. The Catholic church did not finally condemn slavery until 1888, after every Christian nation had already abolished it. Certainly, in this light, we can say that until 1888, the church's teaching on the subject did not conform to what revelation teaches us about being children of God and being made in God's image.[1]

Catholic moral teaching then cannot be posed without the background of the fundamental claims of the New Testament. Similarly, a history of Catholic theological ethics cannot be written or read without that background that feeds and sustains that ever-emerging blueprint of the Christ event.

For these reasons, then, we start with the revelation of the Christ event for people of faith.

Catholic Theological Ethics and the Bible

Asserting that we need the Bible for the foundations of a history of theological ethics does not necessarily mean we have been doing that for a long time! In *Doing Biblical Ethics in the Twenty-First Century: Developments, Emerging Consensus, and the Future*, Lúcás Chan reminds us that for most of modernity, Catholic theological ethics was rarely explicitly invoking the Bible.[2] As we will see in chapter 5, theological ethics from the eighteenth to the twentieth century was based on moral handbooks or manuals that outlined the matters that priests should address in the confessional: sins and vices. During that period, the Bible was used for the most part as a proof-text, that is, simply to confirm a teaching that the tradition had held.

This Roman Catholic history is in contrast to that of the Protestants. Since their inception at the Reformation, all Protestant theological ethics is and has been biblical ethics.

For our purposes now, it was not until the twentieth century that something truly interesting happened in Catholic theological ethics. A Vatican congregation, in 1912, ruled that a German commentary on the New Testament was unacceptable. The congregation ordered that the book be banned and withdrawn from sale because an author had argued in the collection that the Synoptic Gospels depended on two different sources, a position then unorthodox, today universally accepted.

The congregation told the author and the editor that they had to leave their positions in the field of biblical theology, but that they had the option of transferring into other theological disciplines. The author became a prison chaplain; the editor, Fritz Tillmann, became a major moral theologian.

In 1919, Tillmann wrote his first moral theology work, *Personality and Community in the Preaching of Jesus*. It was the birth of biblical ethics in the modern Catholic Church. Later, in 1934, he wrote on the *Idea of the Disciple of Christ*, which was a great success. Many years after its publication, it was recognized as the first Catholic work to talk about the disciple of Christ. Though it is a commonplace today for a priest to refer in a sermon to everyone listening as a disciple of Christ, before 1934, no Catholic preacher and no Catholic parishioner was very familiar with the concept.

In 1937, Tillmann wrote a more accessible biblical ethics text for laypeople, *Der Meister Ruft*. This work had an even greater impact on theology. In 1960 the book was translated into English, *The Master Calls*.[3] It presented a handbook of lay morality not as a list of sins, but as virtues dominated by the idea of the following of Christ and guided by Scripture. By turning to the Bible, Catholic theologians began thinking about love, virtue, and discipleship once again. Before then, at least from the sixteenth century onward, the focus was almost exclusively on sin, vice, and confession.

Strangely enough, as important as this work was, no Catholic moralist attempted another work in biblical ethics until the 1990s. Certainly others, most notably Bernard Häring, based much of their ethics on a Gospel-inspired ethics. But Tillmann was the only moralist who used the Scriptures as his primary text.

Then came the Second Vatican Council.

In the document on priestly formation, *Optatam Totius*, the Council defined seminary education and offered a simple two-sentence statement on moral theology. This comment admonished the seminaries to incorporate the Scriptures in their study of moral theology and to embrace more clearly the virtue of charity and the role of discipleship. Since its promulgation, the paragraph has become a terse manifesto of the Council's agenda for moral theology. It reads:

> Special care must be given to the perfecting of moral theology. Its scientific exposition, nourished more on the teaching of the Bible, should shed light on the loftiness of the calling of the faithful in Christ and the obligation that is theirs of bearing fruit in charity for the life of the world. (no. 16)

Notice three things: the teaching of the Bible, the calling of Christ, and the bearing fruit in charity. All three were together in Tillmann's significant book *The Master Calls*.

In 1984, Paulist Press published William Spohn's remarkable *What Are They Saying About Scripture and Ethics?* Attracting great ecumenical interest, the book quickly became a reference text for providing a typology of the various models of approaching Scripture so as to understand its moral instruction. Therein Spohn offered models that he described as "a sign not of scholarly chaos but of the irreducible richness of the Scripture itself."[4]

Interesting to note, Spohn referred to Protestant biblicists and moralists who wrote in biblical ethics, but when he referred to Catholic writers in biblical ethics, they were all biblical theologians, like Wolfgang Schnackenburg and Pheme Perkins. Interestingly, he did not seem to know any of Tillmann's works, not even *The Master Calls*. Certainly, by that time, there was Gustavo Gutiérrez and later liberation theologians who developed their theology out of the Bible, but they were not moralists, per se. Still Spohn referred to four moralists, Charles Curran, Josef Fuchs, Bernard Häring, and Richard McCormick, who suggested how they thought the Bible should be used for ethics, but they did not begin their theological reflection from the Bible, but rather from the Catholic tradition. Spohn's small book served, then, as an important catalyst that in time generated a great deal of work about Scripture and ethics.

Sixteen years later, Spohn published a sustained argument for his own biblical foundations for ethics. In *Go and Do Likewise* Spohn laid out an integrated vision for a biblical ethics. It was the first Catholic book since Tillmann's works that basically suggested what a biblical ethics could look like. In many ways, however, it resembled Tillmann's book about the "idea" of the disciple of Christ, that is, it was not a book that did biblical ethics, but rather a theoretical foundational book that got us thinking about one.[5]

Later, Lúcás Chan arrived on the scene with two books, both on biblical ethics. His first book, *The Ten Commandments and the Beatitudes: Biblical Studies and Ethics for Real Life*[6] is similar to Tillmann's *The Master Calls*. It is a book that actually *does* biblical ethics. In it he took each of the Ten Commandments and first provided the biblical exegesis of them so that we can know what the writer of the text meant for us to understand when we are told, for example, to keep holy the Sabbath. Then he applied the exegetical finding to a contemporary virtue ethics so that we could see what contemporary lessons we could appropriate from it, what virtues we ought to develop, and what practices and actions we should take up. He did the same with each of the eight Beatitudes, referring to the Commandments and the Beatitudes as the two moral pillars of the Bible.

In his other book, *Doing Biblical Ethics in the Twenty-First Century*, he followed in Spohn's steps in *What Are They Saying* and provided an update about the work in biblical ethics since Spohn's own publication. Like Spohn's book, Chan's work stands as another historical marker for a now truly developing field called biblical ethics. Like Spohn, Chan surveyed the recent literature but now with books by Catholics and Protestants, both biblicists and ethicists. Moreover, while Spohn was looking at biblical ethics just as it was beginning to emerge in Catholic circles, Chan now surveyed the field thirty years later. While Spohn had a few American and European contributors, Chan had a global church writing on the topic.

Additionally, Chan went much further than Spohn by evaluating these contributions. He argued that biblical ethics can only be so-called if the work reflects the competencies of both biblical exegesis and a hermeneutics for applying the exegetical insights to the moral lives of persons and their communities. In effect, he wanted to know the answer to two questions: How competent are biblicists to write on biblical *ethics*? How competent are ethicists to write on *biblical* ethics? Chan argued that biblical ethics requires the competencies of both biblicists and ethicists.

Chan did not make his claims as a simple conceptual argument. Rather, after leading us through the developments of these last thirty years, he walked with us as we encountered the different attempts that biblicists and ethicists made until *they* realized they needed each other's competency.

What about the Ten Commandments?

Quite remarkably, we can note that if we were to retrieve today any specific moral text from either the New Testament or the Old Testament, it would certainly be the Ten Commandments. The key word in that previous sentence is *today*.

The distinctive history of Christian ethics begins with the so-called Council of Jerusalem (see Acts 15) that decreed that new Christians did not have to become circumcised Jews first. This council also determined that the more than six hundred prescriptions of the Law would not necessarily be part of Christian morality. Precisely because Christianity was not constrained by Jewish law, it was free to take what it wanted. One lesson that Christianity did take from Judaism was the Ten Commandments (sometimes called the Decalogue). Over the twenty centuries of Christian moral teaching, the Decalogue eventually became one of the two pillars of Christian morality.

That being said, in the first millennium of the church, the Ten Commandments only appeared, for the most part, in an occasional sermon of the early church fathers. As Dominik Markl, an expert on the history of the Ten Commandments, wrote, "During the first Christian millennium, however, the importance of the Ten Commandments in Christian teaching was relatively limited."[7]

Later, in the second millennium, the Ten Commandments appeared in some early scholastic writings and occasionally merited a commentary, as in Thomas Aquinas's *Explanation of the Ten Commandments*. Later, as catechisms began to appear in the late fourteenth and fifteenth centuries, the Ten Commandments began to emerge as the key organizing moral framework of those texts. As we will see in the fifth chapter, by the sixteenth century, catechetical instruction, by the Reformers like Martin Luther and John Calvin and by early modern Roman Catholic theologians and finally by the Council of Trent itself, all depended on the Ten Commandments as the singular text for presenting Christian moral doctrine. Why and how that happened will be seen later.

Let me conclude that Chan's brilliance in bringing forward the Beatitudes as the second pillar for teaching theological ethics is presently emerging as an acceptable foundational claim, and the story of that acceptance we will discover later.

II. THE NEW TESTAMENT

Introduction

In Wayne A. Meeks's landmark work, *The Origins of Christian Morality: The First Two Centuries*, he did not begin with a foundational chapter on the New Testament. Still, revelation plays in the background of all that he wrote, and he made an extraordinarily broad claim about the aim of the New Testament in its relationship to moral truth. He wrote, "Almost without exception, the documents that eventually became the New Testament and most of the other surviving documents from the same period of Christian beginnings are concerned with the way converts to the movement ought to behave." He added that these documents are "addressed not to individuals but to communities, and they have among their primary aims the maintenance and growth of those communities." That growth is dependent on one insight, that the formation of a Christian moral order would lead to the up-building of community. He added, "Making morals means making community."[8]

This is an extraordinarily important claim. While we think of the Bible as giving shape to the faith that we have, Meeks made clear that it also should give shape to the lives that we live. While this is perfectly clear for most Protestants, there is still residual hesitancy for many Catholics. In part, our hesitancy is due to how moral teachers used Scripture in the past as "proof texts," to how others today use Scripture to support certain "fundamentalist" positions, and to our own ignorance about how to "apply" Scripture today.

Meeks also added something key and that is that revelation insists that by behaving ethically, we will be better able to live as a community of disciples in the world. In short, our happiness depends on this upright behavior. If we are not ethical together, we will not be able to connect as a people of God nor will we be able to share and live the good news. Moreover, Meeks did not suggest that our happiness is solely in our future eternal reward, as in Matthew 25, where the sheep are rewarded with entry into the kingdom for having been merciful on earth. Meeks insisted that the possibility of our present and our future happiness depends on us living lives of moral truth.

Let us now turn to the variety of texts that comprise the New Testament.

Paul

As we begin our considerations of the New Testament, Meeks reminds us that the "first Christians, the Christians who began to invent Christian morality, did not have a New Testament. This obvious fact is often forgotten."[9] Still, as we move to Paul, let us not forget the years and witnesses that preceded him.

Paul's seven undisputed letters—1 Thessalonians, Galatians, 1 Corinthians, 2 Corinthians, Philippians, Philemon, and Romans—were written between 51 and 58 CE. The remaining Pauline epistles—2 Thessalonians, Colossians, Ephesians, 1 Timothy, 2 Timothy, and Titus—are generally regarded as having been composed after Paul's death in his name and spirit to address new problems and conditions that had arisen in the churches.

Paul's letters were for the most part social communications intended to help Christians in the communities that he had founded to deal with the pastoral problems that had arisen in his absence. They were written not so much as theological treatises as practical extensions of his ministry.

In offering advice, Paul offers his own instruction, but that instruction is very much based on his experience of the risen Christ (narrated by Luke in Acts 9, 22, and 26, as well as by Paul himself in Gal 1:13–17). That experience led him to recast his identity in a dramatically different way: "I regard everything as loss because of the surpassing value of knowing Christ Jesus my Lord" (Phil 3:8). Paul unexpectedly came to recognize that knowing Christ Jesus as Lord had become the new center and dynamism of his life. In a manner of speaking, the new experience made him new: "It is no longer I who live, but it is Christ who lives in me" (Gal 2:20).

In Philippians 3:12–16, Paul insists that he still has a long and difficult road to travel on the way to fullness of life with Christ: "Not that I have already obtained this or have already reached the goal; but I press on to make it my own, because Christ Jesus has made me his own" (3:12). Paul's statement acknowledges both the power of his experience of the risen Christ and the struggle that he was to undergo to reach his goal fully.

Paul was convinced that a new era in salvation history had begun with Jesus's death and resurrection. The focus of Paul's theology is, then, on the saving effects of Jesus's death and resurrection. Paul describes these effects in many ways: justification, sanctification, reconciliation, atonement, salvation, peace with God, access to God, and so on. These effects, Paul believed, not only pertain to the end-time but also shape Christian life in the present.

Paul reminds us that we do not *yet* share in the fullness of God's kingdom. In fact, in Romans 8:18–25, Paul paints a vivid picture of all creation eagerly awaiting "the revealing of the children of God" (8:19). He describes the present state of Christians both as having "the first fruits of the Spirit" (through faith and baptism) and as groaning inwardly "while we wait for adoption, the redemption of our bodies" (8:23).

The scripture scholar Daniel Harrington has helped us appreciate a further insight into Paul's moral instruction in his epistles. Harrington turned to Paul's letter to the Romans to explain:

> A fundamental principle in understanding the "ethical" teachings contained in the New Testament in general and in Paul's letters in particular can be expressed in this way: Context is almost everything. Content counts too. In Romans 12–13 Paul supplies a large amount of what can be called "ethical" teaching. Taken out of its present context, much of it sounds like what appears in the Old Testament wisdom books or in the writings of Greco-Roman moralists. But in the theological context of Paul's letter to the Romans, it becomes Christian moral teaching.

Harrington continued: "If context is almost everything for understanding Paul's ethical teachings, then Romans 1–11 in general and 12:1–8 in particular provide ample theological context: the need for Christ, the history of salvation, Christian freedom, eschatology, worship, the body of Christ, and the charismatic community."[10]

These instructions illustrate the attitudes and actions that would enable the church at Rome to be the Body of Christ and the charismatic community described in 12:3–8. These ethical teachings also spell out what it means to be ardent in the Spirit and to serve the Lord (12:11). In fact, Paul's entire letter to the Romans can be viewed as an essay designed to establish that through the Christ event persons of faith can participate in the new creation. In Romans 12:1–2, Paul summarizes the whole process of redemption through Christ as the manifestation of "the mercies of God." As redeemed persons touched by the grace of God, Christians have the obligation to conform their lives to what is their new identity in Christ. It is precisely in the context of Christian identity that Paul presents his ethical directives.

We need to see then that Paul is not speaking to us as if we do not understand what he is saying. He speaks only to those who are like him, children of the new creation. He presents his argument to us waiting for our assent. He is constantly appealing to an internal recognition within us of what it means to be in the new creation; he engages us, expecting an experiential affirmation that what he proposes is necessarily true. What he declares to be our condition begs for our affirmation; his claims are not simply stand-alone statements of fact.[11]

Paul is constantly forging a consensual insight between himself and us, his readers. He is not appealing to a detached, impersonal inexperienced reader, nor is he therefore presenting ethical knowledge as some given *dicta*. Rather his proposals are always submitted for our "Amen." The truth of his proposals is not found independent from the reader. Rather, it is found in the baptism that we share and, therein, our shared identity in Christ.

Paul sees no conflict between describing who we are and what we are called to do. Whatever we affirm about our self-understanding carries within it the burden to realize the understanding ethically. If we are the Body of Christ, we should act like it.

Moreover, as readers of Paul, we should realize that when we say "Amen," we say it in conscience. There we testify to the Lordship of Jesus and there we stand in solidarity with him. For Paul, conscience is where experience and authority meet; from experience, we encounter the authority of conscience as a way of recognizing and testifying to the truth in love. In fact, just as Paul waits for us to respond in conscience to his testimony that Jesus is Lord, so too today we see how in Christian theology the conscience recognizes the call to understand and witness to the truth. The centrality of the personal conscience as the place for hearing the call to respond has had, as we will see, a long history in the church.

The major issue for Paul in Romans 14:1—15:13 is a needed sensitivity to the consciences of others, even in matters that he regarded as morally indifferent. In addressing this issue, Paul points to God as the ultimate judge of all persons, to the pivotal significance of conscience in moral decisions and action, and to the example of Christ who put the needs and the unity of others before his own desires. In particular, Paul stresses why the strong at Rome should be sensitive to the consciences of the weak, and in the meantime, he brings to us the realization that as Christians we *grow* in moral freedom and that we must be mindful that we each grow at different rates.

Paul realizes that the formed Christian, who knows in the depth of his or her being that s/he has been saved by the blood of Christ, does not need to worry about little things like minding fasts or certain church obligations. But neophytes earnestly trying to find the way often need the law as a guide to develop: should not the formed Christian make sure that s/he does not scandalize the not yet developed Christian with a disregard for church law? Paul reminds the strong that they need to be mindful, as Jesus was, of those trying to grow in the faith.

Paul's treatment of the conflict between the strong and the weak at Rome fits well in the context of his entire letter to the Romans. In fact, some interpreters view it as the pastoral goal to which the whole letter was pointing from the beginning: each must help one another to grow in the freedom of Christ so as to be his disciples.

Finally, Paul instructs us on the Eucharist. In 1 Corinthians his words recall the belief that sharing in the cup and bread is really sharing in the blood and body of Christ, and so is both a sign of and a means toward full participation in the Body of Christ. In this context the Lord's Supper serves as a reminder of the basis of all in the Christian community and as an encouragement toward greater unity among Christians such as the "strong" and the "weak" who might take different positions on certain matters.

For Paul, then, the Eucharist has social implications for Christian life and community. As a kind of "trump card" at the end of a long argument, Paul in 1 Corinthians 10:14–22 appeals to the Eucharist as a help both toward promoting mutual understanding within the Christian community and toward sharpening Christian identity vis-à-vis other forms of religious expression.

The Influence of Paul on the History of Catholic Theological Ethics

Although the theme of unity and care for the members is even a stronger theme in John than in Paul, still Paul is constantly working out how his communities must participate in the self-understanding of Jesus. They must understand themselves as belonging to the Body of Christ and that all their moral toil is toward making each and every member a part of the whole.

Paul constantly appeals to his listeners to see how from their own experience they are able to recognize the Word of God and the Body of Christ. Paul appeals then to the consciences of his readers that they may share in the recognition of their need to love one another and to care for one another in the interim times.

Finally, as we will see repeatedly in the history of the church, when Christians want to appeal to conscience they invoke Paul. Whether it is Martin Luther, Martin Luther King Jr., Bernhard Häring, or Dietrich Bonhoeffer, one after another roots her or his appeal to conscience in Paul more than anywhere else in the Scriptures.[12]

The Synoptic Gospels

After Paul's letters, the narrative of the life, death, and resurrection of Jesus began to emerge. As Meeks wrote, "When Mark set down to write 'The beginning of the Gospel of Jesus Christ, Son of God,' he set in motion another decisive movement in the retelling of that story." Now the story begins to approach biography.[13]

Three of the Gospels—Mark, Matthew, and Luke—share particular similarities such that we call them the Synoptic Gospels (*synoptic*, from the Greek, for "seen together"): they tell similar narratives, with similar wording, and similar order. Therein they are presumed to share similar sources and similar points of view. In a word, there seems to be a fair interdependence among them. There are obvious differences, however, from the different infancy narratives in Matthew and Luke, as opposed to none in Mark, to the post-resurrection appearances in Matthew and Luke, as opposed to virtually none in Mark.

Still, there are certain key concepts that emerge from the synopses of the three Gospels to which we should attend: Kingdom of God, Discipleship, Love and Mercy, and Sin.

Kingdom of God

Although Paul preaches Christ crucified, what Jesus preaches in the Synoptic Gospels, is first and foremost, the kingdom of God.

Recognizing that many parables are clustered within the Synoptic Gospels (e.g., Mark 4; Matt 13; 24—25; and Luke 8), Daniel Harrington began his account of the ethics of the Synoptic Gospels with these words: "The kingdom of God serves as the horizon for Jesus' ethical teachings and their goal. According to the parables in the Synoptic Gospels, the kingdom belongs to God, emerges from the 'future,' and marks a decisive change from the present."[14]

While teaching about the kingdom of God is the central theme of the parables, most of Jesus's other teachings also focus on the kingdom. For instance, Jesus teaches us to pray the Our Father (Matt 6:9–13; Luke 11:2–4), which Harrington described as "preeminently a call for the full coming of God's reign when God's will is to be done perfectly on earth as it is in heaven."[15] Similarly, Jesus often heals precisely so that others may understand his authority to preach the kingdom.

The idea that God reigns over all creation is an enduring theme in the Hebrew Scriptures as well as other rabbinic sources, as can be seen in the Psalms, for example. In time, however, Judaism developed an appreciation not only for God's present reign over all the earth, but also began to anticipate and await a future display of God's kingdom, a forthcoming, transformational kingdom where God's reign would be definitely and everlastingly established.

Although other rabbis preached about the forthcoming kingdom of God, the distinctiveness of Jesus's preaching and ministry is his resurrection. Harrington again wrote, "The resurrection of Jesus is a decisive turning point in the New Testament doctrine of the kingdom of God. Resurrection was regarded in many Jewish circles as part of the scenario of end-time events. The claim that an individual should be raised from the dead before and apart from all the other end-time events was quite extraordinary."[16]

In terms of the connection between Jesus and the kingdom he preaches, we as hearers of his Word then are to be attentive to his return in glory, to his kingdom breaking in. By the resurrection, however, we believe that the kingdom of God has already begun to break in. It is, as we say, "already, but not yet." This means that the kingdom of God has already begun to arrive, to be in our lives, our faith, our communities, and our church, but we also know that it is not yet here, that we wait for its full expression, when every tear will be wiped away.

The post-resurrection appearances of Jesus are then the clear instantiations that the new reign of God has begun. Grace is now available. Our redemption has been won. We can walk in the way of salvation, and, above all, we can have a sense of the presence of the Holy Spirit in our lives and in the church.

Pentecost, the breaking-in of the Spirit into the lives of the first witnesses of Jesus's resurrection, is *the* sign that the post-resurrection appearances of Jesus were not isolated moments in salvation history but rather the certain beginning of the coming forth of the kingdom of God. Pentecost is also the birth of ourselves as the people of God chosen to be the disciples of the Lord. Thus, the kingdom is itself the foundation and the measure of the church's integrity.

In terms of the instructional purpose of preaching the kingdom, the hearer is beckoned repeatedly to develop a sense of preparedness, attentiveness, and vigilance for the coming of the kingdom, the return of Christ in glory. While the parables emphasize the inevitable arrival of the kingdom, they also emphasize that the time of the kingdom's in-breaking is only known by God (see Mark 13:32; Matt 24:36). Our preparation for the kingdom, then, is a lifelong task, and given our uncertainty as to the timing, a constantly ongoing one.

Discipleship

In the late Italian director Pier Paolo Pasolini's famous movie *The Gospel According to St. Matthew*, the person of Jesus is seen on the screen preaching and teaching while he is busy hurrying to Jerusalem for his encounter with history. Pasolini's Jesus never stops, sits, or rests. He is always walking at a fast pace and the disciples are always trying to keep up with him. Like the disciples, we the viewers have a hard time seeing him as well. Almost like a silhouette on the screen, he seems to move with deliberate speed; we can hardly make him out. This is a man on a mission.

When he preaches, even in parables, he does not pause. His Sermon on the Mount is like a sermon on the run. He keeps moving forward toward Jerusalem, occasionally looking back to let his disciples know that he realizes they are trying to follow him. Eventually, we realize what he means when he says that he goes before us to prepare our way. In that sense, he is himself the unsurpassable goal who always goes before us, making our call to follow him an extraordinarily dynamic movement.

This image of Jesus as being on the horizon of our vision is a good one for appreciating what Christian discipleship is about. Not only do we await the return of Christ in glory and the coming of his kingdom, but we do so as his followers. Being a follower of Jesus is not like being a follower of Immanuel Kant or Karl Marx. Disciples of these latter figures are interested above all in their thoughts; disciples of Jesus are interested in a personal and communal relationship with him as we follow along the way.

We saw earlier that Fritz Tillmann (1874–1953) was originally a scripture scholar. From 1905 to 1931, he wrote on a variety of themes: Jesus's self-disclosure as the Son of Man, the future coming of Christ, the self-understanding of the Son of God, and the personality and community in the sermons of Jesus. In effect, Tillmann wanted to know as best as possible, what did Jesus really know and understand about himself: Did he know he was the Son of God, the Son of Man, the Messiah? Did he know the people he was choosing as his disciples? What did he mean when he said that the Father and he were one? It is not surprising that in asking such modern questions, Tillmann became himself the subject of investigation.

By his crossing over into the field of moral theology, Tillmann constructed the first major bridge between the studies of Scripture and moral theology; his writings in moral theology followed from his studies in Scripture. As his interests there revolved around the personal effect that Jesus's self-understanding had on the community of disciples, Tillmann naturally developed the theology that the Christian pursuit of the good had to be within the framework of being a disciple of Jesus. Christian moral self-understanding could only be in the light of Jesus's own self-understanding.

Tillmann held that moral theology was the study of following Jesus in the life of the individual and the community: Catholic moral theology finds the source of its search for moral truth in the person of Jesus as the original image and the eventual goal for all of us.

His popular work *The Master Calls* was divided into four parts. The first part, "principles," was a striking departure from those principles in the contemporary manuals of moral theology that taught principles principally about sinful actions. Among Tillmann's principles, the first was the following of Jesus. This principle was an ideal because Jesus himself is an unsurpassable goal of an unattainable value who is always before us and who, in inviting us to follow him, calls us into a dynamic moral life. By following Jesus we become children of God.

In developing discipleship Tillmann claimed that the primary sacrament for moral theology was not penance (which in the beginning of the twentieth century, as we will see, was what most people believed), but rather baptism, which alone supplied the call that is freely given by Christ. As Paul would say, by baptism we enter into a new creation; we are not the old Adam, but we are regenerated, liberated, and elevated by Christ. Here Tillmann offered his "amen" when he wrote that by the Holy Spirit "we are made free to share in the magnificent liberty of the children of God."[17]

By baptism, then, we have a new relationship with Jesus. Like him, we understand God as our Father. Like Jesus, we seek to be conformed to God's will, because God's will makes possible and is the foundation of the moral life. This new relationship calls us then to take notice of the imprint of God's self within ourselves; there, within, we are called to allow the work of God to continue in the development of our interior dispositions and consciences. We are called to become fully alive.

Discipleship in the Gospels is the primary category for the Christian's self-understanding. True, the disciple is a sinner, and in the Gospels we can see that frequently the sinfulness of the disciples emerges, whether of Judas, Thomas, or Peter, for example. But sinfulness is not the key issue that Jesus perceives in hearers of his call to follow him. Rather, he fundamentally wants to know whether we accept the invitation to be his disciples.

Love and Mercy

The call to the moral life is a call of disciples to walk in the way of the Lord, which is the summons for true participation in the life of Jesus. The subsequent three parts of *The Master Calls* are dedicated to the three objects of the love command: God, neighbor, and self. Throughout the three loves, Tillmann regularly invoked Jesus himself as the model and motive of the possibility for our following him. The entire moral life is organized and shaped by our participating in the life of Jesus who teaches us to love.

The double love commandment—love God and love the neighbor—appears in somewhat different forms in Matthew 22:34–40; Mark 12:28–34; and Luke 10:25–28. The historical context for Jesus's teaching is the question about the greatest commandment in the Jewish Law (Torah).

In the Bible, love is not one virtue or command along with others. It is prior to everything: it comes first. It is the foundation to the moral life and as such, it is, as Dan Harrington explains, "a response to the experience of God's love for us." He adds,

> The closest thing to a definition of God in the Old Testament appears in Exodus 34:6: "A God merciful and gracious, slow to anger, and abounding in steadfast love and faithfulness." And the New Testament stresses God's love for us revealed in Jesus: "In this is love, not that we have loved God but that he has loved us and sent his Son to be the atoning sacrifice for our sins" (1 John 4:10). The persistent message of the Bible is that God has loved us first, and the proper response to God's love for us is to love God and to love the neighbor.[18]

It is difficult to underestimate the place that love has in the Christian Scriptures. Harrington gives us a sense of how all-encompassing and foundational love is: "As creator and lord, as Yahweh the God of Israel, and as the Father of our Lord Jesus Christ, the God of the Bible is the origin, source, and goal of love. The proper response to God's love for us according to Jesus' double love commandment is to love God and to love one's neighbor."

But what does love look like in the concrete sense? Well, since there are two loves, that's a double question. First, love of God is a very responsive act and virtue. Thomas Aquinas tells us that love of God finds itself in "union." Love is union, a sense of being one with God, the very act of receiving God's love. Prayer is a certain form of union; by prayer we enter into union with God. By a prayer in which we open ourselves to the love of God, we become active recipients of God's love.

For Catholics, the greatest expression of union is the Eucharist. In the Eucharist, we enter into the very life of God, in the Word and in the reception of the body and blood of Christ. The Eucharist is therefore the central way we receive the love of God and God's offer to enter into union through love.

Second, love of neighbor is deeply connected to the love of God. By receiving God's love, we are capable of loving our neighbor. Many people think that we love our neighbor because God commands it; that is only partially true. The more important insight is that God makes love of neighbor possible.

We know that the clearest way to love our neighbor is to "show mercy." That is after all the directive that Jesus gives at the end of the parable of the Good Samaritan (Luke 10:25–37), wherein Jesus answers the scribe's question: "And who is my neighbor?" That parable is key in the history of the Bible's ability to form our behavior, because it is there that we learn that the love of God makes possible our love of neighbor.

The parable is an odd one because its end is, unless we are not attentive, a reversal of the beginning. The parable is answering the question "Who is my neighbor?" and so, as the story begins, we quickly begin to think that the neighbor is the wounded man on the road. But by the end, the scribe, when asked again the original question, responds that the neighbor is the one who shows mercy.

Jesus's parable teaches us not to look for a neighbor to love, but rather to *be* a neighbor who loves. We give that answer because when hearing the story, we see that the center of the story is not the man lying wounded on the road, but rather the Samaritan. We make the shift to the Samaritan because in hearing the story we cannot get over how merciful he is.

This surprising shift to the agent of mercy made an enormous impact on hearers of the parable. Throughout the tradition many preachers and theologians saw in the story of the Good Samaritan the narrative (in miniature) of our redemption by Christ. Starting with Clement of Alexandria (ca. 150–215), then Origen (ca. 184–254), Ambrose (339–90), and finally, Augustine (354–430), the parable of the Good Samaritan is the narrative of our merciful redemption. Later from Venerable Bede (673–735) to Martin Luther (1483–1546), preachers and theologians appropriate and modify the narrative, but in each instance, the narrative is first and foremost the gospel in miniature, a story of what Christ has accomplished for us, so that we, in turn, can go and do likewise. It is much more than a story of moral instruction.[19]

The basic allegorical expression of the parable is this: the man who lies on the road is the exiled Adam, wounded (by sin), suffering outside the gates of Eden. The priest and the Levite (the law and the prophets) pass him by because they are unable to do anything for Adam. Along comes the Good Samaritan (Christ), a foreigner, one not from here, who tends to Adam's wounds (our salvation), takes him to the inn (the church), gives a down payment of two denarii (the two commandments of love), leaves him with the innkeeper (St. Paul), and promises to return for him (the second coming), when he will pay in full (our redemption) and take him with him (into the kingdom of God).

Although often forgotten today, this interpretation of the parable shows us that it is *first* a narrative of Jesus's redemptive work and *then* a call to imitation; the parable reveals the mercy of Jesus that makes possible our mercy. This is a lesson we must never forget.

The parable is then not one among many. As William Spohn notes, it has a privileged position in the Gospels and a privileged position in the church that hears the Gospel proclaimed.[20]

This privileging of the Good Samaritan is at once a privileging of mercy. Elsewhere, the Scriptures name mercy as the condition for salvation as in the last judgment in Matthew 25. This story is striking in that everyone but the King is surprised by the judgment. Consider, the King sits in judgment and the goats and sheep stand before him. The goats are condemned to hell. "Why?" ask the goats. The King responds, because you did not feed me when I was hungry, clothe me when I was naked, and so on. The goats say but when did we see you hungry or naked? The King answers, what you did not do for the least, you did not do to me.

Similarly, the King summons the sheep to enter his kingdom. "Why?" ask the sheep. The King says, because you fed me when I was hungry, clothed me when I was naked, and so on. "When did we do that?" they ask. The King answers, whenever you did it for the least, you did it to me. While the sheep never realized that in feeding the hungry, they were feeding the King; unfortunately, the goats never realized that by not visiting the sick, they were not visiting the King.

As in Matthew 25, elsewhere in the Synoptic Gospels we see that we will be judged by whether we practiced mercy and we will not be excused if we knew not to practice it. In Luke 16:19–31, Jesus tells the parable of Dives, the rich man, who ignores the daily pleas of poor Lazarus begging at the rich man's gates. When Dives dies and is sent to Hades, he asks for relief, but the Lord says, you ignored Lazarus for his whole life. Like the goats, the rich man in Luke learns this lesson when it is too late. We will be judged by the practice of mercy, whether we know it or not.

How can that be? Like the story of Dives, who ignores Lazarus at his gates, the Gospels presume that we have within us a disposition to hear the cries of the poor. It is not something we have to strain to do. On the contrary, like Dives, we have to actually work to overcome the cries of the poor. Dives, like the goats, deadened his ability to hear and respond to the hungry and the naked.

Here, in seeing how often we are called to respond to the summons of mercy, we discover *implicitly* our own vulnerability, our capacity for recognition, and the subsequent ability to deliberate a course of action in conscience. The capacity we have to hear the poor is in our vulnerability; when we recognize the other, our own vulnerability recognizes the other's. Deciding to respond as both the Good Samaritan and the sheep did, we use our consciences to determine the best ways to do so.[21]

I define *mercy* as the willingness to enter into the chaos of another.[22] We see that God is merciful, precisely because God hears our pleas and enters into our chaos. For instance, through creation God brings order out of the chaos of the universe, through the incarnation the Son of God enters into the chaos of human existence, and through the redemption, God brings us out of the chaos of our slavery to sin. Christ's own entrance into the chaos of death occasions our hope in the risen life, and his pledge to return again is a pledge to deliver us from the chaos of our own lives. Every action of God is aimed at rescuing us. Time and again, we see that being merciful is to act like God.

We will see in the next chapter how decisively the early Christians identified themselves with the practice of mercy, but here we can at least acknowledge the biblical imperative to imitate God through the conscientious practice of mercy. Its reception into the history of the Catholic Church cannot be doubted. Mercy is found in our encounter with God: in response to that mercy, we become imitators of the God in whose image we are made. Likewise, in answer to Christ's call to follow him, we practice mercy.

A turn to the *Summa Theologiae* of Thomas Aquinas proves a worthy conclusion to this section. Thomas asks the question whether mercy is the greatest virtue (*Summa Theologiae* II.II.30.4) and responds that charity is the greatest virtue because by it we are united in love to God; second to charity alone, mercy is the greatest because by it we exemplify God in God's actions and, therefore, we become like God. Charity, in effect, makes it possible for us to be merciful.

Sin

Among many lessons about sin, there are, I think, three in the Synoptic Gospels: sin is the failure to bother to love; we sin not from weakness, but from strength or capacity; and finally, we often do not realize that we have sinned.

Sin is the failure to bother to love, a very biblical definition of sin. Understanding sin in this way follows from the command of Jesus to love God and neighbor. The primacy of the love commandment inevitably leads us to see sin as the failure to do what Jesus commands and makes possible. It captures the sin of Matthew's "goats," Lazarus's rich man, the wounded man's priest and Levite, the publican's Pharisee, and so on. Each of the gospel stories that refer us to sin highlight what the agent could have done and did not do. These are not the only stories; there are others as well: the man who did not invest the talent (Matt 25:14–30), the virgins who were not vigilant (Matt 25:1–13), and the son who did not go into the field to work as he said he would (Matt 21:28–32). In all these sins is the failure to do what could have been done, or what I describe as the failure to bother to love. There's a capacity to act and a failure to realize that capacity.

Despite present conceptions of sin, this understanding of sin helps us to see that almost every "sin" narrative in the gospel is about sinners sinning *not* out of what they were too weak to do, but what they were most capable of doing. When the publican and Pharisee are praying in the temple, the sin of the Pharisee is his own fascination with his strength (Luke 18:9–14). When Dives ignores Lazarus at the gate, his sin is not that he could not help Lazarus, but that he could have and did not (Luke 16:19–31). The steward who asked forgiveness for his debt is forgiven, but he is later punished because he does not forgive the minor debt of his own employee. He is excused for what he could not do (pay his own debt), but he is convicted because of what he could have done (forgive the minor debts against him) (Matt 18:21–35).

In the parable of the Good Samaritan, where is the sin? Those who committed the crime of beating the poor man on the road to Jericho are completely absent. The focus is rather on the Levite and the priest; they could have acted, but they did not (Luke 10:25–37). They sinned precisely out of their own capacity. Similarly, in the last judgment, the goats are condemned for what they could have done but did not bother to do (Matt 25:31–46).

I am not here talking about pride or hubris. Pride is a perfection. When people sin out of pride, they know that they sinned and boast about it. I am interested in something prior to pride, sin itself. Dives, the goats, the steward, and the Levite and the priest are sinners because they failed to respond when they could have. Their ability or capacity is key; if they were unable, no blame would be on them. Yet because they had the ability and did not respond, therein we see that our sins come from where we are capacious, not where we are weak. If Dives, the goats, the steward, and the

Levite and the priest failed to respond because they were filled with pride, then their sins would be, according to Aquinas, "perfect."[23] A person who sins out of pride perfects their sin: this means that they have sinned for so long that they have grown accustomed to their sinfulness. So sinning out of pride only makes the sin itself more grievous.

Many people claim that they sin because they are weak; they invariably think that they have a weakness, like anger, lust, or gluttony. They work hard to overcome the weakness, but eventually succumb to it and count it as sin. They even confess the struggle to an understanding priest. But is that sin as it appears in the Bible or is that what we have misconstrued as sin?

The Gospels do not talk much about those who struggle not to sin. Instead, the Gospel reveals sin as where people could have acted but simply did not act; they were able to recognize the other and respond but did not. Here, I think, in fact, most of us actually do sin, though we frequently confess the narratives of our failed struggles to deal with our weaknesses.

Many people confess as sin where they struggled to do something right, but because of a weakness or two, they fail to do the right. So they confess the struggle. I find this phenomenon revealing. People confess as sins, moral struggles. They have problems with anger, lust, or impatience and try hard to overcome the vice but fail. Is there much sin here if they have been "bothering" or struggling to love? In fact, when they do this, often the confessor will say something like your sin is diminished because you tried to address it but failed.

What people rarely do is confess that they could have done something, and they just did not bother. Yet this is precisely what sin is in the Bible.

Why do we do this? I think, because we forget how deceptive sin is. We forget that to know our sinfulness we have to have God's perspective on our souls. We forget that we need the light of revelation to illumine our ability to examine ourselves. It is for this reason that St. Ignatius, among many others, suggests that we need to *ask* for graced illumination to do any serious self-examination. Only with that grace can we see ourselves as we actually are and therein discover how often we sin by a failure to bother to love out of our own strength or capacity.

What I am suggesting here is that sin is very hidden as it was to the goats, the rich man, the virgins, and all the others, and that we need a theology of sin that captures this biblical teaching.

Worse, when we speak of sin today, we usually presume that one has to have intended the sin to be convicted of sin, but in the gospel stories, there is general surprise at finding out one's sinfulness. Recall again the goats at the last judgment. The goats ask, "But when did we not feed you? When did we not visit you?" They are clueless about their self-understanding as sinners. Similarly, the rich man is ignorant of his fate. Listen to him as he calls from beyond: "Father Abraham, tell my brothers," he pleads from Hades. What about the priest and the Levite who pass the wounded man in the parable of the Good Samaritan? Do they see what we see, that they have failed to be neighbors, failed to respond conscientiously in mercy? Or again the Pharisee, does he know the judgment of arrogance being attributed to him in his prayer?

The Gospels effectively demonstrate that we allow ourselves to ignore others, and that is sinful; we do not bother to see the man wounded on the road, or the hungry, or Lazarus. We think that we only sin when we deliberately choose to ignore. But that is a luxury that the Bible does not tolerate. We think we only sin when we proudly refuse the beggar, but Dives's sin was that he did not bother to heed the beggar.

All of these texts are telling us, I think, that we have a predisposition to *not* believe we are sinners; like the Pharisee, the Levite, the priest, Dives, and the goats, we too would be surprised to learn that we are sinners. Yet we know from lessons in prayer, that whenever we want to do an examination of conscience, we have to ask for the grace to see ourselves as we are. Asking for that grace means asking to know where we have truly sinned.

The Influence of the Synoptic Gospels on the History of Catholic Theological Ethics

As we will see in the next chapter, some of the fundamental claims of the Synoptic Gospels pass easily into the moral teachings of the early church. Love quickly emerges in the early life of the church as the foundation of the Christian moral life as we will see in the writings of Augustine and other church fathers. Similarly, mercy becomes the trademark of Christian practices of the ethical life and eventually evolves into what today are the corporal works of mercy.

In the third chapter, against the background of the call to follow Christ sin emerges. But in time, some of the fundamentals about sin are lost and everything focuses on human failure. Later, penitential manuals are designed and lists of sins are generated. The Gospel insights into sin, about a failure to bother to love, about sinning out of strength, and the ignorance of our own sinfulness are lost: the notion of sin as it emerges in the early medieval period is effectively about wrong actions that we can barely prevent from happening.

Subsequently, sin is no longer our failure to bother to love, but rather a specific, vicious act. Love vanishes from the field of moral theology, almost all together. Even the works of mercy get caught into the obsession on sin. Now the works of mercy are no longer the fruits of the good disciple; they are rather part of the penance of the repentant sinner and eventually become occasions for indulgences so as to avoid the pains of punishment. The rest, as we will see, is history.

The Gospel of John

In light of Meeks's claim that the New Testament is fundamentally "concerned with the way converts to the movement ought to behave," we might be surprised to find him writing later that the Gospel of John "offers no explicit moral instruction."[24]

Meeks is not alone in his assessment. Brian Blount wrote, "John does not do ethics. Or so it seems."[25] Wolfgang Schrage wondered whether a chapter on John even belongs in his book on ethics in the New Testament, though he has one in *The Ethics of the New Testament*, and Frank Matera wrote, "For anyone interested in the study of New Testament ethics, the Gospel according to John is a major challenge....In a word, there appears to be remarkably little ethical content in the Gospel according to John."[26]

As Lúcás Chan pointed out well in *Doing Biblical Ethics*, many scripture scholars who write on biblical ethics are far more competent in exegesis than in ethics. They tend to think that ethics has one of two dimensions, either it is about personal responsibility issues like temperance or fortitude (are you reliable, sober, balanced, and integrated or a ne'er do well, a drunk, a lecher, and simply irresponsible) or about social issues like those related to justice or even mercy (do you act on behalf of the poor, give to each their due, etc.)

There is another dimension to ethics that they often overlook: interpersonal relations of friendship, family, communities. Here, unlike the concerns of justice, temperance, and fortitude, these more interpersonal relational issues depend on what we call today fidelity or solidarity. Just as God is just and merciful, God is also faithful to Israel and to all God's people. Fidelity is in fact the mark of the covenant!

Years ago, Carol Gilligan, a psychologist in moral development studies, argued that too much of moral development studies, outlined by her colleague Laurence Kohlberg, was aimed at a moral maturity in which the personal responsibility of temperance and fortitude and the judgments of justice were the sole double goal of moral maturity. In *In a Different Voice*, Gilligan asked why was it that people who were leaders in the area of justice had terrible problems in their fundamental relations as spouse, parent, or friend.

I understood her question to be, was ethics solely aimed at justice and were matters of fidelity not important? Later, other thinkers in ethics like Paul Ricœur, Daniel Maguire, and Margaret Farley wanted to know whether, in the pursuit of justice, people were also expected to be faithful to interpersonal relationships? What Gilligan brought to the language of moral development became a major category in philosophical and theological ethics. The ethicists argued that justice alone was insufficient, and that friendship and fidelity were also constitutive of the fundamental virtues that humans should pursue.

I write that the virtue of justice guides us in our relations with all people, whether they are friend, foe, or stranger, to be impartially fair and to give to each their due is justice. Other relationships are not impartial; in the name of fidelity and loyalty, friends, families, colleagues, students, neighbors, and fellow citizens look for us to sustain, support, maintain, cultivate, and accompany these specific relationships.[27] When I called my mother, for instance, I did it out of filial fidelity, not out of justice.

When I began teaching with Daniel Harrington a graduate course at Boston College on "John and Virtue Ethics," like Matera, Meeks, and others, I could not find much in the Gospel of John on sobriety, vigilance, or temperance, that is, there is very little admonition about personal responsibility in general or preparedness for the kingdom in particular. Nor is there much on mercy: Luke has the Good Samaritan and the prodigal son; Matthew has the last judgment, but John has nothing per se on mercy. Nor is there much on justice, or the poor, or any other related topic. In John, there is a great deal on Jesus and his encounters with others, on love, and on a very intimate understanding of faith as profoundly relational and intimate. If Gilligan wanted to find a different voice in the Scriptures, it is the Gospel of John.

In his splendid work *Imitating Jesus: An Inclusive Approach to New Testament Ethics*, Richard Burridge treated ethics in the Gospels as coming not from the teachings of Jesus but from the life, death, and resurrection of Jesus. He sees, as Meeks noted, that the Gospels are not books of teachings, but rather biographies. For this reason, Burridge argued that the type of ethical teaching we find in any of the Gospels is not what we find in the major philosophical traditions.[28] If we are to start with the Gospels, then we must start with Jesus, not his teachings per se.

Nowhere is this more the case than in John's Gospel. Burridge began his treatment of John asking, by the end of a reading of the Gospel, is Jesus a great moral teacher or a friend of sinners?[29] The question is key: the Gospel is told through a series of encounters: the call of Peter and Nathaniel, the marriage at Cana, the man born blind, the woman by the well, the raising of Lazarus, the Last Supper with the Twelve. At the end of the Gospel, we have met Jesus by meeting him in each of his relationships, whether with the Samaritan woman or Peter, with Martha or Thomas, with the man born blind or Nicodemus, with the Magdalene or Mary of Bethany. Is Jesus a great moral teacher or a friend of sinners?

While many exegetes argue that there are seven signs in the Gospel, I find that invariably there is an encounter, a robust dialogical encounter, with each sign. In each, the character and Jesus become better known because in most of them Jesus reveals to the other what he knows of them: think here of Nathaniel, the Samaritan woman, Thomas, and Peter (at his call, at the Last Supper, and on the beach). In each, Jesus enters into the life of the other in a transformative way.

In the pericope about the man born blind (9:1–41), Jesus's disciples see the man and ask whose sin caused his blindness, the man's or his parents? Jesus responds that it was neither, but that God's work might be shown, Jesus heals the man by putting mud on his eyes and telling him to wash in the temple pool. When the man is cured and returns to the temple, neither Jesus nor his disciples are present. People are confused when they see the man; could this, they ask, be the same man born blind who has been begging at the temple? He insists that he is the same man and that the one who did it is Jesus. As he is questioned by the crowd, investigated by the Pharisees, abandoned by his parents, and finally rejected from the temple, in each instance he confesses that Jesus was his healer, and that Jesus could not be a sinner because only an agent of God could do this miracle. After his continuing witnessing leads to him being denounced by literally everyone to whom he was ever related, the man is found by Jesus. They speak together and Jesus discloses to him that he is the Son of Man, and the man worships him.

The encounter with the man born blind is a quintessential Johannine narrative, with the interpersonal encounter, the disclosure (that the man is not a sinner), the dialogue, the sign, and the witnessing. At each stage of each of his encounters, Jesus dialogues with the other and there is a new disclosure of both the other and Jesus. Finally, there is the witnessing by Martha of Jesus as the resurrection; by Thomas, as my Lord and my God; by Mary, as Rabbi.

There is something very prayerful about these encounters; we are almost eavesdropping on contemplative conversations. Moreover, these intimate encounters are, for Christians, deeply moral ones: they are based on love, expressed in faith, maintained by fidelity, and usually accompanied by an instruction about an act of hospitality. These four virtues—love, faith, fidelity, and hospitality—are the moral instructions the reader of John learns.

Because so much of John's Gospel focuses on love, each of the encounters are within a context of love. Though a few encounters are with unknown persons, for example, the Samaritan woman and the man born blind, often there is an engagement that is generous, tender, and fairly visceral. The scenes are substantively common and ordinary: Jesus replenishes wine in one, the Samaritan woman offers water, Mary without notice bathes the feet of Jesus while everyone eats dinner, and the Magdalene thinks the risen Lord is a gardener. Even the raising of Lazarus happens while friends of Martha and Mary are grieving. One hardly gets a sense of spectacle. Calvary hardly happens; more of the passion account is about the washing of feet. Jesus's appearances after the resurrection are where the disciples pray, walk, or fish.

Even when Jesus gives the love command, the setting is not public as in the Synoptic Gospels where there is public questioning and answering. In John, the love command, which is more a gift than a command, is given after Jesus has washed the disciples' feet at the supper (John 13:34–35). In fact, the command is incredibly horizontal: Love one another as I have loved you. There is no vertical movement to or from God in the Johannine love commandment.[30]

These encounters prompt deeper and more explicit faith. For John, faith is a moral action. In John, we believe in response to the gift given; to not believe is to reject the gift, the person of Jesus. The testimonies of faith from Martha to the man born blind are all deeply relational commitments to Jesus. To appreciate how "relational" faith is in John, contrast faith with the questions in the *Summa Theologiae* (II.II 1–16). In Thomas, when he writes about love, it is union, and deeply relational, but for him, faith is adherence to central tenets of Catholicism, the creed, for example. For Thomas, faith is assent to truth claims. For John, faith is the loving response to Jesus Christ, whence these witnessing actions are subsequent to the encounters with Jesus.

This faith is to abide with Jesus, to be faithful. Jesus's great injunction on the love commandment is not primarily about doing, but about staying: "abide in me" is his constant injunction.

Sin, then, is precisely walking away from faith. Jesus's resurrection admonitions are remarkably moral, as he reprimands the disciples at Emmaus, Thomas in the upper room, or Peter on the beach. Jesus reprimands those who were slow to believe, those who doubted, or those who abandoned him. Believe and remain in my love, believe and abide in my love, these are Jesus's fundamental injunctions. For John sin is the failure to stay in love and believe.

Finally, if anything concrete ever happens in John's Gospel, it is usually an act of hospitality. Certainly there is the wedding feast of Cana and there are other gestures, like Jesus cooking fish, the Samaritan woman offering water, or the disciples on Emmaus inviting Jesus to stay, but the key hospitable gesture is the washing of the feet. In John, the washing of the feet occasions the teaching of the new commandment, to love as Jesus loves. Moreover, as if by extension, Jesus adds to the love command, the command to wash one another's feet: "So if I, your Lord and Teacher, have washed your feet, you also ought to wash one another's feet" (John 13:14).

I never appreciated how effective the feet washing command is until I attended a Holy Thursday liturgy and the pastor decided that instead of washing feet, we were to wash one another's hands. That ritual was banal. There's something about the humbling of oneself to wash another's feet that makes the action powerful. In fact, that is precisely what Jesus emphasizes, that the one who washed the feet is the Lord. No wonder poor Peter became so awkward.

In the previous chapter, however, Mary of Bethany, the sister of Martha and Lazarus, bathes Jesus's feet with expensive nard and then dries his feet with her hair (John 12:3). This sign of welcome to Jesus leads us to see this foot washing as a central moment preparing us for the next.

The Influence of John's Gospel on the History of Catholic Theological Ethics

Curiously, the emphasis in John's Gospel's on love for one another remained in the early church as that by which disciples were known. John's Gospel specifically prompts in Christians a very specific call to love one another that, of course, became an early Christian trademark. By the same token, besides Paul's preaching against factionalism, John's Gospel is really the foundation upon which sins of schism and other threats to church unity and harmony are based.

The pursuit of a particular relationship with the Lord as a moral action develops as part of the life of asceticism early in the life of the church. But the life of asceticism and the act of praying became only moral actions for those who pursued the life of perfection. For centuries, the so-called perfect life of the vowed religious or clergy will be distinguished from the lives of commoners, but eventually commoners will find themselves being obliged by the life of the church to fulfill certain commands of the church that fortify as moral their relationships with the Lord and his church. Here, above all, are the teachings on the requirement to worship on Sunday, and the development of these laws will be traced in subsequent chapters.

Finally, hospitality became, as we know, deeply tied to asceticism, particularly in the *Rule of St. Benedict*. Nevertheless, by the twelfth century, lay guilds develop the practice of Matthew's works of mercy. After the lay guilds, in the thirteenth century come the religious orders and then the lay confraternities that, like the lay guilds, offer their members the practice of prayer that keep them in love with one another and then the practice of a specific work of mercy. These two movements of coming together in prayer to form communal relationships with Jesus and then to go out and serve those in need of mercy become the trademark of all Catholic communities from the twelfth century to the present, as we will see later in subsequent chapters.

III. TOWARD A CONCLUSION

At the end of his book on the early church, Meeks provided us with a list of seven theses. In a way they are the material that build bridges from the Scriptures to the life of the early church, and they seem to me appropriate to mention here in closing.[31] They are as follows:

1. Making morals and making community are one, dialectical process.
2. A Christian moral community must be grounded in the past.
3. The church's rootage in Israel is a privileged dimension of its past.
4. Faithfulness ought not to be confused with nostalgia.
5. Christians must be polyphonic. ("The fact is that the Christian movement has survived despite—or perhaps because of—a large and often raucous diversity."[32])
6. Moral confidence, not moral certainty, is what we require.
7. God tends to surprise.

These theses remind us that the reception and living out of Christianity in every generation and in every period is not predictable; the initiatives of an era depend on the actual agents' actions and not future projections or forecasts. History develops as history happens. For instance, I began writing this book soon after Pope Benedict XVI resigned (who would have thought!) and then the cardinals elected a Jesuit from the ends of the earth (who would have thought!), but that's history.

Not only do we need to be mindful that history's developments are always affected by an enormous array of conditions (think of how the weather affected the bombing of Hiroshima or the maiden-voyage of the Titanic!), but we need to appreciate that the message of Christianity is not only diversified because we hear the Gospel messages differently but also because the Gospel messages themselves are somewhat diverse. The emphatic concerns of the Synoptic Gospels, of John and of Paul, are not as easily assimilated into an identifiable tract.

This leaves us with two concluding points that will run throughout this entire book. First, an astonishing development in the work of biblical scholarship occurred when women and non-Europeans entered the field. For too long, biblicists and everyone else assumed that all one needed was to do exegesis correctly, that anyone would read the text the same way because, after all, all one needed to do was know the ancient languages. But when women entered the field of biblical scholarship, we began to read the diverse texts diversely! As Lúcás Chan noted, "Earlier exegesis...was considered an objective, non-interpretive science. Anyone with training could exegete the same text as another could and the exegesis would presumably be the same. The social location of the exegete was not important."[33] Today, however, we think otherwise. To make his point, Chan introduced us to the significant work of Sandra Schneiders who prompts us to read Scripture more inclusively.[34] He could also have cited the work of other women biblical theologians who have significantly changed the field like Elisabeth Schüssler-Fiorenza,[35] Phyllis Trible,[36] and Gina Hens-Piazza.[37] More recently, Hens-Piazza, a dear friend of Chan, calls us to read the Scriptures without blinders, to be attentive to minor characters in the text, so that we read the text more justly by not overlooking characters too long ignored.[38] By giving due recognition to those unnamed, to those long overlooked, these scholars invite us to approach the Bible with newer expectations.[39]

In a similar vein, Chan also examined the work of the postcolonial biblical scholar Rasiah S. Sugirtharajah, who also proved yet again the evident relevance of the social location of the scholar.[40] Like Sugirtharajah, Chan, a native of Hong Kong, was a postcolonial scholar.[41] Following his lead by attending to the diverse social locations of biblical theologians, we end up developing a multiperspectival read of the Scriptures. Clearly, we need that multiperspectival, inclusive approach for our study of the history of theological ethics.

Second, as we move forward into history, let us not read history as we would want it to have been, but rather as it was. Let us also read it with the blueprint of the Christ event, assessing that if it happened that way, we still need to ask, should it have happened that way—or at all? Therefore, mindful that fidelity to history ought not be nostalgic, let us also rid ourselves of a very dangerous yet hardly believable myth in the oft-used but very nonhistoric phrase, "as the church has always taught." For decades I have taught my students, as soon as you see those words, get cracking, it is a clear sign that something new is coming across the pulpit.

History is not make-believe. We can only understand our history if we do the work of research and if we try to appreciate the elements that shaped us. But we also need to read it as believers, pursuing Christ and his teaching.

Chapter Two

Mercy

The Social Formation of the Early Church (Up to 500 CE)

This chapter is divided into three parts. The first is about the earliest life of the church, receiving the call to baptism and discipleship, and turning to a new understanding of being both disciple and neighbor. The second is about further developments in appreciating how and why the church established teachings on three matters: participation in the Eucharist; readmitting apostates; and the harnessing of sexual desires. The third leads us to profile the moral teachings of the most significant figure of this period, Augustine.

I. DISCIPLE AND NEIGHBOR

In this part we go through three stages. First, we explore how early Christians first received the gospel news in their communities. Here, we see how, as Christians tried to better understand who Christ was, they also began to understand better who they were. But their grappling doctrinally with Jesus Christ as both truly divine and truly human became an invitation for the disciples to understand themselves as integrated, which led to a new understanding of themselves as embodied and ensouled. In this they also appreciated their neighbor as embodied and found that they needed to welcome newcomers with a vigorous hospitality that led to a new solidarity. Finally, from these virtues of hospitality and solidarity emerged the practices of mercy, both corporal and spiritual, which further reminded the disciples of Christ, that like the one they followed, mercy was to be their standard.

Understanding Christ and the Human Body

Despite the commonplace belief that Christianity has maintained a negative stance toward the human body, a singular point of consensus among historians, scripture scholars, and theologians contradicts that assumption: the Christian tradition valued continuously the human body as constituting the Christian's identity and, in some strands of that tradition, it combatted vigorously a variety of expressions of dualism, which separated body from spirit.[1] This consensus is again renewed in contemporary studies, having emerged from the foundational investigations of important scripture scholars.

Reflecting on the Greek word for body, *soma*, Rudolf Bultmann argued that for Paul "*soma* belongs inseparably, constitutively, to human existence....The only human existence there is—even in the sphere of the Spirit—is somatic existence."[2] Emphasizing human existence as bodily, Bultmann noted that Paul never used *soma* to describe a corpse. Moreover, the body is so integrated into human existence that the human does not have a *soma*, but rather is *soma*.

Robert Jewett developed these insights and begins his work with the remark that "for Paul theology is anthropology."[3] Investigating anthropological terms in the Scriptures, Jewett found, on the one hand, that the word *sarx* (flesh) generally describes those negative desires for righteousness that keep us from God. On the other hand, the word *soma* is used to combat Gnosticism[4] and provides the basis both for the metaphysical unity of the person and for the possibility of "relationship between persons."[5] By considering ourselves as embodied, we realized that we were dependent on one another.

Others develop these arguments. Antoine Vergote contended that the scriptural understanding of "the resurrection event does not imply the thesis of an immortal soul; on the contrary, it suggests the idea that the body is the whole man."[6] This, in turn, had another ramification: the ability of the human body to explain human existence, personality, and relatedness furthered our understanding of resurrection. Through the believer's corporeality, one is and can be related to others and, thus, can be caught up in Christ, who transforms our corporeality. No less than St. Paul makes a similar point: "Christ will be exalted...*in my body*, whether by life or by death" (Phil 1:20).

The New Testament reveals, then, not simply who we are in Christ, but who we will be. If our corporeality encompasses our existence and is the basis for our relationality, then the resurrection of our bodies means that in our bodies we will be one with one another in glory. That promise also leads to the hope that we will never be at war within our bodies again. Would that promise of glorious integration in ourselves and with one another have any bearing on the moral task for a contemporary Christian?

Human fulfillment as embodied in the risen Christ is central for understanding the hopes and moral responsibilities that early Christians held. Brian Daley captured the importance of the early church's hope in resurrection and immortality in establishing the Christian task to seek integration. Of the apologists of the second century, Daley wrote that they "saw the integrated mortality of body and spirit as an anthropological necessity: only the immortality of the whole person can make our present struggle to integrate the body and spirit meaningful."[7] Like the scripture scholars, Daley found in human destiny as defined in the risen Christ the opportunity and the demand for all people to find in their own bodies the fullness of the Spirit of Christ.

In his study of the early church, Gedaliahu Stroumsa announced that integrating the divinity and humanity of Christ was the major theological task and accomplishment of the early church:[8] "The unity of Christ, possessor of two natures but remaining nonetheless one single persona, is, of course, in a nutshell, the main achievement of centuries of Christological and Trinitarian pugnacious investigations."[9] This achievement took practical significance in the ascetical imitation of Christ that called Christians to the duty to seek a unified self like Christ's: as Christ brought divinity and humanity into one, Christians were called to bring body and soul together. Integration became a key task for all early Christians, to "be an entity of body and soul, a Christ-bearing exemplar."[10]

Integration of body and soul was not an aim for the contemporaries of the early Christians. As Meeks and others pointed out, the self in Greek thought was distinct from the body.[11] For Plato, "to know oneself—the reflexive attitude par excellence—meant to attend to one's soul, at the exclusion of the body."[12] Thus when Christianity, on the belief that the human is in God's image, made integrating the body and soul both a theological expression of humanity's integrity *and* a normative task, it proposed to the Western world a new claim on the human body. Stroumsa noted, "The discovery of the person as a unified composite of soul and body in late antiquity was indeed a Christian discovery."[13]

Peter Brown argued in similar ways. Though often understood as a flight from the body, "the doctrine of sexuality as a privileged symptom of personal transformation was the most consequential rendering ever achieved of the ancient and Christian yearning for a single heart."[14] With this presupposition, Peter Brown investigated how Christian doctrine freed citizens from Roman control over their bodies. That control exercised itself in two ways: the human body of the nobility was to uphold the dignity of the state through the citizen's own noble bearing and the human body was to reproduce so as to give the state control over the chain of generative life. Thus, the Roman state was assured both of its pride and of the children it needed and, in return, gave to the citizens freedom to do whatever they would with their bodies so long as they did it with proper discipline. In this exchange, the state vested the human body with a dignity derived from the state's needs and not from the body's own integrity. Christians and Jews resisted this exchange and charged that the city bestowed the human body with a false indeterminacy that in their eyes was created in God's image. Recouping that determinacy meant a rejection of a great deal of sexual liberties, but in doing so, the church liberated the human body from the city's control. Brown wrote,

> Christian attitudes to sexuality delivered the death-blow to the ancient notion of the city as the arbiter of the body. Christian preachers endowed the body with intrinsic, inalienable qualities. It was no longer a neutral indeterminate outcrop of the natural world, whose use and very

> right to exist was subject to predominantly civic considerations of status and utility.[15]

The time of the early church was, then, a remarkably innovative period, when the integrated moral life was understood as a central component for living out of one's call to discipleship. The moral life was, then, a response to the Word of God; it was an application of the rhetoric of preaching to the ordinary life.

Particularly noteworthy was Brown's claim that chastity played a decisive role in liberating women from the claims of the city. In order to provide support to the early church, some wealthy Christian widows did not remarry. Instead of relinquishing their family's income to a second husband, Christian widows remained unmarried and used their funds to support church ministry, which was in their own households.[16] Eventually their daughters imitated their mothers by committing themselves to perpetual virginity, a completely new state of life. Women benefactresses either in their widowed or virginal states freed themselves, then, from the claims of the city to reproduce and became instead models of generosity in the life of the church.[17]

Ambrose writes, for example, about the paradox of the closed womb: it is a sign of the benefactress's openness to the Scriptures, Christ, and the poor.[18] These chaste women became, then, models of and for the church.

In the contemporary world in which personal autonomy is so prized, we might want to ask a question about personal freedom and decision-making in light of these decisions for chastity and hospitality. Clearly the freedom women enjoyed in their decisions regarding chastity and hospitality would be deeply connected to questions of leadership. What role did the widow or virgin who housed a church have in that community? Joyce Salisbury raised doubts about what this meant for women. For her, the closed womb was not a sign of freedom, but another exercise of control. As the woman was to absent herself from all sexual activity, likewise she was to remove herself from all other worldly commerce. In particular, for the true virgin and good Christian woman, the silent mouth became a necessary corollary for the chaste womb. Thus, the Christian community raised her to a privileged position on account of her chastity, but the same community paradoxically silenced her in return for the privilege.[19]

However, Carolyn Osiek and Margaret MacDonald investigated precisely these early house churches and found women's leadership to be evident and pervasive.[20] Certainly, some women are considerably without power, notably female slaves, but still, these authors find women as leaders of the Christian assemblies in their house churches and as leaders of funerary rituals as well as agents of expansion.

The historical account of women's leadership is just now materializing. In 1983, Elizabeth Clark gave us access to some of the actual texts that spoke about or were by women in her *Women in the Early Church*.[21] More recently Patricia Cox Miller provided us with further texts and along with others, introduced us to particular women.[22] In 1984, Clark published *The Life of Melania the Younger*, a fifth-century biography that gave us concrete access to a significant contemporary figure (383–439) of considerable wealth and power.[23] The granddaughter of Melania the elder (350–417), whose own properties and wealth were found throughout the empire, the younger Melania founded monasteries and convents for both men and women in the Middle East and in northern Africa, emulating her grandmother, who earlier founded convents and monasteries throughout the Middle East.

The Melanias were known as desert mothers. Like the desert fathers, these women played an important part in the development of monastic life. As early as the third century there were women living in community or as hermits in the Egyptian desert.[24] For example, in the fourth century, St. Gregory of Nyssa's biography[25] of his sister St. Macrina (ca. 330–79) helped us to see her as a model of virginity, sanctity, hospitality, and leadership. She established a monastery and a convent in Pontus and sets the stage for others, like the later Melanias, or St. Benedict's sister, St. Scholastica, who did for cloistered women what her brother did for cloistered men: setting for them a way of living the ascetical life. Joanne Turpin, who writes on the cloistered Macrina, suggests that Egeria's *Diary of a Pilgrimage*, which gives the firsthand account of a woman's devotional travel through Egypt, Syria, Palestine, and Mesopotamia from 381 to 386, gives "proof of what women were capable of."[26]

In a significant essay, Elizabeth Castelli noted how difficult it is to retrieve the narratives of early women church leaders and notes that St. Macrina, the sister of Basil of Caesarea and Gregory of Nyssa, is a case in point: "We know Macrina because of Gregory's biography but her other brother Basil, whom she effectively brought into the ascetical life, makes no mention of her in his four volumes of writings or any of his 366 letters." Castelli asked, "How many women lost their places in the written record of the church because no one chose to write their biographies and because the men whose lives they influenced omitted any mention of them? How many exceptional women may have been only mentioned and been otherwise lost without a trace?"[27]

Of course, still we ask the leadership question: Was the authority of women sufficiently recognized that they were ordained? A variety of works have pointed us in the affirmative direction, but one in particular, Kevin Madigan and Carolyn Osiek's *Ordained Women in the Early Church: A Documentary History*[28] is summed up as follows: "Finally, readers have a single compendium in English of the evidence that women did hold church office as deacon, presbyter, and bishop, not simply as spouses of male officeholders and not in heretical sects but in their own right and in the Catholic Church."[29]

Let us not understand the entire issue of women leading in the church nonhistorically. Only knowing the question historically, do we recognize the costs such leadership exacted. Scholars of the early church demonstrate, then, that religion and the state wrestled through a kind of dialectic for the social construction of the body. The struggle between the two appears most striking in those arenas where Christians were martyred. As Francine Cardman noted, their deaths were "the most intimate of bodily choices."[30] Surprising though it may seem, the shock of early Christian martyrdom did not come from the brutality of the spectacles: athletic events and, in particular, gladiatorial combat conditioned Roman audiences for slaughter. Rather, the introduction of women into the arena stunned both Romans and Christians.

In many instances, the women were martyred precisely because of their virginity. The claims on women's bodies again became the focal point of the struggle between the two. In fact, during their torments, women became victims of sexual abuse; their chastity praised by the Christian community became the target that their persecutors most sought. Too much weighed upon the persecutors' attempts to wrestle that chastity away from these women martyrs.

As Cardman, who examined the accounts of Felicitas (101–65), Blandina (ca.162–77), Perpetua (182–203), and Crispina (d. 304), among others, remarked, "The dissolution of the social body is mirrored in the destruction of the martyrs' own bodies."[31] Thus, while the state made these women's bodies objects of attack and derision, the church depicted them as gloriously triumphant.

As Cardman reminded us, in martyrdom the Christian finds freedom, not from the body, but from death: the martyr's body triumphs. Like Salisbury, however, Cardman was sanguine about the cost of this victory: "For women especially, the making of a martyr meant the unmaking of the body—her own as well as her world's."[32]

The Virtues of Hospitality and Solidarity

Early Christians strove for the integration of themselves like Christ as individuals, but they also sought to become one like Christ as a people. Understanding themselves as saved by mercy, they sought as disciples of Christ to practice it with and for others. The bridge between one's identity and one's future and between oneself and the community was completely built on mercy, and as we will see later, the Eucharist.

Among all the virtues, hospitality would be the first and most inclusive virtue for the practice of mercy. By being hospitable, one sheltered, fed, clothed, visited, and tended to the other. Paul writes to the Romans, "Contribute to needs of the saints; extend hospitality to strangers" (Rom 12:13). Peter urges, "Be hospitable to one another without complaining" (1 Pet 4:9).

Writing about hospitality, Wayne Meeks underlined just how widely practiced it was: "For Christians, a movement spread by itinerants, hospitality had special significance."[33] Not surprisingly, he found in Paul many texts admonishing the communities to be hospitable: Philemon 22; Romans 16:1–2, 23; 1 Corinthians 4:14; 16:10–11; Philippians 2:19–23; 2 Corinthians 8:16–24. He noted that the Pauline communities actually provided financial support for the missionary endeavors, which made the benefactors "partners in the Gospel" (1 Cor 11:8–9; Phil 1:5; 4:10–20).

In Matthew 25, Meeks found the summons for the early Christian community to welcome those sent to them from the neighboring churches. Likewise, the Letter to the Hebrews (13:2) admonishes the community, "Do not neglect to show hospitality to strangers, for by doing that some have entertained angels without knowing it." Clearly the angels from God who visited Abraham (Gen 18) and Lot (Gen 19) were precursors of the disciples sent by Paul and by Jerusalem.[34]

Beyond Scripture there are many other early texts exhorting Christians to hospitality. The *Shepherd of Hermas* (104.2) describes how bishops "always without ceasing, sheltered the needy and the widows, by their own ministry" and the hospitable persons "always gladly welcomed God's servants into their houses without making a show of it." Likewise, Cyprian (*Letter* 7) and Tertullian (*To Wives* 2:4) as well as the writer of the *Didache* (12) urge Christians to practice the hospitality of sheltering the stranger. Clement often recommends it (1 Cor 1:2; 10:7; 11:1; 12:1) and Melito, the bishop of Sardis, writes a treatise on it, *Peri filoxenias*. In fact, Rome's fame in Christendom was not primarily based on its being the center of apostolic activity; rather, it was the source of such generous benefaction.

Later, the *Rule of St. Benedict* provided a great impetus for the development of other institutional responses to shelter the stranger. Benedict dedicated a chapter (53) of his Rule to hospitality and provided two different structures to respond to those in need. The guest house was designed for persons of means. It provided welcome, stability, and shelter for pilgrims, monks, nobles, and clergy, but the hospice received persons in dire need—beggars, invalids, the aged, and the infirm.

From the second to the early fifth century, the bishop's deacon cared for the needs of five specific groups: foundlings, orphans, the aged, pilgrims, and the sick. Like the foundlings and orphans, the aged had no family to assist them. Similarly, the sick were without family and were more likely newcomers, transients, or pilgrims. The deacons' care for pilgrims and the sick was a particularly onerous duty in pilgrimage centers. These centers of hospitality would eventually appropriately be called "hospitals."

Founded to care for the overlooked Greek-speaking widows (Acts 6), deacons were always associated with providing spiritual and physical support to the other. As their ministry developed, the church constructed appropriate institutions. Emperor Constantine, for example, authorized every city to build and maintain facilities for the pilgrim, the sick, and the poor. Subsequently, from the writings of

St. Jerome we learn of a hospital in Rome; from St. Basil we hear about one he erected near Cappadocia. These institutions eventually divided labor, from which the separate practice of "nursing" emerged. The Christian community of Alexandria records five hundred nurses in 418. In time, nearly all hospitals were under the administration of particular bishops.[35]

In his compelling argument, *The Rise of Christianity*, Rodney Stark argued that "Christianity was an urban movement, and the New Testament was sent down by urbanites,"[36] but those urban areas were dreadful; he describes the conditions as "social chaos and chronic urban misery." This was in part due to the population density. At the end of the first century, Antioch's population was 150,000 within the city walls or 117 persons per acre. New York City has a density of thirty-seven persons per acre overall and Manhattan with its high-rise apartments has one hundred persons per acre.[37]

Moreover, contrary to early assumptions, Greco-Roman cities were not settled places whose inhabitants descended from previous generations. With high infant mortality and short life expectancy, these cities required "a constant and substantial stream of newcomers" in order to maintain their population levels. As a result, the cities were comprised of strangers.[38]

These strangers were well treated by Christians who, again contrary to assumptions, were not all poor.[39] Through a variety of ways of caring for newcomers, financially secure Christians welcomed the newly arrived immigrants. This welcoming then was, as we saw above, a new form of incorporation. Stark noted, "Christianity revitalized life in Greco-Roman cities by providing new norms and new kinds of social relationships able to cope with many urgent urban problems. To cities filled with the homeless and impoverished, Christianity offered charity as well as hope. To cities filled with newcomers and strangers, Christianity offered an immediate basis for attachments. To cities filled with orphans and widows, Christianity provided a new and expanded sense of family."[40]

This new incorporation was distinctive. Certainly, ethical demands were imposed by the gods of the pagan religions. But these demands were substantively ritual, as in bringing food or other gifts for the gods. They were not, however, neighbor directed. While pagan Romans knew generosity, that generosity did not stem from any divine command, but rather simply from a particular person's own inclination. A nurse who cared for a victim of an epidemic knew that her life might be lost; if she were a pagan, there was no expectation of divine reward for her generosity; if she were a Christian, this life was but a prelude to the next where the generous were united with God.[41] Stark concluded, "This was the moral climate in which Christianity taught that mercy is one of the primary virtues—that a merciful God requires humans to be merciful. Moreover, the corollary that *because* God loves humanity, Christians may not please God unless they *love one another* was entirely new. Perhaps even more revolutionary was the principle that Christian love and charity must extend beyond the boundaries of family and tribe, that it must extend to 'all those who in every place call on the name of our Lord Jesus Christ' (1 Cor 1:2)....This was revolutionary stuff. Indeed, it was the cultural basis for the revitalization of a Roman world groaning under a host of miseries."[42]

Stark's claims were effectively developed by the work of other scholars. In a recent book, Peter Brown added that the virtue of hospitality eventually enhanced the understanding of the itinerant stranger as becoming a member of the community and thus contributed to an overall sense of another virtue, solidarity. In *Through the Eye of a Needle*, Brown helped us to see that the practice of hospitality produced an appreciation for the poor as one's sibling.

Significantly, Brown turned to Ambrose to substantiate his claim. Brown wrote that Ambrose insisted "that giving to the poor should be based upon a strong sense of solidarity." Ambrose "did not wish the poor to be seen only as charged outsiders, sent by God to haunt the conscience of the rich."[43]

Brown described how Ambrose incorporated the poor: "On many occasions, Ambrose spoke of the poor as interchangeable with 'the plebeians' and 'the people.' To call them plebians in this way made them members of the same Christian community as the prosperous."[44] Brown concluded, "For this reason, Ambrose went out of his way to make sure Christians did not see almsgiving as a de haut en bas gesture. Rather, they were encouraged to see it as the gracious repayment to their fellow humans of an ancient debt."[45]

Brown wanted us to see that Christianity "could be seen as vertically as well as horizontally all inclusive." The result was that "top and bottom—the very rich and the very poor—faced each other in a one-to-one relationship in which all the intermediate gradations of society had been elided."[46] The bishop, then, did not simply castigate the rich, especially the irresponsible and unmindful rich; he defended and became the advocate for the poor. Brown added, "The intervention of a preacher such as Ambrose, toward the end of the fourth century, showed that the poor could no longer be spoken of only as 'others'—as beggars to whom Christians should reach out across the chasm that divided the rich and the poor. They were also 'brothers,' members of the Christian community who could also claim justice and protection."[47]

For our purposes it is important that we appreciate that the strangers arriving who received hospitality may have been the apostolically sent missionaries, but they were also the unknown immigrants who found a home among the Christians.

The practice of hospitality was fairly widespread. "Hospitality was exercised most often by householders who were able to take in traveling apostles in their own houses, but, as Justin attests, provisions began to be made early on for a communal treasury for such purposes."[48] By the second century, the bishop became gradually the chief patron for welcoming the stranger.

Collections and hospitable practices were not only provided by the wealthy. As Paul instructs, "On the first day of every week, each of you is to put aside and save whatever extra you earn" (1 Cor 16:2). The practices of hospitality as well as the raising of funds for the missionaries were for those with any income. These practices became then institutionalized: Christians had collections, were prepared for the newly arrived, hosted them in the bishop's name, and recognized them as siblings. Meeks saw these practices as highly communal and effectively institutionalized. Moreover, unlike others whose religious practices always were confined to sacred occasions and rituals, the Christian practices were ordinary, constant, and integral to their own self-identity.[49]

Let us close this reflection on hospitality by considering one of the corporal works of mercy: clothing the naked. By becoming naked in his death on the cross, Christ entered into solidarity with us, who were shamed in our nakedness as we were exiled in sin from the Garden of Eden. Clothing the naked is a responsive act in which Christians recall how Christ became naked for us to save us from our own nakedness in sin.

Clothing a stranger appears in the story of St. Martin of Tours (316–97). *The Life of St. Martin* was written by Martin's disciple, Sulpicius Severus (360–425) and is one of the first extended biographical profiles of a saint whose own life was an imitation of Christ. It is meant, in turn, to prompt emulation. In reading the story we may be surprised to see not the well-dressed Martin giving a part of his cloak (as El Greco and so many other famous painters have depicted him), but rather a nearly naked Martin sharing his last remaining bit of clothing. As we can see, the works of mercy were the chief way that all Christians, rich and poor, entered into solidarity with Christ and with one another:

> ACCORDINGLY, at a certain period, when he had nothing except his arms and his simple military dress, in the middle of winter, a winter which had shown itself more severe than ordinary, so that the extreme cold was proving fatal to many, he happened to meet at the gate of the city of Amiens a poor man destitute of clothing. He was entreating those that passed by to have compassion upon him, but all passed the wretched man without notice, when Martin, that man full of God, recognized that a being to whom others showed no pity, was, in that respect, left to him. Yet, what should he do? He had nothing except the cloak in which he was clad, for he had already parted with the rest of his garments for similar purposes. Taking, therefore, his sword with which he was girt, he divided his cloak into two equal parts, and gave one part to the poor man, while he again clothed himself with the remainder. Upon this, some of the bystanders laughed, because he was now an unsightly object, and stood out as but partly dressed. Many, however, were of sounder understanding and groaned deeply because they themselves had done nothing similar. They especially felt this, because, being possessed of more than Martin, they could have clothed the poor man without reducing themselves to nakedness. In the following night, when Martin had resigned himself to sleep, he had a vision of Christ arrayed in that part of his cloak with which he had clothed the poor man.... After this vision the sainted man was not puffed up with

> human glory, but, acknowledging the goodness of God in what had been done, and being now of the age of twenty years, he hastened to receive baptism.

Martin's action was one of entering into the shame of the beggar. In return, Christ enters into the nakedness of the beggar so as to stand in solidarity with Martin and invite him into baptism.

The Corporal Works of Mercy

Mercy defines the early church. But mercy is not simply a disposition; it is an active set of practices. In Matthew 25 the saved are those who performed what we later called the corporal works of mercy—feed the hungry, give drink to the thirsty, shelter the homeless, clothe the naked, visit the sick, visit the imprisoned, and bury the dead. While the first six are in Matthew 25, by adding the seventh, the church created an easier pedagogical device that would in turn later generate other lists of seven, like the seven deadly sins, the seven virtues, the seven spiritual works of mercy, and the seven sacraments.

These many calls to mercy were heeded, in one way or another, as imitations of Christ. In short, we respond to the sick, in part because Christ did. But we also respond to the sick because, like Christ, we recognize their need. Even before someone in need asks for our help, we, like Christ, recognize their need for help. That is why the failure to bother to love is sin: it is the failure to act on the recognition that we already vulnerably experience. Our own vulnerability awakens us to their needs and disturbs us when we fail to bother to reply.

Christ's actions therefore are lessons bearing imitation. Perhaps it might be better to say, however, that Christ's actions awaken in us a further call to recognize, to recognize the person in need and to recognize that Christ would respond. The Synoptic Gospels agree that healing the sick was Jesus's first miracle. The inauguration of Jesus's ministry was marked, in fact, by many healings (Mark 1:32–33; Matt 4:23; Luke 4:40–41). Not surprisingly, then, like Jesus, his disciples attend to the needs of those whose health is in jeopardy. Mary's visit to Elizabeth is the first expression of Mary's own discipleship: she promptly responds to the annunciation by attending to her cousin in need. Likewise, after the Pentecost, the disciples' ministry is marked by the physical and spiritual care of those in need.

In the early church, attending to the sick is a fairly common Christian practice. Cyprian, bishop of Carthage, leads his congregation to respond to victims of the plague in 252. Bishop Dionysius provides a narrative of his community's response to the plague in Alexandria in 259: "Most of our brethren, in their surpassing charity and brotherly love did not spare themselves and clinging to one another fearlessly visited the sick and ministered to them. Many, after having nursed and consoled the sick, contracted the illness and cheerfully departed this life. The best of our brethren died in this way, some priests and deacons, and some of the laity" (Eusebius, *Hist. Eccl.* 7.22.9).

When we turn to the exhortation to visit the imprisoned, Christian history helps inform the meaning of this work of mercy. Early Christians routinely sought to comfort their fellow Christians who were imprisoned; they often sought their blessings as well. Christ himself had been a prisoner. Thus, like Peter, Paul, and many of the apostles, imprisoned Christians were perceived as not only people in need but also people of courage and holiness. Working to visit, console, and liberate them were in themselves their own reward. Clement of Rome tells us in his first chapter to the Corinthians that many Christians ransomed others by offering themselves in exchange for the one held hostage.

Perhaps the most interesting of the works of mercy is the last. While belief in the resurrection is, as Augustine notes, what separates Christians from all others, the Emperor Julian contended that one of the factors favoring the growth of Christianity was the great care Christians took in burying the dead. Although individuals often performed the task, the church as a community assigned it to the deacons, and, as Tertullian tells us, the expenses were assumed by the community. Lactantius reminds us further that not only did Christians bury the Christian dead, but they buried all of the abandoned: "We will not therefore allow the image and workmanship of God to lie as prey for beasts and birds, but we shall return it to the earth, whence it sprang: although we will fulfill this duty of kinsmen on an unknown man, humaneness will take over and fill the place of kinsmen who are lacking."

The Christian community accompanied the dead to their resting place, and their care for the dead extended not only to burying them but also to making offerings for the repose of their souls. The significance of burying the dead is then rooted in the profound respect that Christians have for the human body. The human body created and redeemed by God is to be raised up by God in glory.

Why is the call to mercy made? Normally six motives are found in the writings of the Scriptures and the early church. First, Proverbs 15:27 encourages us to practice mercy for the remission of our sins, that is, in gratitude for God's merciful stance toward our sinfulness. John Chrysostom sees mercy, in this passage, as the queen of the virtues, outweighing all our burdensome sins. Second, Tobit 12:8–9 tells us that for our prayers to be heard by God, works of mercy should accompany them. Several of the fathers, Augustine, Cyprian, Leo the Great, and John Chrysostom, preach on this theme. Third, Matthew 6:20 highlights that works of mercy will lead to eternal reward, a motivation that Augustine often uses. Fourth, Matthew 25:40 reveals to us that any merciful action is for the sake of the Lord. Cyprian calls this the most powerful of all motives. Here, many of the fathers promote the figures of Mary of Bethany and Zacchaeus as models of mercy. Similarly, the celebrated episode of Martin of Tours giving his cloak to the beggar becomes a motif throughout the church. Being merciful is the call to holiness, and being holy is the call to mercy. Fifth, Lactantius and Ambrose urge mercy to fortify human solidarity and to extend the circle of fellowship in the Lord. Finally, Clement of Alexandria, John Chrysostom, and Leo the Great remind us that works of mercy bring us into the life of perfection. By practicing mercy, we become more like the God who entered into our own chaos. These motivations ought not to appear as singular; rather, all six weave together into the life of the church as it moves forward in history.

The Spiritual Works of Mercy

The spiritual works developed in both the Eastern and Western Christianity during patristic times as well. Like the corporal works of mercy, the spiritual works are seven: instruct the ignorant, counsel the doubtful, comfort the afflicted, admonish the sinner, forgive offenses, bear wrongs patiently, and pray for the living and the dead.

Origen recognized that Matthew 25 was not only a call to dress the body with clothes or to feed it with food, but also a summons to tend to the spiritual needs of the other. In many ways, the roots of the call came through the appreciation of the Christian as being one—body and soul, corporal and spiritual. Thus, preachers from Origen through John Chrysostom warned listeners to attend not only to their siblings in need of physical nourishment, but those in need of the Word of God.

Such concerns were often accompanied by another set of issues. The epistles urged Christians to pardon, give mutual support, and exhort each other (as in Eph 4:32; Col 3:13, 16). These biblical recommendations too were looking for a home in the emerging tradition of the church. Indeed, in 2 Corinthians 5 Paul urges his readers to become ambassadors of reconciliation, imitating the very action of God in reconciling the world. If the Christian is the follower of Christ the incarnate one, then the Christian is called to do what Christ did: reconcile.

This call to reconciliation, along with the call to be vigilant about the spiritual needs of the other, eventually coalesced into the spiritual works of mercy. The longstanding development through the tradition finds a comparable occurrence in the writings of Augustine. Around 378, in *De moribus ecclesiae catholicae*, Augustine describes a hodge-podge of concerns; but by 421, when he writes the *Enchiridion*, he proposes the corporal works of mercy and adds a few: console the afflicted, show the way to the lost, and assist those who hesitate.

After proposing these three, Augustine offers a second form of spiritual mercy: pardoning. Augustine sees that pardoning is not only forgiving sins and bearing wrongs but includes correcting and rebuking the sinner.

Augustine realizes that this second set of three is fraught with difficulties and informs us that before we look to the great task of loving of our enemy, we need to recognize our own need for spiritual mercy. For Augustine, the works of mercy are very much a way for the Christian to acknowledge God's mercy. They bring the work of salvation full circle, helping the Christian to see the gift of mercy, which enables us to practice the task of mercy.

Finally, it is after Augustine that the seventh, all-encompassing prayer for the living and the dead emerges. Here, this third form of almsgiving, as it is named, is first conveyed as a general, but deeply felt well-wishing for all people including one's enemies. The third form of spiritual almsgiving is, then, a complement to all the foregoing.

While the corporal works call Christians to respond to those with specific needs that are lacking: shelter, food, water, clothing, and so on, the spiritual works are a little more complicated. On the one hand, like the corporal works, the first three deal with spiritual burdens that the neighbor suffers. Their aim is for the neighbor, primarily. The next three deal with matters of strife and reconciliation. They are appeals to the Christian to take significant steps toward maintaining the harmony of the community rife with many problems. In many ways, they aim to build up the practitioner into being an ambassador for the community. Finally, the last spiritual work, the call to pray, builds up the entire community both through the one who prays and through the one for whom the practitioner prays.

Unlike the corporal works, with the exception of the first and the seventh, the spiritual works are primarily intended for individual practice. We see a strong corporate legacy to each of the corporal works of mercy. Often an early diocese, a medieval religious order, a thirteenth-century lay association, or a renaissance confraternity decided on a corporal task: ransoming the prisoner, sheltering the homeless, feeding the hungry. There were, however, no confraternities known for bearing wrongs patiently or forgiving offenses, nor were religious orders counseling the doubtful or admonishing sinners. They are not works looking for specific groups to assume them, but invitations to all individual Christians to practice them.

II. TURNING TO EMERGING AMBIGUITIES AND CHALLENGES

Of course, not all of the early history of the church is a narrative of hospitality, solidarity, and corporal and spiritual works of mercy. There were challenges and the most evident ones were where the most was and is at stake: the Eucharist. It is there that from the beginning, at the Last Supper, when Judas leaves and when Peter is admonished for his inability to be faithful, that Christians most fully understand that the gift we have been given must be shared. It is there that we realize most clearly that while we do often share, we often fall short, at best.

In this section, we also need to attend to emerging questions of sin and sexuality to see that as the works of mercy have their legacy, these developments have them as well.

Celebrating the Eucharist

Jesus preaches often that the kingdom of heaven is a great banquet and often plays with us about our inability to recognize who will be included in that banquet. In Luke's Gospel he preaches that the unexpected people from the byways will be brought into the feast (Luke 5:34). Likewise, when he preaches to the masses, Jesus expects to eat with them as well. The disciples never grasp this, wishing instead to send the listeners away hungry. But Jesus brings them into his table fellowship by his magnificent multiplication of loaves feeding the five thousand (the only miracle to appear in all four Gospels: John 6:1–15; Matt 14:13–21; Mark 6:32–44; Luke 9:10–17). In addition to the feeding, the miracle yields an extra twelve baskets as a simple reminder of the banquet to be celebrated again at the end of time when he will gather us into the twelve tribes of Israel. John's Gospel takes the miracle's significance even further by following it with his own discourse on the identity between Jesus and the bread that will sustain us for all time: "I am the bread that came down from heaven" (John 6:41). In John, the eschatological and the eucharistic come together in the miracle.

The great scandal for Christians, then, is to ignore the needs of the hungry. The story of the rich man who ignores the hunger of Lazarus is clearly an admonition to the early community: act now, or you will be in Hades with the ignorant rich.

Not surprisingly, then, the first great dissension for the early church concerns eating and inclusion. The Greek-speakers claimed that their widows were being neglected, a charge that led to the appointment of "the seven" (Acts 6:1–6). Likewise, at Corinth, disorder at table fellowship and the failure to leave enough food for latecomers became an issue (1 Cor 11:33–34). The widows, like the latecomers, could have become another Lazarus had the communities been left unaware of their needs. In recognizing their needs, however, they recognized that eating and inclusion are mutually defining matters in the life of the church.

Thus, when we turn to the history of dominical observance itself, we find the long-standing effort to include others into the solidarity of the eucharistic celebration, in which the breaking of the bread is at once the means and the promise of a community becoming one.

It is important to begin with the fact that the early church did not prescribe a day of Sabbath. On the contrary, like the scriptural record of the frequent instances with which Jesus broke the Sabbath ban on work, early Christians seemed similarly to be a busy lot, not resting in any noticeable way on the Sabbath. Paul, for instance, often refers to his own rejection of laziness and acceptance of work (1 Thess 2:9; 2 Thess 3:10–12; Eph 4:28). The general tendency of early Christians was to work seven days a week.

In his foundational work on the development of the dominical observance, Louis Vereecke noted that from the very beginning the early church came together on the first day of the week (see 1 Cor 16:1–2; Acts 20:7–12) to celebrate the supper of the Lord (1 Cor 11:20). Sunday became called the day of the Lord because it was the day that Christ rose from the dead. On that day, on which the new creation began, Christians gathered for the supper of the Lord. So, the first concern was simply to celebrate Eucharist on Sunday; the practice began without any law, neither a law to rest nor a law to worship.[50]

In fact, the first texts of the early church positively exclude any cessation of work on Sunday. Ignatius of Antioch (d. 110), for example, sees the Christian Sunday as in opposition to the Jewish Sabbath. Irenaeus (d. end of second century) argues that Christians keep every day as their spiritual day, but no day as a day of repose. Tertullian is the first to refer to repose on the Lord's Day, but this is so as to celebrate the day the Lord was raised. The *Didascalia* (third century) tells Christians that whenever they are not worshipping, they should dedicate themselves to work always and diligently. Vereecke summed it up: in the first three centuries there is no law banning work; whatever exhortations are solely focused on Sunday and the celebration of the Eucharist.[51]

In 321, Emperor Constantine prescribed Sunday as a day of rest and prohibited judges, professionals, and soldiers from doing public work. However, he permitted personal as well as agricultural work. Eusebius (260–341) translates the edict as giving Christian soldiers and civil servants the time or freedom to worship. As Vereecke noted, the civil law was to permit soldiers the opportunity to participate in the Eucharist; it was to free them to worship in the community and it had no roots in Sabbath law.[52]

While this law came from Constantine, we do not find any comparable ecclesial law or practice, not in any rule of Benedict, Jerome, or others. What we find instead is the summons to work. Not until the end of the fourth century do apocryphal texts from Syria and Alexandria (*Apostolic Constitution* 380; *The Testament of Our Lord Jesus Christ*) contain "orders of the Lord" to give rest to slaves and to those oppressed by work, so that, again, like Constantine's soldiers and civil servants, these too may participate in the Eucharist and receive religious instruction.[53]

At the Council of Orleans (538), the first ban on Sunday work appears: it is a ban on any hard labor that would keep the masses from receiving religious instruction at the eucharistic celebration. In effect, the poor, like the soldiers and slaves earlier, were freed to worship and the weight of the law was borne by the masters of the poor who had to release them from this labor. Later Martin of Braga (d. 580) used for the first time the term "servile work" to designate the work of serfs that was prohibited by the Sunday observance.[54]

Finally, Charles the Great in his *General Admonitions* (789) ruled that, with the exception of produce providers, soldiers in war, and those burying the dead, no man or woman could labor on Sunday. From every part of the church, all are called for the solemnity of the Mass and to worship God.[55]

We see here, then, that the dominical observance laws were designed to free those who had not the freedom to participate in the Eucharist. Moreover, they are brought into the Eucharist to receive the gospel and to enter the community of believers and worshippers, where they also received religious instruction. The laws that were developed to ban servile work were precisely articulated to free serfs to join the rest of Christendom in its taste of the kingdom of God as the bread was broken and shared.

Readmitting Apostates by Acknowledging Sin

In the early church, people thought of themselves as sinners, but there was not much attention to one's specific sins. In liturgies persons did confess being sinners, and there may have been some places where persons called out in the liturgy how they were sinners. We have, for example, certain accounts that at liturgies, people described how they were sinful, but these tend to be exceptions to the rule. In summary, everyone around the table knew that they were sinners, but they did not specify the matter.

With later persecutions, however, apostasy occurred, and the real issue was not that they had sinned but that returning apostates wanted readmission. How to readmit those who denied their baptism? How do you readmit to the community those who renounced the very sacrament that cannot be repeated? Eventually, rituals were appropriately developed for readmitting apostates, and the ritual focused on a renewal of their baptismal promises.

In time, however, some returning apostates were returning with a lot of problematic moral histories. Tertullian, for instance, expressed concern that the practice of readmitting apostates meant, in some instances, readmitting them with their histories of murder and adultery. Consequently, other questions arose about whether these readmitted murdering and adulterous apostates could participate in the Eucharist.

In reflecting on the three sins of apostasy (idolatry), adultery, and homicide, early church leaders in the third century began codifying them to conform to effectively the same worrisome categories at the Council of Jerusalem (see Acts 15:29). Eventually, the practice developed into confessing any of these three matters when an apostate was readmitted, and here begins the practice of confessing sins. You were, however, only readmitted once and therefore only required to confess once.

As persecutions ended, apostates were fewer, but some Christians still murdered and committed adultery. Now the offenses were no longer attached to the question of readmission for forsaking baptismal promises; now it was a matter of whether one could participate in the Eucharist having violated the matters addressed by the Council of Jerusalem.

To remedy this situation, bishops assigned heavy penances for murderers and adulterers, but these penances were so severe that repentant Christians tried to determine when the best moment was to reenter the church. For many, this became a decision to wait until one was too weak to perform the penances and so began the narrative of praying for a happy death and offering to make amends on one's death bed.

As we will see in the next chapter, on the penitentials, this early classification of such major sins became, I think, the beginning of a terrible mistake, for along the way we lost a sense of the gospel meaning of sin as the failure to bother to love. As we developed the habit of naming and numbering wrong actions that we performed, we eventually made sin a set of discreet little categories and, as John Mahoney wrote, subdued and "domesticated" sin and trivialized both sin as well as our need for mercy.[56]

Sexuality

Catholic moral teachings on sexuality evolved somewhat haphazardly over the centuries, with successive generations appropriating earlier positions based on often very different premises. In a manner of speaking, a series of fairly negative accretions were added one upon another, as we will see, until in the eighteenth century we have an absolutely negative estimation of sexual desires. For the most part, the teachings reflect the concerns of celibate men who, while pursuing an integrated life of discipleship (what was later called "the state of spiritual perfection"), found sexual desires to be obstacles rather than aids in the pursuit of that perfection. But the impact these teachings had on members of Christian cultures generally, and Catholic cultures particularly, remains to be learned. Still with reason, James Brundage claimed, "The Christian horror of sex has for centuries placed enormous strain on individual consciences and self-esteem in the Western world."[57]

These desires were not understood as belonging to or needing to be included into a broader understanding of any particular dimension of human personality. Rather, they were as random and as precipitous as they were for anyone who does not have an integrating concept like "sexuality." As arbitrary, powerful feelings, there was little about their nature that lent their being conceptually incorporated into an overarching, integrated reality. The idea of these venereal desires was as unstable as the desires themselves were felt. This helps us to understand that while early Christians understood the difference between *soma* and *sarx*, they did not understand sexual desires conceptually at all.

Language hindered any tendency to understand these desires as belonging to something more integrated or holistic. Pierre Payer's remarks on medieval ideas of sexuality extend to the very beginning of the Christian era:

> A contemporary writer dealing with medieval ideas of sex faces a peculiar problem of language. Treatises entitled, "On sex," are nowhere to be found, nor does one find talk about "sexuality," because medieval Latin had no terms for the English words "sex" and "sexuality." In the strictest sense, there are no discussions of sex in the Middle Ages. Whatever one might think of Michel Foucault's overall thesis about the development of the history of sexuality in the West, his claim about the relatively late date for the invention of sex and sexuality is, I believe, of paramount significance. The concept of sex or sexuality as an integral dimension of human persons, as an object of concern, discourse, truth and knowledge, did not emerge until well after the Middle Ages.[58]

In appreciating the development of Christian teachings on sexual desires, we begin with the Judaic tradition that believed in the moral rightness of spousal sexual intimacy and procreation. Except for certain communal movements like the Essenes, who practiced celibacy, it did not commend the notion of celibacy for its rabbinical leaders. Regarding sexual conduct, the Hebrew Scriptures regularly upheld fidelity and repeatedly prohibited sexual licentiousness. Like their neighboring communities, the Israelites were patriarchal and, therefore, women were effectively considered personal property.

In the Gospels, Jesus promoted the primacy of the love command and had very little to say about sexuality per se: an ethics of interiority that privileged the singleness of heart of the disciple was his major concern. Regarding celibacy, Jesus acknowledged that it was only for those "to whom it is given" (Matt 19:10–12). Concerning gender, the Gospel of Luke highlighted time and again the agency of women as supporters and companions of Jesus on his mission (8:1–3), at his passion (23:27–31), at his death (23:49), and at his burial (23:54–56). Most notably, at a time when the testimony of women had no legal force, they were the first to announce the good news of Jesus's resurrection (24:1–11). The Gospel of Matthew and the Gospel of John privileged the testimony of Mary Magdalene as the first witness and preacher of the good news (28:1–10; 20:11–18, respectively).[59] For this reason many scholars find a near gender egalitarian approach to discipleship. Thus, Christians see in the Acts of the Apostles, as the church is born, that Mary the mother of Jesus (1:14) had a central role in receiving the Holy Spirit with the Twelve; elsewhere, we find other women accorded leadership positions (e.g., Rom 16).

In the Pauline letters, we find more interest in sexuality than in the Gospels. With some expectation that the "end times" were upon him, Paul commended celibacy for those who could wait (1 Cor 7:39) and marriage for those who could not. Effectively, marriage was a licit remedy for sexual desires, while celibacy was the preferred choice for those who wished to be free of anxiety (1 Cor 7:32). Paul's pragmatic view of marriage made no connection with procreation.

Later, as Christians wrestled with questions about integration, Christians turned to the Stoics who saw that a rational purpose of sexual intercourse could be "brought under the rule of reason not by subduing it but by giving it a rational purpose, procreation.... With the adoption of the Stoic norm for sexual intercourse, the direction of sexual ethics was set for centuries to come."[60]

The Stoic purpose came with a price, however. Clement of Alexandria (ca. 150–200), who upheld the moral legitimacy of marriage and argued that it was against the Gospels to condemn sex within marriage, held with the Stoics that sex for the sake of pleasure, even in marital union, was contrary to law and reason. The "Alexandrian rule" about pursuing sex for pleasure would vex Christians for centuries.

The first time that sexual norms were developed is at the Council of Elvira (ca. 305–6), which dedicated nearly half of its eighty canons to sexual conduct. Brundage claimed, "The Elvira canons seem to represent an attempt to define a Christian self-identity. What made a Christian different from a pagan? Part of the answer according to the Elvira canons, was that Christianity observed a strict code of sexual ethics."[61] Although it seems that nearly all clergy of the third century whose marital status was known were in fact married, Elvira was the first attempt to prohibit clerical marriage.

In the fourth century, the development of sexual ethics took further definition as church fathers began writing specifically about venereal desires themselves. Furthermore, by making Christianity the state religion, Christianity began to take on an institutional control of the population much the way that pagan Rome controlled its citizens' bodies in previous centuries. Finally, because integration or single heartedness remained the moral imperative, many of the fathers translated their own personal experiences into a normative framework. In short, Christian theology on sex grew out of the personal struggles of major early figures whose ascetical programs for personal integration encountered an impasse in light of their own sexual urges. The personal influence of these figures is most evident in the lasting impression Augustine of Hippo has made on Christianity, whose teachings we will see below.

The church fathers' focus on sexual activity led to specific judgments about particular sexual actions. If married persons could not intend noncontraceptive sex, then they could not engage in anal or oral intercourse. In 342, the emperors Constantius and Constans outlawed such sex as deviant. As Louis Crompton notes, this same edict also outlawed homosexual activity and was later incorporated into Theodosius's law in 390 and later into the Theodosian Code in 438. By 390, any social tolerance of homosexuality was thwarted by civil law, which specifically opposed homosexual activity on the belief that effeminacy weakened the state. For this reason, the death penalty was imposed on any male engaging in passive sexual activity.[62]

At the same time, as we saw earlier, virginity developed as a significant Christian practice in a communal context. Sexual renunciation allowed women a freedom and a social role that marriage did not. Free of the real and present dangers both of pregnancy and childbirth and of patriarchal dominance, these women were able to explore a life with Christ in an environment largely ignored by the church fathers and a life with other women. In fact, their communities, along with the religious communities of men, actually highlight one instance in which Christianity promoted a certain equality. Notably, the communities of the Benedictines are helpful reminders of the development of the institutional settings in which Christian virginity flourished.

Still, at the same time that monastic communities were developing, the sexual lives of monks came under scrutiny, especially with regard to the "vices" of the "solitary" life, particularly masturbation, sexual fantasies, and even nocturnal emissions. Both John Cassian (365–433) and Caesarius of Arles (470–543) wrote extensively on the need for growth in spiritual perfection and to subdue any influence of sexuality at all. Yet, as Giovanni Cappelli observes, aside from the possibility of a condemnation by Clement of Alexandria, there were no other writings against masturbation prior to Cassian; masturbation was simply not considered a sexual offense.[63]

The Emperor Justinian (527–65) brought a number of reforms to the civil marriage code regarding divorce and the welfare of children of the divorced. He also provided sanctions to protect women from being forced into prostitution. In implementing the edict of 342 regarding homosexuality, however, Justinian expanded the death penalty to all males involved in any homosexual activity.

III. AUGUSTINE'S ETHICS

Any study of Augustine's ethics highlights that they are end-oriented, grace-based, and deeply resonant with human interiority. Unlike much of contemporary ethics that is based on action theory and defines ethics according to the rightness or wrongness of sets of discrete external actions (abortion, homosexual activity, self-defense, lying, bribing, etc.), Augustine's ethics is based on God's right-ordering of the will through virtue. Ironically, his legacy in ethics is more frequently connected to the external dimensions of actions pertaining to lying, war, and sex in marriage than with their interior moorings within the person.

Interiority and the End of Ethics

Whether a person claims it or not, the end of all human beings is happiness (*De moribus eccl* 1, 3, 4 cc. 427). For Augustine happiness is not found in the external goods that contemporary utilitarians or hedonists seek, but rather in an internal experience of peace, order, and love (*De civ Dei* 22, 30). For Augustine, happiness is a sense of human flourishment and well-being, a sense of the right realization of humanity, that is, a sense of completion in the nature of what it means to be human. This is the notion of the end for Augustine as well as Aristotle and Aquinas. For Augustine, the life of happiness is the good to be loved for its own sake (*De doctr Christ* 1, 22) and as Christians, God is our happiness (*De civ Dei* 19, 26). In God is our hope and in God we will rest.

The nature of happiness and the means for attaining it differentiate Aristotle from Augustine. For Augustine, happiness is contemplating God and it is attained by the great work of sanctification and justification. These two features are frequently mentioned by most commentators, but a third difference is found in Augustine's interest in interiority. For Aristotle, the end is found in the flourishment of the community or polis; for Augustine, the end has a deep resonance with the interior well-being of the person where peace, order, and love are attained through Christ.

The accent on interiority does not deny the communal nature of happiness; for Augustine, happiness is found in the kingdom (*De civ Dei* 22, 30, 5 cc. 428), the call to happiness in God is for all human beings, and the common good is always preferable to the private good (*Ep.* 211). Still, happiness is an encounter of God within ourselves, for God is closer to us than we are to ourselves (*Confessions* 3.6.11; *Soliloquies* 1.2.7, PL 32: 872). God then is not something or someone in addition to the human. God is the beginning and the end of the person and of humanity as a whole. For Augustine, we cannot understand the human being in its origins, nature, or destiny, apart from God.

For this reason, then, the order of charity, that is, the order of the triple love command (for God, self, and neighbor) depends on the issue of interiority and closeness. Because God is our cause and is closer to us than we are to ourselves, we are to love God first; because of that union we are to love ourselves then before our neighbor; and, finally, because that union is spiritual and because our union with our neighbor is a fellowship with God, we should love our neighbor before our bodies (*De doctr Christ* 1, 22–28). This order of charity becomes the norm in the scholastic tradition (see *ST* II–II, q. 26).

Augustine brings to ethics a deep sense of the interior, as any reader of the *Confessions* can appreciate. This sense of interiority focuses on the ordering of the will and the passions through the virtues. For this reason too the moral law is interior to us, neither exterior nor foreign, because God impressed the law on our hearts (*Conf* 2.4.9; *De Trin.* 14, 15, 21). Similarly, God formed us with a conscience. Augustine calls us to "return to our conscience," "to turn inward" and to have God as our witness (*In ep. Jo* 8, 9).

Augustine depends on Paul's letter to the Romans (13:1–7; 14:7—15:14), in which Paul speaks directly of the law and the conscience, but Paul's faculty of knowing right from wrong hardly bears the summons for Augustine to introspect. Stendahl calls Augustine's *Confessions* the first great document in the history of introspective conscience, a history that climaxes with the writings of Martin Luther.[64]

Within ourselves we find God, but we also find the law, the conscience, the will and in all this, the need for order. Inasmuch as goodness and badness then derive from our interior lives, sin and guilt are also deeply interior. While objective morality (as it is known today) was often described in the moral manuals of the past four centuries through the value or disvalue that we attached to the intrinsic worth of certain external actions, in Augustine moral objectivity is located interiorly in the virtues that order our passions and our will and in the vices that correspondingly prompt disorder in our lives.

The focus of that interiority is the will. For Augustine, the will was in a state of perfect balance before the fall, but original sin brought disorder into the will and our members. The task now is for the will to resist all evil inclinations (*De imperfectum contra Julianum*, 3.117) and to pursue, by God's grace, love (*De Trin.* 9, 12, 18). The mistress of all moral actions is the will, and it is through the will that God's grace moves us to action. Inevitably, if all depends on the will then anything that is required of us must be attainable. Therefore, God does not command the impossible (*De nat. et gratia*, 43, 50).

Criticism by moral theologians of Augustine is not with his overall ethics of interiority or even his introspecting conscience. Rather, Augustine's singular concern with the will leads others to charge him with a simplistic, reductionist idea of moral praise and blame. Is ethics, after all, nothing more than an act of the will? John Mahoney, for example, argues that Augustine leaves the implicit presupposition that all that is needed in the face of moral challenge is sufficient effort, for otherwise all challenges are surmountable. He argues that most moral challenges are more rooted in every person's familial, social, and historical hardships.[65]

The Virtues

Augustine's view on interior happiness naturally leads to a consideration of virtue and love. Virtues establish the order that leads us to God (*De ord.* 1.9.27). While in his early life Augustine trusted the virtues as a mode for attaining the highest good, later he rejected those who held we could be happy here on earth and achieve bliss by our own efforts (*De civ Dei* 19, 4). For Augustine, nothing good is possible without grace. Grace is always at work for true virtue.

Augustine gives us his brief definition of virtue as ordered love (*De civ Dei* 15, 22; *De moribus eccl* 25). His claim is based on the simple insight that an ordered will is a good love, and a misdirected one is a bad love (*De civ Dei* 14, 7). From that he adds that passions are "evil if love is evil and good if it is good" (*De civ Dei* 14, 7, 2).

Still, because of the need for our will to be ordered by God's grace, Augustine insisted that virtues without charity were not true virtues (*De Trin.* 15, 18, 32) and that no one could have charity without first having faith (*Ench.* 8). Basing his argument on Paul's claim that everything not from faith is sin (Rom 14.23), Augustine argued that all true virtues were rooted in charity and that charity was a gift of faith; without faith and subsequently charity, a virtue could not be considered true (*De civ Dei* 19. 25). This basically means that if a person does not believe in the God of Jesus Christ (who gives us the virtue of faith that makes charity possible), then the person cannot be virtuous. For Augustine, Plato and Socrates are not virtuous, nor for that matter, would Confucius, Mahatma Gandhi, or the Dali Lama be considered as such.[66]

Lying and Warring

Two specific teachings that illustrate well the rootedness of Augustine's moral instruction in the virtues are lying and warring. Regarding lying, Augustine establishes the foundational position that all lies are sins. His argument is based on the claim that a lie is rooted in the desire to deceive (*Contra mendacium* 4.5; *De mendacio* 3.3).

Alexander Flierl finds from the early life of the church that there has always been two schools of thought on this matter: one describing the lie as an absolutely wrong action, for example, Augustine, Aquinas, and Immanuel Kant (1724–1804)); the other, John Chrysostom (347–407), Bonaventure (1221–74), and Samuel Puffendorf (1632–94), referring to scriptural cases (Gen 27; 29:23; 31:35; 34:14–25; 38:13–26; Exod 1:17–20) and validating as morally legitimate certain exceptions.[67]

For his part Augustine did not view the scriptural "exceptional" cases as lies (*Contra mendacium* 10.23). Rather, he presupposed that those whom the Scriptures proposed as virtuous could not be liars (*De mendacio* 5.5).

We cannot, then, overlook Augustine's fundamental stance regarding internal virtue and the intention of deceiving. Augustine's position is not based on the wrongness of the external act of lying or on the consequentialist grounds that lies harm others (indeed he includes among lies those in which we try to protect another by lying), but rather for Augustine to attack something as unethical, it had to be an internal matter. Here, he turned to the vicious intentionality of deceiving others: lying is above all about the interior integrity of the person. Intending to deceive corrupts the agent. All lies are sins, therefore, and anyone who tries to say otherwise is shamefully deceived, since one thinks of oneself as honest as one deceives (*De mendacio* 21.42). The wrongness of the lie is rooted in the intention to deceive.

Virtue roots the teaching on just war as well. For Augustine, war is waged not for motives of gain or cruelty, but to secure peace, establish order, and punish wrongdoers (*De civ Dei* 19, 12;). Like the internal vices of vengeance, a warlike spirit or the lust of power are forbidden in just war (*contra Faust.* 22.74). We go to war, then, for the sake of establishing peace (*Epist* 189), and we punish for the sake of the sinners so as to free them from their evil will (*Epist* 138). The hermeneutics for estimating the legitimacy of war depends very much on the intentionality of the just leader who regrettably goes to war as a last alternative, needing to act so as to restore peace and order.

Still, as Lisa Sowle Cahill notes, the realism of Augustine forces him into the details of warring factions, and as he descends into these details, the original instinct of the interior motives of peace become replaced with specific interests in the actions of war.[68] This is especially the case when Augustine looks to restrain his listeners from vice rather than to guide them in virtue. In issues of restraint, Augustine invariably prohibits us from certain actions and those prohibitions often overshadow his original interest in promoting interior virtue.

Sexuality and Marriage

Losing track of his original claims regarding virtue as the foundation of ethics is especially apparent in his teachings on sexuality and marriage. Certainly, Augustine sees in chastity the virtue that preserves us from the disordered and dangerous vice of lust; in fact, conjugal chastity keeps spouses in good order, even in sacramental life. Still, for Augustine, one senses that chastity is not enough, and firm laws of restraint must be in place: "For although conjugal chastity makes a right use of the carnal concupiscence which is in our members; yet it is liable to motions not voluntary" (*De Trin* 13, 18). Interested in restraining the human from the disorder of sex, Augustine spends more of his energy on negative prohibitions than on virtuous development.

Three broad strokes paint Augustine's vision of sexuality. First, against the Manicheans, he upheld the moral rightness of marriage and its three purposes: children, marital friendship, and sacrament (*De bono coniug* 24, 32; *Gen Litt* 9.7.12). He held the rightness of sexual intercourse when engaged for the purpose of procreation (*De mor Eccl.* 1.35.79; *Adim* 3.1–3). If for mutual pleasure, they sinned though only slightly, venially. If they had sex and intended to avoid procreation, they sinned mortally. While believing then that intercourse for any other reason than procreation was morally wrong, he believed that sexual desires were basically disordered but by submitting them to the purpose of procreation, they were restored to a rational order (*De ret* 2.53).

Second, in his later writings against the Pelagians, he developed a theology of original sin and placed both the greatest effects of the sin in the basic disorder of sexual desires and the transmission of the sin in the act of sexual intercourse (*Gen Litt* 11.31.41). Sex became inextricably and irreversibly contaminated with sin in

Christian theology. This marks a radical departure from Paul who held that marriage was a legitimate alternative for Christians who were seeking the satisfaction of sexual desires (1 Cor 7). Now, married Christians needed a legitimate moral purpose to engage in sexual intimacy.

Third, Augustine's understanding of women was deeply troubling. In many ways, theology was being shaped by men for men based on their self-understanding and, as many of the church fathers were hermits or monks, it seems not only that their sexuality was dispensable, but their relationships with women were also effectively dispensable, as Cahill notes in Augustine's abandonment of his mistress.[69] Mahoney too notes that Augustine could not think of any reason why woman should have been given to man than for the procreation of children "as the soil is a help to the seed" (*Gen Litt* 9. 3.5).[70]

A second look at Augustine, however, helps highlight more positive features. He upheld the primacy of love in the moral tradition and that the pursuit of sex within marriage was basically, legitimately moral. As dark as his sexual views were, he was not a Manichean or a Gnostic.

Still, most commentators are very critical of Augustine's teaching on sexuality.[71] Mahoney argues that Augustine's view of sexuality was deeply reductionistic, that he grossly limited the range of sexuality and overlooked the fundamental complexities of human interrelational experience.[72] Cristina Traina contends that Augustine's belief that even licit marital sex ought to be hidden away has significantly caused us to understand sexuality as a deeply private and nonsocially relevant activity.[73]

In her work on female nakedness, Margaret Miles states that Augustine finds in the nudity of Eve weakness and dependency, which she attributes to Augustine's insistence that human relationships are inevitably ordered by dominance and submission, a point that Bernadette Brooten also makes.[74] Miles contrasts Augustine with Hildegard of Bingen (1098–1179), who sees Eve's body as life giving, while the married Martin Luther (1483–1546) refers to Eve's body as beautiful.[75]

Most are nearly universal in referring to the autobiographical nature of Augustine's stance toward sexuality as problematically privileged: When it comes to the marital and sexual experience of others, Augustine's own experience trumps all others. Indeed, Augustine comments that in all his conversations with persons who are or were married, he never met one who cited the hope of procreation as the reason for intercourse (*De bono coniug* 13, 15). In his history of contraception, John T. Noonan Jr. simply notes that for Augustine "the experience of the faithful is not regarded as a relevant datum."[76]

Still, the legacy of Augustine influenced the rest of the history of sexual ethics, though not absolutely. The idea that intercourse for the sake of pleasure was venially sinful is explicitly rejected by Martin LeMaistre (1432–81) and John Mair (1467–1550) precisely on the grounds of the experience of married couples. In time, theirs becomes the accepted teaching of the church as the experience of married couples makes greater claims on prudential judgments.

With all matters related to Augustine, however, generalizations are often contradicted by Augustine himself.[77] Though the sexual experience of married couples does not calculate into morally objective teachings, the experience of the laity is relevant when Augustine discusses *sensus fidelium*. In its Dogmatic Constitution on the Church, *Lumen Gentium* 12, Vatican II offered a classic formulation of *sensus fidelium* citing Augustine, that "from the bishops to the last of the faithful" (*De praed Sanct* 14, 27), the people cannot err in matters of faith.

Here, then, we come to the conclusion that when Augustine leads us in the pursuit of the good, he has a guarded confidence in humanity and his teaching on virtue is evidently apparent; but when he fears the chaos of our lives, he acts to restrain. Still, any study of Augustine's ethics must inevitably prioritize his interest in virtue, for otherwise we fall into a reductionism that fixates on particular actions rather than on persons, a vice that even Augustine did not avoid.

Chapter Three

Pathways to Holiness

The Fourth to the Sixteenth Century

I. INTRODUCTION

Taking a Different Path

Reading back into history is a challenge. I was first tutored to appreciate that challenge at Weston Jesuit School of Theology by John O'Malley, SJ, who along with Josef Fuchs and Klaus Demmer became my academic mentors. While studying at the Gregorian University I also had the good fortune to take courses with Louis Vereecke, CSsR.[1] Later, after I finished my doctorate on Thomas Aquinas, I read John Mahoney's *The Making of Moral Theology*. This was such a groundbreaking and influential work that when *The Oxford Handbook of Theological Ethics* appeared in 2005, Mahoney's was the only Catholic book to fit among those five books that shaped the field of theological ethics in the twentieth century.[2] Mahoney offered a lucid, well-researched, and fairly compelling account of the history of moral theology.

Mahoney began his eight-chapter work with "The Influence of Auricular Confession." He opened it as follows:

> To begin a historical study of the making of moral theology with an examination of the influence of auricular confession may appear to some an intriguing, and to others an

> unattractive prospect; but however one regards it there is no doubt that the development of the practice and of the discipline of moral theology is to be found in the growth and spread of "confession" in the Church.[3]

Mahoney narrated the history of theological ethics from the patristic era through the penitential and later confessional manuals into the moral manuals. He argued that the moral tradition has been fixated on sin or what he called a "spiritual pathology." By examining early councils, the penitential tariffs themselves, the imposition of the "Easter duty" by Innocent III at the Fourth Lateran Council, the Council of Trent, and the subsequent moral textbooks or manuals, Mahoney marshaled the evidence for his indictment of moral theology's obsession with sin. Whereas many moral theologians criticized the manualist era from the seventeenth to the twentieth century for its emphasis on sin, Mahoney blasted the entire tradition that singularly focused on "man in his moral vulnerability."[4] He wrote,

> The pessimistic anthropology from which it started, and which served inevitably to confirm and reinforce itself, particularly when the subject was pursued in growing isolation from the rest of theology and developed as a spiritual arm of the Church's legal system, drove moral theology increasingly to concern itself almost exclusively with the darker and insubordinate side of human existence.

He called this "miasma of sin" "not only distasteful but profoundly disquieting."[5]

His presentation of the patristic period, in fact, was incorporated into the chapter on auricular confession, little more than a four-page prelude to his commentary on the Celtic penitentials and later confessional manuals. After his chapter on auricular confession, he turned back to "the troubled person" of Augustine and his moral teaching: "It is there that the darkness and the somber pessimism are most in evidence and, it must be said, at their most dogmatic and devastating."[6]

His eighth chapter on the renewal of the church through Vatican II became a clarion call for finding a truly life-giving moral theology. In fact, before *Making*, Mahoney pursued such a moral theology in a collection of inspiring essays, *Seeking the Spirit: Essays in Moral and Pastoral Theology*.[7]

I benefitted immensely by his investigations, but my argument in this book marks a departure from Mahoney's foundational study. While his book remains influential, there has been a good deal of historical research in the thirty years since it first appeared.[8] That research has in turn affected my understanding of the history of theological ethics. As you have seen, my reading of Augustine is, as any comparison would show, remarkably distant from his, but there are two other major differences. First, in lieu of the patristic period as foundational for a sin-oriented ethics that became manifested in the penitentials and the practice of auricular confession, I propose that from the beginning of the church, members sought pathways toward the holy, and the confessing of sin and concern about this matter was only a part of the pathway to holiness and not the overall focus of either the patristic or medieval era. Second, Mahoney read the penitentials as they are. But, as "dark" as they might be, I believe that they appear within the context of what today might be called spiritual direction.[9] That is, the confession of sin by an individual was started not to help a sin-obsessed church deal with its pathologies, but rather as a pastoral development in the context of accompanying someone wanting to become a better Christian. In short, the penitentials did not arise from a vacuum but from a historical context of a people journeying toward holiness. Where Mahoney sees an obsession with sin, I see a struggle within the context of holiness, a context that begins with the Eucharist and a community of faith, but which couples with a myriad of spiritual pathways that develop through the next centuries.

Preparing for the Journey

A major figure in the history of Christian ethics and Scripture, Ceslas Spicq argues that though the Book of Genesis describes the creation of the human as being made in the image of God, this did not imply any command to imitate God.[10] Spicq claims that the people of Israel, who did not dare invoke the name of God, would hardly suggest a course of life of imitating the divinity. The transcendence of the God of Israel could not be understood let alone measured and therefore could not be imitated. The God of Israel gave commandments, laws, and precepts to be followed, not an identity to be imitated.[11]

For Christianity, the story is very different. John tells us that Jesus and the Father are one. John also writes that Jesus is the Way, the Truth, and the Life. Paul calls us to put on Christ. While Judaism did not invoke the language of imitation, Christianity did: in Christ we have the image in whom we are made and the image that is our future destiny. We are to become like him.

This was an insight very much alive in the Renaissance. We can consider Michelangelo's "theology" when at the beginning of the sixteenth century he put the Creation of Adam at the center of the ceiling of the Sistine Chapel and the risen Christ at the center of the Last Judgment in the same chapel, while putting the same face on both Adam and Christ. It captures rightly Renaissance theology: the human is made in the image of the divine; the alpha and the omega are one.

The blueprint of humanity for Renaissance humanists was in fact the incarnation. They were not simply celebrating humanity, but rather the humanity that is revealed in Christ. Still, it took time for Renaissance painters to get to the theology of Michelangelo. Their first predominant image was the Madonna enthroned with angels holding the Christ child. You can see this if you enter the very first room of Florence's great Uffizi art museum that celebrates the birth of the renaissance: the magnificent portraits of the Madonna and child enthroned surrounded by the angels by the three masters at the dawn of the Renaissance, Duccio, Cimabue, and Giotto. Later, they embraced the annunciation as the biblical moment of the stirring of the incarnation. The annunciation becomes the theological summons of the Florentine Renaissance[12] that celebrates not only God made human but also the human putting on the divine.[13] It is not until much later that Renaissance theology reaches its full maturation in Michelangelo's Sistine Chapel.

The Brazilian theologian Ronaldo Zacharias notes this transition well: "As *eikon* (true image) of the Father, Jesus does not only reveal the Father but he also becomes a visible model for the faithful."

He adds that with Jesus, the New Testament emphasizes the moral life as less "obedience to a precept," and more "an increasing conformity with a person," Jesus himself.[14] But as the Scriptures teach us, it is not until Pentecost, through the descent of the Spirit, that we have the possibility of responding to God's invitation to follow Christ. By the Spirit we can understand and follow Jesus and we can become by loving, like him. He is who we are called to be.

We should be careful about trying to project back into history the theological insights that belong to a later era. The claims of Spicq and Zacharias are right, but we should be careful of looking for them in the fourth century. Their theological insights are after all from the twentieth and twenty-first centuries. In fact, as we saw in the first chapter, even the very idea of discipleship as a theological concept is new. When Fritz Tillmann writes on the *Idea of the Disciple of Christ* in 1934, he is proposing a new theological view of who we are as Christians. That does not mean that no one thought of discipleship before Tillmann, for certainly many did, but today in the prayer of the church we hear frequently the term *discipleship* in a way that worshippers in previous centuries would not have heard it.

Tillmann's work had a transformative effect on the church since today we easily recognize church members precisely as disciples. Yet the Christian understanding of discipleship is very specific. When you say you are a disciple of Socrates, Thomas Aquinas, or Karl Marx, you effectively mean you are a devoted follower of their writings or their ideology. You study them to become more familiar with their ways of thinking. To be a disciple of Christ is to follow in his footsteps, to conform one's interiority to one's perception of who Jesus really was. To become a disciple of Christ is to try to understand him, to know him, to imitate him, and to become like him. This is the theology that Tillmann brought in the twentieth century.

In this chapter, rather than looking for models of discipleship or even imitations of Christ, we are going to look more generally at what I call pathways to the moral life and to holiness. I chose this phrasing because as we look at the writings and practices of the medieval world, we find a good deal of spiritual and moral exhortation and instruction using very particular virtues, along with very particular accompanying exemplars. Rarely, however, is the exemplar Christ. Old Testament figures along with New Testament ones and, in time, saints serve as models for the embodiment of recommended virtuous practices. It is not until the twelfth century that we begin to see a shift in the capacity of the Christian to understand her or his calling, and then in the great preaching of the thirteenth century, we have the christological exemplar emerging more and more evidently, as per example, the person of Francis who literally embodies the crucified Christ in his stigmata.

We cannot stop in the twelfth century, however. In this chapter, I want to take you to the sixteenth century so that you can appreciate the long history of virtue ethics and exemplars of both the moral life and of holiness. I want you to see that as the church matured, so did its expectations for who we could become in this life and of course, in the next. I want you to see that forming church members for the moral life is a long-lasting interest of the church; that formation was both in the key of vices to be rejected or abandoned and virtues to be appropriated or received.

Aiming for the moral life was not the only goal that church leaders put before the Christian. From the very beginning, Christianity had the instinct, as in the death of the deacon Stephen, to live beyond expectations, to go further into the land of holiness as Anthony did when at nineteen, he entered the desert in the third century. As Christianity is instructing on the moral life, therefore, there emerged an additional lesson, the invitation to live more than the moral life, to live if you will, the perfect life, that is the life of holiness.

As we will see, the line between the moral life and the life of holiness is not simply found or drawn. Certainly by the thirteenth century we have the line when we distinguish the schools of perfection as the religious life, but as we will see later, not everyone in the schools of perfection was perfect and not everyone living the life of perfection came from its schools. Moreover, as early as the fourth century the Christian beholds her or his calling to be a Christian as a lifelong growth, constantly open to greater and greater betterment. Christian morality is then wildly dynamic: there is never a stage of growth that becomes a finally achievable platform. Rather, Christian growth looks at a pathway that constantly opens up its horizon to greater challenges and expectations.

We must not think that these pathways were, however, Pelagian or Herculean trajectories, that is, that we accomplish this holiness without first and foremost God's invitation and grace. We cannot do this alone. For Christians nothing is possible without grace. Thus, most often we will see humility at the threshold of the journey, a humility that calls the agent to surrender first to the will of God and to abandon the vices already inherent in the novice ready to undertake the journey. In that humble abandonment, the Christian realizes that the journey he or she undertakes is by an invitation from God who supplies an accompanying grace to undertake each of the passages that unfold along the way.

Make no mistake: that journey is decidedly uphill. Early writers used the image of a ladder of ascent to highlight how upward bound the Christian journey to morals and holiness was. We are invited to ascend, to leave the vicious life below and to receive and appropriate the virtues until finally we enter the fullness of virtue in holiness above, but that end point is never visible. Only as we ascend the ladder does the next step become visible. The dynamism of Christianity depends on an interior growth that further expands the capacity of the Christian to fathom and advance ever upward along the pathways of holiness.

In a way, then, the maturation in the life of the Christian plays itself out in the life of the history of Christianity. Certainly, as we will see, the twelfth and the thirteenth centuries are breakaway periods in the life of the church. But, as I mentioned a moment ago, I want to take you to the sixteenth century so that you do not deceive yourself into thinking that at the twelfth century we arrived at the end of the journey, the summit of the ladder. Later, in the works of Erasmus and Ignatius of Loyola to say nothing of Granada and Lanspergius we find a fullness to the pathways that is fairly remarkable and that beckons us to appreciate just how "endless" the journey on these pathways seems to be.

Finally, do not be surprised that as you move up on the ladder of this history you begin to doubt the progress you are making. Christians, because of grace and humility and because they appreciate that they can never know who really is good, hesitate to mark their progress and rightly so. Christians are more comfortable with describing whereby the grace of God they find themselves, nothing more, nothing less. And that insight seems to be an appropriate place to close this introduction.

II. PATHWAYS TO MORAL LIVING AND HOLINESS FROM THE FOURTH TO THE SIXTH CENTURY

In this chapter we will proceed through four different stages. First, we consider the pathways to moral living and holiness that develop in the fourth to the sixth century. Then we turn to the treatment of sin in the famed penitential manuals and the later confessional manuals. Third, we consider the spiritual achievements of the twelfth and thirteenth centuries. Fourth, we close with the subsequent development of ascetical theology and its major contributions from the sixteenth century in the works of Erasmus and Ignatius of Loyola.

We saw in the last chapter that in the patristic era, the church worked through its identity with a self-understanding that was embodied and confident in the resurrection. The Eucharist quickly becomes the center of its practices and the measure of the inclusivity of Catholicism emerges with its insisting that soldiers, serfs, and all other laborers be free for Sunday worship. These liberating and inclusive laws are later known as the "dominical observance laws." Similarly, canonical procedures are developed in order to readmit those who have been alienated by their own apostasy.

Throughout the period, the practice of mercy becomes the trademark by which Christians become known and, according to Rodney Stark, by which they expand their evangelical reach. The practice of mercy is comprehensive with seven corporal works and seven spiritual works. They are deeply connected to the parable of the Good Samaritan that, as we saw in the first chapter, was seen from the second century onward as an allegorical narrative of salvation in miniature. This allegorical exposition passes on for fourteen centuries and helps Christians understand that they were saved by the merciful Samaritan. Knowing that, they are called to be merciful in kind.

The Good Samaritan is the quintessential exemplar of the early church and Martin of Tours, a fellow traveler, becomes himself a more "historically" sanctioned exemplar. Called to Christianity after his response to the beggar, Martin helps the early church to realize that if a pagan like Martin could act this way, all the more should they. But they too hope that in emulating the Samaritan they will encounter the one who taught them to go and do likewise.

Yet not everyone was a Martin. For our purposes, the entry of the nineteen-year-old Anthony (251–356) into the desert after the death of his parents and the distribution of his inheritance to the poor marks the beginning of a continuous Christian narrative of spiritual calling, moral striving, and gracious struggle in general, and a withdrawal from the world and human company in particular. In short, by aiming toward an ascetic ideal filled with personal combat with one's demons and by having that life described by Athanasius of Alexandria (295–373) in *The Life of Anthony* (356–62), the early church was provided with yet another pathway to holiness. In its day and its own way, *The Life of Anthony* became a bestselling classic.

In order to appreciate more deeply the spectrum of the pathways to holiness developed during this time, we turn to three other major texts from the fourth to the sixth century that illustrate how the early church promoted holiness: Ambrose's *De Officiis*, Augustine's *Sermon on the Mount*, and Pope Gregory's *Morals on the Book of Job*. In these works, the dynamism of the Christian life emerges quite quickly, a dynamism of growth, a sense that the Christian could always spiritually and morally improve.

According to Louis Vereecke, three key characteristics define the fourth century, the Golden Age of Christian patristic moral theology: the progressive conversion of the Roman empire to Christianity; with the end of persecution, the eventual realization of the monastic life as the ideal model of Christianity; and finally the beginning of the appearance of strong personalities capable of giving directionality to the life of the church.[15]

Aside from a hermitic exemplar like Anthony, Renzo Gerardi, in his history of moral theology, helps us to appreciate the witness and teaching of the bishops of this time. Their sermons, writings, and conferences are always both based on the Scriptures that inspire the bishops themselves and aimed to form the religious and moral lives of the dioceses.[16]

Early in his life, Ambrose (330–97) developed a capacity for administrative leadership. After his early successful training in Rome, he was appointed governor of Liguria and Emilia with its capital in Milan and afterward was proclaimed bishop of Milan. As bishop he was dedicated to the right administration of the diocese, the moral and religious formation of its members, the care of those committed to the life of asceticism, and the care for the poor and orphans.

His major work in morals is *De Officiis* written between 388 and 390, which originally derived from sermons he gave to the clergy of Milan.[17] The work finds its roots in Cicero's work with the same title from 44 CE, a work on the moral duties that all citizens should develop. Ambrose takes this insight and writes about ways to form the Christian consciences of clergy and laity. He offers his readers governing principles: reason should govern the emotions, due proportionality or moderation is key for addressing life's task, and one must attend to the signs of the times. As fundamental principles commonly found in what today is called "virtue ethics," they highlight how prudence guides the moral person to observe the moderate mean while also anticipating contexts for growth.

Ambrose proposes four virtues for the right realization of one's moral life: prudence, justice, fortitude, and temperance. He then proposes exemplars who embody the four virtues: Abraham, Jacob, Joseph, Job, and David. Here is the first exposition of what becomes a cornerstone of Christian formation: the acquisition of the cardinal virtues, first espoused by Plato, but now made Christian by Ambrose's appropriation and accompanying Old Testament heroes. Essential to understanding Ambrose well is that Christian humility guides the acquisition of the cardinal virtues; as he writes in his commentary on the Beatitudes in Luke 5, humility is "the parent and generation of the virtues."[18] Moreover, Ambrose insists in *De Officiis* that faith, hope, and charity are the defining virtues of the Christian. Renzo Gerardi calls this "the first organic treatment of Christian morals from a practical perspective."[19]

In his magisterial *The Sources of the Christian Tradition*, Servais Pinckaers, OP, proposes the Beatitudes as the foundation of the Christian moral life.[20] Here he turns to Augustine's sermon on Matthew's account and notes that Augustine's first pastoral work is this sermon, occasioned in 391 by his bishop, Valerius, who put Augustine in charge of preaching in Hippo. Augustine spent time preparing the sermon, exegeting the passage, and then offering his commentary. After preaching it, he publishes it, much as Ambrose had done with *De Officiis*: "If any one will piously and soberly consider the sermon which our Lord Jesus Christ spoke on the mount, as we read it in the Gospel according to Matthew, I think that he will find in it, so far as regards the highest morals, a perfect standard of the Christian life: and this we do not rashly venture to promise, but gather it from the very words of the Lord Himself."[21]

In considering the close of Matthew's sermon where Jesus refers to the wise man who built his home on a rock, Augustine concludes his introductory comment writing that the Lord's teachings "so perfectly guide the life of those who may be willing to live according to them, that they may justly be compared to one building upon a rock. I have said this merely that it may be clear that the sermon before us is perfect in all the precepts by which the Christian life is molded."[22] Besides the argument that these Beatitudes are the perfect sum of all Christ's teachings, Augustine sees them to be stages going from one to the next in ascendancy. The Beatitudes then are a course in spiritual growth with the first being the possibility of growth into the second, and the second into the third. He accompanies each Beatitude with a virtue. Not surprisingly, like Ambrose before him, Augustine starts with humility as the virtue for the poor in spirit. Humility is always the point of departure. Lúcás Chan underlines how Augustine—as well as many patristic figures like John Chrysostom and Ambrose all the way to modern theologians like Gerald Vann, Bernhard Häring, and Johannes Baptist Metz—all found in humility the pathway to becoming poor in spirit, the foundation of any Christian anthropology. Humility begins with the acknowledgment of God as the ultimate source and meaning of our lives, which leads us to renounce anything that separates us from God. This requires an ability to be both detached as well as free to share what we have, and both depend on ascetical practices of self-denial. Exemplars are plentiful but invariably they begin with Jesus, who tells us, "Take my yoke upon you, and learn from me, for I am gentle and humble in heart" (Matt 11:29).[23]

For Augustine, the Beatitudes go from the first stage, humility, to the seventh stage, which he sees as wisdom. Augustine only sees seven Beatitudes because he believes the eighth is a summary. Seven Beatitudes leave him to consider therein the perfection of the number itself. He writes, "The eighth, as it were, returns to the starting-point, because it shows and commends what is complete and perfect: therefore in the first and in the eighth the kingdom of heaven is named....Seven in number, therefore, are the things which bring perfection: for the eighth brings into light and shows what is perfect, so that starting, as it were, from the beginning again, the others also are perfected by means of these stages."[24]

Augustine, who loves relationships, sees in the perfection of the Beatitudes a perfect correspondence to the seven gifts of the Holy Spirit. He writes, "Hence also the sevenfold operation of the Holy Ghost, of which Isaiah speaks, seems to me to correspond to these stages and sentences."[25] However as soon as he makes the correspondence, he acknowledges that like a double helix, the ascendancy of the virtues associated with the Beatitudes is inverted by the virtues corresponding to the seven gifts. Speaking of the gifts, he wrote, "There is a difference of order: for there, the enumeration begins with the more excellent, but here with the inferior. For there it begins with wisdom, and closes with the fear of God: but the fear of the Lord is the beginning of wisdom."[26] By now seven has become a Christian number.

Augustine's conception of the Beatitudes as an ascent through progressive stages derives from Ambrose, his mentor. Pinckaers notes that while Ambrose accepts the Beatitudes as eight, the ascent for the Christian is from "detachment from the goods of this world to the crown of martyrdom with each stage or virtue leading to the next."[27] Augustine's ascent of the seven Beatitudes is appropriated by successors. Pinckaers lists them as Peter Damian in the eleventh; Anselm, Hugh of St. Victor, and John of Salisbury in the twelfth; and Thomas Aquinas in the thirteenth century.[28] Clearly, Augustine's sermon becomes a pathway text for the later church, and rightly he turned to the Beatitudes as the foundation for that pathway.[29]

Pope Gregory the Great (540–604) was the son of a Roman senator and becomes prefect of Rome in 574. Wanting something more from life, Gregory dispersed his wealth and entered the Benedictine abbey of St. Andrew's to become a monk. While building monasteries in southern Italy, he was chosen as one of the seven deacons of Rome and in 590 was selected to be Pope, the first monk so chosen. Gregory was a prolific writer. In 592, shortly after his election, he wrote *Liber Regulae Pastoralis* (*Pastoral Care*), a work not unlike Ambrose's *Duties*, wherein a major, beloved early church leader offered his clergy and fellow bishops a set of instructions on the pastoral care of souls. While Ambrose developed virtues for church leaders, Gregory, who had great understanding of psychological and spiritual needs, offered a variety of skills, practices, and activities as well as virtues to help in one's pastoral responsibilities. Gregory descended into the world of specificity. He developed the responsibilities of bishops and clergy, contrasting their responsibilities to the privileged roles of the nobility. The work of the man who preferred the title "servant of the servants of God" is immediately appropriated and remains to this day an invaluable classic.[30] Besides 850 of his letters that survive to this day, he also wrote *Dialogues*, a work in four books on the lives and works of saints, with the second book dedicated solely to St. Benedict.[31]

Gregory's major accomplishment in morals was *Moralia, sive Expositio in Job* (*Morals on the Book of Job*), an enormous work consisting of thirty-five books (today, three volumes of more than 1,750 pages).[32] The administrator who turned his focus on specific pastoral care was also a believer that the Scriptures have a moral wisdom that needs to be understood and taught. A forerunner to the contemporary attempts to develop a biblical ethics that exegetes the text and yet uses a virtue ethics methodology to make it applicable for contemporary moral instruction,[33] Gregory developed a method of three levels so as to break open the texts of the Book of Job to find and teach moral instruction. He first provided a literal or historical meaning of the text, then he moved to a rhetorical or allegorical translation of the text, and finally he provided a moral instruction from it. The boundaries for each level were fairly fluid. Significant for our study was Gregory's development of moral imperatives from Job as truly an exemplar in his patience, humility, and wisdom. These qualities emerge from the texts, but they are recognized as necessary qualities for leadership within the church, for example, in Augustine's own *Confessions*. One reads the text of Gregory mindful of Psalm 139: "Lord, you know me...." In relationship with God, one learns what God knows of me. The one who knows the depths of the sea knows the depths of my soul.

This trust in the wisdom of God served as a key to understand Gregory's extraordinary contribution. His reflections on Job 2:1–13 were quite to the point as we find Job scraping himself with a potsherd, sitting in a heap of ashes. He wrote,

> Paul saw the riches of wisdom within himself though he himself was outwardly a corruptible body, which is why he says *We have this treasure in earthen vessels.* In Job, then, the earthenware vessel felt his gaping sores externally; while this interior treasure remained unchanged. Outwardly he had gaping wounds but that did not stop the treasure of wisdom within him from welling up and uttering these holy and instructive words: *If we have received good at the hand of the Lord, shall we not receive evil?* By *the good* he means the good things given by God, both temporal and eternal; by *evil* he means the blows he is suffering from in the present.

Then Gregory reflected on how the miserable yet trusting Job countered his wife's counsel of despair and resignation, "Curse God and die!"

We should especially notice the skillful turn of reflection he uses when he gathers himself up to meet the persuading of his wife, when he says, "*If we have received good at the hand of the Lord, shall we not receive evil?*" It is a great consolation to us if, when we suffer afflictions, we recall to remembrance our Maker's gifts to us. Painful things will not depress us if we quickly also remember the gifts that we have been given. As Scripture says, *In the day of prosperity do not forget affliction, and in the day of affliction, do not forget prosperity* (see Sir 11:25).

Later, Gregory offered a lesson that ought to accompany us before and after afflictions and before and after graces; they were virtue lessons about hope and the corresponding vices of despair and presumption that arise when moderation was not followed: "Whoever, in the moment of receiving God's gifts but forgets to fear possible affliction, will be brought low by his presumption. Equally, whoever in the moment of suffering fails to take comfort from the gifts which it has been his lot to receive, is thrown down from the steadfastness of his mind and despairs."[34]

At the end of his entire thirty-five volume work, Gregory turned to reflect on himself and the man who counsels the entire church becomes on the final note, confessional. He begins the long conclusion, "Now that I have finished this work, I see that I must return to myself. For our mind is much fragmented and scattered beyond itself, even when it tries to speak rightly." A central insight arose:

> For when I turn inward to myself, pushing aside the leafy verbiage, pushing aside the branching arguments, and examine my intentions at the very root, I know it really was my intention to please God, but some little appetite for the praise of men crept in, I know not how, and intruded on my simple desire to please God. And when later, too much later, I realize this, I find that I have in fact done other than what I know I set out to do.

After having written the most significant work of his life over the course of nearly twenty years (575–95), Gregory described an insight about himself that today we may call, mixed motivations: "We must admit therefore that our intention, which seeks to please God alone, is sometimes treacherously accompanied by a less-righteous intention that seeks to please other men by exploiting the gifts of God." Faced with this insight, Gregory moved toward a point of moderation not unlike Job's: the good of his commentary can never be too good and the wickedness of his own intentions will never be too bad. Like the plight of Job, the good and bad balance each other. In that light, at the end of his text he opts for transparency: "But I think it worthwhile for me to reveal unhesitatingly here to the ears of my brothers everything I secretly revile in myself. As commentator, I have not hidden what I felt, and as confessor, I have not hidden what I suffer. In my commentary I reveal the gifts of God, and in my confession I uncover my wounds."[35]

The scriptural exemplars of the Good Samaritan and Stephen, of Martin and Anthony, of Job and Paul entered into the life of the church and provided in their modeling pathways to holiness. However, these bishops—Ambrose, Augustine, and Gregory—also became in their lives, writings, and confessional transparency, worthy ideals of Christian living. Their theology gave a moral instruction that builds up the church to be not a church that has already attained the grace of its calling, but rather a church that, like its people and its leaders, was on the way through stages of ascent. Rightly they are named doctors of the church because they helped not only its members but the church itself to discover that the pathways to holiness required us to move upward and ahead, that as humble as we are called to be, we are still called to great works whether building monasteries, establishing dioceses, instructing on pastoral care, or developing a theology for a new church grappling at once with its limitations and yet the summons, and along the way our own limitations and our unending need for grace.

The life of the Christian is inevitably dynamic; we cannot miss that insight. No less than Gregory summarized it when he wrote in *Pastoral Care*, "In this world the human soul is like a ship sailing against a river's current: one is never at all permitted to stop, for if it does not always strive at its best, it will sink back to the bottom."[36] Later Bernard of Clairvaux followed the insight of Gregory: "On the way of life, to not progress, is to recede."[37] Later, Aquinas conflated their insights into a motto: "On the way of the Lord, to stand is to move backwards."[38] The call to follow does not let anyone stand behind.

III. CONFESSING SIN FROM THE SIXTH TO THE SIXTEENTH CENTURY

We have seen how persecution prompted major theological and pastoral problems about readmittance. Furthermore, there were questions about those who after having been baptized still committed other scandalous sins that "endangered the community's holiness." By the late second century, in most urban centers the "order of penitents," not unlike the "order of the catechumenate," was formed to assist these public sinners who voluntarily go through a conversion process that is accompanied by and within the church. When the conversion was evidently complete, the sinner was "restored" to the church by the laying on of hands by the bishop in a liturgy. This once-in-a-lifetime opportunity for readmission was also marked by demonstrable forms of repentance and reformation, like prayer, fasting, sackcloth, and ashes. Finally, this experience of shameful, public renunciation and restoration was for only serious sinners, and the only time any of these procedures were private was for one who was dying.

For a variety of reasons, the entire process became further formalized and institutionalized and, by the fourth century, became known as the "canonical penance." By the sixth century this institution began to fade. James Dallen wrote, "Without a clear sense of Christian life as a call to continuing growth in holiness and a sense of solidarity in community," few Christians saw any good of entering into such penitential institutions. By this point, besides the most pious, only those coerced into this form of penance entered into the band. However, at the same time, many other Christians sought private penance for the dying, what was once the "emergency adaptation of an exceptional institution," which, in time, became a well sought-after practice.[39]

Dallen reports that a tradition from early Celtic monasticism developed in which monks and nuns who had no need of something as serious as canonical penances sought advice from spiritual experts about how to take account of their ongoing life of prayer. In the context of spiritual direction at the monasteries and convents, monks and nuns and some privileged nobility sought first spiritual direction and, in time, a process to give an account of their soul. In this context, the practice of confessing one's sins was born. As the practice expanded, this naming of sins was indeed called "confession," a rather remarkable departure from the activity with the same name whereby a community acknowledged their faith together in the eucharistic liturgy.[40]

The practice of private confession developed in this way. Following the transactional language of redemption, committing a sin was considered the same as incurring a debt. On one's pathway to holiness, to have one's debt lifted, one had to pay a tariff.[41] In the Celtic monastic world, a monk would acknowledge her/his sins to the spiritual director who in turn stipulated penitential acts as appropriate tariffs to remit the debt. When the penance was completed, the debt was lifted. With its wider appropriation, more spiritual directors looked to known abbots and abbesses who published their list of tariffs according to the sins confessed and the publications became known as "penitential manuals." Within these manuals, the tariffs were assigned to sins categorized usually according to the eight deadly vices articulated by John Cassian. As any reader of the indispensable *Medieval Handbooks of Penance* edited by John T. McNeill and Helena M. Gamer can see, these manuals were fairly brief and very local, inasmuch as they dealt with sins committed for the most part by those few regional Christians (monks, nuns, clerics, bishops, and occasionally devout nobility) who had a spiritual director to whom they also confessed.[42]

In his study of the Irish penitentials, Hugh Connolly noted the originality in the Celtic practice of confessing sins in that it shows no familiarity with the earlier canonical penances or the "order of penitents."[43] He wrote that in the beginning these "confessions were usually made to a spiritual guide known as an *anamchara*, a Gaelic word that literally means soul-friend. The soul-friend was esteemed within the monastic system. An ancient Irish saying comments that 'anyone without a soul-friend is like a body without a head.' Every monk was expected to have an *anamchara* to whom he could make a manifest his conscience (*manifestation conscientiae*)."[44] The practice became appropriated by many. As Dallen noted, unlike the canonical penances, the monk's mode of proceeding became more attractive: "no public knowledge, no social stigma, no life-long consequences—and it could be repeated whenever necessary." Moreover, these private penitents were not excluded from the community, but they did not receive communion until the tariff was paid. Still, at this time, communion was rarely received.[45]

The development of the penitential practice was accompanied by the development of the penitential manuals. Throughout their history until the eve of the thirteenth century, the penitentials held certain presuppositions. First, sin was committed by the execution of a wrong act. Second, the gravity of the sin was first determined by the act itself. Third, further questions about the egregiousness of the act were determined by the agent's permanent and temporary state in executing the act. Circumstances were considered only inasmuch as they intensified the gravity of the sin: they were not, at first, engaged to reduce guilt. Guilt was further determined by the permanent and temporary states of the penitent. They first judged that those who were more morally competent were held to greater moral responsibility; tariffs for the same grave matter were greater for an abbot than for a cleric, cleric more than a monk, a monk more than a noble person, and so on.[46] The second consideration regarded whether the sinful act was rare, occasional, or habitual.[47]

The penitentials presumed that if an objectively bad act was performed, the confessor merely needed to know just how subjectively bad the agent was. There were no mitigating circumstances; the manuals did not speculate about the possibility that the penitent could have been excused or even good while performing the prohibited act. Neither did they consider right actions being performed out of some subjectively bad motivation. The confessor could only know the penitent's moral worth through the penitent's acts, and then only those acts specified in the manuals. Thus, once an objectively bad act was committed, subsequent questions about the agent were not to determine *if* the agent was guilty but rather *how* guilty the agent was. Questions about the agent were predominantly circumstantial, helping the confessor assign the sentencing.

The Penitential of Cummean gives us a good idea of what an early handbook was like. Listed below is the entire treatment of the first vice, gluttony. The Penitential seems to have been compiled sometime in the mid-seventh century and the manuscript from which it comes was written in the monastery of Lorsch (near Worms, Germany) around the beginning of the ninth century. The rudimentary list helps us to see that the sins came more from the mouths of sinners than the imagination of Cummean. Despite its elemental structures, incipient concerns are very evident.

I. Of Gluttony

1. Those who are drunk with wine or beer, contrary to the Savior's prohibition (as it is said, "Take heed that your hearts be not overcharged with surfeiting and drunkenness or with the cares of this life lest perchance that day come upon you suddenly, for as a snare shall it come upon all that dwell upon the face of the whole earth,") and [that] of the Apostle; ("Be not drunk with wine wherein is luxury")—if they have taken the vow of sanctity, they shall expiate the fault for forty days with bread and water; laymen, however, for seven days.
2. He who compels anyone, for the sake of good fellowship, to become drunk shall do penance in the same manner as one who is drunk.
3. If he does this on account of hatred, he shall be judged as a homicide.
4. He who is not able to sing psalms, being benumbed in his organs of speech, shall perform a special fast.

5. He who anticipates the canonical hour, or only on account of appetite takes something more delicate than the others have, shall go without supper or live for two days on bread and water.
6. He who suffers excessive distention of the stomach and the pain of satiety [shall do penance] for one day.
7. If he suffers to the point of vomiting, though he is not in a state of infirmity, for seven days.
8. If, however, he vomits the host, for forty days.
9. But if [he does this] by reason of infirmity, for seven days.
10. If he ejects it into the fire, he shall sing one hundred psalms.
11. If dogs lap up this vomit, he who has vomited shall do penance for one hundred days.
12. [One who] steals food [shall do penance] for forty days; if [he does it] again, for three forty-day periods; if a third time, for a year; if, indeed, [he does it] a fourth time, he shall do penance in the yoke of exile under another abbot.
13. A boy of ten years who steals anything shall do penance for seven days.
14. If, indeed, afterward [at the age] of twenty years he adds to this any considerable theft, for twenty or forty days.[48]

This short text raises a number of questions, among them: If one was held accountable for a homicide, what was the tariff? If one knew the tariff for a homicide, would anyone ever confess that out of hatred they caused another to get drunk? Were monks often drunk during the singing of the office? How often were they receiving the Eucharist? Why is a boy of ten confessing? These and other questions would arise if we were to see the other six vices as well. Moreover, we can be sure that the more experienced penitential writers had more sins, more concerns, and more distinctions. And this helps us to understand the mindset of those who promoted and participated in the penitential practice that spread over time across northern Europe.

As these practices and their manuals develop so does the sophistication of measuring sin. Similarly, the practice goes from a monastic practice to a much larger institutional one. The question of exactly when absolution was introduced is a case in point. We do not know exactly when absolution was added to the spiritual director's repertoire. In the context of canonical penances, "absolution" was basically the bishop welcoming a known sinner back to the church through a major liturgy. With the rise of clericalization, we find in the ninth century an absolution provided by the priest that signified that there was no further satisfaction needed to remit the debt: by the assigning of the penitential tariffs, the penitent's debt would be remitted, conditional to the completion of the penance. In time, absolution and not the penitent's own satisfying performance of penance, became more and more the sign of the lifting of the debt.[49]

Kilian McDonnell provided a good summary of the influence of the penitentials from the sixth to the thirteenth century: "The penitentials took the baptismal commitment with gospel seriousness, made private confession part of a larger process of discernment and spiritual direction, fought against episcopal intransigence for the principle that priests should grant access to penance as often as a believer sinned, made forgiveness accessible to all, and quite rightly leveled more severe penalties on monks, priests, and bishops than on the laity."[50]

The influence of these sin manuals changed dramatically when the Fourth Lateran Council (1215) imposed on Christendom the "Easter Duty," that is, the obligation to receive communion at least once a year during the Easter season. To fulfill the Easter duty, Christians had to be in the "state of grace," and therefore every Christian had to confess their sins annually so as to fulfill their duty. This obligation made the turn to penance no longer a matter of spiritual election, but rather a required duty. The Fourth Lateran Council gave the classical formulation: the faithful "must confess all their sins... to their own priest at least once a year."[51] "All their sins" became of course an enormous issue, as we will see. The nineteenth-century church historian Henry Lea called the Council's edict "the most important legislative act in the history of the Church."[52]

We should not miss, however, that if communion is being mandated as occurring at least once a year, the frequency with which one received communion seems to have changed from the earlier practices of the church. We do not yet know how great the difference nor why, but mandating it once annually prompts at least these questions.

By introducing confession conditionally into the fulfillment of the Easter duty, not only did the laity now have to learn how to make that confession, but the clergy also had to learn how to hear it. Moreover, since the sins of monks and nuns tended to focus on their vows and religious practices and were generally less complex than those of people with families and businesses, the penitential manuals became inadequate for this much larger and more diverse group of sinners. In the thirteenth century, the *Summae confessorum* that covered a lot more sinful material than the penitential manuals, were published; like their predecessors, they too were organized around the seven deadly sins.[53]

The Easter duty had a profound effect on the newly founded preaching orders, the Franciscans and the Dominicans. While Leonard Boyle reminds us that the Dominicans were recognized by Pope Honorius III in 1217 as the Order of Preachers, they were also given by the same pope in 1221 the mission to hear confessions. While at their inception they had the ministry of preaching, only four years later the Dominicans had two ministries.[54] The result was that the Dominican course of studies was comprised of two very different tracks: the first was for a very few to go for a university education at any of the Dominican "studia" ("houses of study") that were established in Oxford, Paris, Cologne, Montpelier, or Bologna, while the second was for the majority, the "Fratres communes," who were instructed by a house "lector" not only for their years of formation but for their entire lifetime of ministry. Every apostolic community had a lector who presented a "pastoral" formation on preaching and hearing confession to the fratres; these lectors were provided with a wide variety of texts written by those in the first track. These texts were biblical concordats, treatises on virtues and vices as well as the Ten Commandments, and the *summa confessorum*.[55]

The *Summa confessorum* were clearly central to the lectors' repertoire, and they were much heftier than the penitentials. McDonnell described them:

> The summae are manuals for confessors, giving an astonishing number of ways of sinning, classifying them, and providing a list of questions the confessor might pose to the penitent. Where the penitentials objectively and abstractly focus on the sin and the appropriate tariff, the summae center on the person of the sinner, and on the personal relationship between confessor and penitent. They are academic, pragmatic, concise books for the confessor, not the penitent. The early penitentials come out of a monastic context, the summists are, with some exceptions, either Franciscans or Dominicans, persons closer to the laity.[56]

Moreover, according to Boyle, the Fourth Lateran Council became the first of a series of major interventions that gave to the parish priest a spiritual authority never before enjoyed. The priest became adequately paid, literate, and respected, and occasionally even received a sabbatical. And, he had assistance, like the religious lector, but also an industry of big, thick *summae confessorum* along with the treatises on the Ten Commandments, the virtues, and the vices.[57]

It would do us well to look at one of the most famous texts to appreciate how extraordinarily different they were from the penitentials. Thomas Tentler introduces us to the work of the Franciscan Angelus de Clavasio (1411–95), *Summa Angelica de casibus conscientiae* or simply the *Angelica*. The *Angelica* was first published in 1486. It went through twenty-four editions before 1501, being published in Venice, Nuremburg, Strasbourg, and Lyons. From 1501 to 1520 it was published at least nineteen times; from 1550 to 1600 it was still published four times from Venice alone. Its most famous moment was when Luther publicly burned it along with Johann Eck's books and the papal bull excommunicating Luther in December 1520. Luther's objections were that the manual attempted to help the confessor and penitent name all their sins as if, first, that were possible and, second, it would be effective of anything. Luther believed that Christians should be consoled by faith alone; instead, they were being consoled by the priest's absolution.[58] For these reasons, he nicknamed the *Angelica*, the *Diabolica*.

The *Angelica* offered 975 questions that the confessor can pose.[59] Specifically it guided the confessor to receive a complete confession, integral, the result of due diligence.[60] The confessor was to interrogate; to fail to do so, occasioned a mortal sin on the confessor's part. Still, "his questions should be confined to those things which are 'reasonably pertinent' [*rationabiliter pertinentia*] to salvation. Further, the confessor should not be 'excessively scrupulous' [*non debet...esse nimis scrupulosus*] in asking all possible questions about all the possible sins.[61] Angelica says that the confessor should not ask 'all things about everything' [*non omnes de omnibus*]."[62]

What was the impact of the Fourth Lateran Council and the history of the *Summa confessorum*? First, unlike the shameful public penances of the Patristic period, the *summas* were for private confession; private guilt not public shame was the matter of the confessional. Second, they were very popular; both priest and the penitent knew about the texts and their authority, and the penitents were no longer monks in northern Europe, but the entire church. By the thirteenth century, confession had "become a private act, protected by the seal of the confessional, emphasizing the inner preparation and disposition of the penitent seeking help from a sacrament dispensed by a priest."[63]

Still, Catholic penitents mostly confessed sins of commission. There were very few sins of omission confessed in the sixteenth-century confessional: hardness of heart for the poor did not make an entry, for instance.[64] Nonetheless, as we will see in the later casuistry of the sixteenth century, we ought not to think that this was simply a registry of personal sexual sins; the seventh and the eighth commandments became the focus of most manuals. Moreover, we can say with Tentler, "In theory and practice, sacramental confession provided a comprehensive and organized system of social control. Its first principle was the sacramentally ordained priest's dominance." Its second essential principle was "the goal to make people obey not only men, but morality and law." Finally, "the penitent is supposed to derive profound psychological benefits from sacramental confession, and authorities try to ensure that this forum offers consolation as well as discipline."[65] No less than the *Catechism of the Council of Trent* (1566) gives us a sense of the achievement of the Fourth Lateran Council and the subsequent *summa confessorum*: "In the tribunal of penance the priest holds the place of a judge, and pronounces sentence according to the nature and gravity of the offence. Unless, therefore, he is desirous that his ignorance should prove an injury to himself and to others, he must bring with him to the discharge of his duty the greatest vigilance and the most practiced acquaintance with the interpretation of the law, in order to be able to pronounce, according to this divine rule, on every act and omission."[66]

IV. THE PATHWAYS TO HOLINESS OF THE TWELFTH AND THIRTEENTH CENTURIES

The Discovery of the Self

In order to appreciate that these developments do not happen on simple and unrelated tracks, it is important for us to understand that they are happening always along pathways to holiness, for the first stage of any pathway requires the conversion from sin. Up to now we have seen the enormous arc of the sin manuals, from the Patristic order of the penitents to the Irish penitentials to finally the early thirteenth- to sixteenth-century tenure of the *summa confessorum*. It is time for us to return to the eve of the Fourth Lateran Council to ask the following: Was there something in the development of such pathways that could prompt the development of such a structure as the confessional? Furthermore, might we discover that those pathways offered not only manuals for the confession of sin, but more importantly, manuals for the following of Christ?

Assuredly, they did.

"The twelfth century has long been seen as a turning point in the history of Latin spirituality," wrote Bernard McGinn. "There can be no argument that the twelfth century was fascinated with the mystery of the human person as *imago Dei* and brought to the study of this mystery a systematic ordering mentality not seen before." Through Abelard's (1079–1142) insistence on the conscience, Bernard of Clairvaux's (1090–1153) location of the image of God in human freedom, Hildegard of Bingen's (1098–1179) knowledge of the way of the Lord and appreciation of the goodness of the human body and the delight of the passions,[67] and Richard of St. Victor's

(1123–73) understanding of the interpersonal human subject as an image of the three-personed God, the theologians of the twelfth century developed a powerful relational anthropology as a base for their spirituality.[68]

Caroline Walker Bynum agreed with McGinn: "No period was ever busier creating structures for its piety than the twelfth century."[69] Like McGinn she too examines Bernard of Clairvaux, who with "other 'new monks' stress discovery of self- and of self-love as the first step in a long process of returning to love and likeness of God, a love and likeness in which the individual is not dissolved into God but rather becomes God's partner and friend."[70] Bernard's spirituality as well as that of his contemporaries drew deeply from the Scriptures and cultivated in a particular way a devotion to the humanity of Jesus, which moved readers into greater intimacy with Jesus and with those who shared the devotion.[71] In developing a highly relational anthropology, then, the twelfth century never compromised the person and in fact discovered, "the self, the inner mystery, the inner man, the inner landscape."[72]

This claim of the discovery of the self is of particular moment for our study. The discovery of the self did not mean the endorsement of individualism. As Bynum argued, the twelfth century "also discovered the group in two very precise senses: it discovered that many separate 'callings' or 'lives' were possible in the church, and it elaborated a language for talking about how individuals became a part of them (the language of 'conforming to a model')."[73] Religious persons understood that they could specifically and individually hear the call and respond to the call. All these are what we today would call "experiences." Spiritual or ascetical theology expanded greatly at this time, and the individual experience of a Christian became something worthy of consideration.

Into the thirteenth century, these insights flourished and developed into three long-standing beliefs. First, inasmuch as union with Jesus undergirded ascetical theology, charity became the premier virtue for the pursuit of perfection. Thomas Aquinas, for example, insisted that the perfection of the Christian life consisted chiefly in charity;[74] the perfection of charity is the end of religious life.[75] Religious life was instituted to obtain the perfection by exercises whereby the obstacles of charity were removed.[76] Those exercises are the stuff of the religious life, which he called "a training school for attaining to perfection in charity."[77] Perfection, as Thomas noted, was not simply for those in the newly formed religious communities. In fact, religious life was no guarantee for the life of perfection: being in a school of perfection was not a guarantee of growing in perfection and not everyone who was "perfect," was in such a school.[78]

Second, the twelfth-century foundational self-understanding of the practicing Christian as being in the image of God so ennobled Christians that it dared them to develop as a goal for life nothing less than union with Jesus. But in the thirteenth century both this foundation and its goal forged a bridge: the imitation of Christ. Being in God's image, the thirteenth-century devout Christian dared to imitate Christ so as to draw closer to him. This imitation of Christ flourished through a variety of texts and practices. As Giles Constable noted, that invitation to imitate in turn produced a self-understanding of the devout Christian as a disciple: "After the twelfth century the ideal of the imitation of Christ increasingly entered the main stream of late medieval spirituality and became equated with following Christ and, more generally, with the Christian way of life."[79] This prompted a powerful interest in Christ's earthly life, which generated works such as the *Meditations on the Life of Christ* (ca. 1265) as well as the *Lives of Christ* by Michael of Massa (d. 1337) and Ludolf of Saxony (ca. 1348–68). "The most influential exposition," however, was the early fifteenth century *Imitatio Christi* (1418–27) that "summed up and handed on to later generations much of the spiritual teaching of the twelfth and thirteenth centuries."[80] The devotional practice of imitating Christ begins then in the thirteenth century, receives enormous support with the publication of the *Imitatio*, and continues until the present as a devotional means to finding the way to perfection in union with God. Of course, along the way the understanding of Christ develops significantly.

A word needs to be said about the *Imitatio Christi*, a work that has been translated into more languages than any book other than possibly the Bible.[81] Years ago I was asked by a community of religious women living in Rome to give them a day of recollection, and they began it by sharing with one another their image of God. Each one had a different image and therein it seemed we grasped a little of the plenitude of God that so many different images were present. But after a while the plenitude conveyed more the diversity of the community. In fact, one after another had an image that bore an uncanny reflection of themselves. The teacher emulated the Jesus in the Sermon on the Mount. The charismatic sister heeded the Holy Spirit. The administrator followed the king in Matthew 25. The pastoral assistant was Jesus the preacher. In many ways, their attraction to a particular image was more a way of seeing the model for their vocation. In other words, these images of God were rarely free of a lot of subjectivity. Of course, these images are right to have; the exemplar of our lives ought to be one who concretely influences our work in our specific vocation. Still, there is a deeply subjective resonance here.

The *Imitatio Christi* is similarly reflective of the vocation of the writer Thomas à Kempis (1380–1471). However, this text became normative for its readers, becoming more like the goal of the author than say Jesus Christ himself. In fact, the handbook spends so much time on the inner life and the matters of internal consolations that there is little that directs one's external actions. In short, this handbook basically promotes a monastic piety that esteems isolation and eschews human company to say nothing of the thirteenth-century apostolic development of going into the heart of the towns to evangelize, educate, and accompany fellow Christians in need. This extraordinarily successful book led its reader to an inward, private journey rather than an outward, social one.

Still, this was a handbook for individual persons and so the interpretations of how the reader was to abandon the vanity of the world, subdue one's temptations, and focus on Christ were left, if you will, to the designs of the reader: "No man rejoices safely unless he has within him the testimony of a good conscience."[82] In a way, the *Imitation of Christ* marks a much more significant access to a spirituality that the laity could read and appropriate, but it was a spirituality that led to the monastery and not to the world as it existed, that is, to the world where the reader lived. Indeed, there was much that the text commends about self-discipline and attentiveness to God, but while talking about one's spiritual growth there is little about bettering oneself for neighbor love, that is, there was a spiritual growth that was not significantly tied to a moral growth.

The first chapter of the first of four books begins with a clear summons to a form of discipleship, mindful of the power to be in the image of God: "He who follows Me, walks not in darkness," says the Lord (see John 8:12). Through these words of Christ, we are advised to imitate his life and habits, if we wish to be truly enlightened and free from all blindness of heart. Let our chief effort, therefore, be to study the life of Jesus Christ: "The teaching of Christ is more excellent than all the advice of the saints, and he who has His spirit will find in it a hidden manna. Now, there are many who hear the Gospel often but care little for it because they have not the spirit of Christ. Yet whoever wishes to understand fully the words of Christ must try to pattern his whole life on that of Christ."[83]

The imitation quickly became a flight from the world into the monastic confines: "This is the greatest wisdom—to seek the kingdom of heaven through contempt of the world."[84] Later, in the seventeenth chapter, we read, "If you wish peace and concord with others, you must learn to break your will in many things. To live in monasteries or religious communities, to remain there without complaint, and to persevere faithfully till death is no small matter. Blessed indeed is he who there lives a good life and there ends his days in happiness." A little further on, we read, "If you would persevere in seeking perfection, you must consider yourself a pilgrim, an exile on earth. If you would become a religious, you must be content to seem a fool for the sake of Christ. Habit and tonsure change a man but little; it is the change of life, the complete mortification of passions that endow a true religious."[85]

We cannot overlook the significant impact of the *Imitatio Christi*. First, it made ascetical literature available to laypeople. Second, rather than providing them a simple list of prayers or an explication of existing prayers, it provided them with an embodied, relational text for the pursuit of holiness. Third, beyond a doubt, with its publication, no exemplar ever again surpasses Jesus Christ as the ultimate, worthy goal of humanity. The earlier church looked to the prophets and early martyrs, but the developments of the twelfth and thirteenth centuries led Christians to consider imitating the one in whose image they were made. At first there was the Godhead, the Trinity itself, but in time, we understood that we were made in the image of the one who became incarnate for us. Fourth, with the *Imitatio*'s enormous success, Jesus became our indisputable model and therein became approachable. We cannot underestimate this shift: think how the orders of the thirteenth century are named after their founders; by the sixteenth century there's one called Companions of Jesus. The *Imitatio* is indisputably a catalyst for the development of intimately relating to the one who became flesh and died for us. Fifth, the text instructed us to look inward and discover consolation. That invitation, I think, was the key to its success: inviting the Christian to find within oneself where the Spirit dwells and to become refreshed by that encounter. Finding that place would lead others to fathom further the world where consolation and desolation were indicators of the will of God.

Still, in an odd sort of way, the spiritual manuals of the twelfth and thirteenth centuries made the spiritual life available to larger groups of people than were in the monastery. Indeed, these books were read often by singular Christians, but their exercises and their emphasis on subduing the interior led the reader not to enter her or his ordinary lay world but rather the monastic world of its writers: "Very many great saints avoided the company of men wherever possible and chose to serve God in retirement."[86]

Third, not all spiritualities were like the *Imitatio Christi* that led to a monastic life, withdrawn from the emerging towns and cities of the thirteenth century. Many other spiritualities led to coherent religious and lay groups. The thirteenth century is marked by significant evangelical movements that led to remarkable preaching. Previously, those who sought to be followers of Christ in the pursuit of "perfection" chose the monastery outside of any urban place. Dominic, Francis, and Clare, however, changed religious history by leaving the isolated monastic model to pursue the evangelization of the vibrant economic and political urban centers of Europe. These apostolic movements, like the Dominicans, Franciscans, and Poor Clares, made their residence literally in the center of the city. Into that world, the collective spiritualities of Dominic, Francis, and Clare entered preaching the gospel.

Moreover, as we will see, these orders effectively provided pathways to holiness and each order understood their pathway differently. For example, the Franciscans saw that there were three stages of spiritual growth. The first was purgation, where one encountered one's sinful life and realized the need to change one's ways. Then came illumination, an extensive pathway where one sought God, and in the light of Christ tried to learn more from the Lord so as to follow his lead. Finally, there was charity, union with God, which really only lasts forever when one has died and entered eternal life.

The Dominicans, on the other hand, were much more elemental. Their stages were the beginners, the proficient, and the perfect.[87]

Although the orders had different pathways, let us not presume that there were different gender pathways. Inasmuch as Clare of Assisi is the first woman to write a rule for a community of religious women, let us not think that Clare's agenda was different from Francis's.[88] Earlier male hagiographers tended to portray women, like Mary, the mother of Jesus, as the worthy model for medieval women, like Clare. However, Caroline Bynum clearly rejects that: "Where we can compare the biographer's perspective with that of the subject (as we can see in the case of Clare), we find that the woman herself tended to ignore the female model to discuss instead the imitation of Christ."[89] Catherine Mooney agrees: "The evidence within Clare's own writings, which significantly parallels the meanings conveyed in Francis's texts, shows overwhelmingly that Clare understood herself and her sisters to be following Christ's foot-steps, conforming their lives to his, in a word, becoming Christlike."[90]

Nevertheless, gender did make a difference. In her work *Gender Differences and the Making of Liturgical History: Lifting a Veil on Liturgy's Past*, Teresa Berger told the story of how the painter Giovanni di Paolo (d. 1482) captured Pope Innocent IV's visit to San Damiano and how Clare asked the pope to bless the bread on their table. The Pope insisted that Clare bless the bread and as the reluctant Clare offered her blessing it miraculously imprinted on the bread itself. In the painting, *Saint Clare of Assisi Blessing the Bread Before Pope Innocent IV*, we see what Berger calls "the power of female sanctity in the face of male clerical power, and God's surprising authentication of this female power over bread, to which a pope can only bow."[91]

Clare's famous gesture was hardly an alien one. Some of the finest contemporary research on the retrieval of pathways to holiness involves the relationship between medieval women and the Eucharist, as Caroline Bynum's classic *Holy Feast and Holy Fast: The Religious Significance of Food to Medieval Women* demonstrated.[92] In this work we get a sense of the imagination and authority that women exercised as they sought union, in the face of both pedestrian and deeply problematic misogynistic obstacles, with their redeemer and exemplar. Indeed, these works harken us back to the claims we saw earlier of how Christians work out in their embodied selves the ways that they saw themselves saved by the God made man. Although we cannot pursue this inquiry here, let us appreciate that the pathways to holiness were not only multitudinous but each one was wonderfully complex, expressed not only through moral living but also, simultaneously, through communal, devotional, and sacramental lives.

It might be helpful here to turn to Thomas Aquinas, whose work we will explore in the next chapter. For the moment, however, in the second of the *Summa*'s three parts, Thomas presented the seven virtues: the three theological virtues of faith, hope, and charity; and the cardinal virtues of prudence, justice, temperance, and fortitude. These virtues and their attendant vices "pertain to people of all conditions and estates." After covering all seven virtues, he concluded the second part with those things that "pertain to certain people." He divided this final section into three treatises: gratuitous graces, the active and contemplative life, and the states of life. The first treatise was on those who have received the gifts of "tongues," prophecy and rapture, and the grace to perform miracles. In the second treatise Thomas raised the difference between those called to the active and/or contemplative life. There he engaged first the contemplative life and argued that this life is "chiefly intent on the contemplation of truth."[93] Then he argued that the active life is "described with reference to our relations with other people, because it consists in these things, not exclusively, but principally."[94] Curiously, he then asked whether teaching belongs to the contemplative or the active life and argued that before imparting knowledge to one's hearers/students, the teacher first was contemplative by considering and delighting in the truth. Teaching straddles both lives. In the final question of the second treatise, he compared the two lives and at the outset declared, "Accordingly we must reply that the contemplative life is simply more excellent than the active." No sooner had he written that, he argued that in some instances "one should prefer the active life on account of the needs of the present life."[95] He then talked about those who are called from the contemplative life to the active life on account of some urgency and saw this as a movement "not of subtraction, but of addition."[96]

There is much more that we can take from Thomas but not here and now. What we can say is that while always insisting on contemplation as an engagement with the love and truth of God and that therefore contemplation is higher than the active life, nonetheless he presumed that we are called to the needs of this world and that we might have to move from the contemplative to the active and that such a departure is not a subtraction from the pursuit of perfection, but an addition. Not surprisingly then, he concluded the entire *Pars secunda* by asking whether a religious order devoted to contemplation is better than one dedicated to the active life. He answered that the active life must be considered either as simple almsgiving and other external works or it "proceeds from the fullness of contemplation, such as teaching and preaching." This latter way is "more excellent than simple contemplation....For even as it is better to enlighten than merely to shine, so is it better to give to others the fruits of one's contemplation than merely to contemplate....Accordingly the highest place in religious orders is held by those which are directed to teaching and preaching."[97] He concluded asking whether the religious community is better than the solitary life and wrote that the solitary life was for those who have already reached perfection, but for all else a "social life is necessary for the practice of perfection."[98]

Thomas Aquinas signified then a significant shift made by the religious movements of the thirteenth century. He described effectively how in the pathway to holiness the long-standing solitary turn away from the world that began with Anthony going into the desert reversed its direction and went to the center of the public square to teach and preach, while belonging to a group identity. The spirituality caught here was one deeply connected to the moral life, for while this later spirituality directed us not only to the avoidance and repudiation of evil, it also urged us to the pursuit of the good in and for the world and on not only one dependent on God, but also on others.[99]

We should realize that lay groups also became affiliated both with these religious orders and later with local parishes. They often incarnated the charism of a particular religious order and from that particular spirituality developed a series of practices that were aimed to help their own members. Thus, in the thirteenth century, Third Orders affiliated with religious communities like the Dominicans and Franciscans developed. Later, confraternities modeled on the Third Orders emerged and in time promoted not only their own devotional practices but also works of charity that were aimed to serve those outside the membership. This combination of devotional practices for the members and the practice of corporal works of mercy for outsiders became the structure for many confraternities.[100] We will see more about them later on, but for now we can see that the thirteenth century collective turn toward the urban center happened not only for those bound by religious vows but also by lay commitments as well. Out of an agenda to preach and evangelize also came the call to catechize and confess. Teaching instruments for lectors and parish priests were provided throughout, but as sin manuals developed, so did ascetical, devotional, and spiritual ones. Toward closing this chapter, then, let us turn a brief eye to the developments of the sixteenth century. But, first, let us raise some questions about sex, wherein we find the dark side.

V. AN ODD CATHOLIC DETOUR

Sexual Ethics from the Fourth to the Sixteenth Century

In the Catholic Church, it is often on matters of sex that church teaching actually departs from its pursuit of holiness agenda and gets extreme. Studying its history highlights just how much it marks a departure from the overall trends that we find in this book. This position is not simply my own. Charles Curran reminds us that "the vast majority of Catholic theologians writing about sexual morality have challenged the basis for the church's official teaching."[101] While Curran takes a "dissenting" position, I describe the history of its teaching to highlight how through language, the teachings on sexuality had a very different style and trajectory that placed it in a fairly absolutist category, unparalleled with any other moral teachings.

Here we can look at a very simple, uncomplicated Catholic sin, masturbation. I say Catholic because there has been a longstanding "concern" about it that's not found in any similar way with other faith traditions.[102] Indeed, no less than James Brundage, the author of the celebrated study *Law, Sex, and Christian Society in Medieval Europe*, reminded us, "The Christian horror of sex has for centuries placed enormous strain on individual consciences and self-esteem in the Western world."[103]

In the fourth century, the development of sexual ethics became defined as church fathers began writing specifically about their own venereal desires. Moreover, by making Christianity the state religion, Christianity began to take on an institutional control of the population much the way pagan Rome controlled its citizens' bodies in previous centuries. Finally, because integration or single heartedness remained the moral imperative, many of the church fathers translated their own personal experiences into a normative framework. In short, Christian theology on sex grew out of the personal struggles of major early figures who having already decided against a life where sexual relationships were integral and possible, had ascetical programs for personal integration. Nonetheless, they too encountered an impasse in light of their own sexual urges. These figures had a lasting influence on Christianity, as we saw, for example, in considering Augustine's own subjective struggles. Still, as dark as his sexual views were, he was not a Manichean or a Gnostic. Nor was he Jerome (340–420), who held that "not even the blood of martyrdom washes away the defilement of marriage" and argued that it was best for a man to have as few relations as possible with a woman, whether wife, concubine, or prostitute.[104]

The church fathers' focus on sexual activity led to specific judgments about particular sexual actions. Since married persons could not intend noncontraceptive sex, they were not permitted to engage in anal or oral intercourse. In 342, the emperors Constantius and Constans outlawed such sex as deviant. As Louis Crompton notes, their teaching also outlawed homosexual activity and was later incorporated into Theodosius's law in 390 and later into the Theodosian Code in 438.[105] By 390, any social tolerance of homosexuality was thwarted by civil law that specifically opposed homosexual activity on the belief that it led to or validated effeminacy, which, it was claimed, weakened the state. For this reason, the death penalty was imposed on any male engaging in passive sexual activity.

At the same time, virginity developed as a significant Christian practice in religious communities. As we saw earlier, sexual renunciation allowed women a freedom and a social role that marriage did not. Free of the real and present dangers both of pregnancy and childbirth and of patriarchal dominance, these women were able to explore a life with Christ in an environment largely ignored by the church fathers. In time, religious communities, like the Benedictines, were formed in which Christian virginity flourished.

At the same time, as monastic communities were developing, the sexual lives of monks came under scrutiny, especially with regard to the "vices" of the "solitary" life. Both John Cassian (365–433) and Caesarius of Arles (470–543) wrote extensively on the need for growth in spiritual perfection and to subdue any influence of sexuality at all. Yet, as Cappelli, Crompton, and Brundage all observe, with the possible exception of Clement of Alexandria, there were no writings against masturbation prior to Cassian; masturbation was simply not considered a sexual offense.

In the era of the penitentials, from the sixth to the thirteenth century, most of those who assumed the practice of confessing sins were monks and their sexual sins remained mostly about solitary actions and same-sex ones. In the penitentials, these topics received greater attention, and, through them, monks were taught to be preoccupied with fears of same-sex desires, masturbation, other "impure thoughts," and even "nocturnal emissions." In the pursuit of spiritual perfection, the issue of single-heartedness or purity was paramount. Context differed, however. When these penitentials considered the practices of nuns, they considered lesbian relations less seriously sinful, though in the more rural communities, the sins of bestiality were considered in detail and without comparison elsewhere.[106]

Teaching on sex changed, however, when Pope Innocent III imposed upon the entire church the Easter duty. As we saw, the Easter duty required explicitly the reception of the Eucharist at least once during Easter and therefore implicitly required confession of one's sins annually to receive that Eucharist. The shift to annual confessions for all caused then the need for new types of manuals; the simple brief penitentials, which were mostly for abbeys and monasteries, were replaced by more comprehensive and sophisticated "confessional" manuals for the church universal.

The injunctions that once fell against the monks and nuns who were pursuing spiritual perfection were now applied against the laity; and though confessional penances considered not only the sin but also the rank of the sinner (clergy, nobility, serf, etc.), still certain sins were distinguished solely by their matter as grave.

Masturbation, which was not a serious matter in the first four centuries, became, in time, considered gravely sinful. The genesis of that insight was precisely dependent upon the vocational choice of the monk who vowed to abandon sexual pleasure for the sake of the ascetical life. What was a sin for a forty-year-old ascetic with a vow of chastity in the eighth century became, however, the same sin for a twelve-year-old in the thirteenth century. Similarly, whatever concern the empire and the church may have had about a religious's homosexual behavior and whatever policing was done about its "wrongness," now through the annual confession, the church was able to police or socially control the behavior of those with same-sex attractions, not only in the monastery, but anywhere; they were able to now put "the fear of God" in them. In short whatever sexual teachings prompted anxiety in monks and nuns as they pursued spiritual perfection became now sources of anxiety in the laity; the difference, of course, was that there was no context of the pursuit of spiritual perfection for most of the laity. Moreover, unlike the religious, the laity did not have the programmatic spiritual support that those in religion had. Whereas religious may have feared damnation because they did not strive adequately to realize their vocational vows, fifty-year-old laypeople now feared damnation because they masturbated or had impure thoughts, and the latter did not have many of the spiritual resources of the former.

Nevertheless, just as the penitentials before Innocent III were less concerned with the solitary vices or same-sex attractions of women, similarly the confessional manuals after Innocent III were just as disinterested in women, especially if they were not affecting the well-being of men. Nevertheless we need to be cautious about what was the actual self-understanding of human persons regarding their sexual desires. Joyce Salisbury argues that we are only beginning to learn the testimonies of women, particularly religious, and are finding that their take on sex and women is quite positive and hardly like those of the church fathers, abbots, and canonists.[107] Similarly, Jacqueline Murray warns us against presuming that the writings we have encountered give us any idea of what the "average" male's self-understanding actually was. The work of historical research has not yet given us adequate access to the ideas of the common man or woman.[108]

Regardless of how the teachings were received, we need to attend to how they were articulated. John Noonan wrote that prior to Innocent III's bull, there spawned a conceptual category of note, "the sins against nature." The description of these sins was articulated by Ivo (1040–1116) as "always unlawful and beyond doubt more flagrant and shameful than to sin by a natural use in fornication or adultery," summarizing the position as simply "the use of a member not granted for this."[109]

On the overall use of these and other concepts, Noonan commented that the language games used were simply within the ambit of the moral manuals themselves: "There is never any attempt to provide a biological description of the acts condemned. Medical terms are eschewed. The vagina is usually described as 'the vessel' or 'the fit vessel.' Ejaculation is often described as 'pollution.' The term 'coitus interruptus' is never employed, but the usual description is 'outside the fit vessel.'"[110]

For example, in the *Book of Gomorrah*, Peter Damian (1007–72) devoted a section to the topic of different types of those who "sin against nature. "Four types of this form of criminal wickedness can be distinguished in an effort to show you the totality of the whole matter in an orderly way: some sin with themselves alone [masturbation]; some by the hands of others [mutual masturbation]; others between the thighs [interfemoral intercourse]; and finally, others commit the complete act against nature [anal intercourse]. The ascending gradation among these is such that the last mentioned are judged to be more serious than the preceding."[111] Damian's concern is specifically with fellow monks committing these sins.[112]

What these men defined as nature and why they understood one sin as graver than another depends on context. Robert of Sorbonne (1201–74), for example, wrote that the closer one is to a person, the more seriously one sinned. For this reason, he argues that the sin of masturbation, the so-called solitary vice, is the gravest. Later, Peter of Poitiers (1130–1205) agreed and dedicated a lengthy passage to the "monster of masturbation."[113]

On the other hand, Albert the Great (1206–80) bestowed on same-sex intercourse a triple condemnation: a sin against grace (as condemned in both the Old and New Testaments), against reason (because it overrides reason), and against nature (because it "contradicts the natural impulse to species continuity").[114]

What links all these sins together is basically that the semen went elsewhere than the fit or appropriate vessel; that it went elsewhere made it "unnatural."

Moreover, semen did not, for these theologians, belong to the individual male per se, but more appropriately to the future of the species. Thomas Aquinas (1225–74) wrote in the *Summa Contra Gentiles*,

> The seed, although superfluous as to the conservation of the individual, is yet necessary to the propagation of the species, while other superfluities, such as excrement, sweat, urine, and the like, are necessary for nothing. Hence the emission of the latter concerns only the good of the individual. But not only this is required in the emission of the seed; it is also required that it be emitted to be of use in generation, to which coitus is ordained....The disordered emission of seed is contrary to the good of nature, which is the conservation of the species.[115]

Thomas developed this insight when he turned to his later work, the *Summa Theologiae*, where he stated that venereal use "is highly necessary to the common good, which is the conservation of the human race."[116] Here Thomas argued that the natural teleology of the (male) reproductive organ belonged to the common good and in many ways laid the groundwork for presupposing that our reproductive organs existed not for ourselves, but for the propagation of the species.[117]

Basically, from Albert and Thomas until the twentieth century, the moral treatises distinguished between sexual sins "in accordance with nature" and those "contrary to nature." While the former could include fornication, adultery, incest, rape, and abduction, in general the latter sins (solitary or mutual masturbation, contraception, anal or oral intercourse, bestiality) were more grievous such was the obsession with the "teleology" of semen and the "fit vessel."[118]

The sins against nature received further treatment by being coupled with two other conceptual categories: "intrinsic evil" and "parvity of matter." It is important to note that contrary to claims otherwise, Thomas Aquinas never used or developed the concept of intrinsic evil. In fact, it was never used in the thirteenth century. Rather, as John Dedek meticulously explained, intrinsic evil was developed and coined by the most famous detractor of Aquinas, Durandus of St. Pourçain (1275–1334), whose anti-Thomism led to his dismissal from the Dominican order by the Master General

Herveus Natalis (d. 1323).[119] In fact, as Dedek noted, intrinsic evil would not make much sense following the moral reasoning that Thomas developed in the *Summa Theologiae*.

Intrinsic evil was a fourteenth century concept that described a particular type of action as absolutely, always wrong, regardless of circumstances. This a priori evaluation removed from consideration any question of the moral legitimacy of such actions. These were described as such either because the action was against nature or the agent had no right to the exercise of such activity. Classic examples of the latter category would include lying or the direct killing of the innocent. Interestingly, instances of unnatural action embraced by definition both categories since an unnatural action was exercising a forbidden activity.[120] The fourteenth-century category of intrinsic evil coupled with sins against nature and removed from debate the moral liceity of any sexual action in which a man's semen would be emitted into any other place than his wife's vagina.

Nonetheless, the history of sexual teachings became even darker when moral theologians entertained the question of the degree of the sinfulness of sexual actions. Here arose the question of whether any sin of lust could be considered light matter or whether it had what the manualists called no "parvity of matter." Why did this arise?

Subsequent to the scholastics, fifteenth- and sixteenth-century casuists considered actions that did not involve the illicit emission of semen, though these actions could have led to such an occurrence. For example, they asked what was the moral quality of a kiss that aroused a man or a passing fantasy that was not repelled but, rather, allowed to stay, what they called a *delectatio morosa*. Were these mortal sins? Major casuists such as Martin the Master (1432–82), John Mair (or Major) (1467–1550), Martín of Azplicueta (1495–1586), and Tomás Sánchez (1550–1610) were among those who considered these obviously marginal, sexual actions morally light or even licit.[121]

Although *The Catechism of the Council of Trent* (1566) did not enter into the discussion of these more specific issues, it presented marriage among the seven sacraments and defined its three goods as "mutual assistance," procreation, and "as an antidote to avoid the sins of lust." For the most part, the *Catechism* addressed the indissolubility of marriage.[122] Afterward, it addressed venereal desires specifically in its treatment of the sixth commandment, where it began with the observation, "The bond between man and wife is one of the closest, and nothing can be more gratifying to both than to know that they are objects of mutual and special affection." Immediately, though, it warned the pastor not to go into too much detail in explaining the sins of the commandment lest he "inflame corrupt passion," but recommended purity for all, and dedicated almost all its comments (without detail) to the filthy sin of impurity.[123]

Still, what if these kisses and fantasies were not seriously sinful, were theologians then acknowledging that some sexual sins admitted the question of "parvity of matter?" In 1612 the Superior General of the Society of Jesus (the Jesuits) condemned the position that excused from mortal sin any slight pleasure in sought venereal desires. Not only did he bind Jesuits to obey the teaching under pain of excommunication, but he also imposed on them the obligation to reveal the names of those Jesuits who violated even the spirit of the decree.[124] These and other sanctions dissuaded moralists from entertaining any of the circumstantial exceptions as earlier casuists had.

By 1750 the moral manualists locked into place the teaching that all sexual desires and subsequent activity were always mortally sinful unless it was the conjugal action of spouses who assured that their "act" was in itself left open to procreation. Therein they assimilated into the tradition the claims that sins against the sixth and ninth commandments had no parvity of matter. Notably this position did not apply to any of the other commandments.

"Parvity of matter," "intrinsic evil," and "sins against nature" combined to isolate venereal desires absolutely as such. Moreover, the teleology of the reproductive organs as belonging to the common good, the right of the spouse to claim the marital debt, and the denial of the right of the agent to use one's sexual organs for anything other than marital procreation effectively isolated the sexual organs even and especially from the human person as agent. In effect, just as the monk in the first millennium sought through ascetical practices to integrate himself body and soul but at the cost of dispensing with his own sexual desires, so too, in the second millennium after the imposition of the Easter duty, celibate church theologians managed to take away from the laity any sense of the legitimacy of sexual pleasure and any sense that those desires could ever lead to anything good except under certain very clear conditions for marital relations. They replaced any natural inclination to those desires with a mortal fear of them and a moral pathology of sexuality itself.

It is important to note that no other set of issues had such an unequivocal intolerance in the moral tradition, let alone such an elaborate set of linguistic concepts to "subdue" and condemn the activity. Even the prohibition against abortion allows certain indirect therapeutic exceptions (e.g., in the cases of women with a cancerous uterus or an ectopic pregnancy); moreover, the teaching itself prohibiting all direct abortions was only arrived at toward the end of the nineteenth century, when questions of human fertilization and embryonic development were better understood. Even when it became condemned, never was there anything like the issue of "parvity of matter" that pursued people who thought about or considered an abortion or confessors who may have responded to questions about the matter.[125] The other near absolute issue is lying. Yet, even though lying was named by Augustine as always in itself sinful, not everyone in the tradition at every time concurred, particularly on the matter of lying to protect the well-being of another. In fact, two distinctive trajectories of teaching on lying emerged.[126] Only the teachings on sexual ethics were absolute, severe, extensive, and without any exception.

The gospel summons to love and the early church's call to be one in mind and body developed well throughout the centuries but they never touched in any way upon most theological teaching on human sexual desires. On the contrary, as Christianity advanced, it did so by isolating and morally quarantining sex. Until Pope John Paul II introduced the theology of the body, sex would remain definitively the Catholic taboo.

VI. NEW PATHWAYS TO HOLINESS IN THE SIXTEENTH CENTURY

Desiderius Erasmus of Rotterdam (1466–1536) and Ignatius of Loyola (1491–1556)

From the first half of the sixteenth century, Erasmus and Ignatius of Loyola significantly shaped the course of devotional literature. Erasmus offered to his readers a comprehensive theology based on biblical writings, especially Paul's, which moved to practical application, integrating both learning with prayer and the devotional with moral theology. The genres that he developed were just as influential. What Erasmus did not develop, Ignatius did. Ignatius presented the reader with a way of exploring one's self-understanding, affections, and relationship with Christ. He presented a fairly existential model of the Christian disciple that gave new meaning to the kind of intimate relations with Christ that devotional practices promoted. Likewise, he taught readers how to discern their own spirits or affections to make the right choices and to examine in conscience whether they were being led by God or the evil spirits. The devotional child that was born in the twelfth century becomes a full-fledged young adult in the sixteenth century.

Desiderius Erasmus's *Enchiridion Militis Christiani* (*The Handbook of the Christian Soldier*) in 1504 is the prototype for all later attempts to develop a distinctively lay, nonmonastic spirituality that could accommodate the call of all Christians.[127] Erasmus explained that the "good life is everybody's business, and Christ wished the way to be accessible to all men, not beset with impenetrable labyrinths of argument but open to sincere faith, to love unfeigned, and their companion, the hope that is not put to shame."[128] His claim implicitly reappeared and became particularly validated in the twentieth century: from Tillmann's time onward the call to perfection and discipleship for all Christians became eventually a traditional claim. This is affirmed yet again recently by the Irish moral theologian Enda McDonagh who observed, "One of the gains of moral theology presently has been the realization that the call to perfection applies to all Christians."[129]

Erasmus was committed to a vision of theology where one's piety, doctrinal beliefs, and pastoral and moral conduct were not to be categorically separated but rather integrated. The task of theologians was to provide a theology that could integrate these concerns and provide a whole vision to the Christian community. As John O'Malley writes, "Piety, theology and ministry were for him but different aspects of one reality."[130] The foundational text for Erasmus's vision is clearly the Bible; he lamented the fact that theological teachers and ordinary laypeople ignored the wisdom of the revealed Word. For him, Jesus Christ was the teacher whose teaching saves (*Enchiridion* 16); from him, learning was salvific. His Word was the text by which all wisdom, including the wisdom of the philosophers, was to be understood. Thus, unlike many reformers who sought wisdom from Scripture alone, Erasmus culled the wisdom of the philosophers, even the pagan ones, though always through the lens of the Bible.[131]

Erasmus's piety was aggressive. He sought reform of previous devotional practices that associated repetitive external actions as being guarantors of grace and moral goodness. Rather than leading readers to consider imitating actions, Erasmus was completely christological: inviting readers to put on Christ from the inside out. His piety was not only corrective of one's own life, but it was also corrective of previous methods of piety. Finally, his piety was neither rationalistic nor anti-intellectual. Rather, he believed in the importance of learning as a companion to prayer. Believing in Christ the teacher, Erasmus saw the very act of responding to Christ as one of understanding and of prayerful union. For the Christian each was constitutive of the other. Erasmus's demonstration of this intimate relationship was so compelling that no subsequent major devotional writer provided methods in prayer without explanations for the Christian life.

The finest representation of Erasmus's theological vision in the context of piety is the *Enchiridion*. Because the text is so fundamental, a reader might be tempted to compare it to the *Imitatio Christi*. Their differences are, however, both substantive and significant; by considering them, we capture the importance of Erasmus's work. First, the purpose of the *Enchiridion* is aimed not simply at a pietistic attempt to move, console, and direct the reader, but more importantly to instruct the reader. This was not instruction by way of a program of study, but for and through an entire way of life (*Enchiridion* 36). The *Enchiridion* provides the wise insight for complete Christian living: "In the *Enchiridion* I laid down quite simply the pattern of a Christian life."[132] Second, the breadth of the purpose is matched by the completeness of its organizational form: besides a unified structure that keeps the material focused, theses are given and then elaborated, scriptural teachings are offered and explained, and a long set of concrete rules for guidance on the way of the Lord are provided. Third, unlike the *Imitatio*, the *Enchiridion*'s piety was neither primarily monastic nor antimonastic. Rather like its purpose and form, its content was all-encompassing. Through a piety that engaged in human company as a good, Erasmus established a piety accessible and applicable to all regardless of their vows that distinguish them. Fourth, undeniably, not until the twentieth century do we see echoes of Erasmus's theology again. Erasmus did not offer a utopia, but rather a realism, but his realism is more optimistic than others, before and after him. His belief in the flourishing of the human good distinguished him. In sum, O'Malley noted, "To compare it to the *Imitation* is to becloud its originality and is almost tantamount to comparing the *Ecclesiastes* with the medieval *artes praedicandi*."[133]

The comprehensive purpose, form, and content mark the *Enchiridion* as the paradigm that can never be put aside. After Erasmus, writers attempted complete guides to living the whole Christian life. They also recognized the importance of the literary form that they used to converse with their reader and attempted on several occasions the same type of editorial unity by which prayer and learning were brought together. Finally, with Erasmus they were able to imagine and conceive a concrete human spirituality that captured not monastic piety, but rather biblical discipleship.

The *Enchiridion* was divided into two parts framed by an extended preface in epistolatory form and an epilogue that named remedies for particular vices. The first part was an exposition of what human beings are and what wise protection Christians have been offered. Although all came from and goes to Christ, the center of the *Enchiridion* was not Christ, but the human self. Erasmus offered a profile of what human beings could become, for good or for bad; against that profile, he let the readers know themselves. The second part had twenty-two prescriptions with expositions of varying lengths for the Christian soldier. In this part, the rules all point to Christ. Whereas Christ was the background of the first part, he was the horizon for all human activity in the second part.

In the prefatory letter to Paul Volz, Erasmus explained the value of an *enchiridion*, that is, a handbook. Among a variety of contrasts, he commented on the literal and figurative weightiness of the scholastic tomes:

> There are almost as many commentaries on the *Sentences* as you can name theologians. Of makers of summaries there is no end....How can a mass of such volumes ever

> teach us how to live, when a whole life time would not suffice to read them?...Furthermore, suppose that they have defined everything truly and correctly, not to mention the tedious and frigid style in which they deal with these questions, how few men have the leisure to read through so many tomes? Who can carry the *Secunda secundae* of Aquinas round with him? (9)

He admonished theologians for their "debates": "And yet the good life is everybody's business, and Christ wished it the way to be accessible to all men, not beset with impenetrable labyrinths of argument but open to sincere faith, to love unfeigned, and their companion, the hope that is not put to shame" (9). Finally, he reminded Volz that in all this the scholastics have abandoned the "unlettered multitude, for whom Christ died" (9). These people must receive the wisdom of God. He added, "I could see that the common body of Christians was corrupt not only in its affections but in its ideas" (12), "and so it must be impressed upon all men that there is a goal towards which they must strive. And there is only one goal: Christ, and his teaching in all its purity" (16). The singularity of aim led him to criticize those religious who believe and act as if their particular rule of religious life (the guidelines for those belonging to the respective religious orders, e.g., the Franciscans or Benedictines) was more important than the gospel itself (18–20).

Having introduced his text, Erasmus proposed vigilance; no virtue save the three theological virtues of faith, hope, and charity appeared more often in Catholic sixteenth-century devotional than this one. At the beginning of the century, Erasmus gave it its primacy: "One must be vigilant. First of all you ought to bear constantly in mind that the life of mortals is nothing else but an unremitting warfare, according to the testimony of Job" (24).[134] In the light of this warfare, the concept of vigilance inevitably entailed moving to preparedness for conflict: "Although we are all engaged in such a difficult and dire conflict, and must do battle with an enemy so numerous, so sworn and vowed to our destruction, so vigilant, so heavily armed, so treacherous, and so well trained, yet, poor fools that we are, shall we not take up arms against them?" (25). That call to preparedness became a summons to serve in the army of Christ: "Are you not aware, O Christian Soldier, that when you were initiated into the mysteries of the life-giving font, you enrolled in the army of Christ?"

The concepts of spiritual warfare, Christian soldier, and vigilance were intrinsically related as context, personal identity, and salutary virtue. Each explained the need for the other. With roots in the New Testament epistles (1 Tim 1:18; 2 Tim 2:3–5; 4:7–8; Eph 6:13–17), the "soldier of Christ" reappeared in patristic writings and monastic rules often;[135] its later use in devotional texts occurred understandably in times of crisis, especially when one's own fealty to one's confession came under attack.[136] Into this combative framework, Erasmus presented readers with the well-named *Enchiridion*, which translated not only as "manual" or "handbook," but also "dagger," a worthy instrument for the vigilant soldier. Mindful of his earlier complaint about the ponderous texts of the scholastics, Erasmus noted, "I hammered out an '*enchiridion*,' that is, a sort of dagger, which you should never put aside, not even at table or in bed, so that if you are ever compelled to sojourn as a stranger…and would find it burdensome to carry around your full armor you would not allow yourself to be overcome at any moment by that ambusher." The modest size was important: "It is admittedly very small, but if you know how to use it rightly together with the shield of faith, you will easily withstand the violent onslaught of the enemy and will not receive a mortal wound" (38).

The principal components of the Christian soldier's armor were prayer and self-knowledge (30–39). Above all, Christ is true wisdom (39–41). There emerged a positive though dualistic anthropology that described the inner human as the possibility of immortality and truth and the outer human as the merely visceral (41–46). Erasmus made an important link between reason and the inner man: "What the philosophers call reason Paul calls either spirit or the inner man or the law of the mind" (47). Through a Platonic anthropology integrated into a Pauline theology, Erasmus set reason to command the passions: "I am truly ashamed of those who profess themselves to be Christians, the majority of whom are slaves to their passions like brute beasts and are so untrained in this struggle that they do not even know how to distinguish between reason and passion. They think that man is only what they see and feel" (46). With trust in reason and distrust of uncontrolled passions, he named the three evils that the human must be vigilant about as blindness, ignorance, and weakness (54).

As readers concluded the exposition of the first part, they would have found that Erasmus measured human beings more as objects than as subjects. Although he believed that the human was internal and more than the visible, still for all its innovation, the *Enchiridion* was not a text that appealed to human experience as an indicator of right spiritual growth. While he recognized the urgency of self-examination and recommended its practice, he described it more as a task to be done rather than as an experience to be practiced. He was then more a class teacher than personal mentor, more instructor than wise and familiar companion. Unlike Ignatius and other later writers, Erasmus's anthropology was not about who we are; rather, it was a description of what the human being is. In Erasmus, the human being was objectively observable, estimable, and controllable.

The second part of the *Enchiridion* began with the first rule, against ignorance about Christ. The comprehensiveness of the first rule demonstrated how foundational it was: "Since faith is the only avenue to Christ, it is fitting that the first rule should be to understand fully what the Scriptures tell us about Christ and his Spirit, and to believe this not only by mere lip service, not only coldly or listlessly or hesitantly, as does the common lot of Christians, but with your whole heart, with the deep and unshaken conviction that there is not the tiniest detail contained therein that does not pertain to your salvation" (55). He summed up the first rule as "not to have any doubts concerning God's promises" (56).

Erasmus's masterpiece served as a paradigm for later handbooks. He provided instruction with practical directives for living out one's devotional life. Theology, morality, and devotional spirituality were completely integrated; the three became one. Moreover, he provided a vision that was comprehensive, guiding the readers through the dangers of a life filled with temptations. He developed an anthropological understanding of the human being, which intertwined both Platonic and Pauline interests so as to draw the reader to a christological end, that is, to be like Christ. He thus provided the vigilant Christian soldier with a powerful weapon, a handbook that integrated all three fields of inquiry: theology, morality, and devotion. Though Erasmus stands alone in the Catholic repertory as one who did not distinguish works of morality and devotion, he also stands alone from Protestant writers. In many instances, they never developed a devotional theology into an ethics; in other instances, as in the Puritans, they accomplished an integrated theology, but they never developed a love of the stranger or the enemy but remained at best only to consider the needs of the familiar Christian. Moreover, Erasmus's comprehensive (social) charity would not develop again until the twentieth century, when theologians like Walter Rauschenbush, Wolfhart Pannenberg, and Dietrich Bonhoeffer begin to write.

Throughout his writings, Erasmus described humanity and gave handy directions, but his Platonic interests never let him appeal to the reader's own desires or affections. Offering instruction to the reader, he never offered them a way of discerning their spirits. To find such discernment we need to turn to Ignatius's *Spiritual Exercises*. Before we do, we need to realize that as distinctive as the *Enchiridion* was, it was a text that belonged by the sixteenth century to a very successful trade. These texts were enormously popular, and though the *summa confessorum* were plentiful for the parish priest, the devotional manuals were for any Christian and they were abundant. These ascetical texts animated the reader's devotional and moral practices. Certainly, these texts motivated persons to confess their sins, not only for the sake of salvation, but for greater union with the Savior. Without these texts, moral practices were animated by fear of damnation; with them, they were animated by the pursuit of Christ. Thus, they provided a relational context for the motivation of moral practices. In turn, the moral life became considered by the devout as a response to the initiative from God in their spiritual relationship with Christ. Being moral meant being a grateful disciple.

Moreover, ascetical theology's powerful interest in anthropology prompted moral theology to be concerned not simply with external actions that were to be avoided, but also with the virtues to be acquired, virtues that emerge earlier in the ascetical theology of the twelfth century. These virtues were the vehicle for devout disciples to pursue Christ. As such, virtues introduced readers to doing exercises so as to grow in virtue. While the moral manuals directed persons away from sinful actions, the ascetical texts directed readers to the practice of actual concrete positive exercises. In fact, asceticism means "to make someone adept by exercises."[137] Exercise became key, then, for understanding the development of the ascetical and virtuous personality.

Subsequently, the moral life was no longer understood by the devout Christian as the simple avoidance of sin. Rather, whenever ascetical theology amplified moral theology, the latter defined itself as primarily interested in the increase of charity. This increase was accomplished both by devotional practices and the corporal works of mercy, that is, exercises involving the love of God and love of neighbor. These modes of growing in discipleship by prayer and good deeds became the measure of the moral worth of the devout. Failure in these practices then became confessional matter as well. That is, in time, the ascetical manuals prompted the moral manuals to incorporate not only the seven deadly sins, which were the sins of those minimally Christian, but also the sins of the devout. Their sins may have been a failure to be attentive in prayer, an inability to fast as much as they could, or a failure to attend to the sick or imprisoned. The ascetical books actually altered and broadened the moral manuals, not only to consider the sins by which we are damned but also the sins by which we falter in the pursuit of discipleship.

Herein ascetical theology introduced moral effort or striving as a key concept for capturing the moral goodness of the agent. This notion of striving was rooted in ascetical theology's overriding interest in charity. Striving particularly manifested itself in the ascetical theology that accentuated the metaphor of the struggling soldier, who appears throughout the sixteenth century, from the *Enchiridion* to Theatine Lorenzo Scupoli's enormously popular *Spiritual Combat* (1603).[138] When moral theology also appropriated the concept of striving, it located the cause of striving, charity, in the heart of the disciple. This turn to the heart conveyed the goodness of deep human desire, captured human aspiration and longing, and finally prompted moral theology once again to talk about love.

Moreover, ascetical theology presented the passions positively, not as sources of sinful inclinations, but as the force that when properly trained would assist the devout Christian on the way of the Lord. This shift was only accomplished when a positive anthropology (*imago Dei*), a positive goal (union with Christ), and a positive way (*imitatio Dei*) provided the framework that the energy of humanity could be understood as at least potentially positive.

Thus, just as the ascetical texts would foster union with Jesus Christ, devout Christians could also interpret their moral lives as seeking union with the Lord. The intimacy that the ascetical theology proposed was consistently evident in their texts, whether Johannes Lanspergius's lovely *Epistle from Jesus to a Soul* (ca. 1526) or Ignatius of Loyola's *The Spiritual Exercises* (1522). The end of ascetical theology eventually also became the end of moral theology, union with God, an insight that we saw already present, implicitly in Thomas Aquinas's conclusion to the *Pars Secunda* of the *Summa Theologiae*.

Finally, the ascetical works prompted an attentiveness to the ordinariness of life. Though ascetical works began as little more than prayer manuals, in time they became meditations that pursued union with Christ in one's ordinary existence.[139] The engagement of ordinariness demonstrated the comprehensiveness of the scope of ascetical theology; in ordinariness ascetical theology encountered humanity completely. That ordinariness is well captured in the very successful *The Christian Man's Guide* (1630) by Alfonso Rodríguez that went through fifty editions and was translated into twenty-three languages. Each of the two treatises are entitled "The Perfection of Our Ordinary Actions," but these insights were already premised three hundred years earlier when Aquinas insisted that every human action was a moral action.[140] The ordinary rescued moral theology from its restricting tendency to study only sinful or controversial actions. The ordinary gave moral theology the realism and the context for truly working out a contemporary ethics for any generation.

In each of these ways ascetical theology amplified the scope, competency, and subject of moral theology. From its loving motivation through its inclusiveness of the ordinary to its personification in the lives of saints, ascetical theology offered moral theology a way of exploring a broadened and positive agenda for examining the ethical life. The *Enchiridion* represented the paradigmatic shift from the monastic to the contemporary order in the sixteenth century.

We conclude by turning to Ignatius of Loyola's *Spiritual Exercises* (1522). Inasmuch as the *Exercises* were to be made rather than read, we can understand it as leading us through four "weeks" in which the "exercitants" engage in an ongoing encounter with Jesus Christ so as to understand individually what exactly the Lord wants of them. In the first week, mostly through meditations on one's unworthiness, one hears the call to conversion and the willingness to place oneself before the Lord for the purpose of the First Principle and Foundation: "The human person is created to praise, reverence, and serve God Our Lord, and by doing so, to save his or her soul. All other things on the face of the earth are created for human beings in order to help them pursue the end for which they are created." Often, at the end of the first week, exercitants would make a general confession of their sins. In the second and third week the exercitant begins to contemplate salvation history through the life and death of Jesus Christ. At the close of each of these contemplations, the exercitant is encouraged to enter into a conversation with Jesus, placing before Jesus questions that he/she might have, specifically about major life decisions that one may want to make. At the same time, the exercitant is to be attentive to the movement of the spirits of his soul, detecting which are from grace and which are not. With this same attentiveness or vigilance, the exercitant is to bring to one's contemplations a heightened engagement of each of one's five senses. Through these exercises, the exercitant moves more closely to discerning the Lord's presence, actions, and will. The fourth week, celebrating the Resurrection moved into Pentecost, where the Spirit works today in all things. As the retreat ends, the exercitant reenters the church and the world somewhat transformed.

Ignatius shares with us his experience that he had at Manresa where for eleven months he entered into a profound, unique, intimate relationship with God who awakened within him every possible way of furthering his relationship with Jesus Christ. The *Exercises* became then an entry point for a form of spirituality that was not imitative, but rather relational and as submissive to God's will as it was discerning of one's own senses. An invitation to extensive periods of prayer by which the exercitant allowed oneself to be in the revealing hands of God, the *Exercises* became an enormous pathway for those seeking to know, love, and serve God in Jesus Christ. Here interiority was the landscape for the encounter between the Christian and Christ.

As skeletal as the directives were, Ignatius provided the exercitant great freedom to explore that landscape; in fact, he insisted as we will see below, that even the retreat director not interfere in the relationship between the exercitant and the movements of

God. In this, he placed enormous trust and respect in the exercitant's conscience, a point that we will return to below. Still, Ignatius also provided the accompaniment of the director and a set of rules for discernment that kept the exercitant's subjectivity from falling into a narcissism or a solipsism of some kind. Rather, the exercitant became trained to always keep their eyes on Christ.

Clearly, Ignatius's experience builds on the *Imitatio Christi*. He credited the *Imitatio Christi* with starting his conversion.[141] As Moshe Sluhovsky noted, "He even assigned the *Imitation of Christ* as mandatory reading for Jesuit novices, who were required to carry the text with them at all times. For Loyola, then, there was no contradiction or even tension between the monastic/spiritual and the apostolic/ministerial missions of the Jesuits."[142] The christocentric focus as well as the introspection and the attentiveness to consolation are clearly foundational to the text. As he knew the *Imitatio* launched him, he wanted it to help others as they got underway. Rightly, O'Malley refers to the influence as "embryonic."[143]

Ignatius's text, however, has a very different impact. He empowered others to become so exposed and acquainted with themselves as they stood before Jesus Christ or as they meditated or even contemplated on divine love, that they became trained to trust their own relationship with the Lord as they developed a way of proceeding for the rest of their lives. They might return, as Jesuits themselves do, to the experiences of the *Exercises* by an annual retreat; however, learning the rhythm of prayerful discernment in the first place prompts them to go forward for the rest of their lives. Once done, once one experiences the training of discernment, of meditation and contemplation, one does not need a text anymore. Though one needed to regularly consult Thomas's *Imitatio* or Erasmus's handbook,[144] Ignatius's liberated the exercitant for a new discerning docility to Christ himself.

As more made the *Exercises*, they had a very powerful social impact. Something so experiential was effectively incarnational and that led to diverse iterations of its impact. As O'Malley notes, "The Exercises set the pattern and goals of all the ministries in which the Society engaged, even though it was not always explicitly recognized as doing so. There is no understanding the Jesuits without reference to that book."[145] The *Exercises* gave, if you will, a new capacity and with it a new authority to the follower of Christ to work in the manifold ministries of the church and the world.[146]

For the purposes of this book, the foundational experience of the *Exercises* cannot be overlooked in terms of its impact on moral theology. Above all, here we discover the priority of the spiritual over the moral. Because Ignatian spirituality so stressed the initiative of God as prior to the individual's response, then a moral theology in this context is always subsequent to God's movements. Moral theology is therefore a response, to the call as well as the grace of charity that enabled the Christian to hear it and to respond.

Throughout the *Exercises*, there are two striking movements: on the one hand, the exercitant is constantly seeing God's graceful movement toward her/him; on the other hand, the exercitant is constantly being prompted to offer one's whole self, whether in the offering of the meditation on the "Kingdom"[147] or the *Suscipe* in the final contemplation.[148] The offering of self is the offer to become more at the service of Christ whose work of salvation continues to this very moment. These foundational movements gave morality a deep interiority.[149] As we saw earlier, the pathways to holiness did not turn to principles that govern actions, but rather virtues that perfect dispositions. As a morality responding to a spirituality, the former emerged from the depths of the latter. But herein experience brought an appreciation for the uniqueness of the individual, because through the *Exercises* the exercitant is always urged to deepen her/his unique relationship with the Lord by seeing that Jesus Christ has done "all this for me."

Because the *Spiritual Exercises* stressed the unique relationship between God and exercitants, Jesuit moralists upheld the primacy of the individual's conscience where that relationship was most intimately understood.[150] Besides the "First Principle and Foundation" urging exercitants to discern God's will and the Examen giving the context and guidelines for exercitants' own examination of conscience before God, the first annotation urged exercitants to heed their conscience. In the fifteenth annotation, the retreat director was warned to not interfere in the unique relationship that exercitants have with God, but rather to "permit the Creator to deal directly with the creature, and the creature directly with his Creator and Lord."[151]

The examination of conscience became not simply a practice to find one's faults but also one's fundamental agenda, particularly in the triple question right in the very first colloquy of the first week: "What have I done for Christ?" "What am I doing for Christ?" "What ought I do for Christ?"[152] Effectively the questions concern whether one was acting or not: Was one bothered about Christ or not? That question was antecedent to the question of right living or acting. It recognized that "to stand still on the way of God is to move backwards." These questions simply asked, are you doing anything for Christ? This self-examination was not simply a once-for-all event. On the contrary, inasmuch as we are each called to be more and more the persons whom Christ wants us to be, Ignatian spirituality called us to a regular reflection of where we were on our journey with Christ. As John O'Malley noted, the *Exercises* broadened the scope of engagement beyond the retreat itself to "a more general design for a person's spiritual journey through life."[153]

The ongoing reflection was necessary so that by knowing Our Lord and ourselves better, we can better both determine the virtuous ends that we should be pursuing as well as assess the steps already taken. Since the virtues were first articulated, the acquisition of virtue has been known as a dynamic, life-long process of reflection and intended practice.

We need to be mindful that it was not the directives themselves that make the impact on the person, but rather the exercises. The exercises were a training ground: they were not lessons that were simply cognitively learned but existentially embodied; the experience of the exercises entered into the very texture of the Christian.

The training in the *Spiritual Exercises* was not much different from the training in moral exercises. The standard expression that Thomas used to describe how one acquires a virtuous disposition was, in fact, "exercise." The intended exercises of temperance, for instance, led to the acquisition of temperance. This training was central then to both the spirituality of the *Exercises* where the exercitant repeated meditations and contemplations to pursue the invitation to greater union with God and to morality where a person engaged in regularly intended and repeated practices in pursuit of particular virtues. It was not coincidental that Ignatius appropriated a word known both among devotional movements in Spain as well as among proponents of the virtues at Paris.

Finally, the life of Ignatian spirituality and the life of virtue each required a mentoring prudential companion, just as the Irish monks understood when they discovered their *anacaram* or their soul friend. In both cases, however, the mentor was not teaching some rules or principles, but rather was helping the apprentice understand how growth occurs in her/his particular life so as to find the right exercises that would lead to greater discipleship and greater self-guidance. In all this then there was an appreciation for human emotions. Hugo Rahner pointed this out in his important work,[154] that the regular "application of senses" (a clear innovation in spirituality) taught the exercitant the importance of familiarity with one's feelings in order to discern properly.

As a Jesuit reflecting on the impact the *Exercises* has on the lives of those who make them, I would say that they give the exercitant a sense of wonder about the complex resources at the human's disposal for not only discerning God's will but deliberating about the ways to realize the will. The *Exercises*, by inviting the Christian to interiorly explore a variety of forms of prayer, a variety of sensory perceptions, the complete canon of the Scriptures, and the entire purview of one's life, trains the Christian to always live in the hope that responses are possible. In summary, the *Exercises* offers the Christian a mindfulness about moral agency at the service of Christ and his kingdom, a mindfulness of living a life of imagination, exploration, discernment, accompaniment, reconciliation, and moral responsiveness.

We return at this chapter's end to our beginning. Anthony retreated to a cave, as did Ignatius in Manresa where he first did his *Exercises*. Anthony remained near the cave, but Ignatius left the cave and eventually went to Paris and Rome where he began to discern how he should make moral decisions based on his Spiritual Exercises. In a way the pathway to holiness entered into the urban center but it did so through a profound pathway that traversed the human heart and mind and all the passions therein. There in that pathway, the conscience, which is where the human encounters and works with Christ, emerged as central to moral theology. Therein the Christian became like Christ, strangely less mindful of the self, and more responsive to the world ahead.

Chapter Four

From the Twelfth to the Sixteenth Century

The Medieval Scholastic Foundations of Modern Moral Theology

"If one had to choose one word to characterize the difference between Christian thought in the eleventh and twelfth centuries, it would perhaps be 'professionalization.'"[1] Philipp Rosemann, editor of Peter Lombard's *Sentences*, explained how professionalization affected theology: the master of theology was neither a bishop with pastoral responsibilities nor a monk called to contemplation, but rather a master of theology, a professional in his own right.[2] Marie-Dominique Chenu, OP, noted, too, that these masters "organized theology into a science with its own rules."[3] Like other academic disciplines of its time, theology was studied as a discipline in its own right.[4]

In fact, theology was *more* than any other discipline. The medieval historian Marcia Colish described well theology at the university of Paris in the twelfth century:

> If the arts students predominated numerically, the academic jewel in the university's crown was theology. Paris had medieval Europe's first chartered and most eminent theological faculty. As the queen of the sciences and the

> discipline drawing the best minds and the greatest institutional support, and also as the most high-risk discipline, theology at Paris was frequently the field in which the most acrimonious debates within the university took place. Defense of the autonomy of this faculty above all was the goal of its hard-won but successful achievement of corporate independence.[5]

Within these new departments were the scholastic theologians who began to put forward their theology as a developing scientific investigation. Reason would now help give expression to faith and, in that way, it would help form faith. Chenu wrote, "Reason and its various disciplines no longer furnished simply the tools for studying the sacred texts. Reason, by introducing 'well-ordered arrangement' somehow entered into the structuring of the faith."[6] Shortly we will see, for instance, just how Hugh of St. Victor, Abelard, Lombard, Thomas Aquinas, Duns Scotus, and William of Ockham took such steps that in ordering the tradition, they effectively shaped faith.

For their professionalization, these theologians developed their tools for investigation. Key to these were the *Glossa ordinaria*—extensive "glossa" or comments on the Bible from the ninth through the thirteenth century in which the commentaries from earlier patristic and medieval authorities were literally written into the margins or under the very passages themselves. Inasmuch as the Bible was the primary text for all theology, the *Glossa* were indispensable in providing the faculty with traditional, albeit somewhat scattered commentary on all of the Sacred Scriptures.

Along with these texts was the matter of language and a more precise vocabulary. Colish captured these developments as well: "It was largely the scholastic theologians who made a systematic effort for terminological precision."[7] As we will see in our examination of Thomas, the scholastic concepts became the key tools by which each theologian could conduct and report on their own investigation. In this way, everyone spoke and wrote in the same language, creating the possibility of moral agreement, but also the grounds for distinctions, debate, and disagreement—a creative climate of discussion in essence.

Here we need to note that one cannot understand Scholasticism as a monolith; Scholasticism was a robust and fairly respectful debate that extended over the course of four hundred years. Hopefully by the end of this chapter we will not only appreciate the debates, but also develop a little expertise with the language, because it is through scholastic language that we understand Scholasticism and its impact on modern theology. Their language allowed them to innovate.

In this chapter we begin with the groundbreaking work of Peter Abelard (1079–1142), who is the first scholastic to work in ethics, and then turn to the advance of *The Sentences* of Peter Lombard (1095–1160).[8] From there we turn to the work of Thomas Aquinas, OP (1224–74), particularly in his *Summa Theologiae*, concluding with a set of insights into the achievement of Scholasticism. Finally, we turn to the Franciscans, John Duns the Scotsman or Scotus as he was called (1265–1308) and the Englishman William of Ockham (1287–1347). In Ockham we find much as we do with Abelard, their positions on logic and nominalism. By concluding this chapter with the fourteenth-century Ockham, we can connect in the next chapter with his successor, in many ways another Scotsman, John Mair of Haddington (1467–1550), who takes us back to the University of Paris for the birth of modern casuistry.

1. PETER ABELARD (1079–1142)

A short biography of the "calamitous" life of Peter Abelard is never sufficient, but it is important to appreciate the personality of the man who literally broke through a world of theology that played by its own rules. He effectively brought a critical, rational inquiry into theology that entertained the fundamentally logical question of traditional positions: but does it make sense? To make sense of it he had to give it a certain order, and in this way, Abelard made theology subject to reason and, therein, made theology worthy of being considered a science.

Betty Radice, the excellent editor and translator of the *Historia calamitatum* (*The Story of My Misfortunes*) as well as the letters between Abelard and Heloise, described him in this way: "He spoke out against the shortcomings of the church wherever he detected them."[9] I would add that he similarly spoke out against the shortcomings of theology wherever he detected them. Elsewhere she noted, "By temperament, Abelard was stimulated by controversy and one can imagine him bored by finding himself at the top without rival."[10] I would add that he had a holy impatience as well as a formidable resilience. The story of his life helps explain the person who brought the concept of investigation into the world of theology.

Abelard was born into the lower gentry in Brittany and was later trained in the great classical authors of Horace, Seneca, Ovid, Juvenal, and Cicero. He was fundamentally a logician, working in dialectics, holding lectureships (in Melun and Corbeil) in the first decade of the twelfth century. His fame started in debates about universals. Abelard attended the lectures of William of Champeaux (1070–1121), a rhetorician, but quickly began contending against him, winning the attention of other students. Abelard was effectively a nominalist and believed that universals were not metaphysical realities, nor relevant, but rather simple names or labels or linguistic categories: the singular was eminently important and did not need any other class to which to belong. For nominalists, humanity was not an essence that belonged to each member of the species; rather, it was simply a shorthand term for suggesting that we should treat all who are named (hence, *nominalism*) "human beings" the same way. Often considered antiessentialists, nominalists resisted claiming that there was something "essentially" common to each human being. For them, just as horses did not have among them an essence like "horsiness," humans were not shaped by an intrinsic specific quality that made them human beings. We call horses "horses," not because of some metaphysical essence that established them as such; we call every horse a horse because that was what we named these particular four-legged beasts. At best, horses were like one another, not essentially the same.

In this, Abelard was a brilliant twelfth-century forerunner of the fourteenth-century William of Ockham. Both of them believed that we should study the specific, rather than the general. Colish described Abelard's point of investigative departure well: "We acquire ideas of individual things first."[11] Abelard's nominalism developed in fact out of a fairly formidable logic that was its own discipline.[12]

In 1113, Abelard studied theology with Anselm of Laon (d. 1117), who taught both the Scriptures and sacred doctrine; in time, Abelard began to offer his own lectures as an alternative to Anselm, earning him Anselm's displeasure. Abelard moved to Paris and in 1115 met the young Heloise (1101–1164) whose uncle, Fulbert, was the canon at Notre Dame. Abelard and Heloise became lovers. Learning that his niece was pregnant, Fulbert threatened Abelard, who agreed to secretly marry Heloise. Fulbert announced the marriage, but Heloise objected. In her first letter to Abelard she wrote, "God knows I never sought anything in you except yourself; I wanted simply you, nothing of yours." Then she added famously about the marriage: "You kept silent about most of my arguments for preferring love to wedlock and freedom to chains."[13] Abelard helped Heloise find a place in a convent in Argenteuil to protect her, but Fulbert believed instead that Abelard had forced her to become a nun. Fulbert had his men castrate Abelard, who in turn retreated to monastic life at San Denis where he taught logic and theology.

Disciples of Anselm charged that Abelard's new work in theology, *Theologia summi boni*, was heretical, and Abelard was subsequently tried and convicted at a council in Soissons in 1121, where he was forced to burn his work and later fled the monastery itself. A year later he built a small oratory that he named the Paraclete. Students discovered him there and it became effectively, for about five years, a little university. Around 1127, he was elected abbot of St. Gildas, a corrupt monastery; there Abelard tried to become its reformer, but the monks attempted to kill him and so he moved out of the monastery but remained its abbot.[14] Two years later, Heloise and her community were thrown out of Argenteuil, and Abelard donated the Paraclete to her and her exiled community who later flourished there and, in fact, Heloise became its famed abbess. Having to abandon Gildas, Abelard headed to Paris in 1132, where students again flocked to him. There he lectured on logic, the Bible, Christian doctrine, and ethics.

In 1140, William of St. Thierry (1085–1145) denounced him and wrote to, among others, Bernard of Clairvaux (1090–1153). Together they had Abelard summoned to a council at Sens on June 2, 1141. Abelard challenged Bernard to a public debate there, but Bernard convinced the council bishops prior to Abelard's arrival that Abelard ought to be condemned. Abelard arrived at Sens, discovered the tables turned, and fled, appealing to Pope Innocent II, who excommunicated Abelard a month later, ordering Abelard to a monastery and his book burned. Peter the Venerable, the abbot of Cluny, gave him sanctuary and convinced the pope to lift the excommunication; he even brought about a reconciliation between Abelard and Bernard. Abelard gave up his teaching and spent his remaining days there as a revered scholar, dying on April 21, 1142.[15]

Abelard's written work can be divided into two parts: from 1102 to 1126, his logic, and from 1120 to 1142, his foundational theological works. In 1120, he published the first edition of *Theologia*, a work that conveyed, among other positions, his theology on the Trinity; though condemned and burned at Soissons, *Theologia* remained a lifelong project that he continued to edit through to its third edition in 1135. After Soissons, he developed *Sic et Non* (*Yes and No*), a brilliant work that covered 158 different theological issues for which one had two mutually contradictory yet authoritative responses: thus, he created a forum for an authoritative debate on each of the issues. In his *Sic et Non*, Abelard did not provide a resolution to the 158 debates, but rather offered it as "a kind of exercise book for his students" at the Paraclete.[16] Here he illustrated the significant challenge that Scholasticism had to face: the tradition of theology was not at all as consistent as it claimed. In fact, for every claim, there was an authoritative contradictory. The multitudinous debates suggest that an ordering was needed.

There we see the roots of the famous "objections" that Thomas used in his *Summa Theologiae*. Thomas structured the *Summa* with a question that contained several articles, though each article was first expressed in the form of a question. After the question was posed, before answering it, Thomas introduced a series of "objections" that in almost all instances would be contradicted by the answer that Thomas subsequently gave. Thomas not only gave his response ("respondeo"), but after it, he offered a reply to each of the objections that were first raised. *Sic et Non* was the clear forerunner of the *Summa Theologiae*.

Subsequent to *Sic et Non*, Abelard sought an ordering of theology. Earlier, in his *On the Sacraments of the Christian Faith* (*De sacramentis christianae fidei*, ca. 1134), we find that Hugh of St. Victor (1096–1141) ordered theology by creating two parts: the foundation and the restoration. The first began with the creation of the world through to the coming of Christ; the second began with the incarnation, passed through the sacraments, and concluded with the end of the world and the second coming. His ordering was biblically historical, following the order of the Bible from its first book till the last. For Hugh, theology remained a given. Rosemann wrote that Hugh's theological system had not yet made "the transition from an essentially narrative order to the stage where, to use Chenu's words, 'reasoning has entered into the structuring of faith itself.'"[17]

For Abelard, the structure was not to be biblical or historical, but rather a rational, philosophically sound logic to help theology make sense. It started with our experience of faith that turned to God and the divine attributes, descending to the angels and encountering the creation of Adam, Eve, and the fall, which led to the coming of Christ (his incarnation, passion, resurrection, and ascension) and then the founding of the church with the incumbent roles of Mary and the apostles and the establishment of the sacraments of baptism, the remission of sin, the Eucharist and marriage, concluding with charity, and law and sin. Its order is the order of our experience of revelation.[18] Later, we will see how Peter Lombard, in drafting his *Sentences*, had to choose between the two orders of Hugh and Abelard.

At Gildas (1127–31), Abelard wrote on the natural law: *The Dialogue between a Philosopher, A Jew and a Christian*.[19] Abelard presented a philosopher who questions whether one should bother with religious tradition when discussing natural law. As the Jew tried to defend himself for inserting religion into the debate, the philosopher highlighted a clear problem in trying to appreciate how circumcision, dietary laws, and the holiness code were relevant to true ethics. The Christian turned a bit on the philosopher, acknowledging the wisdom of the natural law tradition, and then appealed to the Patristic tradition to say that behind and at the end of all ethical law is faith. Though the Christian saw Plato and Socrates as good out of their love for Wisdom, he believed that it was within their belief in Wisdom that God had implicitly given them this faith. In the end we are left waiting for the philosopher to respond and then for the Christian to become the final word, but Abelard left the reader to resolve the issue by being the ultimate reviewer of the claims.

In 1132, as he began his final tenure in Paris, he wrote his *Historia Calamitatum*. Heloise read it and wrote a reply, thus launching the exchange of letters between the two lovers, now monk and nun. In Paris he wrote his commentary on Romans and lectured on God,

Christ, virtue, vice, sin, merit, and the sacraments, all while reediting for the third time *Theologiae.*

From 1138 to 1140, he worked on his ethics, *Scito te ipsum* (*Know Thyself*), but never finished it. The first part was basically a determination of what constitutes sin; the second part was to be on virtue. The logician, who was a man of faith, defined sin as consent, an attribution for failing to keep oneself from doing what was not to be done. Through a series of stages, he negated what sin was. It was not a mental vice that disposed us to do a bad deed. Nor was sin a bad deed itself, nor finally was it a bad will to do a bad deed. Instead, it was the "consent to what is inappropriate" (7).[20] Abelard's negative theology was significant.[21] He explained that consent was more an attribution to an omission than a positive act. The sinful consent is discovered by its absence: no consent is explicitly made. Rather by doing the grave sinful act, evidently the agent has not exercised due restraint and in that failed restraint is consent. In fact, right after defining sin as consent, he declared his definition to be negative: it is found not in what is explicit but rather in what was attributed as wrongly omitted.

> Thus our sin is scorn for the creator, and to sin is to scorn the creator—not to do for his sake what we believe we ought to do for his sake, or not to renounce for his sake what we believe ought to be renounced. And so when we define sin negatively, saying that it is *not* doing or *not* renouncing what is appropriate, we show clearly that there is no substance to a sin; it consists of non-being rather than of being. It is as if we define shadows by saying they are the absence of light where light did have being. (8)

He returned to showing what sin was by declaring what it was not. It was not a vice, because we can renounce it (7). Similarly, sin was not a bad will, since someone sins impulsively by not keeping oneself from committing the sin (11–15, 20). Sin was also not in the act, because a deed did not in itself make an act any more or less blameworthy or praiseworthy (25). Thus, he adds, "Doing the sin doesn't add anything to the guilt or to the damnation before God" (35). Here, through this process of negative theology, he returned to the insight of paragraph eight and now made consent a negative act or what I call attributing consent for what was wrongly omitted. Brilliantly, he writes, "Now we consent to what isn't allowed when we don't draw back from committing it" (29). He repeated this insight a few paragraphs later:

> Therefore, any kind of carrying out of deeds is irrelevant to increasing a sin. Nothing taints the soul but what belongs to it, namely the consent that we've said is alone the sin, not the will preceding it or the subsequent doing of the deed. For even if we want or do what is improper, we don't *thereby* sin, since these things frequently occur without sin, just as, conversely, consent occurs without these things. (48)

Abelard again referred to the negative notion of consent, or what I am describing as the failure to refrain, when talking about the commandments: "Indeed the Law calls this *consent* to lust 'lust' when it says, 'Thou shalt not lust.' For it isn't the *lusting* that had to be prohibited...but the assent to it" (50). Assent to lust was the failure itself to check our lusty desires. He again gave us a summary:

> To gather all that has been said into one short conclusion, there are four things we have set out above in order that we might carefully distinguish them from one another: (a) the mental vice that makes us disposed to sin (2–7); after that (b) the sin itself, which we have located in consent to evil or in scorn for God (8); then (c) the will for evil (9–34); and (d) the doing of the evil (35–66). Now just as willing isn't the same as accomplishing the will, so sinning isn't the same as carrying out the sin. The former is to be taken as the mind's consent by which we sin, the latter as the result of the doing, when we accomplish in deed what we consented to earlier. (67)

Abelard raised the question of knowing something to be inappropriate and introduced a direct connection to conscience: "There is no sin, except against conscience" ("*non est peccatum nisi contra conscientiam*" 109). Inasmuch as conscience was about knowing the right and wrong, sin was basically failing to heed what conscience dictates. Sin as consent was then a consent to what one knows was not the right to be done or the wrong to be avoided. To make his point, he famously brought in the provocative case of those responsible for crucifying Christ:

> Nevertheless, if someone should ask whether the martyr's persecution, or Christ's, sinned in doing what they believed was pleasing to God, or whether without sin they could have given up what they thought shouldn't be given up, then insofar as we earlier (7–8) described sin to be scorn for God or consenting to what one believes shouldn't be consented to, we certainly can't say they were sinning. No one's ignorance is a sin, and neither is the disbelief with which no one can be saved. (110)

Implicitly he argued, if they in conscience were to kill Christ because in their estimation, he was spreading heresies and that he was therefore an affront to God, then they could not have sinned for otherwise they would have had to violate their consciences.

In his summary, he turned to ignorance: "We judge that only what consists in the *fault* of negligence is properly called 'sin.'… But I don't see how not believing in Christ (which is what disbelief is) should be attributed to a fault in children or those it wasn't announced to, or how anything done out of invincible ignorance or that we were unable to foresee should be attributed to a fault in us" (129). Invariably for Abelard consent was located in the violation of one's conscience. We consent through failure; we do not stop ourselves from doing what we know ought not to done or from omitting to do what needs to be done.

The start of the discussion of theological ethics among the scholastics was initiated by the most exacting, most autobiographical, and most passionate and provocative of all of them. Abelard was a logician, a lover of specificity, and a theologian within a tradition whose contradictions needed more to be understood than resolved. Whether in his natural law, *Theologia*, ethics, letters, or *Sic et Non*, Abelard was a man of faith desiring to engage in a provocative discussion with his students so that the next generations would pursue the science of theology. While Bernard, William, and others wanted to keep theology in their ambit, Abelard released theological ethics to be critically engaged by human reason informed by faith and specifically by the generation that succeeded him.

II. HELOISE (1101–64)

Where was Heloise in all this?[22] In a major work on the relationship between Abelard and Heloise, Constant Mews highlighted that the "difficulty with this fascination in the story of their love affairs is that it has tended to overshadow awareness of Abelard and Heloise as thinkers, preoccupied by issues of language, theology, and ethics."[23]

Mews affirmed that "Heloise's ideal of *amor* as demanding true friendship, without concern for self-interest, is very different from Abelard's understanding of *amor* as irrational passion, at least as he presents it in the *Historia Calamitatum*. She feels that he has betrayed the ethical ideals that she thought they had shared in the messages of love that they once exchanged."[24] Mews added, "A driving theme in Heloise's writings is her concern for true authenticity in all behavior, whether in her relationship with Abelard or in her living out a religious life."[25] Consider Heloise's own words: "Wholly guilty though I am, I am also, as you know, wholly innocent. It is not the deed but the intention of the doer which makes the crime, and just should weigh not what was done but the spirit in which it is done. What my intentions towards you have always been, you alone who have known can judge."[26] The honesty of her lament was palpable: "I offend him more by my indignation than I placate him by making amends through penitence. How can it be called repentance for sins, however great the mortification of the flesh, if the mind still retains the will to sin and is on fire with its old desires?"[27] She added, "It is easy enough for anyone to confess his sins, to accuse himself, or even to mortify his body in an outward show of penance, but it is very difficult to tear the heart away from hankering after its dearest pleasures."[28] Intentionality, the intentionality that we find in Abelard's thought, is precisely the subject of Heloise's complaint with Abelard's oversight.

Along with intentionality was honesty. While Abelard worked on negatives, Heloise's thoughts on marriage were quite clear. Barbara

Newman noted how Abelard attributed to Heloise her assessment of marriage in his *Calamities*: "What harmony can there be between students and nursemaids, writing desks and cradles…? What man bent on sacred or philosophical thoughts could endure the crying of children, the nursery rhymes of nannies trying to calm them, the bustling throng of male and female servants in the household? And what woman will be able to bear the constant filth and squalor of babies?"[29] Heloise was hardly a defender of marriage: "A woman should realize that if she marries a rich man more readily than a poor one, and desires her husband more for his possessions than for himself, she is offering herself for sale."[30] The matter of the marriage is not much different from the matter of the cloister: "It was not any sense of vocation which brought me as a young girl to accept the austerities of the cloister, but your bidding alone, and if I deserve no gratitude from you, you may judge for yourself how my labors are in vain."[31]

Reflecting on Abelard's *Dialogue*, Mews wrote that the philosopher "makes the case that the works of faith do not matter as much as the intention behind them, which is the same position Heloise argues so strongly for in her third letter to Abelard about the relationship between outward observance and the inner disposition."[32] Mews wondered whether Abelard's philosopher was Heloise? Does Abelard wait to see how Heloise herself would finish the *Dialogue*? Mews concluded instead that the *Dialogue* helped Abelard to develop his work on ethics "while indirectly responding to Heloise."[33]

Clearly Heloise challenged Abelard in their love matters precisely with the language he used in the *Dialogue* and *The Ethics*. Newman and Mews prompt us as we go forward in our understanding of Scholasticism to see the *Letters* as texts that helped Heloise and Abelard to hone or be honed in both word and trusted action by the intentions that bind. The *Letters* help us indispensably in understanding the centrality of intention and consent in the work of the forerunners of medieval scholasticism. It also helps us to imagine the development of intellectual history to be a lot more than the singular thoughts of unrelated persons musing aloud about their inner thoughts.

III. PETER LOMBARD (1100–1160)

Because every aspiring master of theology, from the thirteenth through the sixteenth century, was required to lecture on the *Sentences* of Peter Lombard, the *Sentences* became the second most commented upon text (after the Bible) in Christian literature. After the Bible, it became, for every established scholastic, his own first work. The numbers are staggering: as Rosemann noted, "A compilation of commentaries on the *Book of Sentences* that appeared more than fifty years ago (and has since been added to) already listed 1,407 items."[34] These commentaries were very diverse; the distinctiveness of a scholastic's intellectual trajectory was imprinted in that scholastic's first work, almost always, the commentary on the *Sentences*. The theological differences among Bonaventure, Aquinas, and Ockham, for example, were discoverable first in their respective *commentaries*. There they worked out their own theological pathways; as significant as their later developments were, any scholastic's *Commentary on the Sentences* was effectively the foundational opus.[35]

The author of the original *Sentences*, Peter Lombard, was born near Novara in Lombardy, Italy, of an apparently poor background; his mother was described as a washerwoman. He needed sponsorship throughout his studies. He probably studied in his local cathedral school and may eventually have studied in Lucca where the bishop introduced him to Bernard of Clairvaux (1090–1153), who introduced him in turn to the Abbey of St. Victor. There he likely studied with Hugh (1096–1141) on the sacraments, although he undoubtedly also attended Abelard's lectures. In 1159 he was made the bishop of Paris.

Before the *Sentences*, Peter worked on his own *Glossae*, on the Psalter and another on the Pauline Epistles, but in the process he recognized the insufficiency of the *Glossae* tradition. Early on, he became attracted to disputations, not unlike those in *Sic et Non*. In public disputations at this time, students usually debated until the master intervened with the resolution. Later, these disputations would be hosted by the university, especially during the ecclesial seasons of Advent and Lent. As we will see later, they were called *Quodlibetales*, literally, the *Whatevers*, because the host could be asked whatever the audience wanted. Such disputations were exactly what engaged the interests of the scholastics.

In 1150, Peter began to consider a collection of sentences or judgments incorporated logically into an overall work. A first edition appeared in 1156; he taught a second edition in 1158 with more than 1,100 citations from Augustine. He took from Augustine's *On Christian Teaching* the distinction between things and signs. Things were themselves; they were to be used or enjoyed in themselves or as a means to some other enjoyment. For Augustine, only the Trinity could be a thing for enjoyment; everything else was to be used for that enjoyment.

The first of the four books of the *Sentences* was on the Trinity; the second, on the Creation (things to be used); the third, on the incarnation ("God, the ultimate object of enjoyment, allowed himself to become used for salvation")[36] and the virtues ("things to be used through which we enjoy");[37] and, finally, the fourth book, on the signs of grace or the sacraments. In his style of organization, Lombard located himself somewhere between Hugh and Abelard, both personally and as a theologian. He was not a settled Victorine, nor a wanderer like Abelard. He was a priest with a simple residence. He had been effectively teaching biblical studies, trying to avoid the traditionalism of the Victorines, while also avoiding the censorship that Abelard endured.

Through the *Sentences*, Lombard tried to accomplish three things. First, he offered an account of the development of the tradition. Throughout, he cited every significant sentence or judgment rendered by an authoritative source. Second, he suggested where there was a consensus within the tradition itself and therein offered the insight that a consensus had been achieved. Still, Lombard offered subsequent insights that could prompt further considerations, or even disputations. Third, he demarcated where in a disputation there was a legitimate contradiction; here, however, more than just conveying a difference as Abelard did in *Sic et Non*, Lombard effectively moderated the debate, suggesting by further inquiry whether consensus could be achieved in the future. Throughout, the lack of any consensus was not at all unsettling. On the contrary, the scholastics were building the tradition, very mindful of doing it, and wherever there was debate, there was the possibility of further development.

In short, Peter gave an account of the tradition and at the same time moderated and therein shaped the future concourse of the tradition. Moreover, as Rosemann noted, Lombard did it with humility, the premier virtue for the patristic period.[38] In fact, often he did not resolve differences in the tradition, but rather reported simply where consensus had been achieved; he did not end debate and was quite comfortable letting it remain open, as we will see below both in penance and on marriage. This served him and his project well. By not settling questions, he left room for those who later commented on his *Sentences* to enter into the discourse after him. In a manner of speaking, his text, because it engaged such differing currents of the tradition without resolving them, became itself a new *glossa*. Later commentators made observations on his sentences and placed their positions on the side of one argument as opposed to the other. While Scripture was the true object of the *glossa* tradition, the *Sentences* become, by analogy, very much inserted into that *glossa* tradition, with its own elaborate subsequent commentaries.

Here we focus on the fourth book,[39] because there the sacraments were central: How can the sinner be saved unless through the sacraments? The administration of the sacraments provided avenues of grace. We will look briefly at penance and then at marriage. Let us recognize that Lombard provided us a look at penance before the Fourth Lateran Council's requirement of the Easter duty, which we mentioned in the prior chapter.

A new doctrine of penance was taking shape. First, Lombard outlined the three things considered necessary for the sacrament of penance: compunction of heart, confession of the mouth, and satisfaction by means of work (IV. Dist. 16.1.1). Here, confession to a priest was an expanding practice, becoming more and more common (IV. Dist. 17) and one can hear in the text how the contrition of the penitent was being considered as the sufficient mark of the sacrament of penance that remitted the debt: "It is necessary for a penitent to confess if he has the time; and yet, before there is confession by the mouth, if there is the intention in the heart, remission is granted to him" (IV. Dist. 17.1.12). Shortly afterward, however, Lombard wrote that, if possible, one should confess to a priest: "It does not suffice to confess to God alone, if there is time" (IV. Dist. 17.3.1). If we should confess to a priest, which priest? Lombard suggested the type of priest one should look for as confessor: "one who is wise and discreet, who has power and judgment"; if he's not available, "confess to his friend" (IV. Dist. 17.4.6).

Lombard's humility and wisdom appeared often in the way he left conclusions unresolved. For instance, Lombard asked that if a sinner repeats a sin already forgiven does the remitted sin return? (IV. Dist. 22.1). After presenting both sides, citing Ambrose, Augustine, Bede, and others, Lombard wrote, "Proven doctors favor each side of the question, and so, without prejudice to either side, I leave the judgment to the judicious reader." Assuredly, later commentators could not resist adding their insights into their commentary on the very same question.

Similarly, on the question of what is the sacrament and what is the thing when speaking of penance, he opened up the issue: "A sacrament is a sign of a sacred thing; what then here is the sign, and what is the sacred thing of the sign?" (IV. Dist. 22.2.1). He proposed one side of the debate: outward penance is the sign of the thing, that is, inner penance, "namely contrition of heart and humiliation" (IV. Dist. 22.2.2). But against this view he proposed the view of others in which there was great variety. For instance, for some, inward penance is "both the thing of the sacrament, that is, of outward penance, and the sacrament of the remission of sin, which it both signifies and brings about" (IV. Dist. 22.2.5).

Still, when Lombard resolved, his positions were fairly modern. For instance, when he turned to marriage, he asserted that consent alone makes the marriage (IV. Dist. 27.3.2). This consent was to be free and precluded coercion (Dist. 29.1). Moreover, he was not a consummationist, that is, one who held the position that marriage depended on consummating the sexual intimacy of the couple. Marriage occurred with the exchange of consents: "from the time of the occurrence of a willing and marital consent, which alone makes marriage, the bride and groom are true marriage partners" (Dist 27.4.2).[40]

Much of the insights about the goodness of marriage were derived from Scripture and Augustine, but Lombard's own views on marriage and his interpretation of texts might strike the reader as more informed than one might have expected. Consider how he explained "why the woman was formed from the side of the man" (Dist. 28.4.1). He wrote,

> And because she is not given as a slave girl or as one to lord it over him, in the beginning she is not formed either from the highest part, nor from the lowest, but from the side of man, for the sake of conjugal partnership. If she had been made from the highest, as from the head, she might seem created for domination; but if from the lowest, as from the feet, she might seem to be created for subjection to slavery. But she is taken neither as mistress, nor as slave girl, she is made from the middle, that is, from the side, because she is taken for conjugal partnership. (Dist 28.4.1)

As we can see, Lombard was quite clear that husband and wife were fairly equal partners. In fact, we can say that his concern for equity in the "conjugal partnership" was a fairly foundational premise. Later he wrote, "Husband and wife enjoy the same right," to which he adds, "It is also to be noted that, as the Lord grants to the husband the right to dismiss his wife because of fornication, the same permission is not taken away from women" (Dist. 35.1.1). Later, he added another right: "That a husband cannot dismiss a fornicating wife, unless he is innocent of the same offence, and vice versa" (Dist. 35.2.1).

Anyone studying the history of the use of the *Sentences* can see that it very much made the development of the tradition more possible. It effectively became the scholastics' textbook par excellence, used in every university as the introductory text of new masters. But it was also itself an invitation not only to know and teach the tradition, but also to contribute to and develop that tradition. Lombard knew when to recognize that tradition had resolved its differences and when it had not. In this way, the *Sentences* became the conduit for advancing the very much developing tradition and, also, allowed subsequent scholastics the opportunity to make their mark. The text itself, then, complemented the universities' mission to pursue the science of articulating the development of the tradition. In short, it made its mission possible.

Nevertheless, when it came to ethics, the *Sentences* was significantly weak. No less than Marcia Colish, the premier expert on Lombard, noted, "The major difficulty in Peter's theology, both substantively and organizationally, is his handling of ethics." Ethics is really only implicitly in the *Sentences*. Moreover, Colish commented that, problematically, not only did Peter not give us an ethics per se, he also did not develop foundations that could yield such an ethics. Colish referred to the problems we encountered when Lombard treated the virtues under the heading of Christ's own attributes: "Yet, Christ had a human nature freed from original sin and united to the Word from the moment of His conception. By grace, the human Christ had a knowledge beyond that which any mortal can possess. His moral psychology is perforce radically different from that of other mortals, and the sense in which he can truly be a moral exemplar for us is an issue that Peter does not adequately resolve."[41] In short, Lombard did not develop for us a workable moral anthropology and, in that sense, never gave us the foundations for a moral theology.

In fact, when we look at these two enormous figures of early Scholasticism, we see that though they present us with methods of inquiry, a commitment to the critical or scientific investigation of the tradition, and a deep awareness of the heritage of the tradition itself, they offered very little by way of moral theology. Abelard's main text on ethics is exclusively on sin; he never gets to the virtue counterpart. His work on natural law is really about its foundations rather than its function or contents. For ethics in Lombard, we can only look at his fourth book because only in the sacraments do we find anything of moral theology pertinent to human beings. What we need is for someone to develop a new type of text that allows us to entertain the moral life per se, something neither Abelard nor Peter Lombard, for all their contributions to Scholasticism, ever achieved.

IV. THOMAS AQUINAS (1224–74)

Why is it that Thomas Aquinas still captures the interest and the willingness of some scholars to spend several years of their lives to study his writings? Why is it, too, that a return to Thomas's ethics yields insights into his writings that have escaped us for decades, even centuries? Why is he a perennial font of reflection that prompts new writers to find fresh insights at the end of the second millennium?

The answer rests, I believe, in the fact that he captured an understanding of the moral life that is enormously helpful in forming a vision of the type of people we ought to become. In an age like ours that wants to respect the individual conscience while maintaining a sense of the ability to establish and recognize the objectively right and wrong, Thomas provided a framework in which we could achieve both. In order to demonstrate how Thomas accomplished this structurally, I advance ten key points that identify decisions Thomas made in the Middle Ages that served as signposts for understanding why we are interested in him today.[42] Hopefully, we will better understand the fascination new writers find in the thirteenth-century Dominican born and raised in the town of Roccasecca (Dry Rock), Italy.

First, Thomas pursued his vocation in a religious order that combined both the contemplative dimension of a monastery with the active service of ministry through teaching and preaching and hearing confessions all in the heart of urban life. The youngest of nine children, Thomas was dedicated to the priesthood and his ambitious parents sent him at the age of six to the famous Benedictine Abbey, Monte Cassino, where they hoped he would eventually become abbot. As urban areas emerged throughout thirteenth-century Europe, the fifteen-year-old made his first adult decision by leaving the abbey where he was expected to live the rest of his life. He moved to Naples for study and at twenty made his second decision, to enter the relatively new religious order, the Order of Preachers, also known by their founder's name, the Dominicans.

We should note the significance of these two decisions to leave one order and enter the other. The Benedictines vowed to remain forever in the community to which they belonged; the Dominicans did not. The Benedictines, though hardly wealthy, had attractive abbeys and Monte Cassino was among the most impressive; the Dominicans were beggars, more properly called "mendicants." While some Benedictine members became theological scholars within the monastery, Dominicans trained their members to preach and to hear confessions in the cities as well as to teach in the medieval universities. In light of what we saw in the last chapter about Thomas's argument for a religious order that incorporated ministerial action as a part of their contemplative life, Thomas's early adult choices very much defined the man.

If Thomas's family did not take the first decision well, it was certainly even less inclined to the second. Subsequently, when his family learned he joined the mendicant order, his widowed mother and siblings kidnapped him and "detained" him in a tower for a year. They eventually relented and the Dominicans immediately—and wisely—sent Thomas away from his family to Paris for three years of studies (1245–48) and another four years to study with Albert the Great (d. 1280) in Cologne (1248–52). In 1252, he began another tenure in Paris, first as master of the *Sentences* of Peter Lombard (thus, composing his own *Commentary on the Sentences of Peter Lombard*), and then assuming the position of regent master. There he wrote his treatise on truth, *De veritate*; began the *Summa Contra Gentiles* to help Dominican preachers in their work in the Near East; and lectured on the Gospel of St. Matthew. After a brief stay in Naples (1260–61), he moved to the papal city of Orvieto where he completed the *Contra Gentiles* and, following in the footsteps of Gregory, wrote his *Commentary on the Book of Job*, among other works. In 1265, he began his teaching at Rome where he remained for three years before being summoned to return to Paris for a rare second term of teaching as again the regent master. In 1272, after extraordinary productivity, he left Paris and returned to Naples for two years before he died in the Cistercian Abbey of Fossanova. His death is doubly ironic. First, the forty-nine-year-old Dominican who abandoned a vocation with a vow for permanence collapses while *walking* to the council in Lyons. Second, he died in a monastic community not far from his home (Roccasecca) and Monte Cassino.[43]

He was not, then, an inactive man. On the contrary, as an adolescent he decided to break away from the standard summons of religious life and pursued a new religious order with a new, fairly urban vision of the holy. Entering the Dominicans only seventeen years after their founding, this man would later walk from one major city to another and became one of the most travelled men of the thirteenth century. At a time when cities were emerging and the Renaissance was about to be born in the paintings of Cimabue, Duccio, and Giotto, Thomas entered the active life of the centers of learning in these cities. For Thomas, defending a contemplative life in action, the place to teach and learn was not to be the monastery, but the rising city and its universities.

Second, Thomas worked to improve the education of fellow priests and religious. As we saw in the last chapter, the Dominican order was approved as the Order of Preachers in 1217, but in 1221 Pope Innocent III mandated the Dominicans to hear confessions as well. In response to this new apostolic charge, Dominican leaders wrote a plethora of manuals for preaching and for hearing confessions. The seriousness of their mission was evident in the two very different tracks of Dominican formation. For the first track, a few extraordinary young members, like Thomas, were singled out and sent to one of the *studia* (studies' programs), set up at the five major universities: Oxford, Bologna, Paris, Montpelier, and Cologne. The majority, however, remained in their own communities where they were required for the rest of their lives to attend lectures on these practical manuals, especially the *Summa de casibus* by Raymond of Peñafort (d. 1275).

Thomas became interested not only in the exceptional students he taught during his three appointments in Paris, but also with his students back in his province. In *The Setting for the Summa Theologiae*, the Dominican Leonard Boyle (1923–99) wrote that Thomas, while at Orvieto, attended in 1265 the Provincial chapter at Anagni where he proposed establishing an experimental program, or *studium*, for young Dominican students, not among the elite who were sent to the universities, but intelligent enough for something more theologically sophisticated than Raymond's cases. That is, Thomas experimented with Dominican formation, finding that some young men who were not destined for the university were still capable of actually learning theology. Moreover, he foresaw the significance of a theologically formed clergy, something that would not become commonplace until the Council of Trent, three hundred years later. Concretely, Thomas wanted to train this class of Dominicans, and the chapter approved the proposal and he subsequently opened in Rome a personal *studium*, where he first taught his *Commentary on the Sentences*. Eventually he began writing the *Summa Theologiae* for these above-average students who were destined for preaching and hearing confessions. For this reason, Boyle rightly called the *Summa* a "Dominican" work.[44]

We should not miss his audience. The *Summa* was not written for university students. It was written for Dominicans already on a pastoral track. These were not students who, for instance, were trained in any philosophy or any theology. This is so different, I need to confess, from how I was originally trained. In my formation as a young Jesuit, I was taught that I needed to study twelve to fourteen courses of philosophy so that I could study theology. When I asked why, I was informed that without philosophy I could not understand theology and, it was added, how could I learn the *Summa* without a philosophical background? Boyle's claim was that, in fact, the *Summa*'s first students were not trained in philosophy at all. He wrote the text for newcomers for ministry whom he believed should have some fundamental theological competency.

Being mindful of his Dominican order's ministerial need was always a part of the mindset of Thomas. Earlier, he had written the *Summa Contra Gentiles* (1259–65), again, not for scholars but for other Dominican pastoral ministers—this time, for missionaries so that they could have a text on hand to help them in their evangelical ministry, mostly in the Middle East. Similar to the *Contra Gentiles*, his *Summa Theologiae* was designed to show that to be a good preacher and confessor one needed not only practical manuals but also comprehensive theology. Behind that presupposition is its obvious parallel: that one could not become a decent theologian without being a decent preacher and confessor.

Third, within the *Summa Theologiae*, he provided a theological context for ethics. In Rome, after one year of teaching the fourth book of the *Commentary on the Sentences*, Thomas began constructing and writing the *Summa Theologiae* for the young Dominicans in his private *studium*. He divided the *Summa* into three parts. The first part was about God's relationship to us as Creator. The entire second part, by far the longest, was about moral theology in terms of our response to God and was divided into two sections: the first provided the needed foundations for a moral theology, that is, a general anthropological vision of the human, while the second explored the specific moral matter for that anthropology, the seven virtues (the three theological virtues of faith, hope, and charity, and the four cardinal virtues of justice, prudence, fortitude, and temperance) along with the vices and sins that correspond to these seven virtues. The third part was about Jesus Christ our savior and the sacraments that assist us in the way of salvation.

Thomas, therefore, dedicated the core of the *Summa* to moral theology. The first section of the second part called the *Prima Secundae* began with a question about the last end, the ultimate goal for living a moral life. The first two of the question's eight articles were about acting for an end with a rational purpose and depended heavily on Aristotle, but Thomas quickly shifted to Augustine. In the third article, he asked whether the morality of human actions derived from their end; he answered positively, citing Augustine, that if the end is worthy of blame or praise, so are its deeds (I-II., q. 1, a. 3, sed contra).[45]

In the fifth article, Thomas negated the possibility of multiple last ends and argued that what every human desires was the perfect good, a good that lacked nothing but rather completed the person. He cited Augustine's *The City of God* on the perfect being the complete.[46] He returned in the next article asking whether in willing we invariably will the last end and again quoted Augustine, noting that the end of our good was that we "love it for its own sake."[47] He concluded the question with two articles: first, asking whether all human beings have the same last end, replying that our last end was happiness, citing Augustine again,[48] and second, asking whether any other creatures share in that end and replying that only human beings have the same last end, again citing Augustine.[49]

In the second question, Thomas, having determined happiness as humanity's last end, led the reader to understand what our happiness was by discounting a variety of inadequate goods (honor, riches, fame, power) before turning to the last two articles (I-II, q. 2, a. 7–8), and here again he relied on Augustine's authority to make his key claims: first, that the life of happiness is the good to be loved for its own sake;[50] second, that God is our happiness.[51] These articles were in sum the foundations of Augustine's and Thomas's ethics. Although he used Aristotle to develop and expand the theological tradition, Thomas understood the tradition to be Augustinian in large measure, just as Lombard did before him. The context then was fundamentally theological; in fact, it was called the summary of theology and the theology of the thirteenth century was above all Augustinian.

Thomas began the second section of the second part, called the *Secunda Secundae*, with a prologue in which he wrote, "We may reduce the whole of moral matters to the consideration of the virtues, which virtues themselves may be reduced to seven in number, three of which are theological, and of these we must treat first; while the other four are the cardinal virtues, of which we shall treat afterwards." He concluded the prologue on the seven virtues with the claim, "In this way no matter pertaining to morals will be overlooked." Thus, while Abelard wrote on sin and never got to the virtues, and as Lombard explored the human virtues of Jesus Christ, Thomas discussed sin, vice, and even the gifts of the Holy Spirit all within the context of the seven virtues. The first comprehensive treatment of moral theology was completely in the key of virtue, certainly a departure from the penitential or confessional manuals that had the seven vices as their foundational hermeneutic.

Still, it would be good for us to remember not only the structure that Thomas developed but the goals that he sought. His aim was to finish the *Pars Tertia* on Christ and the Sacraments. In a relatively new work, Mark Jordan suggests that readers of the *Summa Theologiae* might do well to read the text from the end to the beginning so as to see the work in the light of the end that Thomas actually reached, Christ.[52]

Fourth, Thomas believed that theology was fundamentally dialogical. As the theologian Marie-Dominique Chenu demonstrated in *Toward Understanding Saint Thomas*, the structure of the *Summa* itself was dialogical: the first part was God's call; the second, our response; and third, Jesus, the Savior who is the Word Incarnate, the dialogue himself. The entire work reflected a dialogue.[53]

Each part was divided into questions, each question was divided into articles, and each article began also in the form of a question. As we briefly saw earlier, prior to giving an answer, Thomas presented a series of objections or considerations from other authorities who, generally speaking, often seemed at odds with the reply that eventually Thomas provided (think here, Abelard's *Sic et Non* and Lombard's *Sentences*). Like those before him, Thomas wanted us to know that there already was a debate on the matter and he insisted that we know what the issues in that dialogue were, before reading his reply. In effect, he structured the articles to appreciate the debate. After he finally replied, he concluded each article with specific responses to each of the earlier considerations. Each article, then, invited the reader into deeper discussions and debates about the standing question. Before moving onto another topic, Thomas proceeded to another article so as to see, as Abelard and Lombard had shown earlier, that every theological issue had a multitude of analogous tangents. This was after all the breadth and depth of Scholasticism's attempt to build the tradition. These related articles were, then, stages of descent into the depths of inquiry first posed by the original question. When Thomas exhausted one question, he moved onto the next. All along, the inquiring intellect of Thomas engaged the reader. Following from Abelard and Lombard, Thomas's *Summa* was then a theological investigation framed as a dialogue within the multitudinous debates within the tradition. In a word it was an inquiry or, as Anselm would have it, faith seeking understanding.[54]

Thomas's life was a dialogue as well. His Dominican biographer, James Weisheipl (1923–84), described that from 1269 to 1272, during his second tenure in Paris, Thomas had four scribes to whom he simultaneously (it seems) dictated: to one, the *Summa Theologiae*; to another, his commentaries on Aristotle's works (e.g., the *Ethics*, the *Metaphysics*, the *Physics*); to another, his commentaries on the Scriptures (specifically, John's Gospel and the Pauline Epistles); and, to the fourth, the polemical discourses particularly in defense of his order, which he wrote for the master general against the antimendicants and the Averroists. One can only imagine what it would be like to pass by the space where these dictations occurred.

Our iconography of Thomas as some large but silent figure then was somewhat peculiar. The man who left Monte Cassino was rarely, except in his last months, speechless. On the contrary, he was lecturing, debating, commenting, discoursing, and dictating with great relish. Moreover, one particular university event that he enjoyed was the *Quodlibetales*. These sessions were held during Advent and Lent, when the entire university was assembled, and random questions were submitted dealing with *whatever* topic the questioner asked. Thomas routinely volunteered to "host" these *Quodlibetales* and answered questions ranging from whether it was morally licit to enjoy a long, warm bath to what the Trinity was or whether there were physical worms and physical tears in hell's punishment.

Thomas, who had joined the Order of Preachers, loved and lived the Word of God. His theology and his life were dialogical. His use of so many sources and his variety of interests demonstrated how convincingly he believed in the gift of human reason. No wonder, then, that he asserted the human is made in God's image by being rational. The *Summa*, then, not only left the reader with new insights; more importantly, it prompted the reader to emulate the probing intellect that wrote it. Thomas drew us into the habit of inquiring deeply, but inquiring as Thomas did—that is, with others.

Fifth, like Abelard, Thomas upheld the primacy of the conscience. Not surprisingly, the man who drew us into inquiry defended the seat of moral agency in each person. In the *Prima Secundae*, Thomas asked whether we could ever contradict the conscience. The question is central: If we do not heed the conscience, then what will we heed? And why? Thomas answered, absolutely speaking, every time we act against our conscience, whether it was right or erring, we sin (I-II, q. 19, a. 5). *Then*, Thomas asked, Are we called good when we follow an erring conscience? Thomas answered, If we could have avoided the error, then we were culpable for not having known what we should have known; but if we could not have known otherwise, then we are excused from our error (I-II, q. 19, a. 6). Here Thomas developed the matter of ignorance and conscience much further than Abelard had. Ignorance could excuse, but if there was something we should have known and could have known, then ignorance does not excuse. Moreover, when Thomas wrote about conscience he wrote about the *dictates* of conscience. He did not describe conscience as an instrument that excused us from responsibility, but one that imposed moral obligation. Thus, Thomas's argument was that we should never disobey that which articulates and imposes moral commands upon us but that we are still responsible to know what we should.[55]

Thomas preferred to call this dictate one of reason, and here we see that his understanding of conscience was one that always needed to grow and be informed. Implicitly within this context conscience was presumed to be fairly dynamic, and it was in pursuit of that dynamism that Thomas fashioned the entire *Secunda secundae*, that is, his moral theology, in the key of virtue. A life spent forever in the quest to acquire virtue was a life seeking to have a fully informed conscience. This was the agenda of the *Pars Secunda*.

Sixth, Thomas insisted that the primary concept in moral theology is the "*obiectum*," in English, the "object." This was perhaps surprising since we often associated ethics with actions, for example, acts of lying, acts of contraception, acts of homosexuals, and so on. But for Thomas, ethics was not primarily about actions as they were performed, but rather about objects we have in mind and, in particular, objects that we intend to realize. In English, the word *object* was like the term *subject matter*; object was something conceptual, rather than physical. The object was the subject matter of ethics. For Thomas, the object was first found in the intention, or as he also called it the internal act, and then later in the external act. Like Abelard, Thomas placed the beginning of the assessment of moral acting in the intention. The beginning of moral acting and of moral investigation and assessment was what was the subject matter of the intention.

Thomas wanted us to realize that what we think, what we intend, what we engage as our purpose is really what we must measure first. Thomas held that we cannot simply look at our external actions; rather, if we want to become more moral, we need to look at how we think and intend, first. For example, if I keep thinking ill of someone, I will probably eventually utter an unkind remark. If I keep having envious thoughts, envy will become more rooted in me. If I wish harm on someone, I will rejoice in their suffering. Thomas realized that rightness and wrongness were something, as Jesus claimed (Mark 7:1–23; Matt 15:10–20), that comes out of us. Therefore, he wanted to make sure that the objects or subject matters that we wanted to consider and intend were, in fact, the right ones.

Seventh, Thomas put the measure of that objectivity in the intention. Today we think of intention in subjective terms. We say things like, "I don't know what your intentions were." We prefer to measure our ethics by our external actions, that is, what we see, rather than by our intentions that are not as visible or evident. Intentions, we think, only take us into the recesses of the mind. Thomas insisted, however, that there was moral objectivity in an ethics that starts with intention. Because ethics required us subsequently to measure whether an action was right or wrong, Thomas began his investigations measuring the internal action first, that is, the intention. We can measure the intention by asking, then, what was the object of the intention. If an envious object was in the intention, then the intention would be wrong; if a temperate object was in the intention, then it, like a just or prudent one, was right. If the intention was wrong, then the external act would likely be wrong. If the intention was right, then for the external act to be right it must be a "fitting" or "appropriate" expression of the intention. If it falls short, then, even though the intention or internal act was right, the external act would be wrong. Thomas appreciated that often we have the right intentions and still get the act wrong, but he always insisted that we started our assessment first with the intention and then with the external or realized action.

Thomas insisted on moral objectivity, always within the context of intention. He could argue this because he claimed that the object or the subject matter, that is, the stuff that one had in the intention, was measurable. By examining our intentions, he could have been suggesting a very introverted agenda, that is, it could have been an investigation into the deeper recesses of a person. As a matter of fact, Thomas's agenda was extroverted, that is, he wanted us to get our intentions right so that our external actions would be right as well. These internal and external actions would become the material that would help the agent to become a more virtuous person because virtues are only acquired by performing intended actions habitually.

The brilliance of his psychology was his insistence that the object in the mind that counts as the intention was that which was most "proximate" to the external action. The moral description of the intention depended on knowing the agent's proximate end, that is, the object of the intention most proximate to the external action, rather than to what he referred to as one of the more remote ends.[56] The proximate end was always the first answer to the question: Why did you do that? The end was proximate in relation to the action subsequently performed by the intending agent.

For example, you might ask me why I wrote this chapter. I would say because I wanted you to understand Scholasticism and the moral life. This is my intention: it is the nearest or most proximate explanation for why I am writing this chapter, but then you ask again, why did you really write this chapter? Now you are looking for more remote reasons, and Thomas preferred to measure these matters as circumstances, that is, as remote ends. He acknowledged that we can measure the objects of these more remote ends as right or wrong as well and that in the long run we should attend to them too, but he insisted that the moral agenda was set in the intention first, that is, the object proximate or nearest to the external act, and that more remote reasons or objects were simply circumstantial.

Thomas is interested in working with the object that most immediately explained why one acts, nothing more and nothing less.

Moreover, Thomas examined this matter on intentions precisely so that we would have the right intentions in the first place. He understood that, unless we act with right intentions, we cannot grow morally. For Thomas, an action was the realization of a person. This active Dominican, who himself *does* a great deal of teaching, writing, walking, reading, thinking, discoursing, preaching, and planning in the city, realized that we each have within us the ability to realize what God has placed within us; these abilities were nascent, what he called inclinations. Looking into the human, he found inclinations and wanted to guide those inclinations by right intentions into the performance of right external actions so that the human could grow virtuously. Likewise, he invited us to look into ourselves so that we could discover our inclinations and guide them into right intentions and eventually into right actions that would help us to grow well.

Eighth, Thomas measures the objects both in the intention and in the external acts as virtuous or vicious accordingly. Not only did Thomas write the whole second part of the *Summa* on the virtues, but while at Paris during that same period, he wrote his commentary on the *Ethics* of Aristotle (1271) as well as his four treatises on the virtues, charity, hope, and the cardinal virtues (1269–72).[57] His ethical reflection was devoted at this time singularly to the virtues. In particular he considered the interdependency of the virtues, that is, that right intention had to be both just and prudent. Justice cannot be virtuous without prudence and prudence cannot be virtuous without justice: the moral and intellectual virtues complement one another (I-II, q. 58, a. 4 and 5).

Moreover, Thomas did not claim that a person is just by simply trying to be just, or that a courageous person is one who simply tries to be courageous. Rather, the just person was one who attempted *and* attained justice; the courageous person was one who actually was courageous. The virtues for Thomas were not about meaning well; as a matter of fact, according to Thomas, they were actually about thinking, intending, and acting well. Thus, in order to attain a virtue, we need, then, to make sure that our acts were right.

To make sure that my intention and my actions were right, I need prudence. My intention in writing this chapter, for instance, is to give you an opportunity to see the value of Scholasticism. To be prudent I must give enough details without giving you too much or too little, that is, I must hit the mean between extremes (II-II, q. 47, a. 7c.).

Prudence helps us to determine in the here and now what exactly we need to grow. In fact, Thomas appropriated from Avicenna (980–1037) the insight that to grow in virtue we need to reflect and exercise (*studium et exercitium*). This suggests that the moral life is like athletics—we reflect on what we need to train within ourselves and then we need to determine the appropriate exercises to realize those inclinations that we want developed. Again, the mean enters because, as in athletic exercise, there is the difference between insufficient exercise and overdoing it. Furthermore, we try to anticipate what areas of our lives need more attention than others and through our intentions set up the way that we will proceed. Thus, prudence is not only about intending this or that particular action; more importantly, prudence is about self-understanding and setting for ourselves both short- and long-term goals for growing in the virtues. The Christian moral life is not about reacting, but about anticipating the courses of my life that I will eventually travel, as my professor Klaus Demmer often argued.[58]

Good parenting is a perfect paradigm for prudence. Parents are constantly trying to get into the heads of their children right ways of thinking about their relations with family members, neighbors, classmates, teachers, and themselves. They want to get their children thinking about right objects. They teach them to constantly set minor, but attainable goals. They teach them to think before they act, to take one step at a time, and to continue moving forward. Like Thomas, they try to teach their children to be prudent.

Ninth, following from this, we should see that Thomas basically believed that we become what we do. What does this mean? Thomas appreciated that anything that we intentionally do makes us become what we are doing. Thomas wanted to get to the right object, that is, to whatever we ought to have in mind, because he recognized that the intention is the seed of our actions and of the people we are becoming. Thomas recognized, of course, that if we only intend, but do not act, then we never realize what we can become. If I intend to speak up to my domineering boss, but never do, I will never attain the assertive stance that I believe is just. If I intend to give up drinking large quantities of beer, but never do, I will continue to be a heavy drinker.

To demonstrate his insight, Thomas distinguished (I-II, q. 74, a. 1c) two categories of acting, those that we make (transient) and those that we do (immanent). If I make a chair, a table, or a cake, the effects of my efforts pass from me into the thing that I make. Yet in those actions that I do, the object of my activity redounds to me: I become what I do. If I dance, I become a dancer. If I run, I become a runner. If I lie, I become a liar. Each of us is called then to become master of our lives by becoming master of our internal and external actions. We become masters of our actions by prudent reflection and exercise, by intending the courses of action that we ought to engage, and by actually doing them. By doing them rightly, we become who we believe we are destined to become. This helps us understand then why Thomas used Avicenna's phrase *studium et exercitium*, "reflection and exercise." These two words mean that we need to prudently choose the right courses of action by reflecting on the virtues we most need to pursue and then, with those virtues in mind, find prudently the right exercises to realize them. In that way, we could choose to do who we wanted to become.

Tenth, a fundamental thesis of Thomas was that "every human act is a moral act" (I-II, q. 18, a. 8). We tend to think of ethics as primarily about contested actions like abortions, divorce, and so on. Thus, if we were to take a course in ethics, we would expect to talk about controversial actions. To correct this way of thinking, I suggest to my students that they take a piece of paper and write down five concerns that they think involve morality. Usually they write, abortion, homosexuality, divorce, war, birth control, and so on. Then I tell them to turn the paper over and to write down five concerns with which they woke up this morning. Those concerns include repairing a relationship, living more justly, drinking less, eating less, getting more sleep, getting more work or more leisure, talking with one's spouse, children, or boss, practicing mercy, being less compulsive or obsessive, confronting a friend, supporting a friend, being more generous, etcetera. This side of the paper, I say, is also moral matter. Ordinary life is the matter for moral reflection, intention, and action.

In fact, Thomas presumed that everything we do is subject to moral assessment and impact. When Thomas asked whether there were any actions that were free of moral meaning, he responded that if we were talking about acts in the abstract, then there could be indifferent acts. Once we discuss actions that we actually intend to perform, then automatically they are for a purpose and that purpose is measurable as right or wrong. However, those acts that we do unconsciously, which he called "acts of man" as opposed to "human acts," he described as "indifferent." He gave an example: "Stroking one's beard, unknowingly." Everything else, for Thomas, was about moral living. Even small acts? Yes, Thomas replied, and used the Scriptures to talk about a simple act like breaking stalks of grain in a field, which caused an uproar when Jesus's disciples did it on the Sabbath (I-II, q. 18, a. 8–9).

The moral agenda for Thomas was extraordinarily full. Anything that we do: how we wake up, drive, clean, write, talk, dress, and so on, are all moral activities. Everything that we do shapes us as either more virtuous or more vicious. For Thomas, there were not one or two moral moments every week, but thousands every day. Every moment was literally an occasion for becoming freer for Christ and neighbor.

Of course, there is a danger here: overload. Prudence reminds us that if our lives are a compulsive expression of a perpetual agenda, then the agenda cannot be right, fitting, or appropriate. Still, we are all busy people and what Thomas was urging us to is not more activity, but of being more aware, more intentional about our activity. Assuredly, Thomas wanted us to become masters of our lives. Thus, Thomas was not asking his readers to do more, but to be more intentional in what they do.

As we move toward closure on Thomas, we need to highlight three integral insights. First, we cannot miss that for Thomas, as he wrote in the prologue of the *Secunda Secundae*, "we may reduce the whole of moral matters to the consideration of the virtues." Believing that all of ethics is in the key of virtue, Thomas developed a moral theology of growth and formation. In light of the way we understand the structure of the *Summa* we should rightly understand that Thomas was interested not only in the virtues that are given to the human, infused by faith, hope and love, but also those acquired: prudence, justice, temperance, and fortitude. To acquire the cardinal virtues, Thomas trained his students to see that human intentionality was the key to the acquisition of virtue.

Herein, the object of any virtue is what the agent ought to have in mind as the governing intentionality of one's thoughts. Thomas was always looking for the right realization of the human through the right intending of the right objects in the ordered person. Getting the object right in one's intention and prudentially realizing that intention in action and making a habit of realizing those virtuous actions was and is the first step in the right realization of the virtues. Aside from the willing reception of the gracious infusion of charity into our lives of faith and hope, avoiding the vices and eschewing the temptation to engage intentionally any vicious objects in the intention and pursuing the acquisition of virtue through the right realization of intended virtuous activity was and remains effectively the moral agenda for Thomas.

Second, when one asks where the natural law in all this is, we should see that a key word that Thomas used when talking about the natural law was the *inclinations*. Inclinations in the human are those natural tendencies that need to be rightly realized. Thomas's ethical agenda then was the right realization of our natural inclinations through the acquisition and development of the virtues. In Question 94 of the *Prima Secundae*, Thomas addressed a number of matters about the natural law. In the second article, he asked about the precepts of the natural law and noted that "according to the order of natural inclinations, is the order of the precepts of the natural law" (I-II, q. 94, a. 2). Then he developed three grand categories of these natural inclinations. First, he compared the human to all substances and argued for this reason all have a natural inclination to the good, which is the end or right realization of the substance. Then he considered the way we are related to all other animals and noted the inclinations to "sexual intercourse, education of offspring and so forth." However, then he considered the third matter, that "there is in man an inclination to good, according to the nature of his reason, which nature is proper to him: thus man has a natural inclination to know the truth about God, and to live in society: and in this respect, whatever pertains to this inclination belongs to the natural law; for instance, to shun ignorance, to avoid offending those among whom one has to live, and other such things regarding the above inclination" (I-II, q. 94, a. 2). Here he laid out the foundations or what we today might call the context for his ethics.

In the next article, he asked whether all acts of virtue are prescribed by the natural law and wrote,

> If then we speak of acts of virtue, considered as virtuous, thus all virtuous acts belong to the natural law. For it has been stated that to the natural law belongs everything to which a man is inclined according to his nature. Now each thing is inclined naturally to an operation that is suitable to it according to its form: thus fire is inclined to give heat. Wherefore, since the rational soul is the proper form of man, there is in every man a natural inclination to act according to reason: and this is to act according to virtue. Consequently, considered thus, all acts of virtue are prescribed by the natural law: since each one's reason naturally dictates to him to act virtuously. (I-II, q. 94, a. 3)

If we think of virtue ethics today, we could say in a manner of speaking that the virtue ethics of Thomas belongs to the natural law that he described. That law provides the context and original inclinations for all that is to be rightly realized through the virtues. Unfortunately, when we see the period of the moral manuals after the seventeenth century, we will see that the natural law is, if you will, pulled away from their integral relationship with inclinations and the virtues and reduced to a set of principles and precepts without really any theological anthropology that considers who the human being is as created, that is, with inclination, or who the human is destined to become, that is through the theological and cardinal virtues. The good fortune of the recent twentieth century is that many scholars, but most notably Jean Porter, has worked assiduously to guide us back to a Thomistic appreciation of the relationship between the virtues and the natural law.[59]

Finally, when we consider whether Thomas was more of an Aristotelian philosopher or an Augustinian theologian, we need to understand that he was first of all an Augustinian theologian, who used Aristotle, among others, to make some corrections in order to develop his own contribution to moral theology. A clear example of expanding Augustine concerns his article where Thomas asked the question of whether virtue was suitably defined (I-II, q. 55, a. 4).

Although he did not name whose definition he was considering, he did not need to: the definition was Augustine's.

In this article, Thomas used Aristotle to develop and expand the Augustinian tradition to depart not from Augustine's premise that only Christians could have the perfect virtues of faith, hope, and charity, but rather from Augustine's premise that only Christians could have the moral virtues as well. According to Augustine, only Christians have true faith; without faith, no one has charity. Without charity, one could not have any true virtue. Non-Christians might *seem* to have virtue, but these would not be true virtues unless they have charity. Thomas believed that while all Christians could have the seven virtues, that is, the three infused or theological virtues given in grace by God to the Christian (faith, hope, and charity), and the four acquired virtues by habitual action (prudence, justice, temperance, and fortitude), non-Christians could still have the acquired virtues, as well. From the beginning of Thomas's writing, that is from his *Commentary on the Sentences of Peter Lombard* (2 *Sent* d41. a2; 4 *Sent* d. 39, q.1, a.2, ad4-5), Thomas recognized that the intention of a pagan Greek or Roman, Jew, or Muslim, if it conformed to right reason (i.e., to justice and prudence), was virtuous or good though not perfectly so (lacking faith, and therefore charity). For Thomas, the questions regarding the domain of the naturally acquired virtues (justice, temperance, fortitude, and prudence) had to be understood as matters of character development conforming to right reason, nothing more, nothing less. These virtues were different from the virtues infused by God's grace that made us "perfect." While the pagan would not know the perfection of faith or charity, the pagan could know and have the virtues of prudence and justice as well as temperance and fortitude.

Before arriving at the definition, Thomas had already used Aristotle to show that humans acquire virtuous habits through right reason (I-II, q. 51, a. 2 and 3). But he made explicit his departure from Augustine, precisely as he examined whether Augustine's definition of *virtue* was suitable (I-II, q. 55, a. 4): Here is the definition: "Virtue is a good quality of the mind, by which we live righteously, of which no one can make bad use, which God works within us, without us."[60] Thomas initiated his response by stating that the definition "comprises perfectly the whole essential notion of virtue." There was a play on words here: the definition is "perfect" because it comprises perfect virtue, that is, faith, hope, and charity. What about virtues that may not be perfected by charity; were they still virtue? This was not a question that Augustine accepted as valid, but Thomas did. Thus, in the article he opted to specify the function of the words "which God works within us, without us." These he wrote are applicable only to the perfect or infused virtues. Then he added, "If we omit this phrase, the remainder of the definition will apply to all virtues in general, whether acquired or infused."

This was an enormous breakthrough in Christian theological ethics. Augustine's position was long held, but Aquinas, precisely while invoking Augustine's own definition of virtue, explained it otherwise, *as if* Augustine would agree. It is after all Augustinian theology with an Aristotelian correction.

Curiously, he repeatedly returned to his difference with Augustine *without* acknowledging his break with Augustine (I-II, q. 63, a. 2; q. 65, a. 2; II-II, q. 23, a.7). For example, he asked whether any virtue can be caused in us by habituation (I-II, q. 63, a. 2). For Augustine, virtue can be acquired but only by one who first was graced with the infused virtues. Thomas did not follow that logic: "Human virtue directed to the good which is defined according to the rule of human reason can be caused by human acts" (I-II, q. 63, a. 2). For Aquinas, not only Christians, but all other persons can acquire genuine virtues through reason, and though they do not reach the perfection of charity, they still have the acquired virtues. Thus, while acknowledging that justice without charity is not perfect justice, for Thomas it was nonetheless a virtue.

Moreover, while Augustine unified the virtues solely through charity, Thomas argued that prudence made the moral habits virtues (I-II, q. 65, a. 1c., ad1, ad3, ad4) and that prudence connected or unified the moral virtues, while charity connected or unified the infused virtues (I-II, q. 66, a. 2). According to Thomas, the cardinal virtues were acquired through reason and, as genuine virtues, did not need charity. For those who believed that dialogue was intrinsic to theology, they made, through this one simple article, dialogue with non-Christians on ethical matters possible.[61]

V. THE ACHIEVEMENT OF SCHOLASTICISM

With Thomas's *Summa Theologiae* we get a sense of not only *his* achievement, but the achievement of *Scholasticism* itself. What have we found? First, this is a tradition very much built on the Scriptures. Each of the theologians taught courses on the Bible: from Abelard and Hugh to Lombard and Aquinas. In a way they were not simply building a tradition on the theological claims from the first century; rather, they recognized that it was from the Scriptures that these theological insights came, whether they were about creation, sin, faith, salvation, hope, the Spirit, Jesus Christ, or charity. The theological tradition was the story of the church's reception of revelation, that is, the Scriptures.

Second, that tradition always needed to be developed. We see that every generation had newer questions that needed to be addressed. Thus, each generation looked back to what earlier theologians said, not to get the final word on the topic but rather to appreciate the way similar topics were engaged by these earlier generations. The scholastics were very aware then of their building a worthy conduit for the forever-ongoing development of the tradition.

Third, toward this end they developed methods and texts that could bear the weight of the tradition as it came from the past and went into the future. The method had to be one that respected and knew the authorities but that did not cede to them too much authority. The *Glossae* already did this: these texts preserved the longstanding commentary on the sacred texts. After the *Glossae* came the *Sentences* of Lombard. The more than 1,400 different commentaries on the *Sentences* were a witness to the worthiness of the text to host the development of the theological tradition, but Thomas's *Summa* was an enormously successful sequel to the *Sentences*: far more accessible and far more engaging.

Fourth, that tradition needed a language, a scientific one. In this section, for instance, you have learned some of the key concepts of the moral theology of the scholastics: the object, the inclinations, the intention, the internal act (or the object of the intention), the proximate end, the remote ends, the external act, the mean, prudence, justice, the imminent act, the transient act, faith, the conscience, and so on. By this language, the scholastics developed a capacity to engage one another. There was no need to translate. Moreover, the language they constructed was built to be clear and accessible as well as to be expanded and adapted. The scientific exactness of the language allowed the scholastics a way that they could not only explain and understand, but more importantly debate. Debate, after all, is what made Scholasticism a living tradition.

Fifth, Scholasticism then was a vibrant debate by masters constructing the tradition, mindful of one another, discerning how best to express the truths being discovered and articulated. For this work not only did the scholastics develop language but texts as well. In a manner of speaking, one could say that Scholasticism endured as long as there was a commentator on the *Sentences*. But scholastics were always experimenting with methods since Abelard came up with *Sic et Non*. Thomas's own repertoire highlighted the extraordinarily wide variety of genres that the scholastics engaged so as to advance the tradition: the commentary on the *Sentences*, the *Glossae*, the *Summae*, the treatises, philosophical commentaries, the scriptural commentaries, the *Quodlibetales*, and so on. In a nutshell, they tried to develop the tradition any way possible.

Sixth, arguably two of the most important commentators on the history of theological ethics, Dom Odon Lottin (1880–1965)[62] and John T. Noonan Jr. (1926–2017),[63] teach us that every time an insight of the tradition became engaged at a particular juncture in history, that engagement alone was enough to transform the tradition: We bring to our grasp of the tradition our own way of looking at it, and through our understanding of an insight, we give it a new translation. No truth remains hermetically sealed from the moment of its first articulation in its own codified way. Our reception of the tradition is itself an act of interpretation and translation.

Seventh, one of the ironies of history is that Scholasticism has long been thought of as a monolithic storage depot of unchangeable truths, but we have seen that it was in fact a continual construction and an ongoing debate that easily extended from the twelfth well into the sixteenth century. It aimed to survive as long as it could, but it aimed at that survival by renovating itself every step of the way; rather than protecting itself from change, it promoted change and development. In a way, it never seemed mindful that it had to protect itself, because as a matter of fact each scholastic innovated.

Now, however, we need to move toward its eventual decline when, in order to address the more specific, it would turn back toward a premise with which Abelard started: nominalism.

VI. ANTICIPATING MODERNITY FROM JOHN DUNS SCOTUS (1265–1308) TO WILLIAM OF OCKHAM (1287–1347)

In order to understand the importance of the contributions of John Duns Scotus and William of Ockham, we would do well to remember Abelard's problem with universals and to see how the Franciscans, Scotus and Ockham, resolved it. Therein we discover how Scotus as a realist represented, if you will, the end of a long tradition, while Ockham in many ways anticipated the initiative of modernity with regard to metaphysics. By considering Scotus, we can appreciate all the more clearly Ockham.

I propose that a good part of the tradition's development between Scotus and Ockham concerned the longstanding question of the one and the many. One of the great Scotus experts, Thomas Williams, explained the question by engaging the topic of universals very succinctly:

> The problem of universals may be thought of as the question of what, if anything, is the metaphysical basis of our using the same predicate for more than one distinct individual. Socrates is human and Plato is human. Does this mean that there must be some one universal reality (hence realism)—humanity—that is somehow *repeatable*, in which Socrates and Plato both share? Or is there nothing metaphysically common to them at all? Those who think there is some actual universal existing outside the mind are called realists; those who deny extra-mental universals are called nominalists.[64]

Williams then identified Scotus in this framework: "Scotus was a realist about universals, and like all realists he had to give an account of what exactly those universals are. So, in the case of Socrates and Plato, the question is 'What sort of item is this humanity that both Socrates and Plato exemplify?'" As a realist, Scotus represented, I think, one of the significant identifications of the medieval era; he believed that Plato and Socrates shared in the real "essence" of humanity. Inasmuch as nominalists denied the essentialism of the realists' argument and inasmuch as Ockham was a nominalist, we ought to see that Ockham did not believe that Socrates and Plato shared essences but rather were called human simply because we named (nominally) them as being human. What distinguished the Franciscans then was that Scotus was a medieval realist scholastic and Ockham was a nominalist scholastic, anticipating modernity.[65]

Before explaining Scotus's resolution, Williams proposed a related issue, individuation: "Given that there is some reality common to Socrates and Plato, we also need to know what it is in each of them that makes them *distinct* exemplifications of that reality." By addressing individuation, Scotus identified the extramental common nature. Williams explained, "Scotus calls the universal the 'common nature' (*natura communis*) and the principle of individuation the 'haecceity' (*haecceitas*)." It needs to be said, that unlike his predecessors, Scotus did not believe that this common nature existed outside of or beyond each individual instantiation or haecceity of it. As Williams wrote, this common nature "has existence only *in* the particular things in which it exists, and in them it is always 'contracted' by the haecceity. So the common nature *humanity* exists in both Socrates and Plato, although in Socrates it is made individual by Socrates's *haecceitas* and in Plato by Plato's *haecceitas.* The humanity-of-Socrates is individual and non-repeatable, as is the humanity-of-Plato; yet humanity itself is common and repeatable, and it is ontologically prior to any particular exemplification of it" (*Ordinatio* 2, d. 3, pars 1, qq. 1–6). We can call Scotus's "haecceity" his "thisness."

Ockham, who appreciated specificity, finds Scotus's "thisness" sufficient and effectively asked why do we need anything more than this? He saw no reason to add that there was any real or essential nature common to both.[66]

Ockham entered the Franciscans as a boy oblate (*puer oblatus*) at the age of seven. He studied at the Franciscan *studium* at Oxford at twenty-three and began lecturing on the *Sentences* from 1317 to 1319. In 1319 he wrote on the connection of the virtues and erroneous conscience and lectured on the Bible as well. By 1321, Ockham was known for his logic and his theology and, three years later, he was compelled or invited (we do not know which) to Avignon to explain his theology to Pope John XXII (1316–34). From 1324 to 1328, he remained in the papal court, but a dispute broke out in 1327 between the pope and the minister general of the Franciscans, Michael Cesena (1270–1342), over apostolic poverty, concerning whether Jesus and the apostles owned any property at all. The Franciscans not only upheld the teaching that they did not, but also that they lived it as a special type of imitation of Christ. Instead, the pope held that Jesus and the apostles had property. Rather than defending himself, Cesena asked Ockham to review and estimate the pope's positions. Ockham concluded that the pope's teaching was heretical and that therefore he was a heretic because, in part, he contradicted his predecessor Pope Nicholas III (1277–80), who in 1279 issued an important bull resolving the question of apostolic poverty.[67]

On May 26, 1328, Ockham left the papal court at Avignon before a verdict on his work was given and eventually found sanctuary in Munich under Emperor Ludwig of Bavaria, enemy of Pope John. Ockham remained in Munich for nineteen years and died there from the plague in 1347.[68]

Ockham was a logician and a nominalist like Abelard.[69] One could add they enjoyed fairly forthright, exacting, and resilient personalities and, in many ways, they were responsible for major innovations in ethics and theology. They were, if you will, "markers," persons who help us demarcate where traditions innovate, for better or worse. For some, Ockham was a problematic marker, a demarcation where, as Servais Pinckaers claimed, the moral tradition went wrong because it was influenced by Ockham's theories.[70] Still, Marilyn McCord Adams noted, "Ockham's moral theory, like his nominalism, finds its place among the most notorious, and yet widely misunderstood, doctrines of medieval philosophy."[71] McCord Adams argued that the source of the difficulty was the assumption that underlying all of his positions was a naïve divine command theory, that the right was whatever God wills. She argued instead that Ockham had a modified right reason theory and that he held obedience to God only after investigating the rightness of God's commands, to say nothing of their generosity. If Ockham were rightly understood, we would see that his willingness to adhere to the will of God was based on a previous, more foundational belief in the omniscience of God. For Ockham, following God's will was, not foolhardy, but rather fundamentally wise.

Importantly, Ockham's nominalism developed in part from his principle of economy, often called Ockham's razor: "do not posit plurality unnecessarily (*pluritas non est ponenda sine necessitate*)."[72] Ockham's economy let specificity have its day: he allowed the specific, the particular, *this* entity to be the first consideration; for him, no longer was the particular an instantiation of something greater, like a universal. Sure, Socrates and Plato were human beings, but really, they do not share a similar metaphysical essence like "humanity." Rather they were each human beings because that is what we name (nominalism) them to be, nothing more, nothing less. His paring down in logic, philosophy, theology, and ethics effectively reduced the world of generalizations and forms. In short, he rejected the metaphysical and the ontological.

For philosophers and theologians, his economy may have reduced the spectrum of their considerations, but for ethicists, he opened doors to spaces that had never been known to be there before. Giving us the particular, the individual, the unrepeatable, he gave us a challenge to treat them each exactly as they were, singular. This was an enormous challenge, and it would eventually lead us to casuistry, the subject of the next chapter.

Chapter Five

Pathways to Modernity I

Casuistry

I. INTRODUCTION

The aim of this and the next chapter is to give you a sense of the development of theological ethics in the sixteenth century that broke open with widespread, imaginative yet prudential investigations about the ethical probability of just about every form of human conduct imaginable. The century remarkably began with enormous creativity that was fueled by doubt about the credibility of earlier teachings, but it ends without a shadow of doubt about its own conclusions.

The movement, from doubting to certainty, was fueled in part by institutional Catholic responses to questions and challenges about doctrine and authority raised by Catholic and Protestant reformers. Obviously, in the background is the Protestant Reformation begun in 1517 by Martin Luther (1483–1546) posting his Ninety-five Theses on the cathedral door of Wittenberg. Later, the Society of Jesus was founded in 1540 and Baroque art flourished throughout the Catholic world. The most relevant issue for the history of theological ethics is the fact that the Council of Trent sat for three sessions: 1545–49, 1551–52, and 1562–63.

About the Council, we should appreciate the recent, sustained argument by John O'Malley that the Council was not primarily a Counter Reformation response, but rather an expression of early modern Catholicism. O'Malley does not see the Council reacting to the Reformation primarily but rather attending to the church's own ongoing agenda as it faced the emergence of modernity. Modernity, at the door of the sixteenth century as Europe invades the Americas and negotiates with the East, confronts the church with a need to reconsider the parameters of life personally, socially, and institutionally. O'Malley explained his reasoning: "I simply acknowledge that the Catholic Church was subject to all the forces at play in the period, and to some degree or other, agent for them. Early Modern Catholicism, in other words, was part of Early Modern History."[1]

One could add that the Protestant Reformation itself was part of early modern history. In fact, in investigating the casuistry of early modern Catholicism we will find that there was not much that seemed mindful of the Reformation. When it does appear, mostly on questions about how to live faithfully in the face of religious intolerance, we find the curious phenomenon that regardless of the side of the Reformation that one was on, the casuistry was similar. We will see a few of these instances later. Moreover, this and the next chapter prove O'Malley's thesis: the Catholic ways of proceeding in the sixteenth century is a reply to the inescapable dawn of modernity.

Catholicism with its sluggish continuities as well as its new realities was bigger than what the other names intimate. Particularly to be said in its favor is that 'Early Modern Catholicism' indicates more straightforwardly than they that what happened in Catholicism in the sixteenth century was an aspect of Early Modern History, which it strongly influenced and by which it was itself in large measure determined.[2]

Significantly, the work of casuistry brilliantly complements these developments by entertaining questions anew so as to offer new arguments for modernity. Moreover, these casuistic engagements themselves allowed for a culture of rethinking and reexamining not only certain forms of conduct but also a variety of social institutions and contemporary conventions. Casuistry prompted enormous change, and critique and invention are rife throughout the sixteenth century. These developments led the church to an understanding of what it needed to become, and this in turn prompted the Council's delegates to establish seminaries, creating for the first time programs for the formation of the clergy that includes systematic theological education. Within this framework, moral theology became, for the first time, one among several specific disciplines, each with its own goals, vocabulary, and distinctive hermeneutics. Their courses needed what would later be identified as textbooks.

Beginning in the late sixteenth century, casuists began bringing together all the different categories in which they developed or argued cases on financial matters, oath taking, business practices, engagement and marital relations, confidences, traveling, maintaining fasts, and so forth. These "summaries," as many of them are called, become the prototypes of the textbook, later called, in the seventeenth century the "moral manuals."

Moreover, when the Council issued its own *Catechism* (1566), which had, at its heart, moral instruction codified according to the Ten Commandments, the church left behind the seven deadly sins and their typologies to organize a more biblically based taxonomy that included both prohibitions and prescriptions concerning not only what was due to neighbor and self, but also to God. This process of summarizing and synthesizing replicated what the medieval canonists and scholastic *summa* authors, such as Thomas Aquinas, had done.

Our Way of Proceeding

Rather than look at the Council, we will look in this history of theological ethics at the development of sixteenth-century casuistry especially, but then in the next chapter at the confraternities, and finally the School of Salamanca as three pathways to modernity. We should realize that we already had a glimpse of another pathway to modernity when we saw how Ignatius of Loyola developed the *Spiritual Exercises* that allowed people to discern from their own experiences the trajectories that they should follow on the way of the Lord. This validation of human experience as well as its incorporation into one's prayer was a move to the modern self just as these other pathways were. Let us see briefly how they developed.

Casuistry comes from the Latin *casus*, which is the past participle of the Latin verb *cado*, meaning, "having happened." Casuistry is the method of moral reasoning that incorporates the particularity of a situation and its attendant circumstances through a short narrative depiction, what we today call, a case. In continental Europe, the method enjoyed considerable popularity throughout the sixteenth century but in other epochs as well, always in times that needed to formulate new moral directives.[3]

If *professionalization* is the catchword for theological ethics from the twelfth century forward, then *casuistry* is the identity word for theological ethics in the sixteenth century and the unfolding of the moral manuals in the seventeenth century and later. Casuistry emerges as a method of moral reasoning to respond to the extraordinarily new issues that materialized in the sixteenth century. In fact, Ockham's anti-essentialism and his preference for nominalism gave attention to the particular rather than to the general and eventually served as the foundation for the great developments of casuistry.

When one hears the word *casuistry* one tends to think of simple deductive logic that begins with a major principle, proposes a minor principle, and then promulgates the conclusion.

Here is an example: all sex outside of the marital act is sinful, masturbation is sex outside of the marital act, so therefore masturbation is sinful. This type of casuistry, which is the simple acceptance of a principled teaching, is an easy deductive logic. Today, it is referred to as "low casuistry."[4] What happens, however, if the major principle itself comes under question? What happens when we ask *is all* sex outside the marital act sinful, *is all* lying sinful, *are all* abortions sinful, and so on? In short, what happens when the principle—the starting point—is itself in doubt. More problematically, what happens when there are questions asked where no principle can be invoked as a simple solution. For example, in the middle of the twentieth century we asked questions about organ transplants that we never considered. Could you donate a kidney, a part of your liver, etcetera? Were these organs mine to donate and if so under what conditions? Or, today we ask questions about artificial intelligence. How can we determine what is correct when the major principles are not yet articulated?

Appreciating these questions lets us enter the sixteenth century, a time when there were too many challenges and not enough principles that were credible. Then, they were not asking questions about low casuistry; rather, they were asking for guidance when the old arguments were inadequate. In response to this void, the sixteenth century developed an inductive, analogical form of moral reasoning that brought a specific case to the fore and examined it by always looking to another normative case to serve in the background as a guide. Then these moral logicians, or "casuists" as they were called, considered differing circumstances in order to determine whether a particular circumstance could change an illicit form of acting into a licit form. Considering those circumstances of the one case, always with that other case in the background, the casuists became masters of what today we call "high casuistry." In a landmark work, *The Abuse of Casuistry*, Albert Jonsen and Stephen Toulmin described the new issues in the public and private arenas of life at that time that prompted the birth of high casuistry.

We will start by talking about the hundred-year-long arc of high casuistry, with John Mair (sometimes known as John Major) (1467–1550) at its dawn and Francisco de Toledo (1532–96) at its sunset. In between these bookends, we will consider several matters: first the achievement of casuistry's breakthrough; then the emergence of the Ten Commandments as replacing the seven deadly sins or the seven virtues as the foundational text of ethics; and then, a fundamental debate about moral authority and casuistry called "probabilism." The ramifications of the casuistic innovation are significant in provoking enormous institutional developments throughout Europe while at the same time assisting the individual Catholic in living out safely her or his conscience in the modern world.

If we think that the Catholic moral life was nothing more than the solutions of casuists and later manualists, then we are sadly mistaken. If casuistry is the historical successor of Scholasticism in the investigation into the ethical life as we saw in the fourth chapter, then the confraternities are the social and institutional successors to the pathways to holiness that we saw in the third chapter. These two trajectories were lived out in the one Catholic person, family, and parish. The moral life lived under scrutiny and needed to navigate through the challenges of the morally debatable forms of early modern conduct. That task was well served by casuistry. At the same time, the moral life was being lived out through the confraternity where its devotional practices of prayer were coupled with an extraordinarily generous, other-directed expression of institutional mercy. So the confraternities and casuistry were the two formative influences on the sixteenth-century emerging modern Catholic Church.

Finally, we must recognize that early modernity brings us into our world today that is unmistakably global. The "global" church becomes by the Second Vatican Council a familiar phrase but an appreciation for the global in the sixteenth century sparked the event of modernity. Rightly we proceed through these two chapters by looking at a third pathway, the incredible development of the school of Salamanca, especially in the foundational work of Francisco de Vitoria, OP (1483–1546), and fellow Dominican Bartolomé de las Casas, OP (1484–1566). We conclude with a few remarks on the Jesuit Francisco Suárez, SJ (1548–1617).

Like all historical developments this has its own lesson: faced with the challenges of how to arbitrate the claims of the native peoples of the Americas, Catholic ethicists did not turn to Mair, nominalism, and casuistry but rather to the instincts of Thomas Aquinas on the natural law. Imbued by the inventiveness that prompted casuistic investigations throughout the sixteenth century, the scholars at Salamanca needed something that in their estimation did not need to be replaced but needed to be applied to a wider world: Aquinas's teachings on law. Using those foundations they expanded from Aquinas into a new area, a field that they called *ius gentium*, the "law of nations."

A Word about the Arc of High Casuistry

In their book, Toulmin and Jonsen posit high casuistry as extending from 1550 to 1650, but they based this claim by ignoring the different types of books of casuistry that one finds from the early sixteenth through the seventeenth centuries. Probably the earliest full successful work of casuistry in Europe is John Mair's *The Commentary on the Book of the Sentences* in 1509. In fact, rightly understood, the work is really a very late form of Scholasticism. Still, finding casuistry in a major scholar's *Commentary on the Sentences* makes sense. Unlike Scholasticism, casuistry never became a school. It just developed as a method to raise and address the continual, variegated challenges that the sixteenth century needed to consider. Responses were needed with some urgency and so casuistic arguments, like the ones we will see in Mair, were just that: one argument made after another. Casuistry, you see, is the bridge that will get us from Scholasticism to the moral manuals.

The first volumes of actual casuistry, like Mair's, were not sophisticated in any way nor with any pedagogical intent or agenda as in, "Here, let me teach you casuistry." Rather, they were postings of cases; they appeared in a variety of different literary forms that gather together the actual case arguments. Later, about sixty years after Mair, others give their judgments in truncated cases, in a way showcasing not their arguments as much as a distillation of the solutions they achieved. These works often bore a title, like Martín de Azpilcueta's *Manual or Handbook of Confessions and Penances* (*Manuale sive Enchiridion Confessariorum et Poenitentium*) (1568), that they were texts to be used by priests for hearing confessions. Here the priests were not interested in the arguments; they just wanted to be told what to do!

Finally, the sixteenth century came to a crashing end with moralists putting not their arguments forward but solely their conclusions, judgments, or norms now set in stone or at least in some type of hardening sediment. Here the century that began with few useful norms, rules, or principles became literally the wellspring of an enormous number of new normative judgments that they gathered, following the model of Toledo, into *summas*. These *summas* were the forerunning texts that became the moral manuals of the seventeenth century. Let us consider these three stages of development.

Mair's most significant predecessor was Martin Le Maistre (1432–81) whose *Quaestiones morales* (1490) was a collection of treatises by Martin on the virtues. He became especially known for his treatise there on temperance. John T. Noonan Jr. wrote of the *Quaestiones* that it was "the most independent critique of the Christian sexual ethic ever undertaken by an orthodox critic."[5] Noteworthy for us is not only his work in ethics, but the influence of nominalism in his work.

In 1474, the year that the teaching of nominalism was banned from the University of Paris and that singular copies of nominalists' books were permitted to be read in the library only if they remained chained to the desks, Martin received his licentiate. Martin ignored the ban and taught Ockham with great success. By 1481, the ban was lifted, a shift completely accredited to Martin.[6] Aside from Martin's work, however, Mair's casuistry of 1509 was otherwise without precedent and Martin's work was not even casuistry but rather a type of virtue ethics that was never developed until the end of the twentieth century.

Although many, including Jonsen and Toulmin, mistakenly believed that it was the birth of casuistry, when Martín de Azpilcueta

(1491–1586) published his famous *Manuale sive Enchiridion*, he was offering only a handbook of the judgments of the cases of casuistry that he already had solved. His work, sixty years after Mair's, was not casuistry. Certainly, he did casuistry earlier, but the published work in 1568 was a pulling together of the judgments that he had achieved through casuistry. His was a work of promulgating his judgments, not an exposé of his investigations. The *Manuale* marks the halfway point between the casuistry of Mair in 1509 and the summary of cases that begin to appear later in 1590. The arc of this period then starts with Mair's work as foundational and ends with Francisco de Toledo's (1532–96) *Summa Casuum Conscientiae Sive De Instructione Sacerdotum, Libri Septem*,[7] as a clear sedimentation of the casuistic period, effectively becoming the first of the moral manuals that will exist until 1960.

Just as Mair's work marked the breakthrough of casuistry, Toledo's marked the beginning of moral manualism. Toledo was the preacher of the papal court and then theologian of the Sacred Penitentiary and the Roman Inquisition as well as consultor to several Roman Congregations. In time, he served seven popes and in 1593 was made cardinal, the first Jesuit to receive that position.[8] He developed his summary from the courses of theology he taught at the Roman College from 1562 to 1569, where he lectured on the priesthood, the administration of the sacraments, the Ten Commandments as they were used for the hearing of confession, and finally the sacrament of marriage. These lectures were the material for the *Summa Casuum*. Copies of these lectures as well as students' notes were probably in circulation before their publication in 1598.[9]

When the lectures were published, they were among the first of a series of Jesuit summaries of cases of consciences that began to appear in the 1590s. Prior to Toledo's work, Pietro Alagona published a compendium of the manual of Martín of Azpilcueta in 1590. Later, Enrico Henriquez wrote in 1591 a summa of moral theology in three tomes, which represented a systematic treatment of the ends of human action including some reserved cases. Finally, Emmanuel Sà published a summa of cases listed alphabetically.[10] Although Sà's work went through several editions, Toledo's work was the first major breakthrough: seventy-two editions and multitudinous translations, remaining in print until 1716.[11] Thus the arc ran from 1509 to 1598, rather than 1550 to 1650; the texts were very different, as were their methods. High casuistry developed through these stages until it was no longer needed.

Previewing the Impact of Sixteenth-Century Casuistry

Before we look closely at the work of John Mair, we need to appreciate the wide variety of contexts in which casuistry appeared. In the sixteenth century, Europeans through their conquest of the Americas and their expansive trade with the east could no longer accept the older moral guidelines of the past. For example, Pope Gregory IX, in 1237, issued the decretal *Naviganti vel eunti ad nundinas*. Of this decretal, John Noonan wrote, "By any standard it is the most important single papal decree on the usury question with the exception of those containing the basic prohibition itself." The issue at hand concerned the first of the three-sentence decretal: "One lending a certain quantity of money to one sailing or going to a fair, in order to receive something beyond the capital for this, that he takes upon himself the peril, is to be thought a usurer."[12] The pope effectively deemed that credit for risk was usury.[13]

The teaching was in the form of principle-based, deductive logic that was an example of low casuistry. All usury (illicit money lending) was wrong; maritime insurance was a form of usury; therefore, maritime insurance was wrong. The teaching was problematic through the thirteenth to the fifteenth century, but at the beginning of the sixteenth century, a prohibition against underwriting expeditions to the west and to the east was unthinkable as trade, exploration, and missionary activity exploded. Merchants therefore petitioned faculty members of the University of Paris and in particular John Mair to render new decisions on the teaching, effectively reinvestigating whether maritime insurance was in fact morally illegitimate. They responded by asking whether the case of an insurer who guarantees the arrival of the worth of a cargo was any different than the case of the captain of a ship who secures the arrival of the cargo itself. The case of the captain served in the background as the norm of right conduct in the hired transport of goods. The question of the insurer was posed as a case and measured against another case, what Jonsen and Toulmin called a "paradigm case," that described already-validated moral activity, here, the case of the captain of a ship. By showing congruency between the two, these writers provided new ways of circumscribing the papal teaching, distinguishing insurance from usury, and proposing ethical grounds to legitimate maritime insurance.[14]

Here is an example of high casuistry being applied to liberate institutions from normative determinations that did not keep pace with other developments.[15] But with this freedom came the need for new expressions of moral guidance and thus casuistry also provided those bankers, merchants, missionaries, explorers, and princes bent on expansionism a new inductive method of moral logic to navigate the unfamiliar waters before them. Eventually, all these cases had to be gathered together, and later they became the grounds for a host of new methodological principles, like the "principle of double effect" or the "principle of cooperation."

Sometimes the newness of moral dilemmas in the sixteenth century was not occasioned by mercantile expeditions. Religious and political conflicts in England at the end of the sixteenth century raised questions that at earlier times were unthinkable. Could a Roman Catholic priest lie about his identity to (the Protestant) Queen Elizabeth's soldiers? Could a Catholic take a loyalty oath and not keep it? Could a Catholic landowner contribute to a non-Catholic/heretic church? Of course, when the English sovereign was a Roman Catholic, the Anglicans and the Puritans asked questions much like the Roman Catholic ones during the reign of Elizabeth. There were few existing principles that addressed these questions and those that did were ill-equipped to answer them. Much like Mair and his successors, these English writers sought to reexamine previous teaching by invoking not principles but rather cases and to make distinctions that were not current in earlier years. A prime example was whether there was a distinction between lying (always forbidden) and pretense (sometimes permitted). The paradigm case that gave them grounds to entertain pretense was the risen Christ who with the disciples at Emmaus acted as if he did not know what had happened in Jerusalem (Luke 24:19) and as if he meant to go on rather than to stay with the disciples (24:28).[16]

Casuistry was not simply a clever game, however. Let us return to the priest. If a priest were to tell the simple truth to a soldier in the queen's army, he would have easily been arrested, probably tortured, and likely executed. The concern was not primarily about his well-being; by entering the realm, the priest was clearly willing to risk his life. His primary concern was to minister to the people who under very challenging times were trying to remain faithful to Rome. If he were arrested, they would have no priest, nor anyone to help them discern. Moreover, the issue was not simply whether the truth be told. Another question was raised: To whom was the truth due? Did the queen's soldier have the right to the truth when, in the eyes of the Roman church, she was not considered the legitimate sovereign? Regardless of the side of the Reformation divide, the questions and solutions were very similar.

On this matter of how similar the matters were regardless of one's church, I want to tell you a very ironic story. Ten years after the excommunication of Queen Elizabeth I by Pope Pius V (1504–72; r. 1566–72) in 1570, a small band of Jesuits attempted to enter England to give support to Roman Catholic "recusants," as they were called, who refused to attend Protestant services. Among them were Edmund Campion (1540–81) and Robert Persons (1546–1610). After one year, Campion was caught in July 1581 and brutally martyred (being hung, drawn, and quartered) on December 1, 1581. Persons returned to the continent and dedicated his life to supporting the recusants. Among his many projects was *The Christian Directory*, a text for those needing to be converted to a more committed Christian life.[17] Originally conceived as the first book of two, Persons's *The First Booke of The Christian Exercise*, as it was initially called, appeared in 1582. Two years later, Persons made major additions. At the same time, the Puritan Edmund Bunny (1540–1619) "puritanized" the text and republished it as a Puritan spiritual handbook.[18] In 1585, when Persons became aware of Bunny's actions, the Jesuit issued his third edition, now named *A Christian Directory*. This edition, amended by Persons, contained a lengthy attack against Bunny and the Puritans. Bunny responded by taking this new edition, attaching his response to it, and complaining that Persons never responded to his first reply![19]

Persons's own unaltered text went through eight editions by Catholic printers and was translated into French, German, Latin, and Italian; the Italian version itself ran through nine editions.[20] Bunny's adaptation of the first and the second edition of Persons's work went through forty-seven editions between 1584 and 1640, enjoying about twice the sales of either of the great Puritan classics:

Arthur Dent's *The Plaine Man's Pathway to Heaven* (1601) or William Perkins's *The Foundation of Christian Religion* (1602).[21] No Puritan text enjoyed such popularity and no contemporary work of devotion compared to it as "the most popular book of devotion among both Catholics and Protestants in Elizabethan and Jacobean England."[22]

The fact that this Catholic text became "puritanized" is drenched with irony. Penned by a Jesuit who sought to reclaim Catholics conforming to the institutional Church of England, it was pirated by a Puritan preacher, Edmund Bunny, who used it not only to answer the needs of his fellow Puritans, but also to convince Catholic readers that the differences between Catholics and Reformers were minor. Bunny was trying to get Catholics to conform to the institutional Church of England.[23] Moreover, the Jesuit author Robert Persons had been tried for treason against the crown, was convicted, and sentenced to death (all *in abstentia*), but later organized along with Dr. William Allen the missionary effort to England, and lastly urged the Spanish invasion of England. No man sought with more passion, conviction, intelligence, and cunning to wrestle the authority of the Reformers away from the crown than Robert Persons; yet his most successful writing achievement not only gave succor to his opponents, it also was used to help devout Catholics in good conscience to accommodate conformity to the established Church of England. As one commentator wrote, "Persons' strategy seriously backfired."[24]

Although Persons's and Bunny's texts are not identical, the puritanizing was not extensive. While Victor Houliston was right to argue that the authors' understandings of the relationship between good works and justification distinguishes them,[25] still Brad Gregory was also right to declare that the differences between the two were hardly noticeable: much more than 90 percent of the text remained intact.[26]

Why was this work so adaptable?[27] Like most devotional works, Persons's work appealed to the individual. Devotional manuals were not like sermon texts that were heard by attentive congregations. Rather, they were received and savored by individual readers. In a particular way, the Jesuits were especially inclined to this individual attention both by their spiritual direction that encouraged a unique relationship with the Lord[28] as well as by their moral theology that defended the individual conscience.[29] In turn, their devotional manuals supported the powerful introspection that both Jesuit priests and Puritan divines promoted among the people to whom they ministered.

Finally, we should conclude this foretaste of casuistry by noting that it was used also in the private forum, particularly for hearing confession. Until the sixteenth century, confessors understood themselves both as physicians who recognized the infection of sin and as judges who determined the fitting penalty for the offense of sin. For these tasks, they turned to the confessional manuals, which used circumstances to establish more definitively the specific nature of a sin.[30] However, in the priestly ministry of the sixteenth century, many religious orders, among them the Jesuits, came into closer collaboration with laypeople through educational institutions, spiritual direction, and above all confraternities.[31]

In the confessional, then, these priests encountered not simply a disease that needed attention or a crime demanding sentencing. Having worked together in the confraternities, priests encountered the spirituality, generosity, and dedication of their penitents; in the confessional, they heard the accounts of struggling Christians seeking relief and consolation. Thus, to appreciate the uniqueness of the penitent's particular struggle, confessors took into consideration as specifically as possible the circumstances affecting the sinner's conduct. These circumstances turned more closely on the person than on the act; instead of being tools for applying the law, they were used to understand the penitent. This descent into the particular took the confessors so far away from the confessional manuals that their directives were no longer helpful.[32] Instead, they turned to casuists who offered confessors guidance by using particular cases, complete with personal circumstances. This study of cases became so important to the Jesuits, for example, that they were recommended to study cases an hour daily.[33]

In the face of antiquated principles, sixteenth-century ethicists attentive to the newness of contemporary projects as well as to the personal struggles of fellow laborers in the field turned for their deliberations to these cases and not to rules or principles. These problematic cases were expressed in a brief narrative surrounded by relevant circumstances. When pivoted analogously against a paradigm case, they generated new solutions, which often highlighted new distinctions. The method appeared to be used in nearly every instance of human conduct: institutional, social, interpersonal, and even the privacy of the confessional.[34]

II. THE START OF THE ARC OF CASUISTRY: JOHN MAIR (1467–1550)

As we look at the arc, we should note that John Mair's *Commentary on the Fourth Book of the Sentences* (1509) and Francisco de Toledo's *Summa casuum conscientiae sive De instructione sacerdotum, libri septem* (1598) appeared thirty years away from either end of the eighteen years that belonged to the Council of Trent. Mair (1467–1550) died five years after the Council began, and until 1530 was the most influential figure in ethics at the University of Paris. Toledo began teaching his popular courses on the priesthood a year before the Council's close; but his work was published posthumously, when Toledo had no more to offer on the cases.

James Farge remarked that the courses of the nominalist John Mair were among the most popular ones at the University of Paris (1506–18, 1521–22, and 1526–31) on the eve of the Reformation.[35] Mair's nominalism afforded him some footing in a world no longer comfortable with older systems.[36] When his scholastic nominalism engaged new practical concerns, the result was a very specific engagement with very particular cases. Mair became, I believe, the father of modern-day casuistry.[37]

Three insights support that claim. First, Mair wanted to experiment with method. Referring to the noted explorer and cartographer, Mair wondered, "Has not Amerigo Vespucci discovered lands unknown to Ptolemy, Pliny and other geographers up to the present? Why cannot the same happen in other spheres?"[38] The new questions that Mair entertained prompted him to frequently reexamine old ways of thinking. Second, as a result, the concept of authority, so significant in the scholastic method, was radically changed. Mair's new insights required to some degree a rejection, albeit nuanced, of the sanctioned views of Gregory the Great,

Huguccio, Thomas Aquinas, and even Augustine. As the world expanded, local cultures and practices demanded newer directives; tradition, failing to provide sufficient insight, had less influence. In a world of competing authorities, Mair and his disciples offered no longer certain, but only probable, arguments. Third, in this probable world, Mair employed the scholastic dialectic, but instead of using it to examine moral and immoral "objects" as the earlier scholastics had done, he drew analogies through a comparison of cases. Mair's desire to explore previous teachings, his ability to contest earlier expressions of authority, and his study of newly emerging cases typify moral theology in the early sixteenth century. Mair entered into any number of specific issues, for example, responding to Catherine of Aragon's request about her marriage and her rights; in that case he affirmed the validity of her marriage to Henry VIII.[39]

To get a better sense of how a casuistic argument was made, we return to his case of maritime insurance.[40] In 1530, a group of Spanish merchants living in Flanders asked the University of Paris to address certain commercial practices. One question concerned maritime insurance, which effectively dealt with the question whether one who assumes the risk that another runs may receive payment for assuming that risk. Mair responded, using the solution from his already published *Commentary on the Fourth Book of the Sentences*. He employed the scholastic method to consider two common objections: that insurance is useless and that it is prohibited. The first objection contended that unlike the soldier or the captain, the insurer does not prevent possible loss of cargo; a sinking ship sinks whether it is insured or not. Mair responded by addressing not the state of the cargo, but the psychological state of the shipping merchant. His worries were allayed because were the cargo lost, its worth would be saved. Moreover, by providing the insurance, the agent entered into a partnership with the owner in which the worth of the cargo and their attendant concerns were borne equally by agent and owner.

Mair then answered the second objection by examining three sets of laws. From Scripture, he noted that all adults are required to work, and referred to the law that we are to eat our bread earned from the sweat of our brow (Gen 3:19) and the injunction that we humans were born to work (Job 5:7). Because the agent only underwrote the cargo, he seemed to fail to heed the Scriptures. Mair again wrote that the agent assumes the merchant's worry and fear of loss, and thus enters into a partnership. Then Mair added a theme that he repeated elsewhere. The children of wealthy families did not work but played and recreated with the amassed riches of their parents. Why, then, were the Scriptures used against the working agents and not against the shiftless wealthy? Next, Mair examined positive law and noted that the law has no injunctions against maritime insurance itself, but instead it outlined conditions for when it would be fraudulent. Finally, he examined the papal decretal *Naviganti* and argued that the Roman pontiff did not prohibit maritime insurance per se, but rather usury, receiving a fee for a loan. The insurance agent did not receive a fee for a loan, but for his share in the partnership and for the service he provided by underwriting the cargo and sharing in the anxiety. A usurious contract was different, then, from a morally legitimate contract of maritime insurance.

This case was an example of high casuistry. Unlike low casuistry, high casuistry erupted in the sixteenth century and addressed dilemmas, used analogies, entertained circumstances, resolved doubt, examined the intentionality of personal agents, and gave its solution. In short, it made its case. It did not presume that the reader agreed, but rather provided argumentation to prompt the reader's assent.

Martha Nussbaum helps us to understand this further when she argues that all great moral logic is waiting for the readers' recognition of the validity of what the writer is proposing. The true ethicist waits for the internal, experiential affirmation by the listener or reader that what is posited is recognized as a true judgment.[41] The authority of the solution rested on two points: what Albert Jonsen and Stephen Toulmin called internal and external certitude. Internal certitude was the cogency of the argument itself. External certitude depended on the recognizable authority of the author. For casuistry, then, a case needed to be credibly made, argued, and demonstrated by an author with evident authority.[42] So we note that Mair undermined the pope's external authority by putting the pope's decretal in a new interpretative context. He did this having subdued the internal certitude of the pope's teaching and thus overrode a three-hundred-year-old prohibition.[43]

Because prudence was the ultimate guide to the judgment, sometimes the casuist realized that his judgment might not yet be prudential for the current audience. To see an example of this, we turn to Mair's investigation of *cambium bursae*, a proposal that aimed to create an institution for a lending exchange.[44] Earlier, rather than define financing as usury (a fee for granting a loan), theologians sought instead another perspective where financing would be morally legitimate. Behind *cambium bursae* was the premise that one could loan another a certain sum and receive back something more than the sum. This difference or fee was not for the loan itself, but because, having made the loan, the lender loses a potential profit that could otherwise have been made. The fee for the loss of this potential profit, in Latin *lucrum cessans*, received some limited support in the late fifteenth century,[45] but *lucrum* only considered the individual instance of an act of financing; with *cambium bursae*, Mair examined the full-time institutional practice itself.

We do not have the space to descend into his argument itself of resolving the objections,[46] but Mair did so convincingly. Despite this, his final judgment was stunning: "The case is illicit; such a state of life is dangerous and dishonest, and needs to be rejected by all prudent men."[47] Mair refused, in the name of prudence, to legitimate this occasional practice into an institutional one. His concern was about the speculation. He feared that the lender would no longer be a merchant; and that rather than receiving the occasional requests from others, the lender would have to seek out others and press them into businesses that they may not have intended. In the end, he wondered what would become of them in such a system.

Mair had the capacity to realize the value of hesitancy in dismantling too much of the commercial structure that provided his merchants the moral stability they needed in a sea of change. If he dismantled the present structures, what would they have in the future?

In his landmark work, *The Structure of Scientific Revolutions*, Thomas Kuhn wisely noted that paradigmatic shifts only occurred when one could disprove the validity of a previous thesis *and* replace it with a fully functional new thesis.[48] Mair operated the same way. He saw that the maritime industry could depend on maritime insurance without ethical compromise. But while he disproved the objections to *cambium bursae*, he could not yet imagine how merchants could safely operate with making such loans. Better to leave the prohibition intact until a new model was available that could make such loans safe. Although he answered and exhausted the ethical objections casuistically, in the end he refused to validate the very position that remained.

Mair provided modern casuistry the method to dismantle long-standing impediments and obstacles to human progress, but unless he could sense that the tangible structures replacing the old ones were safe, he withheld a final judgment in favor of change. Familiar with maritime insurance's validity and safety, he could promote his conclusions; in the absence of *cambium bursae*'s safety mechanisms, Mair hesitated. Although Mair rejected the simple *cambium bursae*, later he upheld the liceity of the famous and famously complicated "triple" or "German" contract, which eventually became the paradigm for licit financial loans. The *cambium bursae* did not sufficiently distinguish a loan's profit from a loss's repayment nor underline the required partnership for legitimate financing. This failure was probably what prompted his hesitation. On the other hand, the triple contract, proposed by Conrad Summenhart (1455–1502) and his student John Eck (1486–1543), embodied the necessary distinctions. When these German writers sought theological approbation from the University of Paris, only one from the faculty responded: John Mair who assented. Mair added, however, that prudence cautioned against preaching the change to the merchants.[49]

We cannot underestimate just how extensive the practice of casuistry was. The inductive analogical method let dozens upon dozens of ethicists entertain inquiries on nearly every complex moral matter, whether about moneylending, paying taxes, mental reservations, dueling, abortion, fasting, investing, and so on. Every type of commerce came under review and yet prudence weighed in at the end as to whether, as Kuhn noted, change was prudential, that is whether the social structures could adapt ethically. This prudential perspective together with the prudential investigation into the ancient arguments themselves allowed casuistry, by the end of its arc, to settle much.

III. THE ACHIEVEMENT OF SIXTEENTH-CENTURY HIGH CASUISTRY

Let me offer several insights about Mair and modern casuistry, insights that become long-standing influences in the field of theological ethics.

First, casuistry was based on the scholastic method. Like Mair using Lombard's *Fourth Book of the Sentences*, casuists proposed a question, presented a series of objections, offered in the corpus a determination, and finally concluded with specific responses to the objections. But unlike scholastic writings, the corpus and the answers to the objections were not about the essentialist notion of a scholastic "object" like usury, loaning, justice, chastity, fortitude, temperance, or the like; rather, the answers were replete with images of licit or illicit, embodied ways of acting.

Second, not only did they describe activities, but they also considered the agents. Mair invoked ordinary figures involved in ordinary affairs; in the cases above, for instance, a ship's captain, the coast guard, and an insurance agent. Often enough, Mair named his main character "Socrates," the restaurateur, fairgoer, or clever investor. Later casuists had their agents as well. But just as such agents were not found in high Scholasticism, neither do they appear in the later work of the summists like Francisco de Toledo at the end of the sixteenth century.[50]

Third, casuistry was a comparison of the congruencies between one controlling insight, the so-called paradigm case, and the case at hand. The controlling insight had to be stable enough to anchor the position. The insight served as a standard for comparison, although the standard was a form of acceptable behavior, not a precept. So, in the case of maritime insurance, Mair fundamentally won his argument at the outset when he asked, if the captain of a vessel can be contracted and paid for providing security, why not the insurance agent?

In early casuistry, finding the right controlling insight was the most important pivot. Casuists looked to commonsense experience, often to invoke a case that was evidently true enough to bear comparison. For instance, on the question of a woman having a health- or life-saving abortion, most comparisons were with a pregnant woman rightfully fleeing a charging bull. If she could "risk" a pregnancy as she sped in flight, jumped into rivers, or scaled cliffs to avoid the bull, could these analogies help us with other internal and external threats to a pregnant woman?[51]

Rather than turning to commonsense, casuists sometimes invoked the Scriptures. When faced with a military expedition in which certain death would result, they needed to distinguish convincingly these actions from suicidal ones; the death of Samson pulling down the temple (Judg 16:30) was frequently invoked in such instances. Similarly, as we saw earlier, Jesus's pretense in the Emmaus story provided substantive grounds for Catholic priests during Elizabeth's reign and Puritan ministers and Anglican priests during James's reign to withhold the truth from most anyone who could do them deadly harm. Each made the same case for their dissemblance as not being a form of lying by citing Jesus's actions during the walk at Emmaus. They particularly focused on his asking them what had happened so as to ward off suspicion; they also enjoyed Jesus's adeptness in "acting as if to go on."[52]

Fourth, herein the importance of nominalism for the birth of modern casuistry became evident. Earlier we saw Farge's assessment that Mair was the most distinguished nominalist at Paris during the first thirty years of the sixteenth century. Though John Mahoney[53] and Servais Pinckaers,[54] two theological ethicists who have written on the history of theological ethics, decried the entry of nominalism into the history of theological ethics, nominalism's premises actually prompted the need and the possibility for casuistry. By denying essentialist and universal claims, the nominalists insisted on the priority of the individual and of the radical singularity of each existent. If the nominalists, then, wanted to determine standards for right ways of acting, they could not refer to essences or objects, but rather to recognizable forms of right acting. Nominalism's proponents, moreover, were forced to look not for the same or universal properties among ways of acting, but only for analogous or similar ones. In the absence of essences, the nominalists looked simply for congruencies, not identities. Nominalists, then, brought with them very different expectations to what we needed to find in moral argumentation.[55]

Fifth, human activity became distinctive. Mair rejected the possibility of determining licit moral activity from animal activity. Because humans were not animals (rational or otherwise), the natural law was not something that bound humans to laws that animals obeyed. In discussing the licitness of conjugal activity for pregnant women, for example, Mair considered the objection that elephants and other animals do not engage in sexual activity during pregnancy and through a variety of objections dismissed the claim: human activity was not bound to be governed by the same rules for animal activity.[56]

Sixth, classical claims lacked force; in its absence, old teachings were subject to renewed investigations. For example, for centuries, one argument used frequently against the legitimacy of sexual activity was that it distracted from simple reasoning. Against the position of many classical theologians before him, Mair asked whether such deprivation was itself wrong. During sleep, while being under ether or anesthesia, or after long hours of study, the brain also shuts down, Mair noted. That something causes a temporary shutting down of the brain was not, in itself, morally wrong activity.[57]

Seventh, just as the method and the specific resolutions were new, so were the perspectives themselves. For example, whenever Mair asked questions about sexual satisfaction and rendering the marital debt, he invoked in case after case Socrates having to satisfy his wife's demands for the marital debt.[58] She was never given a name, but Mair provided a variety of occasions to legitimate her expectations from Socrates.

Eighth, not surprisingly, experience was frequently invoked. For instance, Mair argued that the legitimacy of marital intercourse was limited neither to the purpose of procreation nor to the avoidance of fornication and that pleasure in sexual activity was hardly sinful. Against Augustine and Huguccio, Mair invoked the "experience" of married couples.[59] Attributing greater authority to "experience" than to Augustine conveyed a much more modern bias than a medieval one.

Ninth, without "essences" and universals, nominalists had fairly singular grounds for moral determination. The theologians of the early sixteenth century published commentary on the more specific and codified *Sentences* rather than attempt any synthesis like a *Summa Theologiae*. They were developing legitimate codes of conduct, not theological world views; without these foundations, nominalists turned to law. Considerably different from the rationalism of Thomas Aquinas, the nominalists' casuistry became considerably juridical. These figures were not simply clever yet benign caretakers of the tradition, but rather its judges. In fact, Jonsen and Toulmin noted that when practiced in antiquity by Greeks, Romans, and Hebrews, casuistry was practiced predominantly by judges. The hermeneutics of a legalistic authoritativeness were always there.[60]

Tenth, prudence in this context was considerably different than prudence in the writings of other, earlier scholastics. In Aquinas, for example, prudence was the virtue that all persons engaged to acquire and perfect the moral virtues interior to the agent.[61] The primary end of prudence for these scholastics was to set the proximate goals for the agent's own personal growth. In the sixteenth century, however, prudence sought not to realize and govern one's own internal nature, but rather to realize and govern the external conduct of society. In a manner of speaking, just as for Aquinas prudence perfected the virtues in the lesser powers, so for Mair and his contemporaries, prudence governed the masses, through the judgments of these theologians.[62]

The judge's superiority in making prudential determinations should not be missed here. For example, casuistry led Mair to recognize the liceity of *cambium bursae*, but something like a "political" prudence dictated to him that its liceity was not sufficient for institutional practice. On the triple contract, Mair affirmed its liceity but argued against the advisability of preaching it. Similarly, in arguing that pleasure in licit sexual conduct was not at all sinful, he concluded that this judgment ought not to be preached, but that penitents privately in the confessional could be told that their pursuit of pleasure was legitimate.[63] As explorative as casuistry was for the casuists, it was an authoritative period and therein prudence exercised more juridical influence over the lives of the laity than it did in their exercising personal choices.

Eleventh, from its inception in the sixteenth century, casuistry was not as accessible a method as we may think. Although many of the specific determinations were less oppressive than previous scholastic judgments, the casuists themselves did not seem to make their decision-making process any more an egalitarian affair than their predecessors did. Not only were there prudential decisions to not inform the masses, but there is no evidence that the casuists were interested in teaching people prudence in the first place. On the contrary, their habit of making new rulings with greater frequency suggests that like other eras in the church, the sixteenth century was one of keeping the laity reliant on others for decisions of conscience.

Jonsen and Toulmin's thesis that the casuists did not articulate their method because, among other reasons, they lacked time, presumed that they had a will to instruct others in the method. I find no evidence for that presumption at all. On the contrary, recently Peter Holmes edited, translated, and published the casuistry of Thomas

Southwell (Southwell was a pseudonym for Thomas Bacon, 1592–1637), an established professor at the English College of the Society of Jesus at Liège. One case that I suspect will become a port of entry for many a doctoral dissertation entertained the question of probabilism. The presupposition of probabilism was that it allowed a priest the freedom to follow a legitimate position of one legitimate moralist even if a more probable position existed (we will see more on probabilism later). In this case Southwell entertained whether "a confessor is bound to follow the probable opinion of a penitent."[64] Note the issue was not that a penitent developed her or his own probable opinion. Rather, the penitent had become familiar with the "approved authors" as the casuists and later manualists were called, and was now asking her/his confessor, can I follow X instead of Y. Southwell resolved first that without sufficient cause a confessor cannot refuse to absolve a penitent following probable opinion, and here he invoked a variety of sources. But then he added that almost all those authorities as well as two others (here he included Mair) hold that the penitent was "bound to follow the safer opinion of the priest." Southwell concluded "a penitent is not suitably disposed if he does not wish to obey a confessor who, for a just and grave reason, wishes the penitent to conform to the demands of his judgment."[65] Southwell, as we will see, let Trent's famous "sacred tribunal of the confessional" negate the probable freedom of the penitent. This leaves us to ask, For whose benefit was the casuistry?

The irony about the birth of modern casuistry was that this helpful system was born when moral certainty was most vulnerable. For example, Jonsen and Toulmin acknowledged that they wrote their book after their experience on a national bioethics commission where they found that so much research was entirely new and that existing moral norms were no longer pertinent. They noted that consensus on the committee was achieved when through analogous taxonomies they attained practical conclusions. Disagreement only occurred whenever individual members "explained their individual *reasons*."[66] Thus they agreed to determine one form of conduct as licit, another as illicit, but were unable to argue coherently in agreement with one another.

Precisely because there was no underlying system, Mair looked for moral certainty in acceptable forms of conduct. The validity of the recognized and accepted conduct was simply presumed. But why something was right or wrong seemed more *displayed* than *explained* both in Mair's and in Jonsen and Toulmin's writings. Reasons were and remained lacking. In a way, casuistry can simply avoid addressing the very challenges a society faces, that is, determining *why* certain forms of conduct are correct and others are not. Certainly, casuistry determined which forms of conduct were correct or not, but why they were, that is the lacuna. Casuistry's determinations with their supposed consensus often remain acknowledged but not proven. If, however, a common vision was articulated, argued, and accepted, then out of that context, casuistry could provide illuminating resolutions. Among practitioners who have some common vision, casuistry could flourish.

Let us now conclude this section by locating Mair. Between the two periods of Scholasticism and casuistry, where do we place Mair? Louis Vereecke proposed, "John Mair seems to have been the last scholastic."[67] However, the Scottish historian John Durkan wrote, "If we think of scholasticism as the old learning, then Mair is its last distinguished representative.... Yet Mair cannot be written off as a representative of the old learning, because circumstances forced him to gradually come to terms with the new situation in the world of learning."[68] Others dismissed him as forgettable. In his landmark work, *The Idea of Natural Rights*, Brian Tierney turned to folio 82–85 from Mair's *Commentary on the Fourth Book of the Sentences*, where Mair posited the position that all were obliged to give to those in extreme need. Mair began asking a series of relentless questions: Does a rich man who gives to the needy give what is already theirs? If there were a thousand rich men and only one poor person, would they all be obliged to give? Tierney commented, "All this is standard theological casuistry. The questions are ingenious. The point is that they do not address any of the urgent problems that faced European society at the beginning of the sixteenth century." He concluded, "In discussing the problems of poverty, Mair seems to have been more interested in sophismata of his own invention than in the social issues of his age."[69]

I do not agree with Tierney. The social was Mair's concern, and that concern lands him in modernity with casuistry. In fact, it was precisely about the social issues of the age that Mair came under critique by Bartolomé de las Casas (1484–1566), in his *In Defense of the Indians* written around 1552, about two years after his debate with Juan Ginés de Sepúlveda (1494–1573) at Valladolid (1550).[70] In his last chapters, de las Casas turned to a ringing attack on Mair's third question in chapter 44 of his *Commentary on the Second Book of the Sentences* where he argued that the king of Spain had the rights to depose a native king of a people not yet evangelized ("Since the Indians did not understand the Spanish language and refused to admit the preachers of God's word except with a large army....It is lawful to take them by force."). De las Casas attacked him for being "ignorant of both the law and the facts."[71] For the most part, both facts and law are the instruments that he used against Mair, but early on, he attacked Mair for his point of view: "John Major adds that the Indian king should reasonably put up with this. I do not at all think that John Major would tolerate such evils and crudities, supposing he were an Indian."[72] Mair might have been wrong, but the inference was that he was a significant authority on social issues facing modernity. In his masterful *A Church That Can and Cannot Change*, John T. Noonan Jr. dedicated a chapter ("If John Major Were an Indian") to de las Casas's hypothetical. Noonan, long appreciative of Mair's contributions, saw his limitations,[73] and if Mair's appreciation of the rights of the poor seemed weak, his defense of the colonialists was even more obscene. Indeed, if John Mair were an Indian, he might have seen poverty and enslavement differently.

Still, for all his shortcomings, Mair marked the beginning of casuistry. His inductive method, his commonsensical controlling insights, his engaging analogues and cases, his insatiably curiosity, his investigative personality, his nominalistic philosophy, his inventive casuistry, his willingness to overturn the teachings of popes and saints, and his evident pastoral care, at least for those he knew, all suggest a personality quite at home with what would unfold in the sixteenth century. Even his deeply problematic errors were demonstrative of the lack of experience that such innovators have. Mair effectively invented the tools that steered him and others through the sixteenth century. He is, I believe, the father of modern casuistry, though his failure was precisely his inability to imagine the contexts of those not in his own.

Mair's sixteenth century is a time period much like our own. Both depend on this very specific type of moral reasoning through analogy simply because traditional moral prohibitions and prescriptions that shaped ways of thinking before our times were/are no longer holding. That Mair and a few others led us into this casuistic engagement is why, I believe, Mair is becoming all the more familiar today.

In closing, let us give Mair the final word by returning to the question of pleasure in sexual relations. He began the question with his controlling insight, that though one ate an apple for its nutrition, one also could eat one, solely for pleasure, without sin.[74] The insight was universally accepted. Noonan noted, "Like St. Thomas, Major holds that God put pleasure in intercourse to stimulate the act, but unlike St. Thomas, Major gives this doctrine full value," by drawing the analogy with eating an apple for pleasure. The image of apple-eating to refute the theologian who made original sin a central dogma was certainly provocative. Moreover, when rejecting the opinion of Augustine that marital intercourse to avoid any form of fornication is always venially sinful, Mair noted that "the saints must be interpreted narrowly when they speak extremely."[75] This early modern casuist adeptly brought modernity into the realm of moral reasoning and this new moral reasoning into the age of modernity.

IV. THE DECALOGUE OR THE TEN COMMANDMENTS

We remember that in the penitential and confessional manuals "sins" were categorized according to the seven deadly sins or vices. Similarly in Thomas's *Summa* the entire *pars* on moral theology were written in the key of the seven virtues. In the sixteenth century, the Ten Commandments, or the Decalogue, replaced both, but most especially, the seven deadly sins.[76] This change began through the advocacy of Jean Gerson (1363–1429), the theologian and rector of the University of Paris who called for the appropriation of the biblically based Decalogue as the foundational moral text for catechetical instruction.[77]

Still, it was not until the sixteenth century that the Decalogue took its unquestioned place in catechetical instruction.[78] Martin Luther's (1483–1546) *Large Catechism* (1529) dedicated nearly half of its 120 pages to the Decalogue. Generally speaking, in terms of prohibitions or prescriptions, Luther began his instruction of each commandment by following the specific form of the commandment, but then turned to its corollary. Thus the commandment on killing began with an explanation of the prohibition but turned eventually to consider the failure to do good to one's neighbor: "God rightly calls all persons murderers who do not offer counsel and aid to men in need and in peril of body and life."[79] Moreover, his explanations focused not on particular actions that were in themselves right or wrong, but rather on general dispositions or habitual stances particularly in relationship to another. Thus, the first application of the eighth commandment "is that everyone should help his neighbor maintain his rights."[80] But above all, it was the heart that dominated this treatment of the Decalogue. One saw this easily in his conclusion to the first commandment: "Where the heart is right with God and this commandment is kept, fulfillment of all the others will follow of its own accord."[81]

These three features-matching—the two components of prohibition and prescription; then the emphasis on habitual, relational conduct; and finally the insistence on the charitable heart—were also found in each of the ten expressions in Luther's *Small Catechism* (1529). This was a practical, popular, and accessible text that Luther's disciples could access and use in their parishes or even their homes. For example, the description of the eighth commandment was simply this: "We should fear and love God so that we do not deceitfully belie, betray, backbite, nor slander our neighbor, but apologize for him, speak well of him, and put the most charitable construction on all that he does."[82]

While John Calvin (1509–64) treated the Decalogue briefly in his *Catechism* (1538),[83] it was not until the *Institutes of the Christian Religion* (1559) that Calvin developed the Decalogue at length. There he balanced every prohibition with a positive injunction and again, like Luther, discussed habitual, relational ways of acting. While the sixth through the ninth commandments concerned licentious desires and intentions, the tenth concerned concupiscence, pure and simple. It began,

> The end of this precept is, that, since it is the will of God that our whole soul should be under the influence of love, every desire inconsistent with charity ought to be expelled

> from our minds. The sum, then, will be, that no thought should obtrude itself upon us, which would excite in our minds any desire that is noxious, and tends to the detriment of another. To which corresponds the affirmative precept, that all our conceptions, deliberations, resolutions, and undertakings, ought to be consistent with the benefit and advantage of our neighbors.[84]

The Catechism of the Council of Trent (1566) had the lengthiest treatment of the Decalogue, consisting of some 120 pages and, like Luther, split most commandments into positive and negative "parts." Each commandment had an explication and then a specific application related to a variety of categories of sinful activity. Inasmuch as the Catholic *Catechism* was not for individual or family use but for the parish priest preeminently, the Decalogue basically replaced the seven deadly sins as they were in the penitential and confessional manuals, precisely in categorizing sinful activity. Catholics never learned the Decalogue for their own moral guidance. Their moral guidance was preeminently moderated through the priest in the pulpit, on the altar, and in the confessional.

Moreover, by 1566, the emerging juridical hand in theological ethics that we saw in Mair sixty years earlier became more chillingly apparent. The context of penance was less a sacrament of mercy but more a tribunal. Nowhere was the image more present than in the *Catechism* at the very start of its treatment of the commandments:

> In the tribunal of penance the priest holds the place of a judge, and pronounces sentence according to the nature and gravity of the offence. Unless, therefore, he is desirous that his ignorance should prove an injury to himself and to others, he must bring with him to the discharge of his duty the greatest vigilance and the most practiced acquaintance with the interpretation of the law, in order to be able to pronounce, according to this divine rule, on every act and omission.[85]

The *Catechism* catalogued lengthy descriptions of wrong actions. Under the second commandment, for instance, it devoted a paragraph-long description of each of the following sins: false oaths, unjust oaths, rash oaths, oaths by false gods, irreverent speech, neglect of prayer, blasphemy. The eighth commandment likewise described false testimony in favor of a neighbor, falsehoods in lawsuits, false testimony out of court, detraction, flattery, lies of all kinds, hypocrisy.

Sometimes, the *Catechism* reminded the priest that what may seem to belong to a prohibition did not. Under the first commandment, for instance, were several paragraphs on each of the following "not forbidden" actions: veneration and invocation of angels, and of saints, representations of the divine persons and angels, images of Christ and the saints, and other sacred images. Likewise, the fifth commandment did not forbid the killing of animals, execution of criminals, killing in a just war, killing by accident, killing in self-defense. The purpose of the Decalogue in this catechism remained the same: to determine solely and exactly those wrong activities that contaminate the soul.

Pastoral advice was also offered on how to avoid sinful actions. For example, the sixth commandment described at length such aids as avoiding idleness, practicing temperance, custody of the eye, avoiding improper dress (and conversation, reading, and pictures), frequenting the sacraments, and mortification. None of these prescribed actions were for moral or spiritual betterment; they were simply prophylactic actions to keep us from sinful ones. Finally, several commandments advised priests against unacceptable excuses for sinful actions. For example, in the seventh were developed the pleas of rank and position, greater ease and elegance, the other's wealth, the force of habit, favorable opportunity, revenge, and financial embarrassment. In the eighth were the inexcusable pleas of prudence, revenge, frailty, habit, bad example, convenience, amusement, and advantage. These operated as prudential guidelines for the confessor who sat in the tribunal of the confessional.

The transition from the seven deadly sins to the Decalogue eventually became complete. The appeal was strong. First, unlike the seven deadly sins, the commandments claimed divine sanction: they and not the seven deadly sins appeared in revelation. Second, they were a solid pedagogical tool that resisted embellishment. The seven vices afforded the medieval mind the opportunity to expand and compound each vice into a multitude of sins and fellow vices. The commandments as a scriptural text needed no such expansion. They simply needed explanation. Third, unlike the vices, they offered not only negative prohibitions but also positive prescriptions. Finally, with the possible exception of pride, the vices were primarily offensive to human life; the commandments specified prescriptions and prohibitions regarding our responsibilities toward God and humanity. By the time the *Catechism of the Council of Trent* appeared in 1566, the tradition of the Decalogue as the organizing framework for moral instruction in the church was settled and would remain so for four hundred years until the Second Vatican Council.[86]

V. PROBABILISM

In his *Summa* II–II, q. 70, a. 2, Thomas Aquinas wrote, "In order to act lawfully and rightly, I must have at least moral certainty of the imperfect kind that the proposed action is honest and right." As theologians weighed this teaching, they argued that since perfect certainty about a moral judgment really only belonged to God, when we make a moral judgment, the required degree of moral confidence was imperfect or what was eventually identified as a "moral certainty": a person was at least adequately, though not absolutely, convinced that his intended action was right. The assumption that we are adequately certain of the rightness of our actions did not guarantee that our action would be morally right, but it did assure us that it was not sinful. As the famous twentieth-century Jesuit manualist, Thomas Slater (1855–1928), wrote, "If my conscience was in error, that does not negate the goodness that I intentionally willed."[87]

What if one lacked imperfect certitude? In that case, effectively one experienced practical doubt and one could not act out of conscience with practical doubt. The doubtful Catholic was expected to search for imperfect certainty and, therefore, needed to consult an expert, which at the time was the parish priest. In the consultation, the priest had an array of options to consider. The differences pertained to the quality of argument required for imperfect or moral certainty when recognized authors proposed differing opinions. Here a brilliant question was asked: Must a priest choose a weightier and stricter interpretation of the law even when another opinion is evidently valid though less weighty and less restrictive in its interpretation? In 1577 this question was answered by the Dominican Bartolomé de Medina (1528–80) who argued famously, "If an opinion is probable it is lawful to follow it, even though the opposing opinion is more probable." I find it helpful when teaching probabilism to insert the word *arguable* for *probable* in Medina's assertion: "If an opinion is arguable it is lawful to follow it, even though the opposing opinion is more arguable." My word *arguable* approaches the word *cogent*. Thus Medina was effectively stating that an argument that was cogent and held by a recognized theologian was sufficiently valid to use. The strictness or the greater burdens of another's interpretation of the law did not undermine the cogency of another interpretation that was easier to bear. This approach was called *probabilism* and gave to the priest-confessor the freedom in conscience to accept any opinion so long as it was cogent or well argued and from an authoritative author, which provided both internal and external certitude.

Later, some moral theologians advanced the proposition that if an interpretation granted more freedom, it had to have weightier arguments than the one that was stricter. This position was called the "more probable," or *probabiliorist*, argument. The Dominicans in time embraced this development though they were concerned that probabilism might fall into laxism if there were not adequate controls on it. In the meantime, most Jesuits embraced Medina's original definition of *probabilism* as legitimate. To mediate this difference, the Redemptorists later proposed *equiprobabilism*, which contended that a more lenient opinion ought to have as weighty an argument as the stricter interpretation.[88] Effectively, the Redemptorist position of equiprobabilism when practically engaged was a slightly modified probabilism, but probabiliorism placed an extra burden on the ethicist, the priest, and in turn the layperson by asking for the weightier argument for a less strict interpretation. It effectively suggested that the competency of the ethicist was not to be taken for granted and that the priest could only follow his position if the more probable was evident.

It may be surprising to find that, in time, many ethicists were self-proclaimed probabilists. In the early twentieth century, for example, Slater, who wrote the first moral manual in English (1906), embraced the probabilist opinion, which he defined thus: "When there is only question of committing sin or not, it is lawful to follow a solidly probable opinion, even though the opposite may be more probable."[89] He defended probabilism and concluded with an argument for its adequacy. Here he dismissed the premise that the solution founded on the stronger (more probable) argument was in fact truer:

> The greater the probability of the other view does not make it certain, nor is the supposed greater probability a sure guarantee that the more probable view is the more true. It very frequently happens that an opinion that is considered more probable at one time is thought less probable or altogether improbable at another. Moreover, degrees of probability are very difficult to determine. What seems more probable to one theologian seems less to another, or even to the same at a different time. And even if it be granted that one opinion is certainly and absolutely more probable, the opposite may for all that remain solidly probable.[90]

Still, not all Jesuits were probabilists, nor were all probabilists Jesuits. For instance, one Jesuit moralist, Tirsio González de Santalla (1624–1705), wrote a lengthy work defending probabiliorism and attacked probabilism. In 1680, Jesuit censors blocked its publication lest it seem that the Jesuits were abandoning probabilism and endorsing the more rigid position.[91] González asked Pope Innocent XI (1611–89; r. 1676–89) to support him, and the pope prompted the Holy Office to direct the Society of Jesus to grant freedom to its members to support probabiliorism. From their perspective the Jesuits never had prohibited support for probabiliorism, rather their objection was specifically with González's text. In 1687, at the suggestion of the pope, González was elected General of the Society of Jesus. For a variety of reasons, not until 1694 was he "allowed" to publish his text *Fundamentum Theologiae moralis id est, tractatus theologicus de recto usu opinionum probabilium*. It should be noted that though he was a probabiliorist, he was neither a Jansenist nor an absolute tutiorist who held that only the "safest" position could be adopted.

How does one distinguish these categories? One could say that at one end of the spectrum was laxism, in which theologians effectively were so loose in their interpretations that they eradicated the function of the law, and at the other end was absolute tutiorism.

Both ends were condemned at different times: the laxists by the University of Paris in 1619 and by the Holy Office in 1665, 1666, and 1679, and the absolute tutiorists by Pope Alexander VIII (1610–91; r. 1689–91) in 1690.[92] In between were probabilism, equiprobabilism, and probabiliorism as three different, legitimate schools of thought.

Probabilism had considerable longevity. In the first years of the twentieth century the three most popular English manuals were all by probabilists: Slater, another Jesuit Henry Davis (1886–1946), and Heribert Jone (1885–1967), a Capuchin priest.[93] On the one hand, probabilists gave validity to the writings of almost all manualists and freed clergy to choose to advise the laity from the full range of manualists' opinions. Probabiliorists, on the other hand, contended that the clergy's options should be more restrictive: generally speaking, only the more rigid interpretation was valid unless a weightier argument could be made for a more lenient interpretation. Probabiliorists were concerned about the degree of freedom that probabilists were extending both to fellow manualists and to the clergy who were adopting these differing opinions.

Still, despite a manualist's general hermeneutics of interpretation, there was a gentlemen's agreement among them not to discredit one another's authority. A manualist basically proposed his own position, occasionally arguing that it represented "a common opinion," but rarely did he declare another opinion as illicit, and if one ever did, he rarely identified the proponent. Although nonmanualists like Blaise Pascal mocked or derided one school (in his case, the Jesuit probabilists), the entire hermeneutical "debate" among manualists was shaped by an active, respectful tolerance: each school enjoyed a recognized legitimacy.[94] Only those on the sidelines were known for mean-spiritedness.

VI. THE END OF THE ARC OF CASUISTRY: FRANCISCO DE TOLEDO (1532–96)

In order to conclude our study into the history of high casuistry in the sixteenth century we turn to Francisco de Toledo's *Summa casuum conscientiae sive De instructione sacerdotum, libri septem* (A Summary of Cases of Consciences or On the Instruction of Priests in Seven Books), a work very different from Mair's casuistry.[95] Rather than making cases as Mair did, Toledo provided extensive summaries of his already solved and taught cases; as with all his Roman appointments, his authority was impeccable.

During his tenure at the papal court, two significant events help to describe both the man and the times he lived in. As the theologian for the Sacred Penitentiary and for the Roman Inquisition, he was consulted on the case of Bartolomé Carranza, OP, the archbishop of Toledo and primate of Spain. Carranza had been imprisoned by the Spanish Inquisition on charges by his brother Dominican Melchior Cano, that the archbishop's catechism was a heretical work. Eleven years later, he was brought to Rome to stand before that inquisition, and Toledo was invited in 1570 to judge the archbishop's catechism. He declared that Carranza was free of any heresy, for which Toledo was later personally attacked as being born of Jewish blood. The attack diminished Toledo's credibility and, subsequently, Carranza was not released until he lay dying in 1576, after nearly seventeen years of detention.[96]

The second example ended differently. In 1560, Peter Canisius, SJ, arrived in Augsburg to find that people there had accepted a practice of moneylending called the triple contract, which we encountered earlier in this chapter. Recall that this method of moneylending had been proposed as morally licit by the moralist John Eck and, as John Noonan noted, was an essential innovation that led, in turn, to extraordinary developments in the moral teaching on usury. As we saw, shortly after Eck proposed it in 1515, John Mair also approved it, giving the practice probable liceity.

Appalled at what he perceived was a usurious practice, Peter Canisius forbade absolution for those engaged in the triple contract. A subsequent long-lasting correspondence developed between Canisius and the Jesuits in Rome on the matter. Then, in 1567, Francis Borgia (1510–72), the third superior general of the Society of Jesus, wrote that Pope Pius V had stated privately that the triple contract was licit. In 1570, a Roman commission was established to study the triple contract. Toledo was clearly the most active member of the commission, which submitted its findings three years later, approving the triple contract as licit. Noonan wrote, "This approval is the first decisive evidence of crystallization of official Jesuit thought in favor of the contract."[97]

Toledo's summaries come from the courses he taught at the Roman College from 1562 to 1569, when he lectured on the priesthood, the administration of the sacraments, the Ten Commandments as they were used for the hearing of confession, and the sacrament of marriage. These lectures were the material for his *Summa casuum*; copies of them as well as students' notes were probably in circulation before the *Summa*'s publication in 1598.[98] When the lectures were published, they were among the first of a series of Jesuit summaries of cases of conscience that began to appear in the 1590s.[99] Toledo's work was the first major breakthrough: it went through seventy-two editions and multitudinous translations, remaining in print until 1716.[100]

Ninety years after Mair's *Commentary*, Francisco de Toledo's *Summa casuum conscientiae* did not look like casuistry. Rather than making a case, it gave summaries of cases. Commentators, both historians and ethicists, often failed to differentiate works of casuistry that were demonstrable or argumentative from case summaries that were collections of pedagogical judgments.[101] These summaries did not depend on internal certitude (there were no arguments made), but rather singularly on their external certitude, that is, on the authority of the writer. Moreover, the purpose of the text was not to receive validation from the reader. Mair's cases needed to receive validation from the reader; he made his cases precisely to prompt others' assent and thereby win the day. Toledo, however, was simply interested in guiding his readers. As the advisor to seven popes, he had nothing to prove; his goal was to instruct.

Toledo's *Summa casuum conscientiae* was divided into seven books: priesthood; the administration of the sacraments; the practice of confession; the first three commandments; the remaining seven; the six precepts of the church; and matrimony. The first book answered the question "What is a priest?" Toledo underlined the unique dignity of priests and the heavy responsibilities expected from those acting on God's commission. He began with a definition that he subsequently parsed throughout the first chapter: a priest is a man commissioned by divine authority communicated through specific persons for the true worship of God.[102]

Throughout, Toledo was concerned with power: by power, the priest is ordained; through power, priests exercise their ministry. In chapter 3, he discussed the twofold power of the priesthood: orders and jurisdiction. The former was the power to confect the body of Christ and to administer the other sacraments. The latter was the power of rendering judgment on the excommunicated, granting dispensations, conferring indulgences, and applying the laws of the church.[103] The second book was on the sacramental ministry of the priest, with similar concerns for power and its right exercise. By this point, Toledo had established the seriousness of the priestly vocation, and priests reading this work would probably have been overwhelmed by the onerous responsibility of their vocation. Still, they would want to read further to find the directions about how to exercise wisely and prudently the power that they have. Rather quickly, Toledo established that he was a man of great authority who was willing to share his wisdom in mentoring fellow priests.

Toledo developed a significant agenda: the priesthood was effectively an institutional position to determine the law and to administer the sacraments. Paramount among the latter was the power to absolve in the sacrament of penance. No other sacrament or task scrutinized the complex personal matter of human conduct; no other sacrament or task so definitively relied on the particular skills and judgment of priests; and no other sacrament or task so directly related to the salvation of an individual soul. In summary, no other divine action was so vulnerable to the fallibility of human judgment as absolution, and yet no other divine activity was as significant as that which absolved a person from eternal damnation.

Like his contemporaries, Toledo added a new feature to the confessional: Not only was the confessional singularly for determining personal actions. By focusing the matter of sin on decidedly institutional concerns, he outlined which social structures were morally permitted and which were sinful. He brought the world of commerce under the jurisdiction of the confessional. In simply counting the number of folios dedicated to each commandment, it was the seventh that was the most considered. While nineteen folios were devoted to the fifth commandment and its exceptions, eighteen to the fourth commandment, and a mere twelve to the sixth commandment, eighty-eight folios focused on the seventh commandment, where he discussed usury and related matters. Similarly, the eighth commandment was the subject of thirty-one folios, and the ninth commandment had a surprising thirty-five folios. Finally, Toledo's evident lack of interest in sexual matters was reiterated in his dismissal of the tenth commandment by simply stating that it was treated under the sixth.[104]

Under the seventh commandment, Toledo examined the fundamental structures of financial institutions. Rather than simple personal or even private acts of theft, lying, or concupiscence, the subject matter was the structures of relationships in civil and ecclesiastical societies. After an introduction, he spent eleven chapters (17—27) on restitution, that is, the social repair of an act of theft. Then he turned to usury and stipulated five conditions without which an action was not usurious.[105] In effect many financial transactions remained problematic, but they were not summarily dismissed as forms of usury. Rather, Toledo determined under what conditions these actions were or were not prohibited. After four chapters (28—31) on usury, he discussed mutual compensation for loans (*lucrum in mutuo*) in three chapters (32—34), restitution of gains accrued from usury in three chapters (35—37), and the innovative public pawnshops-turned-commercial banks (*De monte pietatis*) in four chapters (38—41). His longest section (chaps. 42—49) was dedicated to annuities (*census*), and he concluded his comments on the seventh commandment with a discussion on credit agencies (*cambium*) (chaps. 50—55).[106]

After these chapters, the eighth commandment addressed the duties in a court of law. A chapter was dedicated to each of the different functionaries in the court: the accused, the state, witnesses, advocates, notaries, and procurators. The final chapters were about what would constitute detraction. Though Toledo described the ninth commandment as the social impact of avarice,[107] it was actually about the financial responsibilities of ecclesiastics. After extensive comments (chaps. 72—75) on stipends, he turned to six chapters (76—81) on benefices. Here, as elsewhere, he explained what specifically was prohibited. He concluded the fifth book with two chapters (82—83) on pensions and ten (84—93) on simony. By stringing together all his rulings, Toledo helped his readers appreciate important distinctions between the permitted and the prohibited.

Then Toledo presented ground rules, new categories, and clearly drawn lines. These became laws, and their deductive applications were made in a decidedly self-conscious institutional context.

How did these moralists arrive at such a synthesis? Albert Jonsen explained that there are three phases to high casuistry: first, a morphological dissection of the circumstances and maxims at play in a case; then a taxonomy to line up the cases to search for congruency among them; finally, there is the kinetic that develops emerging insights and articulates them into rules.[108] All three were in place in Mair's presentation, but in Toledo, we see only the conclusion of the entire casuistic process: the kinetic phase in its summaries. Within those summaries we find occasional explications that we can call an application of a principle to a case, or what today we call low casuistry.[109]

In the sixteenth century we move from Mair with outdated principles and innovative cases to Toledo with newly articulated rules and principles that are designed to anticipate any subsequent emerging cases. Mair's age was marked by innovation. The fifteenth and early sixteenth centuries allowed moralists to explore every major moral question alive on the European continent. Toledo's voluminous *Summa* was a testimony, however, to how many of these discussions became settled, institutionalized, and standardized. He marked the conclusion of the innovation.

VII. SOME CONCLUDING THOUGHTS ON THESE PATHWAYS

This move from innovative casuistry to institutionalized norms appeared in all the areas of moral theology in the sixteenth century. By the end of the sixteenth century, matters are concluded. Let us consider three issues: abortion, sexual pleasure, and the use of methodological principles.

John Connery showed us that there were two longstanding positions in the tradition on abortion: it was always murder, or in a very few rare instances, it was not. Those who considered exceptions often followed a distinction between an unformed and a formed one, the difference between the two being ensoulment, that is, a formed fetus was one with a human soul. This was based on the presupposition, following from Aristotelian biology, that until a fetus was formed, it was not yet, in its evolution, human. Moreover, those who held to the difference also believed that the male fetus was souled at the fortieth day of development, the female at the ninetieth day. Those who considered the possibility of an abortion were usually among those who believed that there was a difference between unformed and formed fetuses, and even then abortion was only considered for the most urgent of issues, for instance, the mother's life being compromised by the pregnancy. For example, Antoninus of Florence (1389–1459) endorsed a position held by John of Naples (dates unknown) regarding a therapeutic abortion of an early or unformed fetus. Antoninus's stance unleashed a casuistic debate about the grounds and means for what constituted a therapeutic abortion of a not yet formed fetus. In 1588, Sixtus V (1521–90; r. 1585–90) introduced *Effraenatam*, which excommunicated anyone involved in an abortion, and by 1591 Gregory XIV (1535–91; r. 1590–91) had modified it to apply the penalty to the abortion of a formed fetus. This remained the standard position of the church for another three hundred years, and theological debate focused solely on the legitimacy of Antoninus's exception. In 1869, Pope Pius IX dropped any reference to the distinction and, from then on, all abortions were declared murder.[110]

Regarding sexuality, we find before the end of the sixteenth century that casuists like John Mair, Martín of Azpilcueta, and Martin Le Maistre entertained that some sexually pleasurable marital activity that was not intentionally procreative was legitimate. As we saw earlier, however, under the debate over "parvity of matter" in sexual activity, the superior general of the Society of Jesus (the Jesuits) put an end to all this in 1612. His and other sanctions dissuaded moralists from entertaining any of the circumstantial exceptions as earlier casuists had. The theological mentality that followed the close of the sixteenth century, therefore, convinced many that ending debate, establishing standards, and writing summas, rather than doing high casuistry, was the right way to proceed. Indeed, the Council of Trent itself, wanting to set up seminaries, develop textbooks, and establish curricula, was actively promoting this era of standardization. As time passed, the church would claim its newly established norms on each of the commandments as universal and, in time, as ones without any accountability to history, that "the Church had always taught."

Moral theology needed, however, new instruments to navigate between the certainly prohibited and the probably safe. At this time, then, moral theology possessed not only specific moral norms such as those from Toledo, but also a variety of methodological principles, such as the principles of toleration, cooperation, and double effect, which were first articulated in the second half of the sixteenth century. For example, although Joseph Mangan argued that Thomas Aquinas first articulated the principle of double effect,[111] Josef Ghoos proved otherwise.[112] Ghoos showed that the moral solutions from the thirteenth century through the sixteenth century were of isolated concrete cases. In the sixteenth century, Bartolomé Medina (1527–80) and Gabriel Vásquez (1551–1604) began to name the common factors among relevant cases. Finally, John of St. Thomas (1589–1644) articulated the factors into the conditions of the principle as such. Although the principle of double effect was first articulated in the seventeenth century, manualists wrongfully but routinely referred to it as being in the *Summa Theologiae*. Similarly, manualists and others attributed to Thomas positions inimical to his thought. For example, the concept "intrinsic evil" was first expressed by the fourteenth-century Dominican Durandus of St. Pourçain, the most significant opponent to the legacy of Thomas Aquinas; yet still manualists referred to Thomas's use of the concept, though he never had the concept and never would have used it.[113]

At the end of the sixteenth century, as we noted, moral theologians had developed summaries of cases by first studying the original cases morphologically, then setting them into related categories taxonomically, and finally articulating them kinetically. They arrived at the newly minted principles in the same way: by considering cases of actions with two effects, or of those requiring simple toleration or more complex actions of legitimate cooperation. Herein were articulated the famous principles of double effect, toleration, and material cooperation, respectively. These principles gave moralists a flexibility with the small number of instances that were not yet settled. Although much had been determined in the summaries, the theologians anticipated yet unnamed circumstances that could place the summaries into doubt. Thus, by offering the methodological principles, they left us tools to resolve any doubt raised by the circumstances.

These manualists who applied moral principles were not like John Mair, looking, as Amerigo Vespucci had, for new lands to explore; rather, they were careful escorts across the terrain of already discovered landmasses riddled with sinful actions. The authoritative moral theologian was able to guide others, for example, by sanctioning an indirect intention or indirect action, on occasion, so as to avoid an already known morally evil action. Trent ended the speculation that moralists such as Mair and Azpilcueta produced and endorsed a mentality that accepted the summaries of cases as everlasting norms. Moreover, for anything still undefined, methodological principles were in place to guarantee that no new norms needed to be articulated.

Trent left as its moral legacy these textbooks that secured as everlasting the indisputably settled norms regarding moral conduct and the more flexible principles that described other actions by what they were not, for example, an indirect abortion, passive euthanasia, an unprovoked ejaculation, or an indirect attack on civilian populations. In this way they left moralists with norms to apply and, when in doubt, methodological principles to resolve the question. In either case, the application was always done deductively. There was no need for the inductive logic from the fifteenth and early sixteenth centuries. It is no wonder that, for almost four centuries, Catholics were fascinated with the principle of double effect.[114] They had nothing else with which to work.

Chapter Six

Pathways to Modernity II

Confraternities and the School of Salamanca

I. THE CONFRATERNITIES

Along with the sixteenth-century casuists who developed the judgments that catalyzed the emergence of social institutions, there was also a fairly active laity working in collaboration with religious and clergy in responding to contemporary challenges. As we have seen throughout this book, Christians were not simply interested in avoiding sin; rather, they were from the beginning pursuing pathways of holiness. In the sixteenth century, they were just as socially minded as the casuists as they developed major, long-standing confraternities to put their spirituality into action.

Confraternities were local associations that pursued holiness collectively by finding particular practices of prayer that could unite the community to Christ and then initiating a corporal work of mercy that helped the community respond to the needs of the community associations. This twofold movement, the internally directed summoning to come together in prayer and the externally oriented service of mercy to those in need, captured the genius of the logic of the confraternity. By the sixteenth century, the previous establishment of medieval guilds and lay associations, along with the innovations of new religious orders like the Jesuits and

Theatines, as well as the important reforms of the Council of Trent, provided new impetus for laypersons to belong to confraternities. These confraternities wed spiritual devotion with the practice of mercy. They had an enormous influence on the moral formation of Roman Catholics.[1]

Confraternities had their roots in the medieval monasteries and convents that were also centers of the practice of mercy. Besides the nuns and monks, many pious women and men participated in the works of mercy by forming lay associations. These began in Naples in the tenth century and later appeared in Tuscany. By the twelfth century, they were throughout France, Spain, and Italy, assisting the religious and mostly establishing and maintaining hospitals. With the spirit of Francis and Dominic in the thirteenth century, not only did many enter the religious orders, but many other professional laypersons also became inspired and answered the call to mercy with great imagination through lay associations or, later, confraternities. In 1498, Queen Eleanor of Portugal, for example, established the Confraternity of Misericordia. In 1516, it had one hundred members: fifty from the nobility, fifty from the working class, all dedicated to the fourteen works of mercy. By the queen's death in 1525 there were sixty-one branches of the confraternity. From the seventeenth to the nineteenth century, twenty-five confraternities were established in Portuguese colonies. Many still stand today.

These institutions often were very creative, particularly, in cultivating not only the institutions to serve others, but also in developing a membership to lead in that service. For instance, the motto of the lay Order of the Holy Spirit founded in the thirteenth century by Guy de Montpellier was the following: "The sick person is the head of the household; those who assist are the servants in the household." These apostolates, with their unexpected leadership policies, were extraordinarily successful: At its height, the order had founded and staffed in Europe some eight hundred hospitals. One of them, the Hospital of the Holy Spirit, still stands in Rome, a few hundred yards from St. Peter's Basilica.[2] The Hospitallers of St. Lazarus of Jerusalem, founded in 1120, was composed mostly of knights infected with leprosy who administrated and protected the leprosarium there. With the spread of leprosy during the Crusades, any knight contracting the disease entered the ranks of the order. Their capacity to administer the Jerusalem leprosarium extended to those elsewhere. By 1265, Pope Clement IV decreed that local clergy should ensure that all leprosaria were under the administration of the Hospitallers. These were not centers of shame, but instead sanctuaries for those whose contagious disease required them to live apart from others. These communities were found throughout Europe and the Near East and were well known for society's responsiveness to those with Hansen's disease. The leprosaria were administered by knights with Hansen's disease.[3]

Confraternities tended to have a specific apostolate. One of the results of the extraordinary upheaval created by the Crusades was the rapid spread of what today we call "sex work." After the Crusades, "sex workers" were without funds and shelter. By the end of the twelfth century, houses of refuge were established in Bologna, Paris, Marseilles, Messina, and Rome. In turn, some of these sex workers themselves became sponsors of hospitality. Founding the Congregation of the Penitents of St. Mary Magdalene (1225), these women established fifty houses throughout Europe, providing community life for their members and shelter for sex workers in need. One cannot imagine that everyone thought the Congregation was morally acceptable. For many it would have been scandalous. Still, notice the role reversals: in many instances these sex workers became heads of the apostolates. These apostolates were scandalous in their generosity, scandalous in their style of service, and scandalous in their success.

Of the hundreds of confraternities dedicated to specific works of mercy, my favorite cared for those with syphilis. Syphilis was a very sixteenth-century illness, deeply connected to Christopher Columbus's conquests. We now know that syphilis was in the Americas before Columbus arrived and that it was apparent in Europe shortly after the conquests, becoming an epidemic in Europe by 1495.[4] From its inception, syphilis, a contagious disease, was often associated with foreigners. The first European report of it was in Naples, but because the disease entered Naples at the same time that French soldiers invaded it, syphilis became known as the French disease by the people of Naples. In 1497, the *Compagnia del Divino Amore* (Confraternity of Divine Love) was founded in Genoa by Chancellor of the Republic Ettore Vernazza as a group of laity and clergy committed to working for those suffering from shame: the poor, the prostitute, and the syphilitic. Victims of syphilis, having been abandoned both by their families because of shame and by hospitals because of fear of contagion, found a welcome in the confraternity's *Ospedali degli incurabili* (Hospitals for the Incurables). In 1499, the confraternity built the first hospital in Genoa. In 1517, Gaetano da Thiene (1480–1547) together with the confraternity built "Hospital of Mercy" in Verona. Shortly thereafter, Gaetano went to Vicenza to reorganize the Hospital of Mercy, there to serve again the person with syphilis. In 1521, the *Ospedale degli incurabili* was opened in Brescia. In 1522, Gaetano opened a hospital, still standing today as a major secondary school, in Venice. In the same year, a confraternity chapter was founded in Padova, and within four years it opened its hospital. In 1572, a hospital opened in Bergamo and, in 1584, another in Crema.[5] Of all the Ospedali, the most compelling one is the one built in 1510 by the Confraternity of Divine Love for pilgrims arriving in Rome. One can only imagine the horrendous experience of those with syphilis arriving in Rome, originally for pilgrimage but discovering the virus along the way, fearing rejection and stigma and a horrible death, precisely as a foreigner. Instead, to these pilgrims, the care and hospitality of the Hospital of the Incurables was offered at the pilgrim Church of St. James on the Via Flaminia, only a few hundred meters from the main Roman entry gate at the Piazza del Popolo. Moreover, like the hospital in Venice, these institutions were built to last. Today, five hundred years later, the building stands as an obstetrics hospital bringing new life into the eternal city.

To locate just how remarkable the sixteenth century was, let us conclude this treatment on confraternities by taking a corporal work of mercy, visiting the prisoner, and following its social instantiation throughout the history of the church. This corporal work has been practiced consistently throughout the life of the church, in fact, from its outset. No less than Christ had been a prisoner. Thus, like Peter, Paul, and many of the apostles, imprisoned Christians were perceived as not only people in need but also people of courage and holiness. Thus, early church members visited their imprisoned brothers and sisters, worked to liberate them, and sought their blessing as well. About their liberation, for instance, Clement of Rome (35–99) wrote to Corinth in chapter 55 of his *Epistle* that many ransomed others by offering themselves in exchange for the one held hostage.[6] In the late twelfth century and into the thirteenth century, charitable institutions were established for the release of prisoners.

The Trinitarians (Order of the Most Holy Trinity for the Redemption of the Captives), founded by St. John of Matha (1160–1213), were singularly dedicated to ransoming prisoners and laboring to alleviate the conditions of those who remained in slavery. Similarly, the Royal, Celestial and Military Order of Our Lady of Mercy and the Redemption of the Captives was founded by St. Peter Nolasco (1189–1256) for the same task.[7]

Later in the sixteenth century, religious orders were founded, and their members worked along with other ministries for the care and release of prisoners. The Jesuits, for instance, provided a variety of services. The Jesuit historian John O'Malley reminds us first that these prisoners were either debtors or those awaiting trial, sentencing, or execution. In Rome, for example, over half the imprisoned were debtors from the poorer classes; the others, awaiting trial, had not yet had their guilt established. Jesuits took care of the imprisoned by preaching, catechizing, hearing the confessions of the imprisoned, and bringing them food and alms. In Italy and Spain, Jesuits spent a great deal of time raising funds through begging so as to pay off the prisoners' creditors. Elsewhere they begged for money to ransom back prisoners taken by the Turks. Likewise, they preached against slave-taking raids. Sometimes the Jesuits worked to improve the plight of prisons. In Palermo, for example, a confraternity was founded based on one Jesuit's work to improve the sanitary conditions of prisons. Another confraternity organized by the Jesuits, the Confraternity of the Imprisoned, was founded for laypersons in Rome, and it generated other confraternities in six other cities throughout Italy.[8]

Other confraternities of the laity also dedicated themselves to those in prison. In Rome, the Archconfraternity of Charity was specifically for those in captivity, as was the Confraternity of Pietà and Our Lady of Loretto in Milan. In France, confraternities such as the Work of Prisons in Marseilles and the Confraternity of Mercy in Lyons were solely dedicated to prisoners' needs, while the White Penitents and the Sisters of the Dominican Third Order were singularly dedicated to the needs of women prisoners.[9] Another confraternity, in Florence, was dedicated to prisoners awaiting execution, most of whom were political prisoners. They would visit the prisoners and spend the night with them before the execution, praying with them and helping them to identify with Jesus as a condemned prisoner. The following day, a confraternity member would walk to the gallows with each prisoner, walking ahead of him and holding a painted panel of the suffering Christ in front of his face so that the condemned man could keep his gaze fixed on Jesus instead of on the crowds or the executioners.[10]

From these experiences of the prisons, there grew subsequently numerous critical voices that protested prison conditions and started movements of reform to correct conditions among the imprisoned in Spain, Italy, France, and England. We cannot underestimate the relevance of these confraternities. Dozens of them took care of prisoners and captives; others were established for the care of the mentally ill as well as those who are unable to hear or speak. These confraternities were paralleled by the extraordinary number of religious orders that adopted a work of mercy to identify with its own charism. Looking at them historically, we see how in many of our contemporary attempts to respond collectively to those incarcerated, seeking refuge, or having been abandoned that a Christian response has always been there, but that those responses in the sixteenth-century confraternities highlighted the imaginative ways that Christian collectives, out of their own experiences of having received mercy, tried to accompany those whose lives were deeply precarious. In all the innovative developments of the sixteenth century, the confraternities were clearly the ones most focused on responding humanely to those experiencing overwhelming struggles.

The confraternities help us, I believe, to correct two misconceptions. Today, remarkably, people refer to lay leadership as if it were a new phenomenon in the church. Yet, with the earlier guilds and lay associations and, subsequently, the confraternities, we find instead robust and enduring lay leadership across Europe in these centers of mercy where Christians concretely worked out their response to the call to "come, follow me." A variety of historians, having worked on confraternities in their research, have significantly shown how the relations between clergy and laity were complicated and that the confraternities were "social spaces where laity and clergy met, mediated, and sometimes competed and fought."[11]

Second, while moralists were attending through a variety of ways to an instruction of the lay Catholic so that, at a minimum, they not sin, lay Catholics were deciding that the minimum was clearly not enough. At times critics look back to see where moral development in the church really was, looking only to the casuists or the later manualists alone, where there are few indications of the *Magis* or of going beyond. However, it is in these institutions that one finds a wholesale repudiation of Christian complacency with the minimum. Instead, one finds sustained, faithful, financially endowed, and fairly well-run institutions that addressed the challenges of the people of Europe. Though there were significant engagements about the life of the soul in the confessional, it was in the confraternities that the souls individually and collectively really flourished.

Here, then, we recognize another pathway to modernity. These confraternities were not fundamentally medieval even though their apostolic intentions reached all the way back to the early church. What was new in the sixteenth century were the lay boards governing them that members elected with procedures that were fairly transparent and accountable. Their governance was often an amalgam of laity, clergy, and religious; they were marked not by sameness but by diversity. Moreover, they consisted of members who were themselves responding to their prayerful experience of encountering the mercy of God; that subjective experience was the warrant for their own decision to serve those in need. In that innovation they were boundary-breakers: whether by reforming prisons, sheltering sex workers, or offering respite for those with syphilis, they embraced the outcast and actually incorporated them into the city that tried to keep them apart. Finally, they set the foundations for a new form of relationality that made the stranger familial. They led many Christians into a brave new world.

II. SALAMANCA AND BEYOND

We cannot conclude this consideration of early modern developments without taking note of the School of Salamanca and, among its many influences, its interest in developing the foundations of international law, for in this way it provided a final pathway to modernity.

These foundations did not develop in the context of idle speculation; rather, Spanish Dominicans who accompanied the Spanish explorers-turned-conquistadores became appalled at the conduct of their fellow Christians. On December 21, 1511, on the Fourth Sunday of Advent on the island of Hispaniola (today, the Dominican Republic), Antonio Montesino, OP (ca. 1475–1540),[12] delivered a sermon of incredible clarity against the emerging *encomienda* system of the Spanish conquistadores.[13] Informing his Spanish congregation that they "are all in mortal sin and live and die in it, because of the cruelty and tyranny they practice among these innocent peoples," he asked them,

> Tell me by what right of justice do you hold these Indians in such a cruel and horrible servitude? On what authority have you waged such detestable wars against these people who dwelt quietly and peacefully on their own lands? Wars in which you have destroyed such an infinite number of them by homicides and slaughters never heard of before. Why do you keep them so oppressed and exhausted, without giving them enough to eat or curing them of the sicknesses they incur from the excessive labor you give them, and they die, or rather you kill them, in order to extract and acquire gold every day. And what care do you take that they receive religious instruction and come to know their God and creator, or that they be baptized, hear mass, or observe holidays and Sundays? Are they not men? Do they not have rational souls? Are you not bound to love them as you love yourselves? How can you lie in such profound and lethargic slumber? Be sure that in your present state you can no more be saved than the Moors or Turks who do not have and do not want the faith of Jesus Christ.[14]

The sermon was as momentous as the actions that were being described and judged. It was transcribed by Bartolomé de las Casas (1484–1566), a young priest, lawyer, and canonist sitting in the congregation that day. De las Casas in fact defended the *encomienda* system, but in time Montesino's sermon would prompt de las Casas to a conversion in his own life.[15] In fact, after he entered the Dominicans, de las Casas would work with Montesino in Spain to secure the rights of the Native Americans. The sermon would also impact two other figures, notably the island governor Diego Columbus (1479–1526), the son of the explorer, and Francisco de Vitoria, OP (1483–1546), who later, at Salamanca, contested the validity of the Spanish claim to dominion over the Americas. After being denounced repeatedly to King Ferdinand II (1578–1637), Montesino returned briefly to Spain to convince the king of the atrocities that were happening in his kingdom on the other side of the Atlantic. In response, the king met Montesino, heard his reports, and wrote the Law of Burgos (1513), designed to bring greater justice to the system. Unfortunately, the law was not enforced.

About twenty years after Montesino's sermon, the Dominicans developed at Salamanca a school that was somewhat different than what we have seen elsewhere. At Salamanca, there was certainly casuistry, but much more evidently than casuistry and its philosophical sources in nominalism was the reemergence of Scholasticism. That return to Scholasticism launched foundational pathways into the intersection of law and ethics. As we head to the end of this enormous century, we find ourselves back at the beginning. We now treat those who, when trying to find something more systemic than casuistry, returned to Thomas Aquinas's teachings on law and developed them radically so as to enter a realm that had not much troubled the Middle Ages: the unexplored idea of what rights a newly encountered people have.

The Roman Empire had different approaches to the laws of citizens, allied peoples, and slaves or enemies. In the Middle Ages, Jewish, Christian, and Muslim territories sometimes tried to work out a respectful coexistence based on an acknowledgment of each other's legal systems. The encounters by Europeans of non-Europeans brought new questions. When other people seem not to have had their own positive laws, do they have rights? That they do is the bedrock of Montesino's claim.

Later, at Salamanca, Vitoria, using Thomas, entered a space that Thomas never entertained between the natural law, which is a participation in the eternal law through right reason, and the positive law that has its own evident authority in its own actual laws articulated and promulgated by its regional lawmakers. Here, pursuing a concept he called *ius gentium*, the law or rights of the nations that had some roots in Roman imperial practice, Vitoria began to articulate how questions of sovereignty are resolved. As he does, he will lay the foundations for others after him in Salamanca, Paris, Oxford, and elsewhere for how the world might adjudicate future claims for a new world order. After an extensive look at the foundations that Vitoria provided, we will conclude with a word on de las Casas (1484–1566).

Francisco de Vitoria (1483–1546)

At twenty-one, Vitoria became a Dominican. Three years later, he was sent to Paris where he began studying nominalism. In time he came under the influence of Peter Crockaert (1465–1514), who had studied under Mair and was an ardent nominalist; by 1503 Crockaert entered the Dominican order, abandoned nominalism, and became an extraordinary advocate for the renewal of the studies of Thomas Aquinas. By 1509, as a lecturer at the Collège Saint Jacques, Crockaert replaced Lombard's *Sentences* with Thomas's *Summa* as the foundational theological text for his lectures, thus opening the gates for a "second Thomism" in Paris. In Italy, Tommaso de Vio, or "Cajetan" (1469–1534), implemented a similar change.[16]

By 1512, Vitoria similarly abandoned nominalism for Thomism, and while under Crockaert's direction edited with him their edition of the *Secunda secundae* of Thomas. By 1516, Vitoria began teaching in Paris and replaced the *Sentences* of Lombard with the *Summa* of Thomas as his foundational text, particularly focusing on the *Secunda secundae*. In 1523, he became professor of theology and director of studies in Valladolid. In 1526, he was elected to the prime chair of theology at Salamanca, the most prestigious theological appointment in Spain, where he lectured each morning to roughly nine hundred students. Like Crockaert and Cajetan, Vitoria too made the *Summa* Salamanca's primary theological text.[17]

In 1527, he was summoned along with thirty-two other Spanish theologians to Valladolid to discuss the orthodoxy of Erasmus's *Enchiridion* (1503), which had just been translated into Spanish. Vitoria found no heresy, but a good deal of unhelpful ambiguity in Erasmus, and as one of Vitoria's commentators writes, thought him "a jumped-up grammarian meddling in affairs he did not understand."[18] Fortunately for Erasmus, the plague interrupted, ending the proceedings without verdict. Events like this one, however, cast doubts on the claims of some commentators that Vitoria was influenced by the humanists. The man who referred to Lorenzo Valla (1407–57) as a "charlatan" had little interest in them.[19]

For Vitoria's courses at Salamanca he employed a Parisian teaching method of lecturing slowly and deliberately (*dictatum*) so as to allow students to transcribe his words verbatim. Subsequently he never published any of his courses, though his students' excellent notes, or *reportationes*, remain.[20] During his twenty-year tenure, he also gave *relectiones*, which were polished public lectures held on significant feasts that drew enormous crowds that, again, were only published as *reportationes* in 1577, nearly ten years after his death. We will consider several of these disputations.

Between his popular courses and his disputations, Vitoria's evident brilliance prompted his disciples to identify him as the founder of a school of thought, the School of Salamanca.[21] To appreciate Vitoria's significant contributions to theological ethics, we need to see how a series of claims established the foundations of his thought. These claims developed as Vitoria worked through the *Secunda secundae* of Thomas and "brought politics together with moral theology in original ways."[22] Along the way we will look specifically at his *relectiones* "On Civil Power" (1528), "On Dietary Laws-or Self-Restraint" (1537), "On the American Indian" (1539), and "On the Law of War" (1539).

First, we saw earlier Thomas's break from Augustine on the acquired virtues. Unlike Augustine, Thomas believed that any person—believer or not, Jew, Muslim, Greek, Roman, even an agnostic, atheist, or heretic—could develop the acquired virtues. The theological virtues belonged to the supernatural order, were not acquired but infused, and could only be developed by grace through the gift of charity *after* the gift of faith. But without faith and charity, an ordinary person could develop justice, temperance, fortitude, and prudence. In a similar way, Vitoria saw the temporal order as different from the spiritual order and that each had its own sphere of influence as well as its own end. As Andreas Wagner notes, "One of the main tenets of Vitoria's legal and political theory was a strong separation of secular and spiritual responsibilities."[23]

Second, following Thomas, Vitoria was firmly opposed to Reformed positions on law; for him law derived its claim or power from the order of creation and not from the order of redemption or grace, as many Reformers would claim. This meant that the authority of a prince did not change if he were to sin or apostatize. Laws and rights belonged to the human community from God inasmuch as the community was constituted by God as created, rational human beings. Thus, a Christian prince had no right to overtake the dominion of another prince solely on grounds of the latter's faith or state on sinfulness, even in the case of sins against nature, like sodomy. Otherwise, with a touch of irony, Vitoria wrote, "The King of France has a perfect right to conquer Italy."[24]

Third, as Brian Tierney notes, Vitoria developed the idea of "subjective rights," arguing that they came from Thomas, but that Vitoria certainly claimed, advocated, and developed them. In Thomas one finds that justice determines the right that is due to another. But in Vitoria the right is located not primarily in the objective judgment of justice but rather in the nature of human beings. He identified the right in the human subject. This meant that rights belonged to human communities because they were human. Within the human was the capacity to "have" rights: "Whoever has a faculty in accordance with the laws has a right."[25] Tierney concludes that while others saw rights as vaguely diffused throughout creation, Vitoria's insistence that these rights belonged precisely to the human became a "key element in the construction of political theories."[26] Renzo Gerardi rightly insists that Vitoria proposed effectively a moral theology based on human dignity that had its origins in creation, the work of God. Herein Vitoria established the fundamental principle that human dignity and, therein, the equality of all persons and peoples, is founded in being created in the image and likeness of God.[27]

Fourth, as Wagner points out, this idea of rights extended to the right to self-determination or political sovereignty, what Vitoria called *dominium* (dominion), and this right was essential for the growth and development of a people.[28] As we will see shortly, dominion is that which Vitoria argued the Indians had before they were encountered. This was an extraordinary position in that already the Bulls of Donation (1493) by Pope Alexander VI (1431–1503; r. 1492–1503) bequeathed the lands of the Americas to the Portuguese and Spanish monarchs.[29] On that gift, the Spanish and Portuguese conquistadores did not bother to presuppose that the Indians had dominion nor a right to it. (Neither, for that matter, did the popes.) As Roger Ruston notes, they all believed, until Vitoria argued otherwise, that papal and imperial authority had the right of conquest built into their obligation to evangelize and that this authority was a summons to be recognized and confirmed.[30]

Fifth, as Grégoire Catta notes, if each people have the same rights by force of being human, then implicitly, each share an equality with one another. Catta writes, "By arguing that the Indians have their own right of dominion, Vitoria is thus making strong claims regarding the equality of all human beings: All are bearers of the same rights founded in natural law."[31] Moreover, Vitoria's notion of the equality of individuals led to the equality of peoples and nations. Rightly, Gustavo Gozzi writes, "What explains Vitoria's interest in an investigation of international law is the necessary connection that his doctrine obtains between the equality of men and the equality of peoples: just as human nature grounds the equality of men—for they all have the same element in common—and so it grounds the equality of peoples. And here Vitoria goes so far as to put forward the idea, that just as individuals have rights so do the peoples they belong to."[32]

Sixth, these presuppositions helped Vitoria to develop the foundations of what would later be called international law. He did this by inserting a category between the natural law and positive law, the law of peoples or nations, the *ius gentium*. We learned from Thomas that the natural law is a participation in the eternal law.[33] Through creation God inscribed in the human the natural law such that through right reason we can discern right from wrong. Positive law, however, is found in the articulated laws of a nation, whose legitimacy depends on them being right and promulgated by legitimate authority. Nations are governed by positive laws, but what happens when there are a people whose positive laws are not known or expressed? Or what of a people who have no treaties between themselves and another nation? When a people are "discovered," do they have rights if they have not yet been articulated, promulgated, or known? In 1528, in his *relectio*, "On Civil Power," Vitoria briefly speculated on this *ius*: "The whole world, which is in a sense a commonwealth, has the power to enact laws which are just and convenient to all men; and these make up the law of nations." He then added that "no kingdom may choose to ignore this law of nations."[34] In one sense, the *ius gentium* is that which generates and validates the law-making power of any nation. Here, it is prior (metaphysically speaking) to any positive law that a nation develops and promulgates. In another sense, its own power and validity is rooted in the natural law that through right reason we discover and articulate; *ius gentium* depends on and succeeds (again, metaphysically speaking) the natural law.

Ten years later, in "On the American Indians," Vitoria negated through a process of elimination all Spanish external claims to dominion over the American Indians and left the underlying *ius gentium* to emerge as effectively the midpoint between the natural law and the validity of any nation's specific positive laws. That law of nations established the right of sovereignty for any people, including the Indians, a foundational claim necessary to undergird any nation's law-making authority.[35] Similarly, in "On the Law of War" (1539), he remarked, "As many practices in war are based on the law of nations," and thereby demonstrated that even when all civilities between nations cease and war begins, and the positive laws of warring nations are no longer respected by their enemies, another law, the law of nations, expresses itself, which we recognize again through right reason.[36] In the absence of expressed positive laws, whether in treaties or in other expressions, human authorities through right reason can determine through the law of nations right international conduct. As he noted earlier, "No kingdom can choose to ignore."

The law of nations becomes the foundation of all national laws. It becomes evident precisely when there is a need for law, either when one nation tries to dominate another or when warring nations, suspicious of the other as enemy, need some law other than their own to regulate the war. In both instances, Vitoria reminded us before any nation posits its own laws, the *ius gentium* guaranteed the fundamental law-making capabilities and the subjective rights for all nations. Ruston provides a worthy summary of Vitoria's accomplishment here:

> In rejecting the medieval notion of the universal jurisdiction of the church, the theologians were putting in its place another kind of universalism, that of natural law. The medieval order is being replaced with something recognizably modern: the international rule of law rather than the authority of persons with a divine mandate.

> Theologian-jurists such as Vitoria considered that the law of nations was a direct derivation of natural law, to which everyone might appeal, Christian or not...(i)n putting the whole question of unity of the human race on the natural level, where it is in principle intelligible to everyone on earth, it removed it from the supernatural (religious) level, where it is intelligible only to Christians. It is an argument which opposes all theocracy, all claims that only the "just" have the right to rule and all attempts to impose a single belief system on others by force.[37]

Seventh, if nations as nations enjoy similar rights and if there is equality among nations and among their people, then they should be treated equally. Justice demands such equity. In terms of moral judgments, therefore, proportionality must be held throughout: the due for any judgment must have an equality or proportionality to it. Rightly Wagner notes, "Vitoria insisted on proportionality as a central concept."[38] Proportionality emerged especially in his *relectio* "On the Law of War," where questions of the grounds for war, conduct in war, and the treatment of prisoners are all measured by proportionality. Here, we see in Vitoria how harm reductive his proportionality was, for proportionality restrains the options on those who go to war and on those who win. As Gregory Reichberg notes, Vitoria's *relectio* on war is the first "full-fledged work by a philosopher of note....From Molina and Suárez onwards, philosophers and jurists would use Vitoria's writings as an essential point of writing for normative thinking on international relations."[39]

A final key to appreciating Vitoria's discourses is found by returning again to the conviction he has of the separation between the temporal and the spiritual political orders. Like the difference between the acquired and theological virtues, the two political orders are differentiated by their ends. This meant that in their exercise of authority, the temporal and spiritual powers were limited and that neither authority could abrogate the other's. Specifically, just as papal authority could not be compromised by a temporal sovereign, the right to temporal sovereignty could not be eclipsed by papal prerogatives because the pope "may neither confirm nor rescind civil law."[40] Vitoria was very explicit on this matter. Keeping in mind that popes had for centuries exercised themselves otherwise by making decrees on temporal matters, Vitoria wrote that the pope "gives no power to kings and princes, because no one can give what he does not have."[41] Ruston provides here another helpful summation: Vitoria's *relectiones* "demolished the theory of the universal rule of the pope and the emperor, and with it the right of Christian armies to invade and conquer non-Christian, indigenous peoples, and replaced it with a theory of the universal rule of natural law."[42]

With these presuppositions understood, we still might be surprised by the evident clarity and forthrightness of Vitoria's *relectio* "On the American Indian." Despite the earlier denunciation of Montesino and the subsequent *Law of Burgos*, three later moments raised nothing but disgust in Vitoria: the conquest of Mexico (1520–22), Francisco Pizarro's (1476–1541) massacre at Cajamarca (1532), and the assassination of the Inca Atahuallpa (1502–33). In a letter to the Andalusian Dominican Provincial, Miguel de Arcos, in September 1534, Vitoria wrote, "As for the case of Peru, I must tell you, after a lifetime of studies and long experiences, that no business shocks me or embarrasses me more than the corrupt profits and the affairs of the Indies. Their very mention freezes the blood in my veins."[43] He added, "As far as I understand from eyewitnesses who were personally present during the recent battle with Atahuallpa, neither he nor any of his people, had ever done the slightest injury to the Christians nor given them the least grounds for making war on them....I know of no justification for robbing and plundering the unfortunate victims of defeat of all they possess and even what they do not possess."[44] He concluded, "In truth, if the Indians are not men but monkeys, they are incapable of injury. But if they are men, and our neighbors, and as they claim, vassals of the emperor, I cannot see how to excuse these conquistadores of utter impiety and tyranny."[45] The privileged and informed perspectives of Vitoria and others at Salamanca prompted in Vitoria and others a response to the evident injustices being reported.

Vitoria delivered the discourse "On the American Indians," *De Indis*, in January 1539. As Pagden notes, Vitoria began with the question, "By what right [*ius*] were the barbarians subjected to Spanish rule?" Underlying this question was another one that became manifest: "had the Indians in fact possessed dominion [*dominium*] over their own affairs, and over the territories they occupied before the arrival of the Spaniards?"[46] Significantly, even before he gave this lecture, Vitoria, having rejected papal claims to temporal authority in his earlier *relectiones*, had effectively negated the legitimacy of Bulls of Donation (1493). He raised the question about dominion, however, because of another doubt: "When we hear subsequently of bloody massacres and of innocent individuals pillaged of their possessions and dominion, there are grounds for doubting the justice of what has been done."[47] He noted, "As far as I am aware, no theologian of note or worthy of respect in a matter of such importance has ever been called upon to study this question and provide a solution."[48]

He quickly posed the key question in the first article of the discourse's first question: "Whether these barbarians, before the arrival of the Spaniards had true dominion, public and private."[49] To answer the question he referred to both Lombard's *Sentences* IV. 15 and Aquinas's *Summa* II-II, q. 62. From these he argued that there could only be four possible grounds to deny their dominion: they are sinners, unbelievers, madmen, or insensates.[50] In the next two articles he asked whether sinners or unbelievers can be true masters and concluded, after a variety of experiential, biblical, and other textual claims, that "the barbarians are not impeded from being true masters, publicly and privately, either by mortal sin in general or by the particular sin of unbelief. Nor can Christians use either of these arguments to support their title to dispossess the barbarians of their goods and lands."[51] Turning to madmen and insensates, he argued that the barbarians "have judgment like other men. This is self-evident because they have some order in their affairs: they have properly organized cities, proper marriages, magistrates and overlords, laws, industries and commerce, all of which require the use of reason." He added, "They likewise have a form of religion, and they correctly apprehend things which are evident to other men, which indicates the use of reason."[52] Thus by dissolving the four possible grounds, he concluded that the "barbarians undoubtedly possessed as true dominion" as any Christians and then added, "It would be harsh to deny to them, who have never done us any harm, the rights we concede to Saracens and Jews, who have been continual enemies of the Christian Religion." He concluded the question with this verdict: "Before arrival of the Spaniards these barbarians possessed true dominion, both in public and private affairs."[53]

He then turned to investigate those false titles used to overrule the Indians' sovereignty. One after another he dispelled them: the emperor is "master of the world," the pope donated them ("the pope is not the civil or temporal master of the whole world"),[54] "by right of discovery," the Indians resisted evangelization, they are sinners, they voluntarily submitted to the Spanish, and finally, their lands and their people were a special gift from God to Spain.[55] On the resistance to evangelization, quite apart from his earlier argument that rejected the failure to believe as grounds for losing sovereignty, Vitoria engaged in a critique of the evangelical methods of the conquistadores: "I have not heard of any miracles or signs, nor of any exemplary saintliness of life sufficient to convert them. On the contrary, I hear only of provocations, savage crimes, and multitudes of unholy acts."[56] As on this point so to the other unjust titles, Vitoria made clear that the injustice of each of these titles unleashed a great deal of harm and injustice against the Indians.

He then turned to just titles by which the Indians' sovereignty could have passed to the Spaniards. These are rights that belong, as does dominion itself, to the nascent notion of the *ius gentium*, or the rights of nations. The idea is that if the Indians were by the use of force to reject the Spaniards international rights, then "it is lawful to meet force with force,"[57] a claim that he will stipulate in the later *relectio* "On the Law of War." These just titles are all cast as hypotheticals in the subjunctive, meaning that the title could be appropriated but still a case would have to be argued. The titles included the right to travel, the right to evangelize and to protect converts, the right to defend the innocent from tyrants. These could be contestable at least in giving grounds to the Spaniards to strike back if their attempts to exercise any of these rights were repelled by force from the Indians.[58]

He gave a nod to one right in particular: the right to protect the innocent. Vitoria highlighted the claims' actual probability because in the other instances there was no evidence that the Indians had by force denied the Spaniards' claims. In this instance, however, the victims were Indians themselves. The reported matter of cannibalism and human sacrifice led him to say that the "Spaniards may prohibit the barbarians from practicing any nefarious custom or rite."[59] Here is arguably an early claim for the contemporary "right to protect," that is, when the international community expresses its concern about the treatment of certain constituencies within a particular nation and takes measures to extend protection to the threatened or victimized population.[60] Vitoria's position was not however a surprise; these thoughts were already developed in his earlier *relectio*, "On Dietary Laws, or Self-Restraint" (1537).[61]

Vitoria consistently negated any right or duty to punish a prince for a lack of faith or the presence of sin. As we have seen throughout, "Christians have no greater power over unbelievers than they do over Christians,"[62] but what if the issue was not the state of the prince's soul but the physical harm he brought to an innocent under his rule? Was there a responsibility to intercede? He raised this in the *relectio* "On Dietary Laws" that for the most part dealt with anthropophagy, or cannibalism. There, he argued, "It is lawful to defend an innocent man even if he does not ask us to, or even if he refuses our help." For this reason he held that "Christian princes can declare war on the barbarians because they feed on human flesh and because they practice human sacrifice."[63] Still, he immediately followed this argument with a significant limit, one that effectively would protect the Indians' long-term dominion: "If war is declared on the barbarians by this title, it is not lawful to continue once the cause ceases, nor to seize their goods or their lands on this pretext."[64] Moreover, proportionality meets equity when he added, "By whatever title war is begun on the barbarians, it is not lawful to take it further against them than we should take a war against Christians."[65] He continued this thread with another admonition: a Christian prince "cannot put greater burdens on them than on his Christian subjects, either by imposing heavier taxes or by depriving them of their liberties or by any other form of oppression."[66] Finally, not only may the intervening prince not exercise vicious practices, but he has an obligation to rule virtuously: "a prince who obtains sovereignty over them is obliged to make suitable laws for their commonwealth also in temporal matters, so that their temporal goods are protected and increased, and they are not despoiled of their wealth and gold."[67] Among general closing remarks, he added, "Care should be taken to avoid provoking unrest, not only among the barbarians themselves but also among other peoples."[68]

Unfortunately for the indigenous population, the conquistadores used this claim of "protecting" those innocents as the just title that allowed them the right to stay. Wagner observes, "Unsurprisingly, and indicating Vitoria's momentous influence, Spanish justifications of the conquest and imperial rule of the American colonies subsequently relied more on reports of cannibalism and human sacrifices than on imperial authority, heresy, or natural inferiority of the indigenous."[69] Still, as we can see, the intervention that Vitoria legitimated was not the conquest that happened. One wonders how another Dominican, Bartolomé de las Casas, would have reacted had he been at either *relectio*. De las Casas, as we will see momentarily, lived in the Americas and knew that the Spaniards and the Portuguese would not abide by the terms that Vitoria outlined. Did not Vitoria have ample evidence that they would not? Would de las Casas have not intervened, asking Vitoria the critical question: Is the right to intervene negated when the intervening power shows no tendency at all to respect the dominion of the local people? Vitoria's naiveté here is tragic.

Here, then, is the founder of another pathway to modernity, Francisco de Vitoria, who developed Thomas's scholastic claims so as to develop universal norms that could arbitrate local claims. Of course, there are evident signs of casuistry in his writings as Vitoria descended into the particularities of a situation, but by abandoning Mair and nominalism and endorsing the *Summa*, he offered us another pathway into modernity, one that refuted the claims of the sacral when faced with the problems of the civil or natural and did so systematically. Mair could not do that; he abandoned systematic thinking, but Vitoria reformed the system, developing subjective rights (a clear nod to modernity), insisting on the right to local sovereignty and an international right to dominion, protecting the universal natural law from particular religious claims, and articulating the *ius gentium* as a conceptual device that would allow for a contemporary order that had to be civil, in its explorations and even in its wars. Moreover, he established rights within the *ius gentium* that protected travelers from piracy, and immigrants seeking sanctuary as well as local people from any unjust persecution that violated their persons. From his lectures at Salamanca, Vitoria brought the church and the academy into concourse with the modern world, confronting it with a theological basis for a cosmopolitan view of law. His law of nations provided a new pathway that others, most notably the Jesuit Francisco Suárez, SJ (1548–1617),[70] would traverse.

Bartolomé de las Casas, OP (1484–1566)

Bartolomé de las Casas was born a year after Vitoria and lived twenty years longer. Any study of these two towering figures highlights inevitably how oddly complementary they were as they pursued the same goal of finding rights for the Native Americans. They were both Dominicans, though Vitoria lived in Spain, while de las Casas worked throughout the Americas while returning to Spain frequently to advocate for the Indians. Regarding theology, Vitoria was the leading theologian of his day; de las Casas was trained in theology and in canonical and civil law. Vitoria advocated through his classes and public lectures. De las Casas had four strategies: pastorally serving the Indians, creating alternative communities to the *encomiendas*, excommunicating the Spaniards, and routinely advocating before imperial courts. Though we have transcriptions of his *relectiones*, Vitoria hardly ever wrote; de las Casas was prolific, publishing major texts, from reporting on the treatment of the Indians and arguing in their defense to developing arguments for the right methods of missiology and evangelization. Even their use of language was a study of opposites. Ruston writes of de las Casas, "He never uses one word when several words meaning more or less the same thing spring into his mind. This makes for very long sentences that sometimes read like extracts from a thesaurus. It is the very opposite of the spare, logical style of Vitoria, and it does not lend itself to plain translations."[71]

Fundamentally, their differences are based on experience. While Vitoria developed Thomas Aquinas's theology of law and introduced *ius gentium* into Thomistic thought and therein developed the rights of international law to provide a stable construct in which the Indians could live in a cosmopolitan world, de las Casas was singularly interested in defending the Indians, using twelfth-century canonical laws (*ius communis*) and subsequent civil laws to secure their protection. As a result, Vitoria entertained the right to travel, the right to migrate, and the right to intervene when innocent citizens are the victims of their own leaders. De las Casas knew well the *encomienda* system and believed he needed to develop a wall of rights to protect the Indians and so provided counter rights: a right to defend against attack, a right to refuse uninvited entry, a right to protect their own resources, a right to practice their ancestral worship even if it involves human sacrifice, and a right to receive the gospel without any coercion.[72] Vitoria gave a green light to a brief, focused, limited interventionism on cannibalism; de las Casas saw the green light as nothing but an open door for continued pillage, rapes, and massacres. Still, the similarities are remarkable: when no one else argued it, they both believed that Indians had dominion. Unlike the humanists, neither doubted the humanity or the civil and cultural competency of the Indians. Because of their respect for the Indians, they both disdained the *encomiendas*. Neither advocated the removal of Spain from the New World, but both hoped that the Spaniards would eventually find alternatives to the *encomiendas* and become civil residents in the Americas. They both believed that the Christian faith could only spread by persuasion and right example, not by mass baptisms, or worse, the sword.[73]

Let us now explore some particular details of the phenomenal Bartolomé de las Casas. In 1502, at eighteen years of age, accompanied by his father who was returning to the Americas having been on Christopher Columbus's second journey, Bartolomé de las Casas sailed to Santo Domingo where he lived for five years. There he learned the *encomienda* system, through overseeing his and his father's "properties," which took the form of the Indians themselves and their lands. The Dominican David Orique provides a much-cited definition:

> An *encomienda* was a grant, held by an *encomendero*, of indigenous laborers made to Spanish conquerors and settlers in Spanish America. It was the earliest basis for coerced labor in Spanish colonies, whereby the indigenous population was entrusted to Spanish settlers, who often exploited and mistreated the Indians. The *encomienda* grant brought two rights, tribute and free labor, and two obligations, military service in times of emergency (there was no standing army until 1762) and support of church and priests for the instruction of the Indians.[74]

Before this first voyage, de las Casas began studies for the priesthood. In Santo Domingo, he was fully involved in the *encomiendas*, having secured land and Indians and "traveled the island as a provisioner to the Spanish soldiery."[75] In 1507, he returned to Europe, where he was ordained a priest in Rome and "accompanied the Admiral's older brother Bartholomew Columbus to a private audience with Pope Julius II in order to help secure for Christopher's son Diego the inheritance promised by the Catholic Monarchs, Ferdinand and Isabella."[76] He completed studies in canon law at Salamanca and returned to Santo Domingo, this time sailing with Diego Columbus. De las Casas became a catechist of the native people.

During his second stay, he retained ownership of his laborers, though he was also their catechist. While he saw brutalities against the Indians during both his stays, and although he heard and transcribed the Advent sermon of Friar Antonio Montesino in 1511, he believed until 1514 that holding slaves and being a good Christian were compatible. In 1512, he served as a military chaplain for the Spanish conquest of Cuba and witnessed a massacre of two thousand men, women, and children, and then cared for the survivors. Still, de las Casas was awarded Indians and land in Cuba for his service. The subsequent pillage of Cuba, especially for its gold, was so severe that within months the indigenous economy collapsed. Later in his life, he named the sack of Cuba as the transitional moment when he could see reality as it actually was. On Pentecost of 1514, he expressed his first conversion and renounced his ownership of Indians (returning them to the governor!) and the interisland provisions business. He began preaching against the *encomienda* system, but without success. As Ruston notes, "When he realized that appeals to their Christian conscience were getting nowhere,"[77] he began to plan a return to Spain to lobby the king for change.

In 1515, he returned to Spain with Montesino to petition King Ferdinand but found the king on his deathbed. He began his advocacy before the new, young King Charles I (1500–1558) and aimed to end the *encomienda* system, free the Indians, and allow Spaniards and Indians to live in peace with one another. In 1519, King Charles I, having become the Holy Roman Emperor Charles V, granted him land designed to bring Indian and Spanish farmers together in today's northern Venezuela. Sailing from Spain with a select group of compatriots in 1521, the farming experiment quickly became an absolute disaster. In 1522, after six years of working in Spain toward a successful harmony between two worlds, the defeated de las Casas entered the Dominicans, his second conversion, realizing that as a member of an established religious order, he would have better impact in assisting the Indians than as a solitary priest.

After a sustained study of theology and law, he began to develop an argument regarding the evangelization of the Indians, *The Only Way*, which insists that faith in Jesus Christ can only be proposed not through force but through gentleness and right modeling.[78] One cannot fully appreciate the significance of this approach; Rustin reports that "some ecclesiastics of New Spain and even the territory of Chiapas had two or three cages in their house in each of which they put six or seven Indians, and with whips and riding crops in hand they taught them doctrine."[79] Less severe, but still problematic, were the mass baptisms by Franciscans, which de las Casas critiqued: Baptism without sufficient understanding was not valid. De las Casas insisted, using Thomas Aquinas, that the human had a natural aptitude for God and that any progress toward God had to respect the human capacity; neither force nor ignorance was a valid means of evangelizing.[80] He brought this argument to a conference in Oaxaca (1536) between Dominican and Franciscan bishops, and later the Dominican leadership in Mexico sent him to Guatemala where he tried again to set up a community in the New World, free of the *encomiendas*.

There, in 1537, he convinced the governor to allow him and a dozen Dominicans to enter an area where the native people successfully repelled all Spanish conquest called Tuzulutlan, or by the Spaniards, *tierra de guerra* (the land of war). De las Casas negotiated that no Spanish soldiers could enter the region for five years and that Indians who became Christians would be free forever from the threat of the *encomiendas*. De las Casas's teachings from *The Only Way* proved very successful with many, including local chiefs, becoming Christians while establishing churches throughout the region, leading it to become known as *Verapaz* (true peace). In the following year, he was called back to Mexico and then would be sent to Spain to recruit more Dominicans.

As de las Casas went to Guatemala, a fellow Dominican in Mexico, Bernardino de Minaya (1489–1562), sailed to Rome to argue that the native people were capable of receiving and understanding the faith, should not be forced into baptism, and should be free of any threats to their freedom or their land. In response, Pope Paul III on May 29, 1537, issued the encyclical *Sublimis Deus*, in which he first stated that God created humanity with the capacity to yearn for and to seek God through understanding, but that presently others were claiming that the Indians were but "dumb brutes" and should be treated as such. He then declared,

> The Indians are truly men and that they are not only capable of understanding the Catholic Faith but, according to our information, they desire exceedingly to receive it. Desiring to provide ample remedy for these evils, We define and declare by these Our letters…the said Indians and all other people who may later be discovered by Christians, are by no means to be deprived of their liberty or the possession of their property, even though they be outside the faith of Jesus Christ; and that they may and should, freely and legitimately, enjoy their liberty and the possession of their property; nor should they be in any way enslaved.[81]

Undoubtedly, de las Casas's *The Only Way* and reports from Mexico and the plans for Guatemala convinced the pope against the campaigns of others, including Spanish Dominicans and the cardinal archbishop of Seville and the President of the Council of the Indies, Juan García de Loaysa y Mendoza (1478–1546), that the Indians had no such capacity for freedom. The document became known as the "Magna Carta of the Indians."[82]

In 1540, de las Casas returned to Spain, first visiting Salamanca where he reported to Vitoria and others there about the mass baptisms by the Franciscans, securing from his fellow Dominicans theological support for his approach in *The Only Way*, and then beginning to write his *A Short Account of the Destruction of the Indies* to present to the Spanish court as an account of the Spanish conquest.[83] He also developed a plan to present to the king proposing that the Indians would remain under him free, like the citizens of Spain. De las Casas saw in the emperor someone who could protect the Indians from any dominating forces including his own soldiers. The native people could have their own cultural and even religious traditions and have possession of their land and resources. They could be taxed, but he built into his argument the critical provision that political freedom was necessary if they were ever to become

Christians.[84] Ruston writes, "This is his first extensive treatment of political liberty, the liberty that is necessary to any people if they are to accept the gospel."[85]

In the aftermath of the papal encyclical, coupled with recent reports of the brutality of the ongoing Spanish conquest, Charles V convened in Valladolid a consultation in 1542. De las Casas was well prepared with his proposal and his account of the destruction of the Indies. On November 20, 1542, the emperor issued the New Laws, freeing the Indians from slavery and gradually dismantling the *encomienda* system. Ruston writes, "The New Laws of the Indies has been the only body of laws in western colonial history which had as its main content a declaration of the rights and freedoms of the indigenous peoples. Nothing like it was ever produced by the French, Dutch or British states."[86]

Unfortunately, the laws had little impact. The *encomenderos* revolted and refused to abide by them. As he prepared to return to the New World, de las Casas was consecrated in Seville as the bishop of Chiapas on March 31, 1544. When he arrived in the diocese there were forty-five Dominican friars to assist in the work. De las Casas decided to enforce the content of the New Laws, threatening to excommunicate anyone in his diocese for mistreating Indians and to withhold absolution to slave owners and *encomenderos*, even on their death beds, unless all their slaves were set free and their property returned to the Indians.

On October 20, 1545, the New Laws were repealed by the emperor. While the *encomenderos* celebrated and believed themselves validated, de las Casas insisted on his episcopal authority to withhold the sacraments from slave owners and in fact authored a *Confessario*, an instruction for the priests in his diocese to follow his orders.[87] The *encomenderos* were appalled, and opposition to de las Casas became stronger than ever. In December 1546, he left his diocese, appointed a vicar, and set sail for Europe for the last time, arriving first in Portugal and then Spain in November 1547.

In Portugal, de las Casas became familiar with the African slave trade that had started in the beginning of the fifteenth century. Earlier in his life, in 1517, believing mistakenly that African slaves were fundamentally prisoners of war and therefore "legitimately" enslaved, de las Casas posited their availability as a substitute for the Indians in working on the *encomiendas*. He did this on several other occasions in his defense of the Indians. Here historians later argued that the defender of the Indians was hardly a defender of the Africans; rather, he endorsed their enslavement. As Lawrence Clayton notes, the 1517 position "eventually left a black scar on his reputation for the next five centuries."[88]

Still, Clayton notes that African slave trade came neither from de las Casas nor the Spanish but rather from the Portuguese who were long involved in it from the first half of the fifteenth century.[89] Moreover, researchers like Helen Parish, Francis Sullivan, Clayton, and no less than Gustavo Gutiérrez have argued at length that when de las Casas arrived in Portugal in 1547 and saw the extent and awfulness of the slave trade, he condemned it and all slave trade.[90] Furthermore, he acknowledged his own wrongness as he wrote about himself in his *History of the Indies*. Ruston quotes de las Casas: "After he found out, he would not have proposed it for all the world, because blacks were enslaved unjustly, tyrannically, right from the start, exactly as the Indians had been." Ruston comments, "He specifically includes the Moors in this retraction and denounces the slave wars in the strongest terms. Even those who have reservations about Las Casas admit that this was probably the first such denunciation of black slavery by a European."[91]

Nevertheless, we have to acknowledge that though he may have been the first to decry the African slave trade a century before the abolitionist movement started, until 1547 de las Casas was complicit in the wrongful commerce of human beings through the chattel of slavery, even while he was a heroic defender of another people.

After he left Portugal, de las Casas learned that in Spain his *Confessario* was taken to infer that, inasmuch as the king had inherited slaves, he too was a target of de las Casas's rules. In 1548, the Spanish court ordered the burning of the manual, which de las Casas's Franciscan adversaries in Mexico did. To his credit, he continued his argument that slavery was wrong, that the Indians should be free, that the Spanish should live peaceably with the natives, and that the Crown should protect all.

At the same time, Juan Ginés de Sepúlveda (1494–1573), a humanist, tried to publish his *Democrates secundus sive de iustis belli causis*, his argument for the just grounds for taking conquest of the Americas and that the Indians existed to be slaves. The School of Salamanca opposed its publication. Nevertheless, the *encomenderos* saw Sepúlveda as their spokesman. Like many humanists, he took from Aristotle's first book of *The Politics* the argument of the condition of a slave:

> The slave is a living instrument, and the lifeless instruments are used by him; he is the first of a series. He is an instrument of action, not of production, for he does not produce; he only lives and serves his master, and life is action. But he is also a possession [and therefore the agent of another]; for he is intended by nature to belong to his master, though separable from him. He may be defined, "a human being who is a possession and likewise an instrument of action."[92]

He used accounts of cannibalism and human sacrifice to strengthen his argument.

In 1550, the emperor and the Council of the Indies called for a debate before theologians and jurists again at Valladolid to determine "how conquests may be conducted justly and with security of conscience."[93] The debate began with Sepúlveda's argument from his unpublished work. The Indians are barbaric, sunk in vice, and cruel; according to natural law they should submit to those who are wiser so as to be corrected and punished for their sins of idolatry and human sacrifice; they should be protected from their own leaders who offer them up for sacrifice; and they should be conquered so as to become Christian.[94] De las Casas gave a five-day-long response, eventually published as *In Defense of the Indians*.[95] He proved that they had and enjoyed dominion and that they had a natural right to their lands and goods but also "to worship according to their own lights, even if it involves human sacrifice and eating people, until such time as they are persuaded that it is wrong."[96] Invoking some of his earlier positions, de las Casas insisted that they had counter rights: a right to defend against attack; a right to refuse entry; a right to protect their own resources; a right to practice their ancestral worship, even if it involves human sacrifice; and a right to receive the gospel without any coercion.[97]

Neither side was declared the winner, and each argued further his position. In 1552, after Valladolid, de las Casas finished and published the text that he had begun for the first meeting in Valladolid in 1542: *A Short Account of the Destruction of the Indies.* The book had enormous influence across Europe, and by 1600 it had been translated and published in English, Flemish, French, German, and Latin. De las Casas spent the rest of his life near the Spanish court advocating for the Indians, keeping the emperor from giving the *encomenderos* any further validation. He died in Madrid on July 18, 1566.[98]

Vitoria and de las Casas in many ways validate each other despite their differences. Both point to modernity: Vitoria's cosmopolitanism based on equity and de las Casas's pastoral and legal defense of an indigenous people. Rightly, Gutiérrez saw in de las Casas the instinct for the liberation theology that he developed four hundred years later, but de las Casas needed the Dominicans as much as Vitoria needed the witnessing of Montesino and de las Casas. The man who stayed in Salamanca drew much strength from the one who saw Santo Domingo, Puerto Plata, Cuba, Panama, Guatemala, Nicaragua, and Mexico. The ethical credibility of each effectively depended on the other. What we will see evolving in the next and last chapters is how eventually, like these two men combined into one, the ethicist becomes both a teacher and a pastoral companion to a church seeking to do God's will.

Chapter Seven

Reforming Moral Theology

From the Eighteenth Century to the Second Vatican Council

We begin this chapter with two rather significant events in the eighteenth century: the ministry of St. Alphonsus Maria de Liguori, who founded the Congregation of the Most Holy Redeemer (better known as the Redemptorists) in 1749, and the suppression of the Jesuits in 1773.[1] These events have long-standing repercussions in the field of theological ethics. Then we turn to the moral manuals, first appreciating them in the context of the different religious communities from which they came, and then looking at the manualist tradition in the first half of the twentieth century. We next consider the matter of reform as it begins in the nineteenth century, develops in the twentieth century, and prepares for Vatican II. At the same time, we note the resistance of American and other English-speaking moralists to the post–World War II European reformers, an opposition most apparent in the mid-1960s. We briefly consider the impact of Vatican II, in particular on *Humanae Vitae.* We conclude with a reflection on the relationship between history and progress, looking at the writings of John Henry Newman, Dom Odon Lottin, Bernard Lonergan, and John O'Malley, among others.

I. ALPHONSUS MARIA DE LIGUORI (1696–1787)

I suggest that the worthy forerunner of the ministerial papacy of Pope Francis is not a Jesuit, nor even St. Francis after whom he is named, but the Redemptorist Alphonsus Liguori.[2] In fact, if you remember, we concluded the last chapter suggesting that Vitoria and de las Casas were near-perfect complements, both interested in theology and the law but one who stayed in the ivory tower of Salamanca and the other on-site in the New World and the Spanish court as pastor and advocate. Liguori is like the best of each in one person, a composite figure; an advocate for those on the margins though a significant scholar who wrote more than one hundred books. He was not simply a casuist like Mair or a summist like Toledo; he was as ministerial as he was a moralist. There's no one quite like him in moral theology before his time. He integrated the care of souls both in teaching and practice. That balance that he sought was also achieved in the arguments he developed: in the probabilist debate, he feared the laxism that could emerge from probabilism, but he feared even more so the rigorism that emerged from probabiliorists. Lombard might have had a bit of the balance or even Erasmus or de las Casas, but Alphonsus's inexhaustible dedication to both ministry and moral theology was unparalleled. He became such a prototype for those in the field that he was made patron saint of moral theologians and confessors in 1950 by Pope Pius XII (1876–1958; r. 1939–58).

Alphonsus was the first of eight children born into a Neapolitan family of nobility. He received his doctorate in law at the University of Naples before his seventeenth birthday. After a three-year apprenticeship, he became a successful lawyer, winning every case during the next eight years. During this time he belonged to the Congregation of Doctors that followed the model of a confraternity: they prayed together and did a set work of charity. Interestingly their work was attending at the Hospital for the Incurables in Naples, the famed network of hospitals that we saw in the last chapter, founded by Ettore Vernazza throughout Italy, to care for people with syphilis.[3] His biographer, Fredrick Jones, notes, "It was here that he first experienced the real happiness to be found in God's service and it was here that his desire to become a priest developed and came to a positive conclusion."[4]

In 1723, the extraordinarily successful lawyer lost his first case, a rather extraordinary one mired in politics, bribery, and a variety of other issues, which prompted Alphonsus to leave the profession directly and begin studies for ordination. During this time, he joined another confraternity, The Congregation for the Apostolic Missions, or the Propaganda. The works of this confraternity took the form of preaching the good news of Christ's salvation, a popular form of evangelization that would in time shape his own ideas for the founding of the Redemptorists.

While active in the preaching missions, he joined a third confraternity, the Confraternity "dei Bianchi," located right next door to the Hospital for the Incurables.[5] This confraternity of priests and laity attended to the spiritual needs of prisoners; more specifically, the sacerdotal members accompanied those prisoners sentenced to death (the members wore white, whence the name of the confraternity) and subsequently attended to the needs of the widows and orphans. Later, in 1775 and 1777, Liguori published a set of instructions, *Advice for Priests Who Minister to Those Condemned to Death*,[6] noting that such men merited the "greatest sympathy" among any about to die, because of "four anxieties": the fear of eternal punishment for their crimes; the dread of the execution itself, cutting short their lives; the public shaming of the execution itself; and the profound regret of leaving family, wives, parents, and children without benefit of support and protection.[7]

Alphonsus's preparatory studies for priesthood were fairly impressive; the faculty with whom he studied were well educated and relatively open minded, supporting, for example, the habit of frequent communion.[8] Alphonsus's training stood in contrast to many other contemporary Neapolitan priests. As Jones notes, at the time, men in Naples who became clergy did so often for economic reasons and were often "unlettered." Moreover, they used the rigorism of Jansenism that gave them a sense of authority, though in reality they understood little. According to Jones, Pope Benedict XIV (1675–1758; r. 1740–58) suggested that some of the local clergy "did not know whether the Trinity was a mystery of their faith or the name of a mountain."[9]

Alphonsus encountered rigorism in no other area of theology except moral theology, and that subject was based on François

Genet's (1640–1702) famed *Morale de Grenoble*.[10] The Redemptorist historian Louis Vereecke comments that in the middle of the seventeenth century there developed a "laxism" in moral teachings that prompted a rigorist reaction called Jansenism. That Jansenism informed Genet's work.[11] Renzo Gerardi notes Genet assumed that only the most arguable position was legitimate, that is, an extreme form of probabiliorism. Gerardi adds that Genet routinely urged in the confessional that priests systematically withhold absolution.[12]

We saw in the last chapter that de las Casas withheld absolution from those who refused to release their slaves and that his position was tolerated by few in authority. In Genet's case, the matter was hardly something as gravely sinful as enslaving a person; rather, he urged withholding absolution for almost any sin, from an impure thought to breaking the law of abstaining from meat on certain days of prescription. This practice of withholding absolution was among the most detrimental of all ministerial practices because the confessor effectively judged that despite a penitent's confession of sorrow, the confessor believed the penitent was still not sufficiently sorrowful. To systematically make that judgment and urge other priests to follow it routinely prompted in the faithful grave doubts in themselves as to whether they were sufficiently sorrowful, and many became notoriously scrupulous. Among them was Alphonsus himself. Manualists like Genet created a pathological conscience and then with the assistance of priests further tormented the people of God by withholding absolution. At no time did Alphonsus engage in the practice. Though he originally defended Genet's rigorist teachings, he soon abandoned them as he entered into ministry.[13] Although his own scruples remained, Alphonsus recognized that a scrupulous conscience could not find health or truth in rigorism and thereby appreciated the personal and social significance of not capitulating to the rigorists.

Ordained in December 1726, Liguori lived like most other priests in his family home. In 1729, however, he was invited to move into the Chinese College, a seminary that was developed for the education of priests seeking to minister in China. Jones writes that it was precisely from the start of his residence in the Chinese College that Alphonsus's "kindness and understanding as a confessor first became known; penitent after penitent was moved by his sympathetic environment."[14] Hearing confessions was in the context of his overall ministry. During this time he began to serve the poorest of Naples' poor, the *lazzaroti* as they were called. In their neighborhoods, he developed with fellow priests various centers, "evening chapels" they were called, to support pastorally these people through catechesis and other forms of spiritual and corporal works of mercy. These centers were overseen by thoughtful young people and spread throughout the kingdom of Naples. Here his ministry took greater shape: he brought to the poor the good news of salvation and in the confessional accompanied them in their struggle to lead upright lives. Significantly, he took seriously the complexities of their own questions of conscience.

Alphonsus's ministerial disposition not to withhold grace but to extend it especially to the margins became the mark of his ministry. The great Spanish Redemptorist and moralist Marciano Vidal reflects on the first twenty years of Liguori's ministry from 1729 to 1749 and then on to 1765. He investigates how it was that this man who was taught the rigorist model and who suffered from a scrupulous conscience was in his ministry mercifully disposed to bring the presence of Christ into the lives of the poor. He names three key influences of Liguori that shaped him: outstanding personal spiritual directors who helped him to understand and to overcome in some measure the scruples; the readings he did of Jesuits writing moral theology; and his own experience with other priests of entering into the lived complexities of the people they were serving.[15] Ministry effectively validated Liguori's choice: he saw the impact of grace on these long-neglected and overlooked people. Vidal names the form of his ministry a "pastoral kindness" (*Benignidad pastoral*) that stood in the eighteenth century as a contradiction to the black tide of rigorism.[16] Complementing Vidal's essay, Salvino Raponi underlines the universality of Liguori's ministerial work: the news of our Redemption was for all. By going to the margins, Liguori was leading others to see the broad expanse of redemptive grace.[17]

Arguably the most important biographer of Alphonsus, the French Redemptorist Théodule Rey-Mermet, provides an even more focused set of descriptions. First, Alphonsus campaigned against the withholding of absolution:

> Do not frighten penitents by delaying their absolution from month to month, as is the fashion. This does not help

> them but results in their loss. When a sinner acknowledges his sins and despises them, he must not be left alone to fight against temptation. He must be helped, and the best help is the grace of the sacraments. The sacrament compensates for the failing powers of the sinner. It is the teaching of the Jansenists to defer absolution from month to month. Far from drawing people to the sacraments, they make the sacraments useless to them.[18]

Rey-Mermet explains the foundational assumptions for Alphonsus's pastoral theology: his trust in the mercy of God, in "the good will of the sinner who has gone to the trouble of going to confession," and in the effective and transforming grace of the sacraments of reconciliation and the Eucharist.[19] For Alphonsus, then, the mercy of Christ was not to be hoarded; rather, it was to be always made available. For him, withholding mercy was an act against Jesus Christ. Rey-Mermet writes, "Do the preachers and confessors continue the work of the Savior, or do they have another 'profession'? He wanted sinners to be received with open arms. Jesus, he said, did not do otherwise."[20]

Rey-Mermet notes that Alphonsus was not looking simply to grant poor sinners forgiveness but rather to provide assistance and accompaniment to bring them into the life of holiness, particularly the social outcasts of the slums of Naples as well as the "forsaken country people."[21] He names the guidance that Alphonsus provided as "a merciful prudence" not unlike Vidal's pastoral kindness.[22] This prudence sought to understand the complexities of challenges that the ordinary poor person faced: to see that what the poor were required to do had to be resolved within the array of actual options that the poor had. This appreciation for the reality of the struggling Christian was the key focus of both his pastoral and theological ministry.

Meanwhile, the priests at the "evening chapels" began to form intentionally a religious community. Jones, noting that "the founders of religious orders bear little resemblance to the religious portrait we paint of them," comments that starting in 1729, when Liguori moved to the Chinese College, he was "in the depths of spiritual darkness, in his personal journey toward God, tortured with scruples, unsure of his future, hesitant and indecisive as he found himself playing a key role in the establishment of a new missionary society."[23] By 1732, the group had dedicated itself as the Missionaries of the Most Holy Savior, and eleven years later seven within the group took first religious vows and elected Liguori as their leader, a position he held for forty-four years until his death in 1787. In 1749, Pope Benedict XIV gave them formal approval and named them The Congregation of the Most Holy Redeemer.

Liguori's priestly ministry and eventual leadership greatly informed his theology. He wrote on three areas: moral theology, systematic theology, and ascetical or spiritual theology. Rightly, Sabatino Majorano explains that one studies Alphonsus's moral theology "in light of the fundamental traits of Alphonsus's thought: pastoral activity which begins always with the poorest and most abandoned people, the priority and the indispensable character of prayer, a practice of love which places even the most lowly on the path to sanctity and redemption understood as an 'economy' or mercy."[24] Majorano's integrationist claim is important: for Alphonsus, his work in theology was not meant to be three separate fields. Rather, like his pastoral ministry, the spiritual, the moral, and the sacramental overlapped and were mutually dependent. We will see shortly, however, the radical separation of these fields later on.

His work in moral theology was effectively about supporting the guided conscience of the Christian. The key virtue that the person needed to walk in conscience with the Redeemer was prudence.[25] Learning prudence required humble guidance, good mentoring, prayer, and the pursuit of the mean between the extremes of laxism and rigorism. That balance was not between any conceptual extremes but rather the actual extremes that the Christian faced. In that sense, prudence was merciful by descending into the particularity of the Christian's context. Moral theology had to be guided by the mean; a frustrating ideal was as counterproductive as withholding absolution.[26]

Recently, Raphael Gallagher edited and translated from the Latin Alphonsus's "Treatise on Conscience" the first part of Alphonsus's much larger *Theologia Moralis*, first written in 1748, with a second edition appearing in 1753. In 1765, after years of debate and discussion on his "equiprobabilism," he published a synopsis of his own thesis on the moderate use of probable opinion. That became incorporated into the sixth edition of *Theologia Moralis* within the

"Treatise on Conscience" in 1767.[27] In the manualist tradition, often one's own moral manual was built on another moralist's manual, effectively being a commentary on the prior one. This practice mirrored how, from the thirteenth until the sixteenth century, every Master theologian's first scholastic work was a commentary on Lombard's *Sentences*. Until the *Summae*, the *Commentaries* like the earlier *Glossae* were literally edited extensions of earlier theologians' works. The manualists followed in that tradition. Alphonsus used the Jesuit Hermann Busenbaum's (1600–1668) *Medulla Theologiae Moralis* for his *Theologia Moralis*. Rey-Mermet notes that Alphonsus chose Busenbaum's probabilist text because it "came most closely to the ideal he was trying to reach."[28] Busenbaum's work, from 1650 to 1770, saw over two hundred editions.[29]

At the beginning of his preface, Alphonsus explained, "The specific aim of our tiny Congregation of the Most Holy Redeemer is to be free to give missions." That work "comes with the duty of directing consciences by instructions and confessions." Toward this end he wrote this work on moral matters, "that would navigate a middle way between views that were too rigid or too lax."[30] Clearly, his concern was more with rigorism. After all, laxists have no real interest or respect for the law in the first place. He noted, "Both extremes are very dangerous. The first opens up, through laxity, the wide road to perdition." The second "threatens souls with ruin in a double way—an erroneous conscience and desperation. Many having heard this rigid doctrine, slip into mortal sin or, thinking there is mortal sin when there is not, are terrified with the enormous difficulty of it all. Imagining that it is not possible for them to be saved in that way, they interiorly abandon caring about their salvation."[31]

Remembering the difference between internal certitude (the reasonableness of the argument) and external certitude (the authority of the casuist), we can appreciate Liguori's own impulse: "In the choice of opinions, my main concern was always to prefer reasoning before authority."[32] Gallagher notes that when Alphonsus invoked the authority of earlier theologians, he was attracted to those who insisted on "the practicality of theological discourse, the inner link between spiritual and moral progress, and the need to keep theological language as accessible as possible." Conscience for him then was the practice of making decisions guided by merciful prudence.[33]

That reasoning is what prompted him to move away from generalizations and to descend into the particulars. Rightly Gallagher notes that "the choice was not conscience *or* law, but conscience *within law. Mea conscientia*, for Alphonsus is not the lonely drama it was for Luther; it is played out within the community of the Church."[34] Gallagher also notes that in the context of a law-based discipline, Alphonsus developed a conception of moral theology: "The careful way Alphonsus outlines the steps in reaching a moral decision within a system of principles guarantees the dignity of personal conscience. The claim of law to its rights is relatively straightforward. The claims of conscience to its rights is more challenging. Equity in the application of the law is the lodestar to protect conscience from an overbearing legalism."[35]

It needs to be noted that as much as he liked the Jesuits, Liguori was reluctant to follow their probabilism. On the one hand, he believed that one could not follow a position solely because it was probable. Of course, it had to be at least probable or arguable; otherwise, it would be nonsensical. Probability, however, was not sufficient. As he wrote in Article 55, "For an action to be lawful probability alone is not sufficient."[36] But the insufficiency of probability also meant that he would not follow probabiliorism that was known for its rigorism. The Dominican belief that more probability made an argument more valid did not make sense to him. How could more of what itself was not sufficient make for a sufficient argument?

As an alternative to probability's insufficiency, he raised the matter of certitude and doubt. Here he argued that if a law has been promulgated, it was certain and must be followed. But if a teaching (say regarding the proper time of fasting before receiving communion) had not been promulgated, then it is not certain, and if not certain, then it was dubious, and a dubious law could not compel. Thus one would be free to follow a probable opinion not solely because of its probability, but because it has not yet been defined as certain. In effect all probable arguments became equiprobable to the extent that they are not yet defined as the law of the church.[37] Inasmuch as the church had not defined or promulgated much on ordinary matters, merciful prudence would be needed to determine the right course of action. Unfortunately, this fairly insightful teaching prompted Rome, in time, to begin the habit of defining as often as possible. That development in part resulted from the habit of moralists and bishops petitioning Rome to define matters, thus making them certain.

In closing, by his gracious, sensitive, integrated, moderate, and inclusive ministry, Alphonsus emerged as a worthy exemplar for any moral theologian of the twenty-first century interested in guiding those seeking the right pathway to follow Christ.[38] Still, decades later, the substance of his actual legacy changed. In 1987, Gallagher considered the reception of Alphonsus's *Theologia Moralis*. He found that starting in 1840, other manualists begin appropriating both in matter and spirit the work of Alphonsus. Gallagher investigated how faithful they were to Alphonsus in the face of the nineteenth-century resurgence of rigorism in the treatment of penitents who habitually returned confessing the same sins.[39] For instance, Francis Kenrick (1797–1863), born in Dublin but eventually the archbishop of Baltimore (1850–63), wrote his very influential *Theologia Moralis* in 1843 with the aim "to adapt the moral teaching of St. Alphonsus Liguori to the problems of the United States."[40] It was the first written moral manual in the United States and was based on Alphonsus's *Theologia Moralis*.[41] In 1829, Thomas-Marie Gousset (1772–1866) was a rigorist who discovered the works of Alphonsus and became so convinced of the legitimacy of Alphonsus's insights that he vowed to promote Alphonsus the rest of his life. Gousset became the archbishop of Rheims (1840) and later its cardinal (1850) until his death. His own work in moral theology was very successful, going through thirteen editions.

Later, however, as Liguori became more popular, he became more betrayed. Gallagher writes,

> Ironically, the more the moral manuals quote St. Alphonsus, the less they study the nuances of the original text: by the end of the 19th century Alphonsus is interpreted in a more rigid sense than his own texts imply. The tendency, continued into the 20th century, to condense issues into compendia of statements, laws and principles increasingly obscured the theological context and prudential application of principles characteristic of St. Alphonsus. In theory the manuals deferred to the authority of St. Alphonsus; in practice, they transformed much of

> St. Alphonsus' nuanced teaching to the extent where it became abandoned.[42]

He concluded that, had the manuals remained faithful to Alphonsus, they could have been adapted but instead they became fossilized and effectively "wrote their own death sentence, by in practice abandoning some of the Alphonsian views."[43] The position of Liguori became in the nineteenth century the one he campaigned against in the eighteenth. As we will see later, in the nineteenth century most of those who sought to reform that period's rigorism were not at all successful.

II. THE SUPPRESSION AND RESTORATION OF THE SOCIETY OF JESUS

In his work *The Jesuits: A History from Ignatius to the Present*, John W. O'Malley prepares the reader to understand the Suppression of the Society of Jesus that is finally accomplished in 1773. The process was protracted: Jesuits were first expelled from Portugal (1759), then France (1764), Spain (1767), and finally, Austria (1770). Thousands of destitute priests and brothers sought refuge in Rome during these years. Finally, in 1773, anti-Jesuit forces succeeded in persuading Pope Clement XIV (1705–74; r. 1769–74) to issue *Dominus ac Redemptor*, the papal bull suppressing the Society of Jesus.

How did this happen? O'Malley explains, "During their second century, the Jesuits became the focal point of three major controversies of international scope, in each of which their opponents eventually triumphed."[44] The first controversy was the accommodation of Chinese, or Confucian, ritual into Christian worship, a position championed by Matteo Ricci (1552–1610), who entered China in 1583. From the start, Ricci argued that just as Aquinas used Aristotle without compromising Christianity, the introduction of Confucianism should not compromise Christianity either. Yet Confucianism had religious claims that Aristotle did not, although

Ricci tried to argue otherwise.[45] Ricci contended that incorporating Confucianism was incorporating culture not religion.

In 1640, when the Spanish Dominicans and Franciscans arrived in China, they were surprised by the liturgies that the Jesuits conducted and in which the Chinese participated. The Dominicans protested to Rome and in 1645 the rites were condemned. The Jesuits in China sent their own representatives to Rome and received the papal judgment that the rites were "purely civil and political cult" and did not compromise the Roman liturgy. In 1676, a Dominican published a critique of the Jesuits in China; the work was translated into several languages, becoming, as O'Malley notes, "a major resource not only for those who had misgivings about the Jesuits' approach in China but for everybody with a grievance of any sort against the Society."[46] In 1697, another protest against the rites was sent to Rome and this time the Chinese Emperor Kangxi (1654–1722; r. 1661–1722) also responded that the ceremonies were civil not religious. The rites were forbidden in 1704, 1715, and definitively in 1742. Chinese authorities began to exclude the Christians from their societies in response to being excluded from Christian rites. By 1746, anti-Christian laws emerged throughout China. As O'Malley adds, "Papal condemnation of the rites gave the Jesuits' enemies the heaven-sent occasion they had been waiting for. They unleashed an avalanche of vilification of the Jesuits as betrayers of the Christian faith and teachers of the Gospel of Confucius rather than the Gospel of Christ."[47] Jansenists and others led the campaign, but their aim was much bigger than the Chinese rites; they now aimed at the suppression of the order.

The second controversy concerned the actual confrontation between the Jesuits and the Jansenists. In his posthumous work *Augustinus* (1640), Cornelius Jansen (1585–1638) made the case that Augustine's theology of grace was effectively compromised by the Jesuits. The Jesuits tried to have Rome condemn the book, but in time failed. Instead, Antoine Arnauld (1612–94) developed his arguments against the Jesuits over the moral laxity they were accused of espousing. The Jansenists articulated six arguments against their counterparts: they were too optimistic of human nature, believed in frequent communion, were too worldly (witness Baroque art), were enamored of pagan practices as in China, were arrogant, and endorsed probabilism.[48]

In 1643, Arnauld published two critical attacks against the Jesuits, on their moral theology and on frequent communion. From 1656 to 1657, Blaise Pascal published his *Lettres Provinciales* in which, through satire and ridicule, he portrayed a well-meaning but absolutely clueless Jesuit straw man who repeatedly proved that he did not understand how much he was leading others into perdition.[49] He made the Jesuits a laughingstock. Reciprocally, Jansenism was being attacked in Rome, but in Paris the archbishop, Louis-Antoine de Noailles (1651–1729), turned on the Jesuits. There, from 1716 to 1729, the Jesuits were banned from preaching, hearing confessions, and any other form of ministry.[50]

The third controversy concerned the Paraguayan reductions, serving roughly 150,000 Native Americans, mostly members of the Guaraní tribe located in Paraguay, Argentina, Bolivia, Uruguay, and parts of Brazil. Unlike other missionary projects where the Jesuits were associated with the Spanish conquerors, here living simply among the peaceful Guaraní, the Jesuits helped organize "permanent settlements that were meant to protect the Indians from slave traders, teach them skills so that they might support themselves and pay the onerous taxes imposed by the government, and, finally, provide an atmosphere conducive to the practice of Catholicism."[51]

Although Jesuit presence in Spanish Paraguay went back to 1585, it was not until 1607 that a Jesuit commitment to the Guaraní developed. By 1630, there were a robust twelve thousand Guaranís in the reductions, but Portuguese slave traders made continuous assaults and kidnappings of the tribe's people. By 1639, the Jesuits secured royal permission for the Guaraní to be armed and to resist the Portuguese. In 1641, Jesuit brother Domingo de Torres led a group of Guaraní forces and defeated the Portuguese in the Battle of Mbororé, and subsequent attacks on the reductions diminished notably.[52] By the beginning of the eighteenth century, the reductions were flourishing, growing to 150,000 members with schools, self-governance, robust catechesis, and a lot of cattle. Artists and musicians also emerged from the communities.[53]

In 1750, just as the reductions were at their peak, Spain and Portugal settled the Treaty of Madrid, establishing new boundaries among their colonies. Seven of the reductions, roughly thirty thousand people, found themselves suddenly in Portuguese territories, but the treaty included their relocation to Spanish territories, while at the same time removing the Jesuits from the reductions. Guaraní resistance ("The War of the Seven Reductions") followed until 1756 when nearly ten thousand natives were killed.[54] By 1767, all Jesuits had been expelled from the Spanish territories.

O'Malley notes that the Marquis de Pombal (1699–1782), prime minister to King Joseph I (1714–77; r. 1750–77), used the war to discredit Jesuit loyalty to the Portuguese crown. On September 3, 1758, an attempt was made on the king's life and Pombal accused the Jesuits of complicity. On September 3, 1759, the king expelled the Jesuits from Portugal and its colonies, thus beginning the protracted suppression. France, Spain, and Austria followed until finally the forty-five-paragraph papal bull was promulgated on July 21, 1773: "We suppress and abolish the said Society; we deprive it of all activity whatever, and we likewise deprive it of its houses, schools, colleges, hospitals, lands...in whatever kingdom or province they may be situated."[55] The bull added that Jesuits were not to comment on it. As a result, 23,000 Jesuits were disbanded and over 700 schools closed; thousands were exiled and many of these died at sea, in prison or as refugees.

A month after the bull was released, the Jesuit General, Lorenzo Ricci (1703–75) and his five assistants were arrested and imprisoned in Castel Sant'Angelo. Ricci's windows were boarded up, his food rations were cut in half, heat in winter was denied; he was forbidden to write or to celebrate the liturgy; when he died, he was refused a Christian burial.[56] The Florentine church of San Giovanni, located literally across the Tiber from the Castello, petitioned the pope for the corpse of their native son and in time held funeral rites. He was later buried in the crypt of the Gesu.

The suppression had to be promulgated locally, and in a few places, it was not. In what was soon to become the United States, there were roughly twenty Jesuits in the region of Maryland, and being the only Catholic priests there, they submitted to the bull but formed another association among themselves eventually establishing, in 1789, Georgetown Academy, the first Catholic school in the United States. More significantly, in 1772, Catherine the Great of Russia (1729–96; r. 1762–96) encountered the Jesuits when she began the partition of Poland; there were two hundred of them staffing four colleges in present-day Belarus. Catherine saw them as instrumental for developing education throughout her territories and refused to promulgate the papal bull. The Lithuanian-Polish superior Stanislaw Czerniewicz (1728–85) asked Pope Pius VI (1717–99; r. 1775–99) for guidance; the pope answered, "May the result of your prayers, as I foresee and you desire, be a happy one."[57] In response to the Jesuit need for manpower, Catherine secured papal permission for Czerniewicz to open a novitiate in 1780. Eight novices entered. Moreover, exiled Jesuits from other parts of Europe learned from Czerniewicz of the empress's tolerance and arrived at these Jesuit institutions. In 1801, Pope Pius VII (1742–1823; r. 1800–1823) confirmed the Society in Russia. Elsewhere the Society began to reappear, in England (1803), Sicily (1804), and the United States (1805). In 1814, Pope Pius VII universally restored the Society.

Still, we cannot think that the restoration was simply that.[58] O'Malley notes that after the French revolution and its aftermath, the Europe of 1815 was one looking very much to the restoration of order and monarchy, the *ancien régime*, with little interest in modernity to say nothing of liberty, equality, and fraternity. He writes, "This was the context in which the restoration of the Society of Jesus occurred. The young men who now entered it were perforce creatures of that context. Although there were exceptions, the Jesuits of the nineteenth and early twentieth centuries were inimical to the values of 'the modern world' or at least highly skeptical of them."[59] Moreover, with their properties, libraries, and most of their documental heritage destroyed, their actual connection to their past was literally missing, save for a few known documents: "Missing in the Society's attempts to recreate itself were the traditions that were actually lived. The result was an often wooden, moralistic, and legalistic interpretation of the normative texts."[60] It would not be until the 1960s that the Jesuits would return to their original documents and retrieve their charism.

With the emergence of the historical critical method, a turbulent awakening began in the Society in the late nineteenth century. Some theologians like George Tyrell (1862–1909) embraced it, but Pope Pius X (1835–1914; r. 1903–14) resisted and repudiated it and any other evidence of modernity.[61] In the middle of the storm was Luis Martín (1846–1906; general 1892–1906), Superior General of the Society who supported the historiographical reform of the Society but dismissed Tyrrell.[62] It would not be until the 1930s and 1940s that Jesuit theologians emerged as leaders in these reforms.[63]

III. THE MORAL MANUALS

By looking at the work of Francisco de Toledo, we saw arguably one of the first instances of the manual tradition. Then, with Alphonsus and his reforms on equiprobabilism that effectively replaced the question of probability with the matter of whether a teaching had been promulgated, we see manualism at the height of its moral and pastoral capabilities. Still, as Gallagher noted, by the mid-nineteenth century, a discipline that was already set in stone became all the more rigid. Shortly, we will see how they fare in the twentieth century, when we investigate the contribution of Thomas Slater, SJ (1855–1928).

We should note first that the moral manuals were developed out of the community of clerics to which one belonged, and this created forms of allegiances in which we already saw, for instance, how the Dominicans tended toward probabiliorism, the Jesuits to probabilism, and the Redemptorists to equiprobabilism. For instance, the Jesuit manualists included Jean-Pierre Gury (1801–66); Antonio Ballerini (1805–81); Augustin Lehmkuhl (1834–1918); Gennaro Bucceroni (1841–1918); Edouard Génicot (1856–1900); and Hieronymus Noldin (1838–1922). Gury's manual was the Jesuits' first after their restoration (1814). Remembering that Liguori based his manual on the Jesuit Busenbaum's, it is worth noting that Gury espoused the moral theology of the Redemptorist Liguori. Rather quickly Gury's manual became, as Charles Curran writes, "the most influential manual of moral theology in the nineteenth century."[64] With Gury's death in 1866, Ballerini edited Gury's seventeenth edition; inasmuch as Ballerini had a distinctive read on conscience and morality, his edition of Gury prompted a lively, sustained, and critical debate between the Jesuits and the Redemptorists on conscience and the law.[65] With Ballerini's death in 1881, Jesuits in different countries made the Gury-Ballerini manual their own by adapting it to their own contexts. As Renzo Gerardi notes, "At the beginning of the twentieth century, it was the most diffuse manual of moral theology in the theological schools."[66]

In the United States, a Jesuit from Naples named Aloysius Sabetti (1839–98) began teaching Jesuits moral theology at Woodstock College, Maryland, in 1873, where he remained until his death twenty-five years later. In 1884, he edited his Gury-Ballerini edition and called it *Compendium theologiae moralis*.[67] Curran, who has written extensively on Sabetti, described the title page as first written by Gury, updated by Ballerini, and "shortened and accommodated for seminarians of this region by Aloysius Sabetti."[68] Sabetti's manual went through thirteen editions in his lifetime and his successors edited another twenty-one editions, the final being published in 1939. Curran notes, "Sabetti's manual was the most influential and long-lasting of the nineteenth-century moral manuals written in the United States. In addition to its use by the Jesuits, ten of thirty-two seminaries training diocesan priests in the mid-1930s still used Sabetti's textbook."[69] In the nineteenth and early twentieth centuries, the history of the moral formation of the Dominicans, Redemptorists, Franciscans, and diocesan priests followed similar tracks of developments. The Redemptorists began with the phenomenal Alphonsus Liguori[70] and later with Jozef Aertnys (1829–1915). The Dominicans followed Dominikus Prümmer (1866–1931) and then Benoit Merkelbach (1871–1942).

At the beginning of the twentieth century, the most important moral manual in English was by Thomas Slater. We now examine at length his work as basically representative of a tradition dating back nearly to the Council of Trent. By examining him we can see how legalistic and constraining moral theology became.[71] Slater represents, I believe, a tradition that does not begin in 1900 but in 1600. Thus, later in this chapter when we see the enormous developments after the Council, let us realize that the reforms in moral theology were of a tradition and its hermeneutics that fairly consistently dominated the church not for 70 years, but for 370 years. Moreover, unlike the period of Scholasticism that spans effectively from Abelard to Mair (the twelfth to the sixteenth century), the manualist period was not only dramatically more juridical and singularly concerned with sin, but also had much more claim on the ordinary lives of Catholics in their family life, the raising of their children, their work lives, their marital intimacy, and even the way they dressed. There was a tangible claim on the life of the Catholic during these centuries that peaked with *Humanae Vitae* and was no longer sustainable, in part because Catholics, after two World Wars, discovered their need for the conscience was greater than their hierarchy's reach and control. Responding to the conscientious summons of the laity became the task of theological ethics after 1970, but until then, that is, from at least Alphonsus onward, the moralist was basically the interpreter of hierarchical dictates of all kinds.

It was not until the second half of the past century that Catholics began to ask of these claims, "But are they true?" This was exactly the question that the theologian James Alison asked in 2003 after the Congregation for the Doctrine of the Faith published its *Considerations Regarding Proposals to Give Legal Recognition to Unions between Homosexual Persons.*[72] Alison acknowledged that the claims were articulated and effectively "promulgated" but added, "Yes we know this is church teaching, but is it true?"[73] Although stated in one instance in 2003, it was the new question that the laity and their priests asked when *Humanae Vitae* was promulgated. In fact, as we will see, even some of the hierarchy began to ask the same question.

Slater studied canon law and ecclesiology at Rome's Pontifical Gregorian University and won a reputation for precision and clarity, evident in his first work, *De justitia et de jure* (1898). His lengthy *Principia theologiae moralis* (1902) was clearly foundational to his later works but a publishing failure. His subsequent *Manual of Moral Theology* (1906),[74] however, was for twenty years the most consulted manual in English, going through five editions, the last appearing in 1931. The *Manual* was later accompanied by his two-volume work, *Cases of Conscience for English-speaking Countries* (1911) and another large compendium, *Questions of Morality* (1915). By 1911, unable to see well, he retired from teaching and assisted at a parish in Liverpool as a confessor for his last seventeen years, writing occasional essays.[75]

After three hundred years of being published in Latin, twentieth-century manuals appeared for the first time in the vernacular. Slater's *A Manual of Moral Theology*, the first English language manual, followed the initiative of authors in German, Spanish, French, and Italian. We will first look at introductory and foundational material and then his treatment of the fourth, fifth, and sixth commandments. In the preface, Slater noted that the manuals "are necessary for the Catholic priest to enable him to administer the sacrament of penance and to fulfill his duties."[76] Noting that they "should not be censured for not being what they were never intended to be," he added,

> They are the product of centuries of labor bestowed by able and holy men on the practical problems of Christian ethics. Here however, we must ask the reader to bear in mind that the manuals of moral theology are technical works intended to help the confessor and the parish priest in the discharge of their duties. They are as technical as the text-books of the lawyer and the doctor. They are not intended for edification, nor do they hold up a high ideal of Christian perfection for the imitation of the faithful. They deal with what is of obligation under the pain of sin, they are books of moral pathology.[77]

Slater acknowledged that if readers were looking to learn how to become better disciples, they should look elsewhere to the manuals of ascetical, devotional, or mystical theology, where they would find the "high ideal of Christian perfection." "Moral theology," he added, "proposes to itself the humbler but still necessary task of defining what is right and wrong in all the practical relations of the Christian life. This all, but most especially priests, should know." Slater concluded the stunning preface by bisecting the natural law's fundamental principle to do good and avoid evil: "The first step on the right road to conduct is to avoid evil." By mandating the doing of the good, that is, Christian perfection to ascetical manuals, Slater held that the natural law had only a singular task: to guide us to avoid evil.[78] This expectation was far from Thomas Aquinas's, and, more importantly, the call of the Gospel.

Slater's *Manual* was classical in form and divided into two parts. The first was two hundred pages long and made up of five "books": human acts, conscience, law, sin, and the theological virtues. The second part consisted in four books: the Ten Commandments, contracts, the commandments of the church, and the specific duties of clergy, religious, and "certain laymen" (physicians and those with different roles in the courts). These 460 pages focused on fairly institutional issues. Alone, the commandments covered 270 pages, with 112 dedicated to the combined seventh and tenth commandments and another ninety to the book of contracts.[79] While thirty pages each were dedicated to the first and fourth commandment, a mere twenty were dedicated to the fifth, and ten each to the second and third. Only sixteen pages were dedicated to the combined sixth and ninth commandments, with one topic, consummated sins against nature (masturbation, sodomy, and bestiality), appearing in Latin, so as not to lead a less educated reader into sin.[80]

At the outset of the first part, in the treatment of human acts, Slater defined the task of moral theology: "To frame rules for human conduct according to the teaching of the Catholic Church, to decide what actions are good and what bad according to the principles of Christian faith."[81] In the second book, on conscience, he wrote that "conscience signifies a dictate of the practical reason deciding that a particular action is right or wrong."[82] He then invoked "certainty": "In order to act lawfully and rightly, I must have at least moral certainty of the imperfect kind that the proposed action is honest and right."[83] Because perfect certainty about a moral judgment was often elusive, the required degree of moral confidence was imperfect certainty: Are we at least adequately convinced that our action is right or not? The assumption that we are adequately sure of the rightness of our action does not guarantee that our action will be morally right. Slater added that if one's conscience was in error, that would not negate the goodness that one intentionally willed.[84]

Still, if one lacked imperfect certitude, then one experienced practical doubt; acting out of such a conscience was not lawful. Now doubt is being used differently than it was in Alphonsus's time; there it was about whether the law was in fact promulgated. Now doubt is raised about the adequacy of certainty in Catholics' deliberative agency about ordinary matters. Here, then, is an indication of Gallagher's rigorist development of Alphonsus. Raising doubt to them about their consciences was like refusing absolution to the penitent Catholic. As we will see on the matters of the commandments, the question "are you adequately certain" became, by its frequency, a debilitating, rather than an empowering question. It was meant to suggest that the laity had need of consultation on most matters. The scope of the social control over the Catholic person by this question was broad and deep and far exceeded any of the impact that Scholasticism had when Thomas talked about certitude.

Slater directed that the conscientious but doubtful Catholic must search for imperfect certainty and, therefore, needed to consult an expert, the parish priest. In the consultation the priest had an array of options and Slater's provided predictably probabilist latitude.[85] Inasmuch as he was endorsing a hermeneutics that held that any credible manualist with a credible argument was a legitimate moral choice, Slater gave greater validity to the writings of most manualists and freed clergy to choose to advise the laity from the full range of manualists' opinions. Probabilism notably was about the freedom of the confessor to choose an array of manualist opinions. It was not a matter that directly affected the lay penitent.

In the second part, Slater turned to the "matter" of morality. Throughout Slater made his case and cited authorities for his positions, using a wide variety of experts. If a matter was "settled," that is, if he could call it a law, he invoked a pontiff's teaching, a national law, or some other form of legislation; otherwise, if it was not yet settled, he invoked another moralist or offered his own opinion. All these matters were framed by the Ten Commandments.

He divided the fourth commandment into seven chapters; each framed some issue of authority and subservience: duties of children to parents; parents to children; guardians to children; between parents; masters and servants; masters and scholars; and rulers and subjects. In the first chapter, he briefly discussed the piety and obedience children owe their parents, stating that the obligation of obedience ceases with the child's emancipation in England at twenty-one years of age. To this he appended a note regarding the different state laws in the United States on the emancipation of a minor. He began the second chapter with love, piety, and emotional and material support and then specifically mentioned the obligation to breastfeed: a mother "is bound at least under venial sin to nourish it with her own milk, unless some good reason excuse her."[86] He quickly turned to education:

> The Church condemns all non-Catholic schools, whether they be heretical and schismatical, or secularist, and she declares that as a general rule no Catholic parent can send his young children to such schools for educational purposes without exposing their faith and morals to serious risk, and therefore committing a grave sin.[87]

Still, he added that only a bishop, and not a priest, could deny the sacraments to parents who acted against this teaching. Here he cited the Third Plenary Council of Baltimore (November 9–December 7, 1884), and then argued that if a bishop (as happened in St. Louis) expressly prohibited all parents in his diocese from sending their children to a non-Catholic school, then no priest could absolve such parents if they continue to send their children.[88]

Later, he turned to university education, noted that the Holy See allowed English Catholics to attend Oxford and Cambridge, but granted no analogous permission in the United States, since the Third Plenary Council was not at all in favor of such a policy. Still, exceptions were granted by the Council.[89] Clearly, no other topic was as extensively parsed by Slater as this one, simply because on this matter the Holy See and the specific episcopal offices made their decisions law. Morals were set by whatever was defined.

In the third chapter, he turned to matters of custody; for these, national policies from England and the United States were invoked. The fourth chapter, only two pages, concerned duties between husband and wife and, with the exception of Ephesians 5:22–24, Slater cited no authorities. A wife was to be subject and obedient to, but not a slave or servant of, her husband; if she showed great contempt for him and neglected his commands, she sinned grievously. Likewise, the husband was bound by justice and piety to support his wife and sinned grievously if he treated her with harshness or neglect. Slater concluded, "The wife would not be guilty of sin if she took from her husband without his knowledge what was necessary for decent support of family."[90] Finally, Leo XIII's *Rerum Novarum* (May 15, 1891) was invoked five times in the fifth chapter, and in most instances, at length, stipulating the duties of employers to employees on just working conditions, respectful treatment, and fair wages.

On the fifth commandment, Slater treated six issues: suicide, capital punishment, justifiable homicide, killing the innocent, war, and dueling. Throughout, he appealed to applications of the principle of double effect.[91] In the first chapter, he established that since "God is the Author of life and death, He has reserved the ownership of human life to Himself," "we have not the free disposal of our lives." Thus suicide, which has one's death as "the direct and immediate object of the will," was prohibited,[92] but that did not mean that one could not do something that could cause one's own death. He applied the principle of double effect to the case of the captain of a ship who, fearing in wartime that his ship will be seized and become a danger to his own country, destroys the ship, knowing that he and his crew will lose their lives. The captain "does not intend the destruction of human life; the immediate effect of his action is to prevent the ship from falling into the enemy's hands. The public advantage counterbalances the loss."[93] With his usual economy, he differentiated in one single paragraph suicide from foregoing extraordinary means to preserve one's life. He gave two instances of such means: a painful and costly operation and one that required travel. Regarding the latter, he considered the case of one who would die if he were to spend the winter in England; Slater judged he "is not bound to expatriate himself and go and live in a milder climate."[94]

He justified capital punishment with arguments from Romans 13:4 and "natural reason." He began the chapter on justifiable homicide stating simply, "In defense of my own life from unjust attack I may use whatever violence is necessary and even to the length of killing the aggressor." He then added that no one should use greater force than necessary, nor act out of vengeance or anticipation of attack. Under these limitations, one may use such violence to defend limbs, property (as long as it is of considerable amount), and chastity. He noted that some theologians once held that one could commit justifiable homicide over an insult but noted that Popes Alexander VII and Innocent XI condemned these positions.[95]

On killing the innocent, he noted that not even the good of the state makes it right to take an innocent life, though he invoked the principle of double effect to demonstrate the liceity of civilian deaths in an attack on a "beleaguered town." He declared the direct procuring of abortion as an intrinsic evil but noted that a pregnant woman may appropriate life-saving means even if that means were indirectly to cause the fetus's death. Finally, he argued against the direct killing of a fetus to save the mother's life, "even if otherwise both child and mother were certain to die." His position is historically interesting inasmuch as it had been held until the end of the nineteenth century that a woman could defend herself against a fetus that threatened her life.[96] His argument is worth reading, in part because of its reversal in depicting the mother as the unjust assailant:

> Some theologians used to think that such operations were lawful if the mother's life could not otherwise be saved, because the child might be considered a material unjust assailant of its mother's life, and so be lawfully killed....

> However, in no sense can it be allowed that the child is an unjust assailant of a mother's life; it is where nature placed it, through no fault of its own, and it has a right to be there and to be born. If either is an unjust assailant of the other's life, it is the mother, who voluntarily undertook the obligations of motherhood....This doctrine is now theologically certain after the repeated declarations of the Holy See that no operation which tends directly to the destruction of the life of the fetus is lawful.[97]

He appended no references to other moralists holding similar positions.

While in three pages he invoked several popes and the Council of Trent to demonstrate the unequivocal wrongness of dueling, in four pages he upheld the certain teaching of Catholic theology on just war.

One should not think that the brevity on the sixth and ninth arose from any lack of interest; rather, in light of the teaching that there was no parvity of matter to the sixth commandment, there was nothing to be considered since almost everything was already forbidden. He wrote, "All sins of impurity of whatever kind or species are of themselves mortal."[98] The sins were in three categories: consummated sins of impurity, consummated sins against nature, non-consummated acts of impurity. Under the consummated sins of impurity were fornication, adultery, incest, criminal assault, rape (!), and sacrilege. On the consummated sins against nature, there were masturbation, sodomy, and bestiality. Clearly the parsing of the first sin evidenced widespread pastoral anxiety.[99] Sadly, in the final chapter he treated touching, kissing, and embracing as sins.

With Slater's moral theology and truncated natural law, we are a long way from Aquinas's integral *Summa Theologiae* where that work's second part on moral theology is on virtue and situated between the first part on God and the third on Jesus Christ and the sacraments. For that matter Slater's preface was a long way from Alphonsus's as well. By Slater's time, moral theology was focused solely on moral pathology and that was progressively determined more by the hierarchy than by the moralist. The pursuit of the good was no longer part of the moral agenda, but rather an elective for those seeking spiritual or ascetical guidance.

Still, the historical trajectory of moral theology from Slater's manual to *Humanae Vitae* is even more disappointing because, as we will see, there developed an even more progressive tendency of regulating ordinary matters coupled with the further pathologizing of the laity's consciences. Sin itself was essentially violating whatever Rome prohibited. Moreover, in this highly itemized world of legislation, the teaching on doubt made the penitent even more inclined to the priest than ever before. The dependency was palpable.

After Slater, the manualist period became more and more like an offshoot of canon law. In fact, in 1911, the Jesuit Arthur Vermeersch (1858–1936), teaching both moral theology and canon law, founded the very successful journal *Periodica de re canonica*, which in 1920 became the *Periodica de re canonica et morali* and by 1927 was known as *Periodica de re morali, canonica, liturgica*. As its website today notes, before Vatican II there was not a "neat and clear distinction" among the fields as there was afterward. Still, it bears noting that the journal returned to its original title only in 1991.[100] Moral theology looked like canon law because it was about rightly legislated (or interpreted) norms of conduct *and* it was coming from Rome.

In the twentieth century, Vatican congregations instructed on moral matters with greater frequency and specificity. These instructions changed moral theology from being a guild of arbiters of the moral tradition to becoming more and more interpreters of contemporary hierarchical utterances. The shift cannot be underestimated.

The neo-manualist work of John Ford (1902–89) and Gerald Kelly (1902–64) is instructive. Kelly, for example, can rightly be called the father of medical ethics in the United States because of his teachings on ordinary and extraordinary means of life support. In 1950, for example, he asked whether oxygen and intravenous feeding had to be used to preserve the life of a patient in a terminal coma and argued, "I see no reason why even the most delicate professional standard should call for their use. In fact, it seems to me that, apart from very special circumstances, the artificial means not only need not but also should not be used, once the coma is reasonably diagnosed as terminal. Their use creates expense and nervous strain without conferring any real benefit."[101]

Ford, a moral theologian at Weston School of Theology, became well known for an electrifying essay against obliteration bombing right in the crucible of World War II, that is, in 1944.[102]

Ford did what his European colleagues on either side of the war did not do: criticize and condemn the saturation bombing of cities. In this, as in his argument that alcoholism was more frequently a medical rather than a moral matter,[103] Ford was a significant and compassionate innovator.

In 1964, Ford and Kelly's two-volume *Contemporary Moral Theology* served as a last-ditch effort to sustain the manualist tradition, long since abandoned in Europe.[104] Their dependence on the agenda that Rome had set was summarized in a stunning statement:

> An earnest student of papal pronouncements, Vincent A. Yzermans, estimated that during the first fifteen years of his pontificate Pius XII gave almost one thousand public addresses and radio messages. If we add to these the apostolic constitutions, the encyclicals and so forth, during the same period of fifteen years, and add furthermore all the papal statements during the subsequent years, we have well over a thousand papal documents....Merely from the point of view of volume, therefore, one can readily appreciate that it was not mere facetiousness that led a theologian to remark, that even if the Holy See were to remain silent for ten years, the theologians would have plenty to do in classifying and evaluating the theological significance of Pius XII's public statements.[105]

What were these statements? Let us go back twenty years to 1943, when the Jesuit Henry Davis (1866–1952) published the fourth edition of his very successful, four-volume work, *Moral and Pastoral Theology*.[106] In the preface, he wrote:

> Some emendations and additions have been made in the fourth edition of this work, which are necessary in view of both recent Instructions issued by the Sacred Roman Congregations, and replies given by the Pontifical Commission for the Interpretation of the canons of the Code of Canon Law. The Author has embodied in this edition all necessary material published in the *Acta Apostolicae Sedis* up to December 1941 inclusive.[107]

The two "recent" instructions referred to were the problem of a social tolerance of prostitution and the issue of female dress. On the latter instruction, first issued on January 12, 1930, Davis presented a two-page "faithful translation" of the twelve main points. A look at these is instructive in terms of appreciating the direct influence of the Sacred Congregation on ordinary life. The first point stated that "parish priests most of all and preachers, should, on occasion, address words of severe admonition to women that they should employ dress that bespeaks modesty and serves as an ornament and a safeguard of their virtue." The second and fourth points called on parents and school mistresses respectively to foster modesty and chastity in the girls. The third point told parents to "deter their daughters from public gymnastic exercises." The fifth through eighth points instructed school mistresses, women of religious institutes, and pious associations of women to aim at checking abuses in modest dress and to ban those who violate such codes. Remarkably, the ninth resorts to excommunication and as such should be quoted in full:

> Girls and women who dress unbecomingly are to be refused Holy Communion, and not allowed to be sponsors in Baptism or Confirmation, and should occasion demand, they shall be forbidden admittance into the Church.[108]

The tenth urged that feast days of the Blessed Virgin be used as occasions to preach on modesty. The eleventh instructed diocesan councils every year to develop strategies "for the more efficacious promotion of female modesty" and the twelfth required bishops and other local ordinaries "to give an account of these matters every third year to the Sacred Congregation."[109] In 1943, at the height of World War II, the only Vatican instruction that appeared at length in the fourth edition of Davis's work was this one. The concern about the education of children in Slater developed into a fixation on the dress of girls and young women by Davis's time. Vatican directives coupled with punitive sanctions were published more and more often without any questioning.

As these excerpts demonstrate, manualist theology at the beginning of the twentieth century shaped the clergy's own disposition toward the pastoral care of Catholics on moral matters. Manualists operated out of a very legalistic world in which the principles themselves were safeguarded by their very interpreters. These principles were indelibly linked to a vision of moral truth that was fairly certain, universal, and arbitrary.

By the eve of Vatican II, the manualists had become primarily dependent on Vatican dictates, and therefore the agenda of moral theology was altered by these teachings. While the Vatican teachings regarding war and killing were few, their attentiveness to the necessity of Catholic education, to prohibitions of theological books, to matters of birth control, and to the dress of women highlighted that their interests were more set on controlling life within the church. As time went on, Catholic manualists, like the hierarchy in Rome, became more and more concerned not with facing the challenges of the world but rather conforming to the rigors of the church. Moreover, with greater research into human psychology, the manualists viewed the conscience of the lay Roman Catholic as not only uncertain but wounded. While Slater had only one page on the scrupulous conscience,[110] nearly thirty years later Davis gave a startlingly long list in twelve pages of categorically problematic consciences (the false, doubting, perplexed, scrupulous, and lax conscience), allowing us to see just how dubious and crippled they considered the penitential Catholic conscience.[111]

After Davis and World War II, the European worldview of the Catholic conscience dramatically changed, but in the United States, moralists only further trained their priests to look for and tend what they esteemed was the crippled Catholic conscience. For instance, in the first volume of *Contemporary Moral Theology*, through the appropriation of scientific literature that focused on psychological impediments to genuine human freedom, Ford and Kelly instructed their priests on the questions they needed to understand about the confessional and the lay conscience. Half of the volume, a full 175 pages, are dedicated to "Imputability and Unconscious Motivation," "Imputability under Stress," "Juridical Aspects of Subjective Imputability," "Alcoholism and Subjective Imputability," and "Psychiatry and Catholicism."[112]

Although the manualist was always known as a physician of souls, now he became in the mid-twentieth century the psychiatric caregiver of the inculpable, because incompetent, sinner. The question that the sinner might be tortured not so much by her or his conscience, but rather by the controlling teachings of Rome and the pastoral practices in the confessional was rarely raised.

Moreover, because Rome insisted that there was no parvity of matter on the sixth commandment, the confessor and penitent often focused on sexual matters like impure thoughts, masturbation, and, significantly, birth control. This was especially the case after the promulgation of the papal encyclical *Casti Connubii* (1930), which not only reiterated the condemnation of birth control, but now accentuated that this teaching was unchangeable and that the distinctive nature of Catholic moral theology (as opposed to the Church of England, among other churches) was that its teachings were not subject to change but remained eternal because they were from God.[113] By *Casti Connubii*, the church's teachings on sex had become so exceptional and petrified that they held a unique claim on the consciences of the Catholic couple who sought the only relief they could imagine: acknowledging their admitted weakness, they sought an understanding priest who would consider their impoverished state. The nearly forty years between 1930 and 1968 was a difficult time to be a Catholic couple raising a family in the United States.

Finally, the anxious penitent burdened by many claims was rarely encouraged to think in any way of the social order.[114] Although on May 15, 1891, Pope Leo XIII (1810–1903; r. 1878–1903) promulgated *Rerum Novarum*,[115] and therein launched the highly significant tradition of "social encyclicals," this "moral matter" made its way into the moral manuals, as we saw earlier, but only briefly. Now it developed into its own field with its own hermeneutics and its own trajectory quite apart from the moral manuals and their directives for the confessional.[116] In order to appreciate, then, how rarely the manualist directed the confessor to the social order, we should note that besides Slater's manual, the other most popular contemporary moral manual was by Heribert Jone (1885–1967), a German Capuchin. His *Moral Theology*, first published in 1929 and translated into many different languages, remained effectively the same in later editions. Interestingly, a manual helpful in Germany passed seamlessly after World War II into confessors' hands around the world. In the handy, pocket-sized manual that Jone wrote for busy priests, confessional matters were either personal violations of the commandments or of church laws. The war efforts on either side to say nothing of the social forces that exhibited enormous control over people during these years were not viewed by Jone or others as confessional matters. First translated into English in 1945 (!), the manual was so successful in English that in 1963 the eighteenth edition of the English translation appears.[117] Interestingly, in 2009, the eighteenth edition was reprinted for contemporary American use.[118]

Of course, moral theologians eventually recognized the need to reform their field, but as they did, the manualist as the magisterium's servant became more and more opposed to any innovation. In particular, he chided those who looked for moral theology to be more integrated with fundamental and/or ascetical theology. In fact, as other church leaders tried to persuade the manualist to turn toward this more holistic direction, the more the manualist receded from moral theology into canon law. Finally, the principles that the manualists followed were unable to address the real critical issues of the day. One only has to see that girls' dresses and male sperm received more attention than atomic weapons to appreciate how distant the manualists were from the world as it tried to emerge from World War II.

IV. EUROPEAN REFORMERS

As it rose from the rubble of World War II, European moral theology had a radical reorientation. If the Council of Trent is the locus for the birth of moral theology as a specific science, then the savagery of World War II wherein 47 million people died marked the most critical moment in its modern history. Moral theology would either shrivel and die from its complete incapacity to speak to the now haunted conscience of the postwar, modern world or it would need to reconstitute itself completely, repudiating what the moral manual had become and offering an entirely new framework, method, and vision for the moral formation of conscientious Christian communities.[119]

Interestingly, the seeds for the development of a new framework were sown long before the war. In fact, they were planted in Germany in the nineteenth century. We will now consider three visionaries, but we should note at the outset that they were not directly influential outside of Germany, as Charles E. Curran has noted, nor were they accepted by their hierarchies during their own lives.[120] Still, eventually they influenced the German reformers of the twentieth century, most assuredly Fritz Tillmann and Bernard Häring, who successfully extended the reform beyond Germany.

Johann Michael Sailer (1751–1832) was a pivotal person working in the fields of ethics, theology, and philosophy, who founded what today is known as pastoral theology. Effectively a reformer who maintained good relationships with Protestant theologians as well as an appreciation for some of the aims of the Enlightenment, he was above all a leader in making theology attentive to the appropriate pedagogy for the laity. In fact, his three-volume manual was addressed to both clergy and laity; there he argued that Christian morality could not simply be about the specter of sin in the shadows of the commandments, but also about the grace given for the teachings of the Beatitudes.[121] On his orientation toward the laity, Richard Schaefer remarks, "He remained faithful to the basic Enlightenment view of the perfectibility of human reasoning through education, and unremitting in his insistence on reason as part of the common stock of human ability. For Sailer, 'This higher reason is why the savage in Canada sees many things just as the philosopher in Athens and Rome.'"[122] As Kathleen A. Cahalan also argued, it was Sailer's work that influenced Häring to write a manual, not for the priest confessor but for the laity.[123] The same can be said for his earlier influence on Tillmann.

Johann Baptist von Hirscher (1788–1865) saw in the kingdom of God the form and matter of moral theology. In 1835, he published his three-volume work of moral theology, *Die Christliche Moral als Lehre von der Verwirklichung des Göttlichen Reiches in der Menschheit* (*Christian Morality as the Doctrine on the Realization of the Divine Kingdom in Humankind*), a title that marked a clear departure from the moral manuals.[124] As Donald Dietrich noted, "In Hirscher's opinion, the Christian was a citizen of his specific political state as well as of the kingdom of God. In fact, God's will was ultimately to activate both the political and spiritual communities in which men lived, making both one."[125] He was a moderate reformer; antimodern in that he believed that the church was necessary for the social order. But he was not an ultramontanist looking to Rome for guidance. Rather he pushed for synodal gatherings much to the chagrin of the hierarchy. Dietrich described him well: "Hirscher bemoaned the industrial revolution, condemned the sovereignty of the people, and accepted participation of the laity in the public affairs of Church and state only because he saw democracy as a devastating epidemic that had to be controlled through inoculation."[126] He believed, however, that the church could and should influence the political life by being true to itself and the gospel vision of the kingdom of God. Therein, in the midst of the changes of the nineteenth century, Hirscher saw the church having a central role in the life of society. Dietrich concluded noting that Hirscher never succeeded because he "lacked influence among the hierarchy who feared the challenges of their era."[127]

Franz Xaver Linsenmann (1835–98) wrote his own manual of moral theology, but unlike others, saw the life of grace as a call to discipleship, a term he used but did not develop as robustly as Tillmann later did.[128] The moral task of the Christian life was to realize Christ within oneself by following in his footsteps. For that task Paul taught that Christian liberty empowered us to realize the call of Christ. Undoubtedly, in the writings of Vatican II and Bernard Häring, Linsenmann's emphasis on freedom was influential, but Renzo Gerardi noted, like his predecessors, that he had little impact until the mid-twentieth century.[129] Moreover, Linsenmann also innovated not only on the general foundations of moral theology but also in the particular. In his work on the death penalty, James Megivern noted that Linsenmann stood apart from all others: while not denying the biblically based claim to capital punishment in theory, Linsenmann argued that the practical need for such punishment was no longer evident inasmuch as containment was now available in late nineteenth-century Europe. Through the use of empirical data he also showed that capital punishment was neither necessary nor in fact a deterrence to capital crimes.[130] Similarly in his courses on Christian marriage, he proposed that marital coitus had an objective and a subjective purpose; the former was its procreative function, but the latter was through effecting the spiritual union of the couple, a claim again overlooked until *Humanae Vitae* in 1968.[131]

Significantly, these theologians help us to appreciate that the reformers of the twentieth century built on the work of their reforming predecessors, a reminder that though the manualists of the nineteenth century belonged to a tradition not known for innovation, still a few recognized that there had to be a better way to bring the message of the Gospels to the people of God.[132] While not influential on most of their contemporaries and in particular on their hierarchies, they influenced the major reformers of the twentieth century, to whom we now turn.[133]

In 1912, a scripture scholar, Fritz Tillmann (1874–1953), was censured for a work he edited, and he was subsequently ordered by the Vatican to vacate scripture studies but given the option to enter another field of theology. He chose moral theology. In 1934, he wrote a ground-breaking work, *Die Idee der Nachfolge Christi*, and effectively proposed "discipleship" as the primary identity for the Christian, a fundamental concept not in theological use before this work.[134] Seventy years after its publication, Karl-Heinz Kleber wrote that in the search to express what the foundational principle of moral theology ought to be, Tillmann came forward and named it: the disciple of Christ. Others followed Tillmann's lead. Kleber names: Gustav Ermecke, Johannes Stelzenberger, Bernard Häring, Gérard Gilleman, and René Carpentier.[135]

In 1937, he published his own moral manual not about sin, but rather about discipleship. More significantly, *Der Meister Ruft*, translated into English in 1960 as *The Master Calls*, was written not for the confessor but for the lay Catholic and was a more accessible text than the earlier work, with practical explications of charity as the love of God, self, and neighbor. Throughout, he highlighted the grandeur of the Christian vocation: "The goal of the following of Christ is none other than the attainment of the status of a child of God."[136] The language, vision, and agenda of Tillmann's handbook marked a major, remarkable alternative to the trajectory of the manuals of moral pathology.

In 1947, Gérard Gilleman (1910–2002) defended his dissertation on the role of charity in moral theology in Paris under the guidance of René Carpentier (1894–1968). After defending his dissertation, Gilleman was assigned to teach in India and Carpentier agreed to edit and publish Gilleman's *The Primacy of Charity*.[137] It is hard to overestimate the influence of Gilleman's work. His charity gave Tillmann's discipleship the interior virtue that would make it possible for moral theologians to see the field not primarily as a study of how to avoid sin, but rather about how to follow in love of neighbor as a disciple of Christ. Together these two moralists began to change the field in Europe on the eve of the Council.

The Benedictine Dom Odon Lottin (1880–1965) began his work as a historian but later became a critic of the manual tradition. His enormous four-volume investigations into Scholasticism demonstrated that the history of ideas was complex, and that progress can never be fully adequately preconceived because the discourse of ideas is subject to a variety of historical variables.[138] Lottin's historical-critical method was developed from a set of assumptions very different from those of the manualists who were his contemporaries in moral theology. Lottin wanted to investigate how medieval theologians developed their arguments. Truth was not, for him, a series of always held, ahistorical, universal utterances. He did not believe he would find one position held by all always. He presumed, instead, that the scholastics did not all share the same understandings of free will, conscience, law, norms, and so on. On the contrary, they debated and contradicted one another and sometimes even themselves. Although the concerns were similar, their quests for moral understanding and truth led them to differing positions. The tradition, then, was not monolithic; it was a series of debates and engagements that developed historically. He wanted to know the history of that development.[139]

Lottin looked historically for the actual roots of moral theology so as to let moral theology flourish in its own proper theological setting. As Lottin noted, after the scholastics, moralists forgot the virtuous ends, both natural and supernatural, of the moral life. Instead fixated on sin, the authors of casuistry and the later confessional and then moral manuals progressively uprooted moral theology from its dogmatic sources and eventually transplanted morals into the field of canon law. These investigations led him to repudiate the claims of the moral manuals. In 1946, he published his first moral theological synthesis, *Principes de Morale*. Rather than being a manual for hearing confessions, it was a theological foundation for anyone interested in the formation of conscience.[140] Later, in 1954, he published his revolutionary *Morale Fondamentale*, where he critiqued the wretched past of moral theology, blaming the priest confessor's singular focus on sin as the principal cause for moral theology's failure.[141] He attacked recent developments wherein canon law had come to dominate moral theology, forcing it to focus exclusively on external acts, when, in fact, historically speaking, moral theology had been primarily interested in the internal life. Overtaken by canon law, moral theology lost its moorings in dogmatic theology and in the biblical and patristic sources of theology; not only had it abandoned its pursuit of the Christian vocation, but it lost its deep connection to ascetical and mystical theology.[142]

In this work Lottin, like his predecessors, turned to the conscience as foundational to the moral life and argued that priests were called to help the members of the church lead conscientious lives.[143] Lottin wrote at length on the virtuous life and "formation" of both the conscience and the prudential judgment. By turning to prudence, Lottin liberated the Christian conscience from its singular docility to the confessor priest. Now the layperson's conscience could grow according to the longstanding virtue of prudence that guided the scholastics. Moreover, Lottin instructed church members to become mature self-governing Christians, insisting that they have a lifelong task, a progressive one, as he called it, toward growing in virtue.[144] By turning to conscience, Lottin urged his readers to find the mode and the practical wisdom for determining themselves as better Christian disciples within themselves, their community, their faith, the church's tradition, and the Scriptures. Finally, in *Au Coeur de la Morale Chrétienne*, he commented on the "poor manuals *ad usum confessariorum*" wherein not a trace of biblical inspiration could be found. He returned to the question of why the moral manuals were so singularly interested in sin, and this time blamed the very numerous mediocre lay Christians who asked their confessors to give them minimalist expectations for the moral life.[145] Lottin cleared the space for further innovation.

In 1936 the young Redemptorist Bernard Häring was asked by his superiors to prepare to teach moral theology: "I told my superior that this was my very last choice because I found the teaching of moral theology an absolutely crushing bore."[146] Häring realized that if he found little benefit in its study, so did the laity. But his own experience of the war intervened and shaped the breadth and depth of his project: "During the Second World War I stood before a military court four times. Twice it was a case of life and death. At that time I felt honored because I was accused by the enemies of God. The accusations then were to a large extent true, because I was not submissive to that regime."[147] Here was social context so absent in the manuals. Häring witnessed how many Christians recognized the truth, were convicted by it, and stood firm with it. There he understood moral truth not primarily in what persons said, but in how they lived. The war experiences irretrievably disposed him to the agenda of developing a moral theology that aimed for the bravery, solidarity, and truthfulness of those committed Christians he had met.[148]

At the same time, he also witnessed to "the most absurd obedience by Christians toward a criminal regime. And that too radically affected my thinking and acting as a moral theologian. After the war, I returned to moral theology with the firm decision to teach it so that the core concept would not be obedience but responsibility, the courage to be responsible."[149] He believed the manualists were responsible for this conforming, obediential moral theology, one that was worried solely about following church rules; instead, he summoned conscientious Christians to a responsive and responsible life of discipleship. In the same year that Lottin's *Morale Fondamentale* appeared, Bernard Häring published in German his 1,600-page magisterial manual in three volumes, *Das Gesetz Christi* (in English, *The Law of Christ: Moral Theology for Priests and Laity*).[150] Of his 104 published books, this was his landmark contribution. The opening words of the foreword were decisive: "The principle, the norm, the center, and the goal of Christian moral theology is Christ."[151] Not sin, but Christ surrounded by his disciples became the subject of moral theology. Among its innumerable contributions are five central themes: an entirely positive orientation in the pursuit of the good; an emphasis on history and tradition; human freedom as the basis of Christian morality; the formation of the conscience; and the relevance of worship for the moral life. These themes emerge, not surprisingly, in *Gaudium et Spes*.[152]

After 1945, Western European seminarians were trained in this vibrant moral theology shaped by Tillmann, Gilleman, Carpentier, Lottin, and Häring. Their work is noted for its rootedness in the Bible, its focus on Christ, its emphasis on discipleship and conscience, its dependence on virtue, and its appreciation of the signs of the times. Others like Émile Mersch, Phillippe Delhaye, Josef Fuchs, and Louis Janssens also entered the classroom and took this new moral theology further forward.[153] In their classrooms were the future Council fathers, influenced not by the rigidity and self-centered moral theology of the manuals, but by the other-directed moral manuals of the postwar world.

V. ENGLISH-SPEAKING RESISTANCE TO REFORM

Unlike in Europe, the end of World War II did not prompt in the United States or in other English-speaking lands a repudiation of the manuals. That repudiation came in 1968, in the wake of *Humanae Vitae*. Until then and in marked contrast, the role of the moral theologian as primarily the interpreter and parser of the church's laws for the sake of the confessor that was rejected in 1946 by the Europeans and replaced by a "revisionist" agenda (as it became called) had an extended life span in the United States, giving this development a chilling maturity that is still with us today. Charles Curran in his compelling *Catholic Moral Theology in the United States: A History* makes a similar point. As opposed to the newer approaches from Europe, "Catholic moral theology in the United States continued to use the manuals as the textbook for the discipline and followed existing approaches in sexual and medical ethics. As a result, theologians in this country were not prepared for the new perspectives ushered in by the Second Vatican Council."[154] While Europeans anticipated the renewal of moral theology by nearly twenty years before the promulgation of conciliar documents, in the United States the Council is long over before it has any impact on the field.

From 1940, American moral theologians writing the "Moral Notes" in *Theological Studies* vetted the European developments. John Lynch and then John Ford and Gerald Kelly were the gatekeepers of European contributions, and they were parsimonious in granting entrance. While a survey of the works of the journal's first twenty-five years (1940–65) shows substantive innovations in the field of social ethics, whether from John Ryan, Paul Furfey, John LaFarge, or John Courtney Murray,[155] hardly any innovation can be found in the moral theology by Lynch, Ford, and Kelly. The divide between the fields remained until roughly the end of the twentieth century. In his award-winning study of Ford, Eric Genilo shows us that these moralists resisted any innovation, unless the magisterium had not *yet* declared on a matter.[156]

In fact, they were in some ways more rigid, authoritative, and intolerant than even their predecessors like Slater and Jone. For instance, Ford and Kelly inverted the order of authority that the early manualists used, acknowledging the authority of the papacy and of Roman dicasteries *before* and, in fact, sometimes *without* considering the authority of the argument itself. A magisterial claim was, for Ford and Kelly, itself the guarantor of its truthfulness: "It is only through conformity with the teaching of the Church that the individual conscience can have security from error. The 'autonomy of the individual conscience' cannot be reconciled with the plan of Christ and can produce only 'poisonous fruit.'"[157]

Their intolerance of European innovation was evident. Ford and Kelly ridiculed Gilleman for his work on the primacy of charity.[158] John Farraher derided Bernard Häring for *Das Gesetz Christi*: "In much of his complaining, Häring, like many who make similar complaints, seems to confuse moral theology with ascetical and pastoral theology."[159] The divide becomes more frequent and regular when Europeans entertained the legitimacy of oral contraceptives. Lynch developed an entire note to refute and dismiss the now famous groundbreaking articles by W. Van der Marck and Louis Janssens on the topic.[160]

We saw earlier the reference to Yzermans by Ford and Kelly in 1964. It was a very American understanding of the role of the moral theologian: effectively the same stance that rejected the innovations of Sailer, Hirschman, and Linsenmann in the nineteenth century. Ford and Kelly's approach was eventually critiqued by their peers. Daniel Callahan described the authors as "loyal civil servants" and "faithful party workers" and dismissed their work "as years behind the (theological) revolution now in progress."[161] Later, in a significant study of Catholic medical ethics in the United States in the twentieth century, David Kelly identified the American period from 1940 to 1968 as "ecclesiastical positivism."[162]

VI. THE SECOND VATICAN COUNCIL (1962–65)[163]

When *Optatam Totius* (The Decree on the Training of Priests) was promulgated at the Council in October 1965, it offered a simple two-sentence statement on moral theology. This comment not only validated the work of the reformers, it gave a directive to the syllabus and style of moral theology. Häring was its draftsman and as simple as it was, its emphases on Scripture, charity, and the exalted vocation of discipleship captured the synthesis of the type of moral theology that Europeans were developing to replace manualism:

> Special care should be given to the perfecting of moral theology. Its scientific presentation should draw more fully on the teaching of holy Scripture and should throw light upon the exalted vocation of the faithful in Christ and their obligation to bring forth fruit in charity for the life of the world.[164]

Among others, Josef Fuchs (1912–2005) made this directive the key to understanding Vatican II's mandate to moral theologians.[165] In a fifty-page article, penned in 1966, Fuchs unpacked the document on a variety of levels, noting first that the summons of "perfecting" moral theology should be understood as being that the "Council requires, above all, that moral theology—and other theological disciplines shall be renewed."[166] In five parts he laid out the implicit agenda of the two-sentence summons for renewal. The first part was the most fundamental and the most relevant for us: "The Basic Truth: The Exalted Vocation of the Faithful in Christ." Fuchs wrote, "The Council requires that moral theology shall be taught not only and not primarily as a code of moral principles and precepts. It must be presented as an unfolding, a revelation and explanation, of the joyful message, the good news, of Christ's call to us, the vocation of believers in Christ." He added, "The fundamental characteristic of Christian morality is a call, a vocation, rather than a law; Christian morality is therefore responsive in character."[167] Then Fuchs underlined the closing words of the conciliar mandate, "for the life of the world": "moral theology must stress the importance of every individual's moral life for the true life of the world. Beyond all doubt, personal morality has social significance."[168] In short, by being restored to its moorings in biblical, foundational, and ascetical theology, moral theology was now able, through the admonition in *Optatam Totius*, to become "a genuine theological discipline."[169]

The conciliar summons in *Optatam Totius* was repeatedly invoked and explored in basic texts of moral theology around the world. Universally, *Optatam Totius* became the first of all reference points for moralists' reception of the Council. Rightly so, as Richard Gula noted, it is the "only explicit statement of the council on moral theology."[170] But that statement validated the renewal movement in moral theology, a movement later identified as "revisionism," after this very summons to renew the discipline.[171] We need to remember that the early revisionists like Carpentier, Gilleman, Tillmann, and Lottin had already helped form the theological background of the European episcopacy from World War II to the Council. Their influence on the Council fathers was significant, as we will see later regarding the reception of *Humanae Vitae*. Moreover, during the Council, Häring had considerable input, but we cannot overlook two others deeply connected to the Council. First, there was Louis Janssens at the University of Leuven who influenced both the French and the Belgian Council fathers, and second, as the Council was going on, another moralist, Josef Fuchs at the Gregorian, underwent a profound rethinking of his theology while a member of the papal commission considering birth control.[172] By the end of the Council, thcsc thrcc—Häring, Janssens, and Fuchs—would have an incalculable influence on their peers in interpreting the Council and offering the foundations for a new theological ethics. The Council, however, not only validated their enterprise; it gave them an entirely new framework to consider in particular in shaping the ethical vision for the church, especially in *Gaudium et Spes*.

While Häring was secretary of the editorial committee that drafted it and was referred to as its "quasi-father,"[173] his actual influence was eclipsed by the work of others, noticeably Archbishop Gabriel Garrone and Cardinals Leo Joseph Suenens and Paul-Émile Léger as well as theologians like Marie-Dominique Chenu, Yves Congar, Joseph Ratzinger, Karl Rahner, and the social scientist Louis Lebret. None of these were moral theologians but each of them knew and were influenced by the emergent work of the revisionists. For this reason Joseph Selling calls *Gaudium et Spes* the "manifesto" of the revisionists.[174]

Revisionism is replete in the document. Its anthropological vision was based on the human as a social being (*GS* 23–25) and moral issues were not treated as primarily individual, but rather as communal and even global. While sin was frequently invoked (§§10, 13–4, 22, 25, §§37, 40–41, 58, 78), the overall vision was that the church stood with the world in joy and hope (§1). A new moral theological foundation was emerging. Here, the church conveys a deep sympathy for the human condition, especially in all its anxieties, and stands in confident solidarity with the world. The entire experience of ambivalence that so affected the world in its tumultuous changes of the 1960s was positively, but realistically engaged.[175] Finally, in looking at contemporary moral challenges, the church encouraged an interdisciplinary approach in understanding and promoting a globalized vision of modernity (§§77–78). In a manner of speaking, *Gaudium et Spes* lays the ecclesial context for the revisionist agenda and had enormous influence on the renewal of moral theology.

Four particular dimensions of *Gaudium et Spes* bear mention. Its theology of marriage was remarkably different from *Casti Connubii*: Marriage was a "communion of love" (*GS* 47), an "intimate partnership" (§48); it was no longer seen as a contract, but as a covenant (§48). Rather than asserting procreation as the singular end of marriage, the Council fathers wrote, "Marriage to be sure is not instituted solely for procreation; rather, its very nature as an unbreakable compact between persons, and the welfare of the children, both demand that the mutual love of the spouses be embodied in a rightly ordered manner, that it grow and ripen. Therefore, marriage persists as a whole manner and communion of life" (§50). Such positive, nonlegalistic, but deeply affirming language was a new phenomenon for church teaching on marriage. In a way, these elements on marriage influence *Humanae Vitae*, as well as the encyclical's "conscientious" reception.

Out of this same framework the Council shaped its teaching on conscience, evidently indebted to Carpentier, Gilleman, Lottin, and Häring's extensive work.[176] Their work anticipated, inspired, and formed the now famous conciliar definition of *conscience* in paragraph 16, which is, I believe, the emblematic expression of the hopeful expectations raised by the revisionists and affirmed by Vatican II:

> Deep within their conscience men and women discover a law which they have not laid upon themselves and which they must obey. Its voice, ever calling them to love and to do what is good and to avoid evil, tells them inwardly at the right moment: do this, shun that. For they have in their hearts a law inscribed by God. Their dignity rests in observing this law, and by this they will be judged. Their conscience is people's most secret

> core, and their sanctuary. There they are alone with God whose voice echoes in their depths. Through loyalty to conscience, Christians are joined to others in the search for truth and for the right solution to so many moral problems which arise both in the life of individuals and from social relationships. Hence, the more a correct conscience prevails, the more do persons and groups turn aside from blind choice and endeavor to conform to the objective standards of conduct. Yet it often happens that conscience goes astray through ignorance which it is unable to avoid, without thereby losing its dignity. This cannot be said of the person who takes little trouble to find out what is true and good, or when conscience is gradually almost blinded through the habit of committing sin.[177]

Significantly, *Gaudium et Spes* rooted the possibility of conscience in freedom (§17). There were many reasons for the turn to freedom: the Fascist and Nazi movements that imprisoned millions across the European continent; the subsequent developments in the philosophy of existentialism; the control of the manualists and the ever-encroaching dictates from the Vatican; and Soviet expansionism into Eastern Europe. However, this freedom was above all rooted in Pauline theology, which taught us that our freedom was secured by Christ and the Spirit. This freedom that guaranteed that one not only could but should follow the conscience's dictates[178] became the very opening salvo of *Dignitatis Humanae*:

> People nowadays are becoming increasingly conscious of the dignity of the human person; a growing number demand that people should exercise fully their own judgment and a responsible freedom in their actions, and should not be subject to external pressure or coercion, but inspired by a sense of duty. At the same time, to present excessive restrictions of the rightful freedom of individuals and associations, they demand the constitutional limitations of the powers of government. This demand for freedom in human society is concerned chiefly with the affairs of the human spirit, and especially with what concerns the free practice of religion in society.[179]

Through conscience, all moral agents needed to discover and articulate the moral judgment that would set the standard of moral objectivity. Just as moralists articulated moral truths by reflecting through their consciences on the Scriptures and the tradition on matters confronting them, now all people, the clergy and the laity, were invited to do the same. These teachings became, then, enormous catalysts for moral theology's ongoing renewal. The German Josef Fuchs, the Australian Terence Kennedy, and the American Charles Curran each published their own collected essays on the topic.[180] Full-length books were written by Eric D'Arcy from Australia, Linda Hogan from Ireland, Kevin Kelly from England, Anne Patrick from the United States, Osamu Takeuchi from Japan, and Paul Valadier from France.[181]

Third, in providing the ecclesial context in which the renewal of moral theology could flourish, *Gaudium et Spes* prompted moral theology and social ethics to take down the wall that let them be two autonomous fields. The revisionists' move toward the social meant that their anthropological core could not remain individualistic and solitary. The moral virtues could no longer be solely about chastity, temperance, fortitude, obedience, a cautious prudence, and fear of the Lord; charity demanded justice, mercy, an ambitious prudence, and a late-arriving solidarity. Nevertheless, although the revisionists insisted on the social, it was not until the Council that the fields actually began to engage each other. *Gaudium et Spes* was written in such a way that the lines that demarcated them are no longer acceptable, or for that matter, visible. For this reason, few self-identify today as moral theologians or as social ethicists, but are more at home with the appellation of theological ethicist.

Fourth, while there is little instruction about ethics (natural law, moral principles, and virtues were referred to as dependable, but with no appreciation for revisionists' radical rethinking of each of the three areas), still the Council was deeply concerned about discourse between the world and the church. Upholding repeatedly the conscience, particularly of the laity (conscience is cited twenty-eight times in *Gaudium et Spes*), the Council fathers argued that no one can "indulge in a merely individualistic morality" but "must consider it their sacred duty to count social obligations among their chief duties today" (*GS* 30). Together through discourse the foundations of good order in the church and the world depended on the well-formed consciences (§43; see also §§16, 26, 41). Moreover, as the laity pursued solutions, they needed to be mindful "that their pastors will not always be so expert as to have ready answer to every problem, even every grave problem" (§43) and that in differing opinions, "no one is permitted to identify the authority of the church exclusively with her or his opinion" (§43).

A new humility was being proposed about Catholic discourse, certainly not seen in Davis, nor in Slater, nor certainly in Toledo: "The church is guardian of the deposit of God's word and draws religious and moral principles from it, but it does not always have a ready answer to every question" (*GS* 30). In a clear nod to Cardinal John Henry Newman (1801–90),[182] the Council noted that now theologians were being asked to develop more efficient ways of communicating church teaching: "for the deposit and truths of faith are one thing, the manner of expressing them—provided their sense and meaning are retained—is quite another" (§62). Now the church attended to boundaries: "The political community and the church are autonomous and independent of each other in their own fields" (§76). This did not endorse, however, the "pernicious opposition between professional and social activity on the one hand and religious life on the other" (§43). Still, it did mean that church teaching must heed the variety of competencies that are needed, that theology must keep pace with scientific findings (§62), and that "the faithful, both clerical and lay, should be accorded a lawful freedom of inquiry, of thought, and of expression, tempered by humility and courage in whatever branch they have specialized" (§62). This description of discourse empowers theological ethical inquiry to be conducted in the public square where a new tolerance for conscientious pursuit of the truth was promoted. Nothing like this had ever been given to theological ethics.

VII. *HUMANAE VITAE* (1968) AND THE COLLAPSE OF MANUALISM

The eventual end of manualist theology in the United States and the rest of the English-speaking world was caused by its greatest achievement: the encyclical *Humanae Vitae*. In 1960, Dr. John Rock, an American Catholic, developed the birth control pill precisely to provide Catholics with a "natural" recourse to acceptable birth control, that did not use "barrier methods" or "obstacles to conception" like intrauterine devices or prophylactics. By developing the pill that would naturally allow a woman's body to become infertile without any artificial devices, Rock thought he had found a legitimate Catholic way to regulate human fertility.

Quite apart from Rock's intentions, the pill now made it possible for most women who had access to it to regulate their fertility. This provoked for the Catholic Church, as it was preparing for an ecumenical council with a charismatic pope seeking to engage reforming theologies, an enormous challenge in light of the irreformable teaching of *Casti Connubii.*[183] To not harness the Council with the unfolding discourse, Pope John XXIII (1881–1963; r. 1958–63) eventually decided to take birth control out of the Council in 1963 by establishing a "Pontifical Commission for the Study of Population, Family, and Births."[184] A year later at the Council, the hopes of developing church teaching on the topic hit an enormous impasse during a week of tumultuous debate over birth control in the final stages of the preparation of *Gaudium et Spes.*[185] Eventually the Council fathers wrote, "In questions of birth regulation the daughters and sons of the church...are forbidden to use methods disapproved of by the teaching authority of the church in its interpretation of divine law" (*GS* 51).

Meanwhile, the commission was meeting. During the first meetings of the papal commission, Häring was believed to be convincing the members of the importance of reforming the teaching on birth control. Purportedly, in an effort to counterbalance his influence, the new Pope Paul VI (1897–1978; r. 1963–78) appointed a number of more conservative archbishops, bishops, and theologians to the commission, among them Fuchs. Earlier, in 1955, Fuchs had written on the natural law. There he claimed that the magisterium's "duty within the actual order of salvation is to form the consciences of all men, primarily those in charge of public life."[186] Many believed that it was Ford who suggested his fellow Jesuit Fuchs to the pope, believing that the man who wrote in 1955 would continue to think the same way and as a Roman theologian would be a formidable opponent of Häring. On the commission, however, already disposed to the revisionists like Lottin, Fuchs began listening to the testimony of married couples and eventually abandoned his conviction that moral truth was founded singularly and primarily in long-held norms articulated by the magisterium. By listening to others, Fuchs slowly recognized that his original supposition was inadequate, and began to explore critically a key question: whether the method of directly applying a norm to a case was also adequate for determining moral truth. If that question were posed to Fuchs in 1955, his answer would have been a resounding yes; by 1968, it was an equally decisive no.[187]

To Ford's surprise, Fuchs became the draftsman of the commission's majority report that essentially advocated that decisions on birth control be made in conscience.[188] There he wrote that the competency of a moral decision depends on the ability to consider adequately the various claims on an agent (*GS* 26). From listening to the testimonies of the married couples on the papal commission and heeding the conciliar document *Gaudium et Spes*, he saw that their understanding of the various claims on them was more comprehensive than the general teachings of Rome and acknowledged that the Christian finds moral truth through the discernment of an informed conscience confronting reality. This did not mean that the moral principles did not guide us to moral truth, but rather than they did so generally, a point that Fuchs took from Thomas Aquinas, that is, that principles apply *ut in pluribus*. Discernment was effectively a descent from the differing principles into the particulars, and that descent was, in Fuchs's estimation, the human search for moral truth. The majority report was effectively the first revisionist church document after the Council.[189]

Still, in the interim between the report being submitted and the publication of *Humanae Vitae*, Ford became indomitable in convincing Pope Paul VI that he could not change *Casti Connubii* (1930) nor accept the majority report of the birth control commission. He also became the draftsman of the commission's minority rebuttal.[190] However, while Ford was lobbying and the pope waited nearly a full year between reception of the majority report and the promulgation of the encyclical, the clergy and laity around the world were growing impatient. As the wait became progressively interpreted as a studied reluctance to reiterate the irreformable, the eventual promulgation was even more problematic.

Much can be said about *Humanae Vitae*. For our purposes, we should see that it is to some degree the first papal rejection of the revisionists' innovative approach and the first significant papal endorsement of neo-manualism after Vatican II.[191] Nevertheless, the local hierarchy received the encyclical differently. The two tracks that we have been following determined very much its reception. Just as the Council fathers from Western Europe gave us the conciliar teachings that led to the renewal of moral theology, similarly we find that their episcopal conferences (the French, German, Canadian, Scandinavian, and Dutch) provided a variety of responses to *Humanae Vitae* that basically exhorted the laity to follow their consciences as they considered the claims of the encyclical. Without rejecting the encyclical, the European hierarchy insisted that the ultimate judge of a moral claim was the conscience. Unfortunately, the U.S. episcopal conference along with other English-speaking ones stood univocally with the reception of the encyclical, with hardly a word on conscience.[192]

Still, while the American hierarchy and their manualists ignored the call to conscience, the clergy and the laity did not, and they began to look for insight elsewhere. There followed first the critical evaluation of the encyclical and second a renewed engagement with the Europeans and, in particular, the Council. Two people led the way on both matters: Charles Curran (1934–) and Richard McCormick (1922–2000).[193] While their styles were very different, together they made possible the reception of *Humanae Vitae* through the Council's teaching on conscience. In fact, they led us to appreciate how by receiving the Council, we could as a community of faith go forward to develop a more life-giving, disciple-based moral theology. Similarly, in Ireland, Enda McDonagh and Vincent MacNamara and, in the United Kingdom, John Mahoney and Kevin Kelly led their theologians into the renewal process of theological ethics in light of the Council. By the mid-1970s the reformers' project was growing on both sides of the Atlantic. Ironically, the repudiation of the neoscholastic manuals led to the conciliar summons to return to the sources of moral theology and that led the revisionists to provide a renaissance in the studies of Thomas Aquinas. These investigations led in turn to two other expansive developments on the nature of natural law and the virtues. In seeking to find a way to go forward, like Lottin we realized the need for history, in particular the history of theological ethics before the manualist tradition.

VIII. CONCLUSION: LEARNING TO THINK HISTORICALLY

We saw the dynamic first century of both the Jesuits and the Redemptorists; we also saw, in time, a resistance to their own developments. In one sense, the resistance came from outside: the Jesuits were suppressed by their enemies and the Redemptorists, and Liguori in particular, were repeatedly questioned for not surrendering to rigorism. But in another sense, both the Jesuits and the Redemptorists became self-censoring; they tempered their own charisms whether knowingly or not. It is not until each order revisited the traditions of their founders that they rediscovered their original charism. For instance, more than 150 years after their restoration, the Jesuits had a certain "refounding" that arguably occurred during the Generalate of Pedro Arrupe (1907–91; general 1965–83). In a similar way, the work of Vidal, Gallagher, Jones, and Rey-Mermet called their members to their founding charisms. Their return to the sources was not a retrenchment, but rather a tapping of the inspiring call that their founders shared. In many ways these renaissances were like Lottin's historical investigations into Scholasticism as a vibrant debate rather than a treasure trove of immutable truths. Lottin similarly inspired us to realize that the Thomism of the manuals was not the dynamic Thomism of Scholasticism.

Just as the Jesuits and Redemptorists were being tempered, John Henry Newman wrote in 1845 his "Essay on the Development of Christian Doctrine."[194] James Gaffney points out how the notion of development for Newman began from a great truth being first apprehended but then becoming increasingly comprehended.[195] Moreover, as Gerard McCarren helpfully notes, the very process of development is not incidental but intrinsic to its truth: "Having admitted the impact of the vicissitudes of history on Christian doctrine, Newman deemed doctrinal development the only hypothesis capable of explaining how Christianity could have remained faithful to its doctrinal patrimony."[196] In a way, the tradition must develop, progress, and unfold in order to live.

In his essay "Does Church Teaching Change: The Development of Doctrine at Trent, Vatican I, and Vatican II," John W. O'Malley notes that "for winning acceptance of the idea that change affected even doctrine, no book was more important than John Henry Newman's *Essay on the Development of Christian Doctrine.*" Commenting that Newman's work belonged to the same age as Charles Darwin's "On the Origin of the Species" (1859), one preoccupied "with evolution, development, progress, and the implications of the historical process," O'Malley adds,

> By using different analogies, Newman showed how teachings evolved while remaining true to their origins. Teachings were both continuous and discontinuous with their earlier articulation. The book, still the classic in the field, put the problem of change in doctrine on the stage of theological discourse to a degree unknown before. Although published well before Vatican Council I, it had no significant impact on the council's debates, but in the decades leading up to Vatican II most Catholic bishops and theologians accepted its basic premise in some form or other.[197]

The acceptance of development as constitutive of the life of the tradition is a nineteenth-century proposal that, like all the other innovations we have seen in the nineteenth century, was not really accepted until well into the twentieth century.

Though rightly we acknowledge that Yves Congar (1904–95) proposed a dynamic notion of the tradition,[198] the Canadian theologian Bernard Lonergan (1904–84) developed the connection between the givenness of the tradition and the developing articulation of it.[199] In 1967, he published three articles that profoundly affected our understanding of moral truth by making a distinction between a classicist worldview and a historical-mindedness.[200] Over the next thirty years, these three essays would influence moral theology considerably.[201] Lonergan's distinction was not a difference in kind, however, but in degree; no one was a pure classicist or historicist.

For classicists, the world is a finished product and truth has already been revealed, expressed, taught, and known. The moral law is found in that which has always been true, never changed, and always applies. The truth claims of a statement are demonstrated when we can claim possession of the same truth eternally: Consistency in historical transmission generates phrases like, "as we have always taught." Change in moral teaching is, then, problematic; it suggests that at one point a teaching was right and, in a later (or earlier) instance, wrong. Similarly, classicists resist contextualization. The truth cannot be compromised by local claims; if it is, it is dismissed as culturally relativistic. The universality and constancy of the truth claim is central. A fine example of classicism is *Casti Connubii* (1930), to say nothing of the entire tradition of manualism.

Historical-mindedness theologians look at the world and at truth as constantly emerging. They argue that we are learning more, not only about the world, but about ourselves. As subjects we are affected by history: we become hopefully the people whom we are called to become. What the world and humanity will be is not yet known, but rests on the horizons of our expectations and the decisions we make and realize. The moral law then looks to determine what at this period corresponds to the vision we ought to be shaping. It admits that the final word on the truth is outstanding but emerging.

Contrary to their detractors, historicists do not argue that truth is constructed or manufactured; rather, truth is "discovered" in history. Truth has its objectivity, but it is only gradually being grasped by us in our understanding over time, through experience, maturity, and judgment. Though historicists believe in the importance of the situation and of circumstances, they are not situational ethicists. That ethics developed by Joseph Fletcher argued that the moral agent has no mediating norms between the self and the concrete: only the law of love is to be radically expressed in the here and now. We have seen, however, from Lottin to Curran that every revisionist believed in the need for mediating moral guidance through the already received stances and values that we need for right acting from Scripture and tradition.[202] Conscience does not operate in a vacuum but relies on revelation, church teaching, and human experience.

Experience differentiates the two perspectives of classicism and historicism. The manualists did little to recognize and incorporate human experience, though the confessors themselves did. When it comes to moral teaching, classicists see experience as an attempt to diminish the truth claims of an evident teaching. Historicists are anxious, however, about whether they adequately grasp and understand human experience. They are suspicious of deductive logic; in their estimation, real truth is found through analogy. They believe that truth is found by comparing one situation to another. They are modest about their judgments and assertions, and usually quite tentative about any truth claim; they tend away from unequivocal clarity and entertain circumstances as significantly and substantively relevant. The particularity of the situation is needed.

Historicists, then, are much more inclined to context. Unlike the manualists, they accept change in teaching on usury, capital punishment, or contraception when that change illustrates a greater approximation to the law of love. Like Lottin, they study history to see how the community of faith tries to understand from one generation to another the values and visions of the emerging moral law. In sum, the classical worldview depends on what is already known; historical mindedness responds to the knower: our ability to recognize the truth as it emerges through the data of experience very much depends on our own moral nature. Following Aristotle, historicists acknowledge that we see reality as we are. The governing notions of objectivity are, nevertheless, very different, not only about history and universality but also about the agent. For the classicist, the agent does not enter into the equation of moral truthfulness: the moral truth remains the same for all. If I want to know the truth, I should be as detached from the situation as possible. For the historicists, the agent is integrally involved in the morally objective judgment.

Finally, the church's identity is deeply affected by its self-understanding as moral teacher. Inasmuch as the church understands itself in the classicist mode, it will resist innovation as beyond its competency, where teachings have already been defined. Noteworthy, for us then, is that *Gaudium et Spes* was providing a historicist perspective, an interesting move inasmuch as church teaching was never more classicist than in the three hundred years preceding the Council document. This call to experience and the concomitant belief in the development of doctrine did not arrive in 1965 unannounced. The three issues that prompted the suppression of the Jesuits were also deeply related to the major rallying cries for the progress of peoples during the second half of the twentieth century: probabilism and the primacy of conscience, the Chinese rites and inculturation, and the Paraguayan reductions and the sovereignty of minority populations.

The integral insight that moral teaching is dependent on both human experience and human progress is similarly seen in Alphonsus Liguori. His actual engagement in ministry becomes the impetus for developing a more progressive moral theology. Encountering the *lazzaroti*, he decided that he could not permit them or others to succumb to the useless ideologies of the rigorists who resisted the progress of peoples. On the contrary, their worlds needed to develop. It is key to understanding the developments of the twentieth century that the experience of Liguori, like the experience of the Jesuits with the Chinese or with the Guaraní, was transformative: integral to understanding humanity was, therefore, an appreciation of humanity's need for development and progress.

Of course, when moral theology became reacquainted with the spiritual pathways that animated it previously, moral theology discovered therein its call to progress. Indeed the insight of progress was deeply connected to the self-understanding of the disciples of Christ who effectively, in their experience, discovered in their call to follow Christ the source of a new moral imperative: to advance. Gregory the Great (540–604; r. 590–604) wrote, "Certainly, in this world, the human spirit is like a boat foolishly fighting against the river's rush: one is never allowed to stay still, because unless one forges ahead, one will slide back downstream."[203] Later, in the twelfth century, Bernard of Clairvaux (1090–1153) argued, "To not progress on the way of Life is to regress."[204] Thomas Aquinas (1225–74) summed up their insights: "To remain standing on the way of the Lord is to move backwards."[205] For them, the Lord who leads us on the way expects us to move, to follow. To not follow is to retreat.

Finally, on a personal note, I was trained by two major theological ethicists: Josef Fuchs and Klaus Demmer (1931–2014).[206] There, in Rome, I learned that working with the tradition was fundamentally a progressive work, for progress is constitutive of the tradition. From Demmer and Fuchs I learned that while history narrates the development of the tradition, theological ethics must occasion such a development. Josef Fuchs wrote that the Christian has received a new competency through Christ to overcome evil with good, and therefore is called continually to improve the human world through innovation.[207] Precisely for this reason, this book focuses on the "innovators." Likewise, Klaus Demmer argued that the moral task of reversing bias and decline in human history shares analogously in the death and resurrection of Christ.[208] More recently, Marciano Vidal invoked recent papal statements to find their endorsements of the necessity of moral development or what Vidal called "progress."[209]

Our historical investigations served then as correctives to the manualists' general claims regarding the unchangeability of moral truth. It also reminds us that we might want to retrieve what we once abandoned, whether the insights of the nineteenth-century innovators or the type of nondeductive casuistry of the sixteenth casuistry. In fact, with the collapse of the manuals, a few European Catholic ethicists began returning to casuistry. Both Jean-Marie Aubert and Klaus Demmer explored the foundations of casuistry as germane to the revisionist project. Aubert saw casuistry as providing the mediation between law and liberty;[210] Demmer noted that casuistry calls us to recognize the historicity of truth in moral reasoning.[211] For Demmer, every time a principle was applied to a new case, the principle itself was being reinterpreted: the hermeneutics of the application of casuistic principles to cases was a sure guarantee for the historical development of doctrine. Later, Demmer's student Thomas Kopfensteiner advanced the position that casuistry was used to liberate institutions from normative determinations that did not keep pace with other developments.[212] John T. Noonan Jr. studied the mutation of old rules by the introduction of new cases that shape both the meaning and the application of the rule. After a lengthy process of application and development, new prescriptions were eventually articulated.[213] In such ways, the moral tradition advances critically. By looking back historically, we can discover the dynamism of our thoughts and beliefs.

Chapter Eight

Moral Agency for a Global Theological Ethics

With an awareness of how our histories affect our agency, we turn then to our own time, when now more than ever theological ethicists turn their responsive gaze nearly exclusively to human suffering. In order to raise greater recognition to the causes and plight of human suffering, they incorporate into the tradition of theological ethics the common good tradition to develop a much more robust, inclusive, and competent ethics that can address suffering both globally and locally. To understand this development, the chapter is divided into two parts: "The Moral Agency of the Theological Ethicist in Breaking Boundaries" and "Recognizing Human Suffering, Descending into the Particular, and Going Global."

I. THE MORAL AGENCY OF THE THEOLOGICAL ETHICIST IN BREAKING BOUNDARIES

The moral agency of the theological ethicist changes dramatically from a very clerical identity who both hears confessions and guides confessors while writing on sin to a much more inclusive agency of both genders living with very different commitments to one another. What keeps them together is their turn to human experience and in particular to human suffering, and that turn prompts them to break down the barriers that define their fields so as to respond to urgent concerns with a more comprehensive method of theological ethics. This section is an attempt to explain how these steps were taken.

Toward the end of the twentieth century, the face of moral theology began to change to reflect the more common features of everyday Catholics. Today, for example, the majority of theological ethicists in the United States and in some parts of Europe are laypeople, a growing number are women, and many of the laity are married, often with children. Not surprisingly they bring their experiences to bear on theological ethics. The change from an exclusive field of clergy to a diverse one of both men and women, lay, religious, and clergy began in the 1970s.

Through a variety of inquiries, I have put together an account of how mostly in the United States women religious and other laypeople[1] entered the field of theological ethics in the 1970s.

Changing the Face of the Field

In 1973, Margaret Farley, RSM, defended her dissertation under the direction of James Gustafson at Yale University and joined the faculty there.[2] In that same year, Walter Conn defended his dissertation at Columbia University and Thomas Shannon defended his at Boston University. In Germany, Dietmar Mieth studied with Alfons Auer at Tübingen, concluded his habilitation in 1974, and began teaching at the University of Freiburg in Switzerland. In that same year James Walter defended his dissertation in Christian ethics at Katholieke Universiteit Leuven (KUL) and entered the field of Catholic Bioethics. All of these men were members of the laity.

Still in 1974, Mary Emil Penet, IHM, began teaching moral theology at St. John's Seminary in Plymouth, Michigan, and then moved to do the same in 1975 at Weston Jesuit School of Theology in Cambridge, Massachusetts; Penet had done a doctorate of philosophy in 1951 at St. Louis University, but in the early 1970s, he became Fuchs's personal assistant so as to develop a competency to teach in the field.[3]

William E. May, who did his doctorate in Philosophy in 1968 at Marquette University, began teaching moral theology at the

Catholic University of America in the mid-1970s.[4] In 1976, Lisa Sowle Cahill defended her dissertation at the University of Chicago, where she was mentored by Gustafson, and began teaching at Boston College.[5] Under the supervision of Louis Janssens, the American Joseph Selling completed his dissertation on the reception of *Humanae Vitae* at KUL in 1977. In 1979, Christine Gudorf defended her dissertation in religious social ethics at Columbia University in a joint program with Union Theological Seminary. In that same year, Patricia Beattie Jung defended her dissertation at Vanderbilt University. Similarly, in that year, Germain G. Grisez, who did his doctorate in philosophy at University of Chicago in 1959 and later was a close collaborator of John Ford during the latter's tenure on the papal commission on birth control, began teaching moral theology at Mount St. Mary's University in Emmitsburg, Maryland.[6]

Significantly, almost all the new lay doctorates in the United States were achieved not at Catholic universities, though in Europe they were. Thus, not only were the candidates new, but their studies' programs were new and, in some instances, their positions of teaching as a theological ethicist were new. For example, Farley takes a position at one of the premier academic institutions in the United States. Thus, boundaries are being reconfigured. Moralists are no longer singularly clerical priests, their training is not necessarily at Catholic institutions, and their professional positions are not always episcopally controlled. Not surprisingly, the matter of theological ethics changes as well once the boundaries between fundamental moral and social ethics are actually removed.

From the 1980s on, laity continue entering the field of moral theology in the United States, Canada, and parts of Europe; by the end of the century, women began entering the ranks of theological ethics in Latin America and East Asia as well. Like the Filipina Agnes Brazal who bridged systematic and moral theology in her KUL dissertation (1998) on method and feminist perspectives emerging from liberation theology, they scaled over boundaries and were not easily compartmentalized. Moreover, some of these women were already teaching in their departments before finishing their degrees. For example, Christina Astorga was Professor and even Chair of the Theology department at the Ateneo de Manila starting in 1994, though she did not defend her dissertation in moral theology at the Ateneo until 2000. Similarly, in Latin America,

Chile's Verónica Anguita Mackay began teaching in 1996 and received her degree in 2000, while Maria Inês de Millen received her doctoral degree in 2003 from the Pontifícia Universidade Católica do Rio de Janeiro.

From India, Sr. Vimala Chenginimattam, CMC, defended her dissertation on "Psycho-moral Development of Girls and Women, according to Carol Gilligan," at the Alphonsianum in Rome in 2006, becoming India's first woman moral theologian. Over the past fifteen years she has developed arguments to launch platforms for women's voices in ethics, letting us know not only that we need to hear their voices but also that they have been expressing themselves for some time.[7] Today there are more than thirty trained women moralists in India and more entering doctoral studies every year.

In Africa, the development was just as significant. In 2010 there was only one African woman, Vivian Minikongo, from the Democratic Republic of the Congo, with a PhD in the field. By 2018 there were more than twenty-five women with doctorates in theological ethics, many mindful of bringing the voices of women into the academy, the public square, and into Catholic fora.[8]

A major inspirational force behind these African women was Sr. Anne Nasimiyu, LSOSF, who in 1986 became the first African Catholic theologian with a PhD, not in theological ethics, but in systematics. She did her dissertation on Vatican II and inculturation at Duquesne. Like Teresia Hinga, who earned her doctorate in religious studies and African Christianity from Lancaster University in 1990, and then Philomena Njeri Mwaura, who secured her doctorate from Kenyatta University in 2002, these women were pioneers in the broad field of theology. Not until 2010 did women in Africa begin pursuing degrees in the field of moral theology.

Nasimiyu published various articles and book chapters on contemporary African experience. Among many essays, in 1989 she wrote on "Christology and an African Woman's Experience."[9] In 1992 she published two essays in one collection on women and African tradition, "Christianity and the African Rituals of Birth and Naming" and "Polygamy: A Feminist Critique," showing how she could raise up one practice within a tradition and criticize another in the same tradition.[10] In 2010 she was a plenary speaker at the international conference of Catholic Theological Ethics in the World Church (CTEWC) in Trento, Italy, and there she spoke on

"The Missing Voices of Women," surveying the missing voices of women in the Bible and the tradition as well as in the contemporary world in Africa.[11] Throughout her work, she posited that women were not only translators of value but inventors of value: their creative contributions that arose from their own experiences needed to be recognized.

The emancipatory style of Nasimiyu impacted not only women but also all those who were oppressed by unaddressed social structures. In 2001, in a very provocative essay, "Is Mutuality Possible: An African Response," she denounced the hegemony of Euro-American culture. She wrote,

> It is the task of the Western theologians to educate their people that Christianity has been too Euro-American centered to open up to other cultures in the world. The monopoly of Euro-American cultures in Christianity has hampered the adornment of the church with the colors and cultures of other peoples in the world. It has to be recognized that all cultures are relative and equally important. It is only in this realization that the church will move from a Euro-American centered church to a world-centered church.[12]

Nasimiyu was both the coordinator of the Circle of Concerned African Women Theologians in East Africa and the African women's coordinator of the Ecumenical Association of Third World Theologians. With a distinguished background of championing women's voices from girl-children to the elderly and with a long record of leadership among African religious women, she came to Boston College to work during a brief sabbatical on a collection of essays entitled *The Moral Right to an Education for Women Religious*, which was published through *Asian Horizons*.[13] The collection had contributions from theologians in Africa, Asia, Europe, and the United States and became a capstone in her legacy.[14] Tragically, Sr. Anne Nasimiyu died suddenly on February 22, 2018, just after returning home, where she contracted malaria.[15]

Even in more isolated and remote parts of the world church, women would hear the same call to rise up in the field. In 2006, Sr. Nhu Y Lan Tran, by defending her dissertation at Weston Jesuit

School of Theology, became the first woman moral theologian of Vietnam.[16] In 2010, Zorica Maros was invited to teach at the University of Sarajevo, and when she was awarded her doctorate in 2013, she became the first woman moral theologian of Bosnia and Herzegovina.[17]

An extensive study of such firsts remains outstanding.[18]

Resistance

I would be remiss not to note that within the narratives of many of these pioneers are the instances of their opposition by hierarchy and clergy who tried to undermine the women's emergent leadership. From clergy they encountered mockery and ridicule in their classes; from the hierarchy, more formidable, humiliating opposition.[19] At the same time, they received welcome support from other members of both groups, but these accounts further indicate and validate the urgency for these voices to find their places and their platforms.

This opposition has not been simply local. Years ago, Carmel McEnroy gave a significant account of the women at Vatican II, noting that they were "guests in their own house."[20] Yet each of these women heard the call that the late theologian Catherine LaCugna articulated when she wrote that if women were looking to express moral agency through leadership, they should become theologians.[21]

Just as these women found resistance from some clergy and hierarchy, so too did some of the existing theological ethicists among the clergy. As religious women and other laypeople were attracted to the ranks of theological ethics, hierarchy moved against some clerical theologians writing in the spirit of Vatican II whom the hierarchy deemed had gone too far. Chief among these priests was Hans Küng, whom Franjo Cardinal Šeper, Prefect of the Congregation for the Doctrine of the Faith, declared on December 15, 1979, could "no longer be considered a Catholic theologian nor function as such in a teaching role."[22] This disciplinary action let theologians know that the Congregation could and would take away what some clergy had and what religious women and other lay theologians were presently seeking: the authority to teach theology.

The censure of Küng followed an earlier form of censorship begun after the promulgation of *Humanae Vitae*, when priests in the United States, following the position of the European hierarchy who held that the encyclical had to be read in the light of the demands of conscience, publicly stood with that interpretation, when their own U.S. hierarchy did not. Notably in Washington, DC, Cardinal Patrick O'Boyle disciplined the priests who publicly protested the encyclical by removing their clerical faculties to celebrate the sacraments.[23]

As others were subsequently disciplined for their positions on liberation theology, the ordination of women, or the divinity of Christ, these public actions had a profound impact on theologians throughout the 1970s and onward. More specifically, for theological ethicists, issues relating to birth control and the LGBTQ community garnered much more attention. Moreover, actions by local and Roman hierarchy, from cancellations of speaking engagements and investigations into orthodoxy to actual long-term censure continually let theological ethicists know that their own conscientious inquiries into ethical issues were not without review. Behind all of this was the hierarchy's concern of the "confusing" impact of a theologian's work on the "faithful," but rarely were these disciplinary actions transparent and rarely was there any coming together of theologians with hierarchy to find a less threatening and more resourceful way of going forward.

Instead, censorship against theological ethicists advanced. In the United States, the most significant case began on August 2, 1979, when Charles Curran was notified by a letter from the Congregation for the Doctrine of the Faith that he was under investigation. Seven years later, on July 25, 1986, the Congregation declared that Charles Curran would "no longer be considered suitable or eligible to exercise the function of a Professor of Catholic Theology."[24] Three weeks later, the chancellor of the Catholic University of America notified Curran that he was initiating the withdrawal of Curran's canonical mission to teach there. Curran did not simply submit to the discipline; rather, he insisted on the legitimacy of his position within the church by invoking the concept of dissent, arguing that it was necessary for the church's own commitment to truth that it allow and respect dissent by those whose task it was to investigate the truth claims of the church's magisterium.[25] In fact, Curran's position was hardly a reaction; for years, in the face of *Humanae Vitae*, Curran along with others had articulated the essential necessity of dissent for the church's own integrity in its teaching ministry.[26] The Vatican and the U.S. hierarchy did not concur. After nearly three years of litigation, on February 28, 1989, the removal of Charles Curran's tenure at CUA was complete.

In 1989, Richard McCormick wrote about "The Chill Factor in Contemporary Moral Theology" within a book entitled *The Critical Calling: Reflections on Moral Dilemmas since Vatican II* and therein documented innumerable accounts of other investigations, imprimatur withdrawals, public questioning of theologians' orthodoxy, and subsequent condemnations that created a climate that left many theologians in a precarious situation.[27] The article named well the impact of these disciplinary actions, though undaunted, many more religious women and other laypeople as well as clergy continued to enter the field in the spirit of Vatican II.

Besides some members of the hierarchy, a few others also thought the discipline was warranted. The Dominican moralist Benedict Ashley wrote a review of McCormick's book and named it "The Chill Factor in Moral Theology." There he argued that McCormick put too much confidence in the theologians' own inclination to self-critical debate and saw instead that the Congregation's exercise of discipline was more of a help than a hindrance, arguing that it was not causing a chill but rather offering an invigorating, refreshing breeze.[28]

More than twenty years later, however, the scrutiny moved beyond clergy.[29] On June 4, 2012, the Congregation declared that Margaret Farley's *Just Love: A Framework for Christian Sexual Ethics*[30] had "doctrinal errors present in a book whose publication has been a cause of confusion among the faithful."[31]

Changing the Location of the Field of Theological Ethics

The difference in the impact of the disciplining of Curran and Farley deserves comment. Farley's work was a constructive study that offered to the field of academic theological ethics a proposal for a contemporary sexual ethics. Certainly, Farley's work as an academic theologian was, like that of most Catholic ethicists, indebted to the pathways for freedom that Curran pursued, but the book's project was not directly to change or even counter church teaching or for that matter to dissent, but rather to propose a sexual ethics that might resonate with people from a variety of traditions who believed that living out our lives sexually requires us to bring into the public arena the virtues, values, and norms for that form of living.[32] Not without notice, Farley won the prestigious Grawemeyer award for her contribution in 2008.[33]

In light of the Vatican charge that her book "affirms positions that are in direct contradiction with Catholic teaching in the field of sexual morality," Farley responded to the "Notification" saying that her book was not intended to express "current official Catholic teaching" but rather to help people "think through their questions about human sexuality."

Farley noted,

> This book was designed to help people, especially Christians but also others, to think through their questions about human sexuality. It suggests the importance of moving from what frequently functions as a taboo morality to a morality and sexual ethics based on the discernment of what counts as wise, truthful, and recognizably just loves. Although my responses to some particular sexual ethical questions do depart from some traditional Christian responses, I have tried to show that they nonetheless reflect a deep coherence with the central aims and insights of these theological and moral traditions.[34]

Farley's work is a Catholic attempt to work out a space for critical ethical reflection in a church whose hierarchies are intent on monitoring adherence to what they define as irreformable teachings. Neapolitan ethicist in Berlin Antonio Autiero reflected on the search for this same space in the church that Farley seeks. He contended that the problem "is above all the knowledge that normative and strictly deductive superstructures expressed in authoritarian control suffocate the space of authentic liberty in the existence of adult subjects who are mature enough to make autonomous and responsible moral choices. Now it is time to ask whether and how far the Church presents itself to postmodern people as an inhabitable home from this point of view also." Reflecting on "the most recent developments," he added, "One cannot deny that there is a movement away from the Church, quite explicitly or sometimes even simply pragmatically, precisely on account of the Church's insistence on moral themes public or private, marked by normative solutions that make little sense to the critical consciousness of contemporary men and women."[35] Is there some way to offer a space for those looking for their faith in freedom that does not necessitate an exit strategy?

In many ways, both Curran and Farley have been looking for the "space" where these critical investigations can occur *and* be engaged: Curran's was quite clearly in the church, in the seminary, and even in the confessional. Thirty years later, Farley's space is more where theological ethicists and their interlocutors are gathered: the academy. Although Farley was not teaching at a Catholic university, she was writing for Christian theological ethicists and others deeply connected to the academy. Autiero's hope for a space within the church where critical discourse can happen without the sanctions found elsewhere would be the university and, in particular, the Catholic university.

On the same days as the Farley "Notification" appeared, Tobias Winright posted a very thoughtful essay entitled "L'Affaire Farley and the Ongoing Chill in Contemporary Moral Theology," reminding us that the chill factor continues.[36] Winright also highlighted Lisa Sowle Cahill's observations that "theologians do not see or present their work as 'official church teaching.'" Cahill added that "few of the faithful are confused about this fact. Readers of *Just Love* hardly need to be warned that this is not official church teaching; they will feel free to question, disagree and improve the points of the author, as is no doubt her intention."[37]

Cahill argued that magisterial teaching and contemporary theological investigations are different in form and purpose. In fact, Cahill noted theological investigations today are not per se located in the seminary but more likely found at the university where there is academic freedom and academic theology.

Earlier in 1987, Curran commented on the emerging "academic context of moral theology":

> For all practical purposes, moral theology and all Catholic theology in the United States were not looked on as academic disciplines before the 1960s. Theology was primarily identified with seminary education....It is true

> that theology was taught at Catholic colleges, but for the most part it was treated as a catechetical rather than an academic enterprise.[38]

The turn from catechetical instruction to academic investigation is noteworthy. Curran noted that in the United States, Catholic colleges and universities began to see in academic freedom a context that could shape the excellence of Catholic higher education. Curran reminded us of the Land O'Lakes Statement issued by twenty-six leaders of Catholic higher education in the United States and Canada in 1967 that was a catalyst for this remarkable shift. He turned to the opening paragraph of their statement:

> The Catholic University today must be a university in the full modern sense of the word, with a strong commitment to and concern for academic excellence. To perform its teaching and research functions effectively the Catholic university must have a true autonomy and academic freedom in the face of authority of whatever kind, lay or clerical, external to the academic community itself. To say this is simply to assert that institutional autonomy and academic freedom are essential conditions of life and growth and indeed of survival for Catholic universities as for all universities.[39]

Effectively, Curran noted that theologians today are not teaching the magisterium per se as they once did. Rather, today "the academic context of Catholic theology in the United States means that the theologian cannot see one's role and function in terms of a commissioning to teach given by the hierarchical magisterium in the Church." Still, he added, "Theology very definitely is in the service of the Church, but it is also an academic discipline as such."[40]

Thirty years later, Cahill, while defending Farley's work, notes,

> It is important to understand the nature and role of academic theology or theological scholarship as "faith seeking understanding." Theology is rooted in faith and practical concerns. But the main purpose of theology—unlike pastoral teaching or guidance—is the understanding of

> God and of humans in relation to God. Understanding involves intellectual justification and cogency. Finally, theology is a process of seeking. Theology is a process of inquiry and exploration in a dynamic and critical relation to other theological positions.[41]

Clearly, there needs to be space where any Catholic, including even members of the hierarchy, can engage critically what we believe to be the right course for Christian living. But that space cannot be hermetically sealed. It needs to be dialogically engaged with and within the life of the church.

Like the social encyclicals that were written for all people of goodwill, theologians posit their investigations to support and sustain the faith, hope, and love of both Christians and others looking for the right realization of both individual disciples and community of disciples. To support this work, recently Todd A. Salzman and Michael G. Lawler have written about the possibility of a more dialogical relationship between theologians and the hierarchy. Their invitation is interesting in that in 2012 the Committee on Doctrine of the United States Conference of Catholic Bishops issued a declaration on the "inadequacies in the theological methodology and conclusions" of Salzman and Lawler's new book, *The Sexual Person: Toward a Renewed Catholic Anthropology*.[42] They made this gesture because "the new, more pastoral, theological, and dialogical climate created by Pope Francis is more conducive to dialogue between theologians and the magisterium than was the case during the papacies of Popes John Paul II and Benedict XVI."[43] Despite the persistent attempts at censorship, Catholic ethicists continue to propose both the space and the dialogue that are critically needed to go forward.

Changing the Boundaries of Catholic Theological Ethics

No social change, in my estimation, more significantly affects the future of theological ethics than the fact that the makeup of the faculty of Catholic theological ethics today are men and women, who are from the clergy, religious life, and the laity. This did not just happen. By naming each of these women and men, we see that a personal decision, a moral agency, became manifest by a vocational response to enter the ranks. That moral agency was clearly animated by the call of Vatican II. That call and its spirit summoned the hearts and minds of people, whom the tradition rarely ever engaged, to become proponents in the field of theological ethics.

These pioneers' decisions to become theological ethicists shaped the fields of research. The repercussions are striking. With many married ethicists, the study of sexual ethics became far less about the ends of marriage and the meticulous matter of the ends of the sexual organs and much more about the nature of human relationality. Today, the ethics of marriage is rarely reduced to the marital act, and more frequently it is about its relationship to family, faith, work, leisure, and, in turn, the common good.[44]

Probably the most significant change is that these persons, who exercised their own moral agency by breaking through the barriers of "for clergy only," broke down the walls that compartmentalized the different fields of theological ethics. As Charles Curran noted, until the 1970s, morals was segregated; fundamental morals, and with it the fields of medical ethics and sexual ethics had literally their own hermeneutics. Indeed, there was a greater credibility to the hermeneutics of social ethics and its more inclusive style that gave greater recognition to human experience. In fundamental morals, and, in particular, in sexual ethics, appeals to human experience were often simply ignored.[45]

Notably, ethicists like Farley and Cahill insisted that sexual and medical ethics needed to be read through the lens of the personal *and* the social and looked to the common good tradition to develop a more engaging set of resources for their own work in sexual and medical ethics.

In particular, Cahill has been a pioneer of the inclusive agenda of connecting feminism to the Catholic social tradition and bringing that connection to the major areas of applied ethics. In 1985 she wrote on an ethics of sexuality and, while exploring the sources of Christian ethics (Scripture, tradition, human nature, and experience), she viewed them not as distinct, but rather as interrelated and mutually defining. In this context, she developed certain concepts that became foundational for her own positions: feminism, the common good, and moral practices.[46]

She advanced a sexual ethics that is deeply relational, while promoting gender equity, invoking the Scriptures (in particular, the narratives of practices that formed communities of faith and justice), and contended that sexuality should not fortify privacy but rather integral relationships within the common good.[47]

In 1992 she further defined her ideas on sexuality ("sex is fundamentally and above all a relational capacity"), looking at the experience of women, and mindful of ethics' need to use the resources of other disciplines.[48] In 1996, in *Sex, Gender and Christian Ethics*, she proposed that human sexual differentiation and sexual reproduction "stand as experiences which begin in humanity's primal bodily existence, and which all cultures institutionalize (differently) as gender, marriage and family. Human flourishing, as sexually embodied, depends on the realization of the *equality of the sexes*, male and female; and in their sexual union, on the further values of *reproduction, pleasure and intimacy*." She added two other integral components: that social institutions ought to be ethically responsible to these values and that though local cultures develop their own social institutions, we must look to standards of justice so as to promote cultural claims rightly.[49] On this last point, Cahill argued that though norms emerge from local cultures, she believed in the consensual establishment of universal norms as not only a possibility but a necessity.[50]

Throughout her writings, on sexuality, family,[51] and marriage,[52] she employs Catholic social teaching to break down any inequities. She is then a self-described Catholic feminist[53] who scrutinizes ecclesial and social practices that undermine the very values promoted by the narrative of its own tradition.[54]

More recently, she turned to bioethics.[55] Then she turned to the common good, solidarity, structural injustice and sin, and the option for the poor, and brought the Catholic social tradition, once practically hermetically sealed unto itself, into bioethics.[56] The result was an extraordinarily practical and relevant bioethics. In it, she examined the economic realities that drive so much research while at the same time disenfranchising those most in need, chided the glorification and fascination with a technology that is more market than person-driven, and remained in solidarity with women throughout the world, particularly those most alienated from medical advances today.[57]

Cahill's purpose in writing is to bring about actions, practices, and policies that promote greater solidarity and equity throughout the world. It is for this reason when CTEWC gathered for its first international conference in Padua, Italy, in 2006 with four hundred theological ethicists from fifty-two countries, Cahill was invited to be one of the main panelists. There she spoke and said moral truth "corresponds to the reality of human interdependence and to the possibility of our being in solidarity with one another to relieve human suffering."[58]

As we will see later in the second part, the focus on suffering prompted ethicists to do two things: to consider all the specificity of suffering regarding its impact and its causes *and* to consider the plethora of resources that could be incorporated in responding to suffering. The turn to suffering was a game changer.

Cahill added,

> Modern terms such as "human dignity," "full humanity," "democracy," "human rights," "equality," "solidarity," and "equal opportunity" are ways of challenging inequitable access patterns. Such language represents a social, political and legal ethos in which participation in the common good and access to basic goods of society is universally shared, even though on many possible cultural models. This is the modern definition of social justice, and social justice is an indispensable constituent of contemporary moral theology.[59]

Cahill brings the resources of the Catholic social tradition in its advocacy for justice into the framework of fundamental moral theology, sexual ethics, and bioethics.[60] She insists that as we do theology we examine narrative claims, social practices, and institutional structures. She advocates an action-oriented ethics that seeks to extend the parameters of discourse and participation and is mindful of the biases of classicism, sexism, and racism. As for most of her contemporary peers, the parameters of theological ethics now embrace all the related fields of ethics rather than being marked by the nice, neat containers that once defined them.

Why did this happen? As we can see, ethicists' investigations today into theological ethics are not simply about what was once called "fundamental morals." Rather, they recognized that the agent in theological ethics was not simply a hermetically sealed individual but rather a social being defined by relationships with others and to the common good. Recognizing the moral agency of the conscientious Christian as both personal and social, ethicists were prompted to look for an ethics capable of including the two.

Yet their understanding of the agent as subject was not the only cause of the change for a more robust and integrated theological ethics. The other change was that these new ethicists changed their gaze from looking to Rome as Ford and Kelly did, to looking to human suffering itself. Just as the subject of theological ethics changed, so too did the object of theological ethics. Now instead of asking what Rome teaches, they ask why human beings suffer and how we can respond.

II. RECOGNIZING HUMAN SUFFERING, DESCENDING INTO THE PARTICULAR, AND GOING GLOBAL

From the Synoptic Gospels and John's Gospel and Letters to Paul's Epistles, from Augustine to Aquinas, to finally the achievement of the twentieth-century reformers Gilleman and Tillmann, theologians have long held love as being at the heart of the Christian moral life.[61] The great commandment to love God and neighbor as self has indelibly been the well-spring of all theological ethics, unequivocally.

Recognizing human suffering, however, is fairly new. Even when we reviewed the manuals used during World War II, suffering was rarely brought into the reflections in fundamental moral theology though it did appear somewhat in recent social teachings on both war and labor.

Still, for the most part, suffering was not the subject of moral theology, though it was the object of concern that led to the practice of the works of mercy and later the founding of religious congregations, and, even later, to professional guilds and confraternities that sought to alleviate human suffering. In the matter of the actual texts of moral theology, however, moral theologians reflected primarily on church teachings and not the matter of human suffering. Responding to suffering was a moral practice but not a matter of moral theological engagement.

Earlier, we saw that the moral manuals focused singularly on what was and was not sin and that most of the matter of sin was about what a person did, rather than what one did not. Strangely, even though the Gospels frequently cast the sinner as the one who failed to show mercy (the Last Judgment in Matthew, the Rich Man and Lazarus and the Good Samaritan parables in Luke), the moral manuals, generally speaking, did not attend to the failure to respond to the one suffering. Rather, by itemizing first the infractions of the seven deadly sins and then the Ten Commandments, sin was cast as an intended wrong action. In fact, even before the manuals, someone like Aquinas, who recognized that sin could be understood as the human failure to love or be merciful, still usually defaulted to sin as an intended wrong act.[62]

What would happen if like the Gospels, theological ethics would turn its gaze to human suffering and, equally, to turn to sin as the failure to bother to love?

Indeed, suffering erupts on the theologians' horizons in the early 1970s and actually nearly dominates the entire landscape of theological ethics. Witness Pope Francis's encyclical *Fratelli Tutti*, on the call to recognize the suffering of our brothers and sisters.[63] This is a significant shift from *Casti Connubi* and *Humanae Vitae*, which focused on church teaching on birth control; it is also a shift from *Evangelium Vitae* or even *Veritatis Splendor*, which focused on human life and church teaching and its tradition but not on human suffering. Although suffering is not foreign to Pope John Paul II's apostolic letter *Salvifici Doloris*,[64] *Fratelli Tutti* is very much a *moral* encyclical, while John Paul II's is a theological meditation on suffering in the church's tradition. *Fratelli Tutti* presumes that suffering is at the heart of the moral agenda. How did that happen?

In the 1970s suffering erupts on the theological scene. Two systematic theologians are among the major, though not only, catalysts: Gustavo Gutiérrez and Edward Schillebeeckx.

From Latin America, liberation theology brought with it a deep concern for oppressive suffering and promoted in its responses the formation of base communities and the option for the poor.

Gustavo Gutiérrez (1928–) above all awakened the world to the experiences and voices of those long ignored. He announced that the bursting in of the poor was a new historical event: they were previously absent from theology.

In 1971, in *A Theology of Liberation: History, Politics, Salvation*, Gutiérrez summoned readers to make an option for the poor, by politically and religiously standing in solidarity with those marginalized by power and economic forces.[65] The option for the poor became a hermeneutical principle for interpreting the legitimacy and purpose of theology.[66] Through it, he endorsed a critical reflection on praxis and made his readers realize that we were summoned to respond to the world of suffering inhabited by the poor.

In the world of suffering are interlocking patterns of oppression and domination established by unexamined yet causal discriminating structures of economic and social power. These structures became the subject of analysis and in time were called "structures of sin," and people in positions of authority were seen as morally responsible for them. Later, social sin was attributed not only to those in designated power, but to the societies themselves whereby ordinary members' implicit tolerance and complacent ignorance of these structures allowed them to be beneficiaries of the very structures that continued to alienate and oppress the poor.[67]

There had been no theological agenda like this. Relying on the developments of theology, particularly as an outgrowth of *Gaudium et Spes*, Gutiérrez brought poverty and politics into theological context and discourse. Later, in *On Job: God Talk and the Suffering of the Innocent*,[68] he turned to other resources from the tradition, both biblical and historical, to assert that the (unrecognized) call to attend to human suffering had always been there. In *Las Casas: In Search of the Poor of Jesus Christ*,[69] Gutiérrez proposed the liberating figure of Bartolomé de las Casas as an example of a life responding to suffering. Four hundred years after his death, de las Casas became a model for Christians, and I would add, for theological ethicists in particular.

Other major figures followed Gutiérrez, above all the Brazilians Leonardo and Clovis Boff[70] and the Argentine-born, Mexican philosopher Enrique Dussel.[71] More recently from El Salvador, Jon Sobrino called for theology as an *Intellectus Amoris* and insisted that theology is always in relationship to actual concrete realities, locating itself in the profound suffering of the world.[72]

Sobrino's theology depends on the historicity of Jesus.[73] We are saved singularly by the historical passion, death, and resurrection of Jesus; that moment is the intervention in history of God. Sobrino sees the historicity of Jesus as key for understanding the promise of the kingdom.[74] Thus just as God in Jesus Christ did not abandon the historical world to its wretchedness, nor can we. That *imitatio Christi* is then the embodiment of the spirituality that we need to follow Christ in administering to those who suffer.[75]

As liberation theologians awakened us to suffering in the world and prompted us to respond to the call of Christ by opting to respond to the poor, European theologians also brought to our gaze their considerations on human suffering. In his famous book *Christ*, the great Dominican theologian Edward Schillebeeckx (1914–2009) described how different religious societies address the question of suffering and remarked that while each religion has a different specific response to one who suffers, they share "the fact that they give the last word to the *good*, and not to evil and suffering...their deepest concern is to overcome suffering."[76]

For Schillebeeckx, Christians see God and suffering as "diametrically opposed; where God appears, evil and suffering have to yield. So there is no place for suffering." Unlike Job's friends, Jesus "breaks with the idea that suffering necessarily has something to do with sinfulness." Looking at the description of the man born blind in John's Gospel (John 9:2ff.) and the account of the murdered Galileans in Luke's Gospel (Luke 13:1–5), we see "that it is possible to draw conclusions from sin to suffering, but not from suffering to sin." That is, we cannot assume that one's suffering is due to one's sinfulness.

Schillebeeckx then turned to the Christian notion of redemptive suffering and again dismissed the notion of a Christian God who sends suffering our way. Schillebeeckx provided strong testimony regarding Christian faith and suffering that in some circles is often misunderstood. Although he acknowledged that some suffering may actually help some individuals to become more sensitive and compassionate and, in some instances, actually transform a person, still he says decisively, "There is an excess of suffering and evil in our history."[77]

Schillebeeckx confirmed our experiences: "There is a barbarous excess, for all the explanations and interpretations. There is too much *unmerited* and *senseless* suffering for us to be able to give an ethical, hermeneutical and ontological analysis of our disaster." He surmised, "Human reason cannot in fact cope with concentrated historical suffering and evil."[78] But he added that not only human reason, but the Scriptures too cannot explain away suffering. He wrote,

> The Christian message does not give an *explanation* of evil or our history of suffering. That must be made clear from the start. Even for Christians, suffering remains impenetrable and incomprehensible, and provokes rebellion. Nor will the Christian blasphemously claim that God himself required the death of Jesus as compensation for what *we* make of our history.[79]

Schillebeeckx offered us, however, another way of looking at redemptive suffering and that is by giving it an ultimately liberating significance. This was the suffering that persons assume in their responsible concern to overcome others' greater suffering. Here was love electing suffering to help another, and the primary model for this love is God.

Here another Dominican, Mary Catherine Hilkert, discussed the importance of solidarity with those who suffer by reflecting on the lives of the four American church women (Maura Clarke, Ita Ford, Dorothy Kazel, and Jean Donovan) who were killed in December 1980 in El Salvador. There we saw the nature of one's commitment to stand in solidarity with those who suffer; in these four women's testimonies we witnessed how, when, and why embracing the suffering of another is an imitation of Christ, an act of vulnerable love. Hilkert wrote, "These women embraced solidarity with the poor not out of any glorification or romanticization of suffering, but because it was among the poor of the world that they discovered the good news of the reign of God at work in the world despite all evidence to the contrary."[80] The decision of these brave women who were brutally murdered on December 2, 1980, stands as a clear example of vulnerable love or redemptive suffering.

Reading Schillebeeckx on suffering is very helpful, then. He noted what all religions have in common: the religious response to suffering is to find a way of eliminating suffering. Moreover, he corrected those false impressions of Christianity (which too often

Christians promote) that seemed to make suffering an expression of a loving God's will, and he offered us a palpable notion of redemptive suffering but in the key of solidarity, mercy, and liberation. It provided a pathway for moral theologians to develop a new telos to theological ethics: to recognize and respond to human suffering. By 1980, the work of Gutiérrez and Schillebeeckx had placed before the church and her theologians an astonishingly new agenda, although the plight of human suffering was always there. Fortunately, many heard their call.[81]

Before moving to the theological ethicists incorporating into their work the attendance to human suffering, we need to recognize two other major theologians, Johann Baptist Metz and Dorothee Sölle. Johann Baptist Metz (1928–2019) found in the Holocaust a dangerous memory that had to prompt us to a political theology of action. While he did not object to the question of where was God in Auschwitz, he wanted to know where humanity was. In 1968 he wrote *Poverty of the Spirit*, which effectively became a spiritual companion for those seeking to respond in hope to human suffering.[82] It became the manual for political theology.

If Sobrino insisted on the historicity of suffering, then Dorothee Sölle (1929–2003) in her work *Suffering* emphasized the embodied nature of human suffering.[83] Both made our considerations of suffering more tangible, more concrete, and more human.

Moreover, all these authors contested against a pious Christian complacency of accepting suffering, which believed that God caused suffering and that God was and reigned in a place that was completely untouched by suffering. The mindset that God was the source or the overall controller of who suffered and who did not was a fairly pervasive and uncritical Catholic assumption; regardless of one's location, before the 1970s there was not yet a critical engagement to challenge these assumptions with evidence from the Scriptures and the tradition. As we will now see, these theologians were remarkably successful in persuading their colleagues that suffering was not to be accepted but resisted. Indeed, the work of God was to accompany and alleviate those who suffered, and we were called to work with God to respond to all those who had hitherto been left to fend for themselves.

By the 1980s, suffering was no longer overlooked in theology nor was our response to suffering muffled by simplistic utterings like

"God has his reasons." Rather, suffering, like the poor themselves, became the object of the theologians' investigations and, in time, it emerged as the predominant interest of theological ethicists.

At the first CTEWC International Conference in Padua, the Australian ethicist Robert Gascoigne proposed suffering as one of the sources of moral reasoning. Suffering, he said, "threatens to render Christian proclamation null and void, to overwhelm our attempts to envision a life of goodness and hope and to understand the complex threads of human experience as held together by a God-given dignity. Yet, although it is suffering that most confounds our search for ethical intelligibility, it is likewise suffering that is the most profound source of insight and conversion."[84]

Suffering prompts us to face the fact that we are often the cause of others' suffering. For this reason, theological ethics turns to a conversion that responds to suffering through compassion.

Today, theological ethicists around the world issue a call for a humane answer to the cry of suffering, a suffering deeply rooted in the decisions of other human beings. From Tanzania, Laurenti Magesa discusses the horrendous suffering in Africa:

> A significant part of the history of Africa and its peoples is slavery and colonialism. There has never been a tragedy in human history to rival these experiences in cruelty and destructiveness of human dignity and identity. In a very fundamental way, they have formed the concrete perception of the African peoples all over the continent in their own and other people's eyes as really "non-people," whose life and civilization are not of much significance, if indeed any at all, for humanity. We can refer to this as only a process of "negation." It was at bottom a denial of the humanity of the African people and consequently of their civilization.

Magesa continues:

> If there is hunger, mismanagement of human and material resources, civil strife and war in Africa today, the source of it can be traced back directly or indirectly to these experiences. On the material economic scene, the

> poverty of Africa, a continent incredibly rich in material resources, is a direct result of the exploitation of imperialism and colonialism, both of which continue to devastate the continent and its peoples under the name of globalization.[85]

From Brazil, Ronaldo Zacharias writes about miserable suffering and an outright insensitivity throughout Brazil to the plight of suffering among the world's poor:

> Poverty, in all of its dehumanizing forms, has become a scourge that is manifested in many different ways: the lack of food, housing, work, health care, and basic respect for the human dignity of every person. The country stands by watching as extreme forms of poverty give rise to a series of explosive social upheavals. The globalization of misery places before us a challenge of incalculable proportions: how do we begin to respond to the needs of the excluded, the marginalized and those who have lost everything.[86]

From Sri Lanka, Vimal Tirimanna writes about the overwhelming inequity in distribution of goods:

> The pathetic part of this story is that if something serious is not done in the concrete level to check this injustice, the "winners" are going to continue to gain more and more, while the "losers" are going to continue to lose more and more. The scandalizing gap of inequality is ever-widening, in each passing year, as the HDRs (Human Development Reports) since 1990 have revealed so convincingly....The distance between the incomes of the richest and poorest country was about 3 to 1 in 1820, 35 to 1 in 1950, 44 to 1 in 1973, and 71 to 1 in 1992.

Tirimanna adds, "In the midst of a globalized world, 10.7 million children every year do not live to see their fifth birthday, and more than 1 billion people survive in abject poverty on less than $1 a day."[87]

These powerful citations show that although the irruption of suffering into Catholic theological ethics is fairly universal, it appears regionally in the theology of local ethicists on each continent. The emergence of local theological ethicists establishing a local agenda appropriate for their own continents has meant that Catholic ethics is no longer singularly European. Indeed, European theology has been often in the guise of a "universal theology" but World War II and then Vatican II brought to the fore that European theology was just that, European, and not universal. The Europeans themselves took that stance by recognizing the turn to the local as a necessary imperative for all. Indeed, in a superb collection on the *Catholic Ethicist in the Local Church*, that he edited with Laurenti Magesa, Antonio Autiero notes,

> The ecclesiality of the theologian is seen as situated in the context of the local church, in dialogue with its world and its culture. For the moral theologian, this shift of emphasis demands and produces a sensitivity and a particular competence in reading the features of the history of the persons and the people who make up the theologian's own church, in order to envisage creatively the responses to the question about meaning and to the existential questions that are proper to one's own culture. Theological investigation and ethical research are motivated, not by Roman centralism, but by fidelity to the history of the people who live in a local church.[88]

In the same collection, Kenneth Himes demonstrates that the shift to the local was made earlier by regional and national episcopal conferences that "took up the challenge of developing statements that were theologically substantive efforts at naming and reflecting on their local situation." Himes comments that the Latin American leadership of CELAM (*Consejo Episcopal Latinoamericano*) provided the pathway.[89]

The turn to the local to respond to suffering will invariably invoke the church's tradition of social justice as the well-spring of resources that might give hope to the multitudes. Since most of the human suffering that ethicists address is the suffering caused by others, the resources of the social justice or common good tradition can correct the unjust policies, stances, and structures that generated the harm that yielded the suffering. Invoking justice to respond to suffering is the local option universally appropriated whether for criminal justice systems in rural India where George Kodithottam invokes "Justice as Healing" or for people with disabilities in urban United States where Mary Jo Iozzio advocates for "Counting the Uncounted."[90]

To appreciate how ethics has been shaped by local cultural experience and theology responding to suffering, we turn first to the descent into the particular and then, finally, to each of the continents and their own agendas for moral theology today.

Descent into the Particular

The turn to suffering was also a turn to the particularity of human experience. Still, that too took a long time in coming.

I have noted in my book on the twentieth century that for all the innovation of European moralists in the twentieth century, above all in respecting and promoting the primary claims of the human conscience through an autonomous ethics, they explored mostly conceptual and attendant philosophical concerns.[91] They were not averse to mentioning suffering and poverty, but they approached these topics generally speaking. Normally, they did not descend into the particularity of human suffering. Moreover, the ambit of their experiential concern was mostly limited to the community of academic theologians from which they came. The specific challenges of human life, the experiential encounters with human suffering, and the multitudinous causes of suffering both socially and structurally were infrequently addressed or even named by the major European fundamental moral theologians whom we studied in the last chapter.

From the last century, exceptions included Marciano Vidal,[92] Enda McDonagh, Kevin Kelly, Enrico Chiavacci, and Antonio Autiero, who attended to the more concrete needs of the marginalized. As McDonagh noted, "The sense of the margins and the people at the margins of society and church began for me" at the beginning.[93] For McDonagh and Kelly, their pastoral experiences led them into their own option for their national poor. Not surprisingly, they were two of the first ethicists to write about HIV/AIDS.[94] Thirty years ago, Chiavacci wrote on peace and globalization, developed a comprehensive theological ethics with deep social claims, and later addressed the question of justice and globalization.[95] Besides writing on the stranger and the other,[96] Autiero was also among the first to write on HIV/AIDS[97] and the environment.[98]

Their descent into the specifics of HIV/AIDS, war and peace, and climate change was a significant move of engaging the particular. We need to remember, the last time moral theologians collectively entered into the particular was the time of high casuistry in the sixteenth century. Afterward, moral theology had become accustomed to the "broad sweep" and "the general norm," when it began the syntheses of the moral manuals marking the end of casuistry. That span from the seventeenth century to the end of World War II is a period marked predominantly by the universal with only exceptional notices of the local with its particularities. Then, in the search to reconstruct moral theology, Europeans like Häring, Fuchs, Janssens, and Demmer began their own reflection on human agency and discipleship and proposed the fundamental outlines of the conscientious Christian responding to the call of Christ.

That call became in time concretized by descending into the particular, as I like to say.[99]

In 1988, in their work *The Abuse of Casuistry: A History of Moral Reasoning*, Stephen Toulmin and Albert Jonsen effectively reproduced the method of casuistry from the sixteenth century.[100] They did this to highlight that moral reasoning that tries to simply deduce answers by applying cases to general principles is fraught with problems that fail to recognize relevant circumstances that can and should influence the rightness or wrongness of a decision. They suggested the moral inductive approach of comparing cases that allowed people to entertain the particular details of a case.[101]

Theirs was not a simple conceptual discussion; rather, as members of the National Commission for the Protection of Human Subjects of Biomedical and Behavioral Research, they knew that looking for general principles alone was inadequate. Rather, they needed to respect the particular so as to adequately find a solution in which justice and prudence were achieved. Their concrete experience of new emerging questions in biomedical issues prompted them to revisit and reconstruct an inductive method that could satisfactorily guide them in trying to find right pathways in a brave new world.

Their argument garnered attention around the world with interest in the history of moral reasoning[102] and dovetailed with contemporary exigencies like HIV/AIDS that raised a variety of moral quandaries never before anticipated.[103] The particular could not be ignored. Eventually, casuistry would be recognized in a wide variety of cultures.[104]

This descent into the particular followed with questions not only on other biomedical issues but also on public health, sexuality, gender, family life as well as issues of work, war, finance, trade, patenting, and so on. Moral reasoning looked less frequently to the general and more to the concrete particular across the field.

The descent into the particular is both a move to the local and to the circumstantial. The Catholic tendency toward the universal finds progressively from the 1980s on a movement toward the local that does not break from the universal but rather sees itself as a particular instantiation of the universal. It is difficult today to find an essay in moral theology that does not take the local seriously, yet rarely is it engaged without an eye to the universal. Similarly, just as we descend into a locality, still we need to descend into the circumstantial. As in the sixteenth century, the complexity of a question is taken seriously and is not reduced to a matter that can be generalized.

Let me introduce you to just one collection to highlight this descent into the local and the circumstantial so that you see the particularity of contemporary theological ethics. A recent collection of essays on sustainability, published in the Catholic Theological Ethics in the World Church (CTEWC) series, illustrates both the descent into the local and the circumstantial yet turns to a panoply of resources from the common good tradition to illuminate a set of local, specific responses. *Just Sustainability: Technology, Ecology, and Resource Extraction*, edited by Christiana Z. Peppard and Andrea Vicini, is divided into four parts: Locations, Structures, Theological Stances, and Sustainable Relations.[105]

Under "Locations," ethicists report from Brazil, Congo, Germany, India, Japan, Mexico, Micronesia, Nigeria, and the United States. Each account is different, but the aggregate of narratives overwhelmingly and clearly convinces us that where the local is impacted, the global is affected. Still, the solutions regarding moral agency require attentiveness to the details of each particular context and to the persons in that context.

In "Structures," we see that social structures and policies conspire to make climate crisis even more difficult to resolve. Other forces, created by equally incompetent agents, give us an "intersectionality" wherein these structures overlap with the crisis, calling us to further appreciate its urgency and complexity. In a superb essay opening the second part of eight essays, John Sniegocki looks at the differing structures of political economies and their push and pull on sustainability.[106] Mark Graham examines analogously the "unsavory gamble" of contemporary industrial agriculture,[107] while Kenya's Teresia Hinga considers at the political structures that instrumentalize food itself as a weapon.[108] Cameroonian ethicist Azétsop Jacquineau investigates the drain that health systems are on social structures, especially where HIV/AIDS demands attention.[109] From South Africa, Peter Knox looks at the social structures promoting resource extraction as invariably unsustainable.[110]

If the second part highlights the complexity of the climate crisis, the third provides us with multiple resources and strategies for the prophetic pragmatism that guides and empowers rightly moral agency. Mindful that we need to engage multitudinous traditions to respond to this unprecedented challenge, these authors develop new and shared responsibilities across a variegated landscape, and therefore we must mine those sources that can guide collective agency rightly. From Catholicism's repertoire of the common good tradition along with the contemporary Catholic ethicists' uncanny knack to breakdown artificial boundaries that sector off one resource from another, Ann Marie Mealey taps into feminism;[111] Nancy Rourke engages straight-talking virtues;[112] Christine Firer Hinze unpacks the Catholic social justice tradition with its linguistic riches like the common good, solidarity, subsidiarity, and the option for the poor;[113] and Daniel DiLeo explores Ignatian spirituality.[114]

In short, this text helps highlight how the investigative work of theological ethics today is continuously responsive to human suffering, and as such, frames its investigation with a clarity about the local or cultural context and then enters into the particular circumstances that highlight both the probable causes and remedies for the suffering. At the same time, there are considerations of the resources that could be applied so as to further the relief and disarm the structural sources of oppression that caused and promoted the suffering in the first place.

In light of this example, it is time, now, to give you an appreciation of the regional as we finally turn global.[115]

Latin America

In Latin America, moral theology has a deep resonance with the proposals of liberation theology: a critical reflection on praxis, a call to respond to human suffering, the option for the poor, and the naming of social sin and the structures of sin. While solidarity helps it to become more social and more communal, liberation theology still depends on and develops the autonomous conscience.[116]

In Latin American theological ethics, Chile's Tony Mifsud develops over the course of twenty years two comprehensive handbooks for the ordinary Catholic to discern in conscience on contemporary issues.[117] Peru's Francisco Moreno Rejón articulates a moral theology that incorporates the perspective of the poor, the social sciences, and a Scripture-based understanding of the kingdom of God.[118] The Brazilians Antonio Moser and Bernardino Leers propose a christological ethics to form the conscience through a conscientization of the forces impeding the kingdom through the idolatries of power, money, technology, pleasure, and superiority.[119] Another Brazilian, Rogue Junges, considers moral conduct in the light of the Christ event. Launching his investigation from the ethical meaning of the kingdom of God, revealed in Jesus of Nazareth, Junges reelucidates the fundamental categories of theological ethics: fundamental option, moral conscience, moral values and norms, the sentiment of guilt and sin, theological and moral conversion, moral maturity, and virtues.[120] In the area of bioethics, Marcio Fabri dos Anjos reflects on how a liberation theology allows us to reflect on issues of power and vulnerability that so dominate the field of bioethics.[121]

A significant recent development in liberation theology is the irruption of women into liberation theology. Ivone Gebara defines the option for the poor as an option for poor women, analyzes women's experience of salvation and evil, develops a distinctive spirituality for women, and writes on the environment from an ecofeminist perspective.[122] Maria Clara Bingemer proposes a theology of Mary as both the Mother of God and mother of the poor.[123] Bingemer is also a prolific theologian, having published manuscripts on *Latin*

American Theology, the power and vulnerability of love in Simone Weil, and the woman's body and the experience of God.[124]

Women in Latin America,[125] like Uruguayan Ana María Bidegain[126] and Costa Rican Elsa Tamez, bring together women's voices and contributions across the Latin American terrain. Latinas in the United States also provide bridges between Latin America and feminist movements. In the United States, the Mexican-born María Pilar Aquino argues that women have a different epistemological horizon than men. She uses feminist methods to recognize and describe women's history; to unmask and dismantle theological formulations that perpetuate the interpretation of humanity in patriarchal terms; and to reflect on women's use of the Bible in their quest to understand and speak about God. Throughout she calls for a hermeneutic of suspicion and daring.[127]

The late Cuban Ada María Isasi-Díaz proposed *Mujerista* strategies for women, particularly a strong political agenda in which salvation and liberation are seen as two aspects of one process. She wrote, "As Latinas become increasingly aware of the injustices we suffer, we reject any concept of salvation that does not affect our present and future reality."[128] Isasi-Díaz advanced liberty, both psychologically and socially, without buying into the myth of individual achievement and justice as both a disposition and a way of acting.

The cause of liberation theology in Latin America did not develop with ease. In 1968 the Latin American Episcopal Conference (CELAM) met in Medellín, Colombia, and endorsed liberation theology, with its attention to the base communities and the option for the poor. From 1972 to 1984, Bishop Alfonso López Trujillo was general secretary of CELAM and used his influence to curtail the conference's support of liberation theology. Still, in 1979, at the CELAM meeting in Puebla, despite his efforts, Trujillo's agenda was opposed by supporters of liberation theology.[129]

Advocates of liberation theology found themselves at risk on two main fronts. First, a variety of assassinations undermined their advocacy for human decency. The killings in El Salvador alone were extraordinary. On March 12, 1977, Fr. Rutilio Grande was murdered. Three years later, after five other priests were assassinated in El Salvador, Grande's friend Oscar Romero, the archbishop of San Salvador, was gunned down on March 24, 1980. Seven months later, on December 2, three American Sisters and a lay woman were murdered by a military death squad. On November 16, 1989, the El Salvadoran army attacked the Jesuit compound at the University of Central America and assassinated six Jesuits (among them, Ignacio Ellacuría, Segundo Montes, and Ignacio Martín-Baró), their housekeeper and her daughter. The only Jesuit to escape, Jon Sobrino, was lecturing in Asia at the time, but since then he has been the compelling witness to their martyrdom.[130]

Second, the Vatican maintained a constant public questioning of the traditional orthodoxy of liberation theology. In 1984, Cardinal Joseph Ratzinger issued his critical *Instruction on Certain Aspects of "Theology of Liberation"*;[131] in 1986, the cardinal issued a less critical and more moderate analysis of liberation theology, *Instruction on Christian Freedom and Liberation.*[132] At the same time the Congregation for the Doctrine of the Faith investigated liberation theology's leading advocates. In 1985 it issued a critical notification on Leonardo Boff's book on the church;[133] in 1993 the congregation sent complaints to the Peruvian bishops regarding Gustavo Gutiérrez; in 1995 the congregation silenced Ivone Gebara for two years; and in 2006 it published its *Notification* on the books of Jon Sobrino.[134]

Despite these setbacks, concepts like option for the poor and structures of sin, critical reflection on praxis, liberation, and the overall call of theology to respond to the irruption of suffering into theology are now constitutively foundational to theology in general and moral theology in particular. Today, we cannot do theology without attending to the defining concerns of Gutiérrez, Boff, Gebara, Sobrino, and others. Yet today there are voices that are organizing across all of Latin America in a way that their predecessors never before did. Here I think of Emilce Cuda[135] and Pablo Blanco from Argentina, Ronaldo Zacharias, Maria Inês de Millen, and Alexandre Martins from Brazil, Verónica Anguita from Chile, María Isabel Gil Espinosa from Colombia, Anna Perkins from Jamaica, Jutta Battenberg from Mexico, and the indomitable Maria Teresa Dávila[136] from Puerto Rico.

Africa

The irruption of the suffering poor did not enter African theology as a delayed afterthought. If there is one part of the world that most people think of when they consider human suffering as a social reality, it is Africa. The world has become more familiar with Africa through globalized communications that narrate frequently the advance of HIV/AIDS, the enduring tragedy of malaria and tuberculosis, and the internecine struggles that pit poor aggressor against poor aggressor. As Magesa noted, however, the questions of how this has happened are rarely presented.

African theology has been attentive not only to the challenges facing Africa, but also to the gifts animating it. If liberation theology is the offering from Latin America, then an inculturation theology that is critically approached through liberation theology is Africa's contribution to the church and the world. African theologians find that by understanding and appreciating its past, it can establish the future.

At the conference in Padua, Mawuto Roger Afan described the fundamental challenges facing Africa today: an identity crisis, the postcolonial moves to democracy, and the reconstruction of Africa itself. With African nations experiencing greater instability, the ethicist is urgently called to retrieve from the African traditions a rootedness that could stabilize social upheaval.[137]

Years ago, the Cameroonian Engelbert Mveng considered the pervasive suffering of Africa as affecting the very personhood of an African and proposed reflection on the "structural sin" of "anthropological poverty."[138] Magesa incorporates this phenomenon into his own reflections: "African self-doubt is perhaps the most embracing factor in African 'anthropological poverty,' the kind of poverty which is not merely material but affects the personality itself. It has enormous ethical consequences, one of which is the psychological situation which instinctively obstructs initiative in many areas of personal and social development."[139]

Writing about African suffering and identity is not without risk. On April 22, 1995, Mveng was assassinated. He had been the leader of a variety of movements, all related to forming intellectual, theological, and artistic communities for the building up of a more just Africa. He encouraged, founded, and led greater associations among these constituencies to help retrieve and shape African identity.[140] A vocal critic of political and ecclesial life, Mveng's colleague Jean-Marc Ela went into voluntary exile immediately after Mveng's assassination. Ela was the father of African liberation theology. Aside from a year as the Joseph Professor at Boston College, he spent his exile in French Canada. Ela died there on December 26, 2008.[141] With Uganda's John Mary Waliggo's death eight months earlier on April 19, 2008, Africa lost some of its premiere theologians.

Many Catholic ethicists teach outside of their country and often outside their continent. From the Democratic Republic of Congo, Bénézet Bujo teaches at the University of Fribourg in Switzerland and the Congolese Juvénal Ilunga Muya teaches in Rome at the Urbanianum. In the United States, the Ugandan Emmanuel Katongole perviously taught at Emory and now teaches at Notre Dame, the Kenyan Teresia Hinga teaches at Santa Clara, the Nigerian Paulinus Odozor teaches at Notre Dame, and another Nigerian, Anne Arbome, directs a center at Marquette University.

As African theological ethics takes shape, some ethicists are reminding others of their forbearers. Bénézet Bujo and Juvénal Ilunga Muya edited a homage to nine French-speaking African theologians who paved the way for contemporary African theology.[142] Premier among them was Bishop Tharcisse Tshibangu (1933–), the only African expert at Vatican II and among the first members of the International Theological Commission. In 1960, he developed a specifically African theology, proposing that certain African epistemological insights and local practices were different from European ones.[143] The Belgian Alfred Vanneste, dean of the faculty of theology in Kinshasa, responded, affirming the universality of theology and denying the specificity of an African theology.[144] Vanneste was fundamentally espousing his European presuppositions as universally normative.

Forty years later, Bujo notes that Tshibangu implicitly contested the presupposition that "the African tradition has been precisely the weak point of the Africans in the face of Western civilization." Moreover, while many want to reduce the "whole question of African theology...to social and economic problems," Tshibangu's proposal offered "an inculturation worthy of the name (that) necessarily ends up in an integral human liberation and development."[145]

Earlier in 1945 a Belgian Franciscan missionary, Placide Tempels (1906–77) published *La Philosophie Bantoue.*[146] Despite the way the work succumbed to wild generalizations about a singular religious philosophy pervading the entire African continent, the text began a discussion about the coherency and relevance of an integrated African vision of humanity, divinity, and the world. Shortly after Tempels's work, John Mbiti (1931–2019), an Anglican priest, offered to English-speaking Africa a foundational African theology. In 1969 he wrote *African Religion and Philosophy*;[147] in 1970, *Concepts of God in Africa*;[148] in 1973, *Love and Marriage in Africa*;[149] and finally, in 1975, *Introduction to African Religion*.[150]

Later, Bujo and Ilunga Muya published a second volume on *African Pioneers* wherein Charles Nyamiti (1931–2020) was considered "the vibrant pioneer of African inculturated theology."[151] Nyamiti was well known for his contributions in Christology and Ecclesiology and his ability to look at them in the context of African ancestor worship.[152] Tshibangu, Mbiti, and Nyamiti were trailblazers in leading others to the African need for inculturation.[153]

Since then, Bénézet Bujo, along with Magesa, have become the most noteworthy promoters of African inculturation in moral theology.[154] Proposing a "palaver" (meaning "word") ethics, Bujo sees it as effective: through discourse the community comes to resolve crisis, heal the sick, and determine itself for the future. Palaver is how the community comes to fuller realization of itself. As Muya writes,

> In the logic of the palaver, everyone has the right to speak. In this sense the palaver guarantees equality and everyone's access to speak in view of building up the community. The final decision arrived at its end is not the result of compromise or of voting according to the majority, but of a solid consensus among all members. The fundamental experience at the basis of the word is that of communion....Communion is not true unless it promises and guarantees the originality of each member, and unless each member is conscious of not being free except in relation with the community....Individual freedom is not therefore a value absolute in itself, but in relation to the community, in the same sense that the community is not an absolute value but one linked to the individuals.[155]

Muya makes it clear that the communion-oriented stance of a palaver ethics does not deny autonomy, an important interest of Bujo and others.[156] Relationality does not compromise autonomy, nor does autonomy compromise relationality.[157] Still, while focusing on community, Muya points out that the palaver is tridimensional as it engages the ancestors, the living and the not-yet-born. By nature, then, there is always a plurality of perspectives, both among the living individuals within the community and by contact with those from the past and expected from the future. This plurality extends, then, beyond the confines of the community.

Bujo develops the dynamics of his ethics as it pertains to leadership:

> The chief must pay attention to everything that happens in the community. Above all he is obliged to receive everything by patient listening and then to try to digest it well. Being a good listener and digesting the word are linked in general to Black Africa....He is the last to speak, after having carefully examined all the aspects of a problem and digested the word well. But first he must propose his own word for debate, at least in the palaver of the elders. In other words, the word must be made available for rumination.[158]

To make the discourse effective, the chief and all the participants in the palaver must have large, broad ears and they must distinguish themselves as listeners before they speak.[159] When they speak, they must be willing to share the word with other members of the palaver, since it is too large and wide for the mouth of one individual.

One critical area in which inculturation plays a major role is HIV/AIDS. In Africa there is overriding insistence that the HIV infection cannot be understood, inhibited, or treated by a simple clinical study of the disease. Only by understanding the African context in which this infection has itself become inculturated can we respond to those at risk, infected, or suffering from full-blown AIDS. Toward this end, Laurenti Magesa looks at practices of the African religion upholding a pan-African life ethic as the standard for more effective teaching on HIV/AIDS.[160] The Ugandan Emmanuel Katongole becomes suspicious of "miracle Western medicines" and asks, What are appropriate medical approaches for Africa?[161] Bujo works with now Cardinal Michael Czerny in developing the theological reflections specific to AIDS in Africa,[162] while Uganda's Peter Kanyandago reflects on the nature of God in a time of AIDS.[163] Still, inculturation does not guarantee unanimity in addressing the challenges of AIDS: the debate over whether condoms are an appropriate part of HIV prevention strategies is a case in point.[164]

Finally, through the African Jesuit AIDS Network (AJAN),[165] we find another set of distinctive contributions. Paterne Mombe looks for signs of hope in the management of HIV;[166] Ghislain Tshikendwa Matadi applies the wisdom of Job to the experience of those afflicted with AIDS;[167] and Peter Knox looks at local beliefs, particularly regarding ancestors, as a resource to minister to the sick and suffering in Africa today.[168] On the thirtieth anniversary of the outbreak of HIV, the coordinators on AJAN held a conference and published papers on how HIV/AIDS is read through Christian faith and ethics.[169]

As important as inculturation is in Africa, Jean-Marc Ela was actually somewhat suspicious of it. If the African church becomes more truly African, will it become better? If African society heeds its ancient cultures, will it actually move forward? In short, is the retrieval of African culture coupled with any critical reflection?

Ela preferred a liberation theology approach: the African church, its leaders, and members need to heed the liberating Gospel, which confronts local cultures with the kingdom of God as expressed in Jesus Christ and in the love, justice, equity, and option for the poor that characterizes the Gospel message. Ela offered a ringing corrective to African contextual theology. As a noted sociologist and theologian, he demanded a concrete and not a conceptual liberation: we must know the Africa that we are talking about, not to accept it, but to liberate it.[170]

Ela challenged the communities of faith to "make an effort to redefine themselves in terms of service to persons stripped of their rights." Indeed, "our primordial sacrament should be the poor and the oppressed, those disturbing witnesses of God in the warp and woof of our history. African reality imposes on the church a kind *of pedagogy of the discovery of situations of sin and oppression*—situations that rear their heads in contradiction with the project of the salvation and liberation in Jesus Christ."[171]

The influence of liberation theology is palpable. Tanzanian Aquiline Tarimo looks for resources from Ignacio Ellacuría and develops a constructive human rights agenda.[172] Feminists like Teresia Hinga,[173] Mercy Amba Oduyoye,[174] and Anne Nasimyu[175] bring a definitively feminist liberation approach to their theology by reflecting on women's experience, patriarchal dominance, the practices of local culture, and the fundamental call of Scripture to hear the cry of the poor.

If Ela has brought liberation theology into African theological discourse, Laurenti Magesa considers it as a companion and not a replacement for inculturation.[176] While identified with liberation theology,[177] Magesa equally promotes a theology of inculturation, especially in his landmark work on the pan-African culture of life that imbued African religion.[178]

John Mary Waliggo was concerned about the effectiveness of theology in responding to suffering and empowering the poor. Waliggo attended less to theological reflection and more to activism in response to the situation of suffering. If he resonated with any particular theological premises, it would be the emerging African feminist ethics, which links liberation to the very specific context of economics and power.[179]

Like Magesa, Waliggo wrote on inculturation too,[180] but the specificity of the context Waliggo addressed was always a globalized world that compromises a good deal of equitable justice for the presence and future of Africa.[181] Still, Waliggo always exuded hope, as is in his tribute to the AIDS activist Noerine Kaleeba[182] and in his comment on the African Synod of 1994.[183]

Finally, if Bujo, Magesa, and Ela have given the framework for a contemporary African theological ethics that fuses inculturation with liberation theology, then I find Agbonkhianmeghe E. Orobator the most creative theologian who instrumentalizes the new African framework. Earlier, he demonstrated how the sociological category of crisis correlates with the theological conception of *kairos* and contends that the identity of the African church is measured by its response to human suffering.[184] Pressing for new paradigms of a discourse on sexual ethics from an African perspective, he finds describing the experience of women as instructive, not only because they are the predominant victims, but because they are on the frontline for the care of people living with HIV/AIDS. Their non risk-averse combating of AIDS should prompt church leaders to risk sacrificing some of their own "disincarnate moral fixations" for a more context-based approach to sexual integrity.[185]

Orobator has also written on the church as a practical institution with a historical tradition rooted in hope while facing ethical challenges. He reflects on the church as family, a very African line of thought, the specific image of the church used at the synod.[186] In another book, through the use of African narratives, Orobator explores central issues of contemporary faith: from the (non)naming of God to the Trinity, from Christology to mercy and grace, and from the kingdom of God to the Communion of Saints. This master storyteller draws his material from the traditional stories of his fellow Nigerian Chinua Achebe's *Things Fall Apart*.[187]

He also co-authored with Elias Opongo a manual on the social justice tradition for local communities. Using simple, sample cases, for example, the right to land and housing, standing up against corruption, and encountering ethnic discrimination, the authors lead communities to understand how they can analyze contemporary challenges and act to resolve them. The manual promotes the social, moral formation of parishes.[188] Similarly, Tanzania's Richard W. Rwiza offers a book on the connection of conscience with virtue ethics and argues that the acting person is called to self-development as both critic and member of her or his culture.[189]

In all of this, we can see a liberating inculturation theology entering in Africa its second generation. With Orobator's most recent book, *Religion and Faith in Africa: Confessions of an Animist,* we can see just how far African ethics has come from the judgmentalism of Vanneste.[190]

Asia

Until recently, theological ethics in India was taught using a moral manual written by the German Karl Peschke.[191] Later, Soosai Arokiasamy emerged as a pioneer for a contemporary Indian theological ethics. His interests embraced ordinary people, liberation theology, cultural context, the need for dialogue, and the critical reconstruction of the tradition.[192] Bishop Gali Bali provided a description of Arokiasamy's contributions:

> The thrust of theological thinking of Fr. Arokiasamy is in the line of people's theology and inculturation in the liberative sense....Arokiasamy further affirms that in the new method of people's theology, Scripture will be appropriated through a re-reading of it by the people, and tradition will be discerningly re-interpreted by, and integrated into, the people's dynamic and context-related praxis of faith.[193]

In India, Arokiasamy and others have argued that until the option for the poor embraces the most marginalized, the *dalits*, its theological ethics will not realize its call to be liberating.[194] Like them, John Chathanatt, who wrote on Gandhi and Gutiérrez as two liberation paradigms,[195] argues that an Indian liberative inculturation must turn to concrete economic questions and structural issues of marginalization.[196] For this more inclusive agenda, Indian ethicists often turn to the language of human rights.[197]

The late Clement Campos portrayed India as rife with cultural complexity and social inequality and examined a host of the major issues his nation faces: globalization, environment, access to health care (in a land with great health care resources), discrimination based on gender, caste, and religion, violence, and the failure to recognize human rights. In each instance, he highlighted the work of contemporary Indian theological ethicists responding to these needs, but invited them to go further: to move both beyond the confines of a seminary setting so as to become more involved in political debate on issues of urgent social concern; to respect the consciences of the laity on ethical matters; to dialogue with other religions and cultures and the poor so as to participate in humanity's search for the truth by which we all live; and to develop a moral theology that is contextualized, truly Indian, authentically human, and socially liberative.[198]

Finally, ethicists write with greater awareness of Mother Earth. Campos noted, "What Indian eco-ethics also stresses is the need to repair the rape of nature by rendering justice to the victims of such exploitation."[199] The poor, the first victims always, have a claim to the earth's resources for the fulfillment of basic needs of decent human living.

In facing the challenges of globalization from the Philippines, Agnes Brazal highlights the multitudinous resources that creative

Filipino ethicists engage.[200] The Catholic social tradition and the Scriptures are a central source of ethical norms and "images" necessary for what Fausto Gomez calls "good globalization/localization."[201] Elsewhere he invokes a theology of the Eucharist to develop an ethic of global justice.[202] Finally, using the teachings of Thomas Aquinas on justice, property, and the poor, Gomez argues that "'superfluous goods' belong in justice to the poor."[203]

Ronaldo Tuazon sees that the narratives from the margins further the Filipino grasp of justice and the common good.[204] Christina Astorga looks to Filipino history, particularly the experience of the people power revolution, as providing a resource to strengthen national resolve to respond to globalization.[205] On issues of gender, Brazal turns to the self-understanding and experiences of women across Asia,[206] while Astorga reflects on the feminization of poverty especially among migrant workers in and from the Philippines.[207]

Beyond these theological and ethical sources, Brazal and others insist on the resourcefulness of interdisciplinarity.[208] She gives evidence of both the need and the failure to utilize interdisciplinary resources in her discussion about sex education and HIV/AIDS in the Philippines.[209]

This inclination to interdisciplinarity is an Asian virtue. Asian writers are not hesitant to use a variety of sources incorporated into local contexts. For example, Osamu Takeuchi brings the writings of Josef Fuchs on conscience into a Japanese context.[210] Haruko K. Okano invokes a feminist understanding of moral responsibility to critique her own culture.[211] Among the specific problems in Japan, she names "the potentially dangerous side of homogeneity or nationalistic togetherness, that is, the crass distinction between 'us and others'" and the "principle of harmony" that "not just ignores those who are different or strange" but actively excludes them. While acknowledging the good of fundamental national principles, she brings to them an ethical critique in their encounter with the other.[212]

Witnessing to the newness of theological ethics, from Hong Kong, Lúcás Chan Yiu Sing developed a biblical foundation for a contemporary Catholic ethics. While writing and working in Ireland and the United States, he developed two major book-length projects. In *Biblical Ethics in the 21st Century: Developments, Emerging Consensus, and Future Directions,* Chan put forward an argument that biblical ethics needed to invoke two competencies, the exegetical one that biblicists had, through which they could explain the meaning of an ancient religious text, and the moral interpretative one that applied the lesson learned from exegesis to ordinary life. Chan proposed virtue ethics as a worthy hermeneutical or interpretative instrument for bridging the ancient with the contemporary.[213]

To highlight the method he provided in *Biblical Ethics*, Chan wrote *The Ten Commandments and the Beatitudes: Biblical Studies and Ethics for Real Life*, in which he took each of the commandments and Beatitudes and provided the exegesis, the ethical virtue, its practices, at least one exemplar, and finally, its possible social impact.[214] As one who lived, studied, worked, and taught in Hong Kong, the Philippines, Cambodia, England, Ireland, and the United States, he became interested in issues related to migration and national and international hospitality and wrote twice about lessons to be learned from Boaz in the Book of Ruth.[215] Later, for *Theological Studies* he wrote a note about how biblical ethics was developing globally.[216]

At the same time, Chan explored the use of virtues for cross-cultural dialogue: to better understand scriptural ethics, Confucian ethics, and the possibility of discourse between the two.[217] Eventually, he became somewhat concerned that cross-cultural dialogue could allow some more dominant societies to refashion another culture's foundational terms and so wrote he "Bridging Christian and Confucian Ethics: Is the Bridge Adequately Catholic and Asian?"[218]

Chan died suddenly of a heart attack at forty-six years of age on May 19, 2015, but by that point he had already begun editing with Brazilian ethicist Ronaldo Zacharias an international collection on biblical ethics[219] and together with Shaji George Kochuthara designed and planned the first Pan-Asian Conference of Theological Ethicists that was held a month after his death. *Doing Asian Theological Ethics in a Cross-Cultural and an Interreligious Context* is the name of the conference and the collection that published its most successful papers.[220] As we will now see, the variety of papers highlights how Asian theological ethics has come of age and how Chan's bridge-building leadership and hospitable style helped the distinctiveness of Asian ethics to emerge.[221]

From India, both Cardinal Oswald Gracias of Mumbai and Campos made foundational claims and argued that the descent into the local where a variety of cultures and religious families resided had to be inclusive and therefore underlined the necessity of doing cross-cultural and interreligious ethics.[222] From these foundations, contemporary challenges could be addressed: Stanislaus Alla highlighted the impact that the right wing Hindu movement, *Hindutva*, has on contemporary India, while Morris Antonysamy explored the roots of sexual assault against women, and John Karuvelil studied the caste repression of rights and its concomitant promotion of corruption.[223] Among resources, John Crasta recounted how the Chotanagpur tribes provided a model response to local environmental impact, while Vimala Chenginimattam described the promise of engaging religious women as new experts in theological ethics.[224] From the Philippines we find again the call to appreciate the cross-cultural and interreligious, yet these summons are against the challenges of such diverse topics of land grabbing or trying to access some relief to reproductive health, though as Christina Astorga reminds us, in each instance women in particular are the most at risk to be oppressed and marginalized.[225]

Even when looking at political repression, the narratives from Hong Kong, Malaysia, and Myanmar were strikingly different and neither could be paired with another.[226] Although there were issues about the plight of women, the narratives from Indonesia, India, and the Philippines were ultimately culturally specific, whether about farming, maid trade, or seeking an education.[227] Of course, where silencing within societies was most frequent, those whose sexual self-understandings were at stake were often the most oppressed, and here issues of overlap or intersectionality only furthered the suffering and concomitant alienation of those most at risk.[228]

A final word from Asia must note the leadership by Shaji George Kochuthara, especially in shepherding *Asian Horizons*. Kochuthara often focuses on the development of theological ethics within India, by hosting significant conferences for Indian moralists.[229] In 2012, however, Kochuthara hosted one in Bangalore to which he invited Chan to introduce to the Indian ethicists a Pan-Asian perspective, "Doing Catholic Theological Ethics: Some Reflections on the Asian Scenario."[230] But after working with Chan in the design and execution of the 2015 Pan-Asian Conference, *Asian Horizons* emerged as a significant host of Pan-Asian theological ethics, with volumes dedicated to many issues from how *Amoris Laetitia* is received in Asia[231] to "Biblical Theology in Asia."[232] An international journal, *Asian Horizons* is itself a bridge like its editor, helping to forge and integrate an Asian theological ethics.

North America, Particularly the United States

Because of its geographical proximity and more importantly its deep historical (and often oppressive) involvement in Latin America, moral theology in the United States was deeply affected by the irruption of liberation theology onto the theological scene.[233]

In 1970, Philip Scharper with Miguel D'Escoto cofounded Orbis Books and published Gutiérrez's *Theology of Liberation* in English. From then on, through Scharper's initiatives, Orbis became a publishing powerhouse of liberation theology.

Later, a variety of U.S. writers promoted the new theology from the south: Penny Lernoux,[234] Arthur McGovern,[235] Thomas Schubeck,[236] Alfred Hennelly,[237] Roger Haight,[238] and then Dean Brackley[239] and Kevin Burke.[240] Although many of these authors were describing the theological arguments from Latin America for Latin America, central premises from liberation theology began to be incorporated by North American theologians into Catholic social teaching and the overall theological foundations of Catholic theological ethics:[241] "structures of sin,"[242] social sin,[243] and the option for the poor.[244]

These theological insights directly impacted the church in the United States. On May 3, 1983, the United States Conference of Catholic Bishops issued their long awaited, transparently drafted, landmark statement, *The Challenge of Peace: God's Promise and Our Response*.[245] This prophetic and ethically well-argued statement gave the church in the United States a sense that working for justice was its mission. Later, the architect of the pastoral Joseph Bernardin developed a broadly inclusive consistent ethics of life through a series of thirty-five lectures.[246] Three years later, on November 13, 1986, the bishops addressed the ethical issues related to the economy in *Economic Justice for All*.[247] These events empowered Christians around the country to reflect on the relationship of justice, the church, and the world.

A leader in this reflection was the social ethicist David Hollenbach. Hollenbach has written on a wide array of issues: mediating claims in conflict, promoting a new perspective for an equitable justice, developing the respect of human rights, analyzing issues of war and peace in a nuclear age, and deepening the notion of common good to reflect better the world in which we live.[248] Later, he has addressed the issues of refugees and forced migration.[249] In all of his writings, he instructs his fellow ethicists to be vigilant about the miscarriages of justice and to be effective in the pursuit of a more equitable world.[250]

The clearest connection between liberation theology in Latin America and theological movements in the United States is Black theology. One year after publishing *Black Theology and Black Power*,[251] James Cone published *A Black Theology of Liberation*.[252] Then, in response to reviews that criticized Cone's dependence on European theologians, he offered a theology of Black traditions and experience in *The God of the Oppressed*.[253]

Later, Cone published *The Cross and the Lynching Tree*,[254] which the noted theological ethicist Bryan N. Massingale calls a meditation on lynching, "the brutally savage, extrajudicial, sadistic torture and killing of African-Americans, mostly men." Cone's meditation "details how these executions—which included shootings, hangings and burnings, often accompanied by excruciating dismemberment—were public spectacles and widely advertised events that occurred with the 'widespread knowledge' of government officials and the 'tacit approval' of white churches."

Massingale writes,

> Cone sees in lynching an "analogy" with the cross of Jesus. He believes that the cross and the lynching tree need each other. The cross needs the lynching tree "to remind Americans of the reality of suffering—to keep the cross from being a symbol of abstract, sentimental piety." But without the cross, the lynching tree "becomes simply an abomination," devoid of hope. The cross, then, enables Christians to stand in solidarity with the victims

of unjust suffering who endure contemporary social crucifixions.[255]

M. Shawn Copeland, a womanist who reflects on the experience of women of color, particularly African American women, is arguably the most prolific Catholic theological writer in Black theology. She has written about liberation theology for women;[256] the nature, method and, traditions of Black theology;[257] the intersection of racism, sexism, and classicism;[258] and the experience and narratives of suffering of Black women who live a theology of resistance, coupled with some sass.[259] Through her books she has developed from those narratives a theology of freedom[260] and testified to the "Uncommon Faithfulness" and the "Witness" of African American Religious Experience.[261] Finally, Copeland has also investigated the building of American Catholicism through white supremacy and anti-Blackness.[262]

Bryan Massingale is Black Catholic theology's leading theological ethicist. In his dissertation he studied the social dimensions of sin and reconciliation in the works of James Cone and Gustavo Gutiérrez.[263] In the 1990s he wrote about racism and Catholic social teaching,[264] and critiqued U.S. academic theology's failure to reflect on racism and the civil rights movement.[265] In 2000, responding to Massingale's essay, Michael Fahey, the editor of *Theological Studies*, dedicated an issue "to make amends for its shameful avoidance of the evil of racism in the United States."[266] The collection celebrated the thirtieth anniversary of *A Black Theology of Liberation* by inviting Cone to reflect on Black Catholics.[267] There, Massingale also returned to Cone to compare his work with recent Catholic episcopal teaching on racism.[268] Since then, like Copeland, Massingale presses his readers to see the racism they perpetuate and the profound relationship it has with poverty.[269]

Another way that liberation theology has flourished in the United States is through feminism, which as Elisabeth Schüssler Fiorenza explains, is a critical theology of liberation.[270] We have already seen in the United States the work of feminists like Farley, Cahill, Pilar Aquino, and Isasi-Diáz, but here, considering this ethics itself, we see that feminist ethics is opposed to discrimination and patterns of domination and is necessarily pro-women. It is suspicious of traditional interpretations of women (and men), any form of inequity, and any deductive logic that guides moral decisions. Systemically it manifests itself in very diverse ways.[271]

While agreeing that the contemporary diversity of feminism is significant, Susan Ross underlines fairly constant points of agreement: the priority of experience, attention to difference, appreciation for embodiment, opposition to patriarchal control, and care for the environment. While inclined to context and social location, it has recently moved toward greater cross-cultural discourse and justice-based transcultural standards.[272]

While systematic theologians gave feminism its fundamental theological foundations,[273] feminist ethicists have definitively extended their claims into the concrete world of sexual,[274] social,[275] and bioethics.[276] Iozzio, for example, in acknowledging that women bear the disproportionate burden of HIV, assembled an international group of twenty-five women theologians to tackle regional challenges emerging from HIV.[277]

Cross-Cultural Discourse, Ethics in the Church, and Globalization

At the end of the twentieth century, Catholic theological ethics became inclined to cross-cultural discourse. This was a long time coming. Since 1965, the journal *Concilium* in its seven linguistic editions has more than any other journal promoted international discourse. In 1965, Richard McCormick took the reins of the "Moral Notes" at *Theological Studies* and mediated an international conversation that continues today after more than fifty-five years. More recently, Christine Gudorf and Regina Wolfe edited *Ethics and World Religions: Cross-Cultural Case Studies*.[278] In *Catholic Ethicists on HIV/AIDS Prevention*, thirty-four ethicists from more than twenty-five countries worked together for the first international project on a globalized threat.[279]

When four hundred moral theologians gathered in July 2006 in Padua, Italy, for the first international conference on Catholic Theological Ethics, cross-cultural discourse in moral theology hit a new plateau. The meeting of CTEWC itself was successful and the conference papers were published in English, Spanish, Italian, Portuguese, Filipino, and Indian editions.[280] Since then the network of CTEWC has promoted a great deal of collaboration. Starting first with an East Asian meeting in Manila in 2008,[281] they met internationally again in 2010 in Trento, Italy,[282] and in 2018 in Sarajevo.[283] Besides fortifying the international network, they worked regionally to strengthen connections there, meeting in Nairobi (2012), Berlin (2013), Krakow (2014), Bangalore (2015), and Bogotá (2016). Besides the volumes on *Just Sustainability, The Bible and Catholic Theological Ethics*, and *The Catholic Ethicist in the Local Church*, their CTEWC book series also includes collections on Feminism, Migration, and Street Homelessness.[284] Their conference papers, their website (www.catholicethics.com), their monthly newsletter, *The First*, and other projects have made contemporary theological ethics both local and catholic by being connected.

In a way, the mission of CTEWC, which was developed as a network of engagement not dominated by the northern paradigm,[285] offers the best summary of where we are today and serves as the point of departure for our days ahead:

> Since theological ethics is so diffuse today, since practitioners and scholars are caught up in our own specific cultures, and since our interlocutors tend to be in other disciplines, there is the need for an international exchange of ideas in Catholic theological ethics. Catholic Theological Ethics in the World Church (CTEWC) recognizes the need: to appreciate the challenge of pluralism; to dialogue from and beyond local culture; and, to interconnect within a world church.
>
> While pursuing critical and emerging issues in theological ethics, CTEWC engages in cross-cultural, interdisciplinary conversations motivated by mercy and shaped by shared visions of hope. It does so by supporting new as well as isolated scholars in theological ethics, fostering the exchange of ideas via its online platforms and regional networks, and publishing a book series.[286]

Epilogue

It was not until recently that nurses, who were often previously understood as the supporting staff of physicians, became identified primarily as patient advocates. The shift was significant as allegiances changed when sometimes nurses found themselves confronting physicians about patient care.[287] A similar shift occurred among moral theologians who, as Ford and Kelly taught, were previously the spokespeople for popes and cardinals who proclaimed Catholic magisterial teaching. By the 1970s, however, like the nurses, the moral theologians began to accompany those who are suffering. As we have seen, this shift was groundbreaking.

With the election of Pope Francis, the shift has become validated. Conor M. Kelly argues that Pope Francis, in the wake of his apostolic exhortation *Amoris Laetitia*,[288] has implicitly given us the charge of accompanying the members of the church in their struggles to discern in conscience.[289] Echoing Pope Francis's admonition, "We have been called to form consciences, not to replace them" (*Amoris Laetitia* 37), Kelly notes that the moral theologian has to become more listener and fellow pilgrim than magisterial instructor.

With *Fratelli Tutti*, Pope Francis has taken us further ahead by also validating our commitment to respond to human suffering. There is Catholic irony here that, after fifty years of ethicists struggling, their priorities are now the agenda that Rome has set.

Notes

PREFACE

1. James F. Keenan, "In Memoriam: Klaus Demmer, MSC (1931–2014)," posted September 1, 2014, accessed November 30, 2021, https://catholicethics.com/news/in-memoriam-klaus-demmer-19312014/.

2. James F. Keenan, "Champion of Conscience," *America*, April 4, 2005, https://www.americamagazine.org/issue/526/other-things/champion-conscience#.

3. John Mahoney, *The Making of Moral Theology: A Study of the Roman Catholic Tradition* (New York: Oxford University Press, 1989).

4. John Gallagher, *Time Past, Time Future: An Historical Study of Catholic Moral Theology* (New York: Paulist Press, 1990).

5. Renzo Gerardi, *Storia della Morale: Interpretazioni teologiche dell'esperienza Cristiana* (Bologna: Edizioni Dehoniane, 2003).

6. See, e.g., her work on the influence of the Via Moderna on the moral theology of the late Middle Ages, Sigrid Müller, *Theologie und Philosophie im Spätmittelalter: Die Anfänge der via moderna und ihre Bedeutung für die Entwicklung der Moraltheologie (1380–1450)* (Münster: Achendorff Verlag, 2018).

CHAPTER ONE: JESUS IN THE NEW TESTAMENT

1. John T. Noonan Jr., *A Church That Can and Cannot Change: The Development of Moral Teaching* (Notre Dame, IN: University of Notre Dame Press, 2005).

2. Lúcás Chan, *Doing Biblical Ethics in the Twenty-First Century: Developments, Emerging Consensus, and the Future* (Mahwah, NJ: Paulist Press, 2013).

3. Fritz Tillmann, *The Master Calls: A Handbook of Christian Living* (Baltimore: Helicon Press, 1960).

4. William Spohn, *What Are They Saying About Scripture and Ethics?* (New York: Paulist Press, 1984), 3.

5. William Spohn, *Go and Do Likewise: Jesus and Ethics* (New York: Continuum, 1999).

6. Lúcás Chan, *The Ten Commandments and the Beatitudes: Biblical Studies and Ethics for Real Life* (New York: Rowman and Littlefield, 2012).

7. Dominik Markl, "The Decalogue in History: A Preliminary Survey of the Fields and Genre of its Reception," *Zeitschrift fur Altorientalische und Biblische Rechtsgeschicte* 18 (2012): 279–94, at 281. See also Dominik Markl, ed., *The Decalogue and Its Cultural Influence* (Sheffield: Phoenix Press, 2013).

8. Wayne Meeks, *The Origins of Christian Morality: The First Two Centuries* (New Haven: Yale University Press, 1993), 5.

9. Meeks, *Origins of Christian Morality*, 3.

10. Daniel J. Harrington and James F. Keenan, *Paul and Virtue Ethics: Building Bridges between New Testament Studies and Moral Theology* (New York: Rowman and Littlefield, 2010), 49.

11. I found Nussbaum developing this claim about the writings of Aristotle, but I believe it even more applicable to Paul. Martha Nussbaum, "Aristotle on Human Nature and the Foundation of Ethics," in *World, Mind and Ethics: Essays on the Ethical Philosophy of Bernard Williams*, ed. J. E. Altham and Ross Harrison (Cambridge: Cambridge University Press, 1995), 86–131.

12. Harrington and Keenan, *Paul and Virtue Ethics*, 211–16; see also Eric D'Arcy, *Conscience and Its Right to Freedom* (New York: Sheed and Ward, 1961).

13. Meeks, *Origins of Christian Morality*, 197.

14. Daniel J. Harrington and James F. Keenan, *Jesus and Virtue Ethics: Building Bridges between New Testament Studies and Moral Theology* (New York: Rowman and Littlefield, 2002), 35; hereafter, *Jesus*.

15. *Jesus*, 37.

16. *Jesus*, 38.

17. Tillmann, *The Master Calls*, 23.

18. *Jesus*, 81.

19. See, e.g., Augustine, *Quaestiones Evangeliorum*, 2.19; Bede, *Lucae Evangelium Expositio*, III (PL 92, 467–70). See also Patrick Clark, "Reversing the Ethical Perspective: What the Allegorical Interpretation of the Good Samaritan Parable Can Still Teach Us," *Theology Today* 71, no. 3 (2014): 300–309; Robert Stein, *An Introduction to the Parables of Jesus* (Philadelphia: Westminster, 1981), 42–52; Riemer Roukema, "The Good

Samaritan in Ancient Christianity," *Vigiliae Christiana* 58, no. 1 (February 2004): 56–74; D. Sanchis, "Samaritanus ille. L'exégèse augustinienne de la parabole du Bon Samaritain," *Recherches de Science Religieuse* 49 (1961): 406–25; "Who Is My Neighbor?" in *The Great Commentary of Cornelius à Lapide: Volume 4: St. Luke's Gospel*, trans. Thomas Mossman (Edinburgh: John Grant, 1908) 256–62; "Venerable Bede and the Parables (Part 2)," in *A Chorus of Voices: The Reception History of the Parables*, a blog by David B. Gowler, https://parablesreception.blogspot.com/2015/08/the-venerable-bede-and-parables-part-2.html.

20. William Spohn, *Go and Do Likewise: Jesus and Ethics* (New York: Continuum, 1999).

21. James F. Keenan, "Building Blocks for Moral Education: Vulnerability, Recognition and Conscience," in *Theology of Conscience and Catholic Education*, ed. David DeCosse and Kevin Baxter (Maryknoll, NY: Orbis, 2021); see also "The World at Risk: Vulnerability, Precarity and Connectedness," *Theological Studies* 81, no. 1 (2020): 132–49; "Linking Human Dignity, Vulnerability and Virtue Ethics," *Interdisciplinary Journal for Religion and Transformation in Contemporary Society* 6 (2020): 56–73.

22. James F. Keenan, *The Works of Mercy: The Heart of Catholicism* (Lanham, MD: Sheed and Ward, 2007).

23. Aquinas, *Summa Theologiae*, I-II, q. 78, a. 4c.

24. Wayne A. Meeks, "The Ethics of the Fourth Evangelist," in *Exploring the Gospel of John*, ed. R. A. Culpepper and C. C. Black (Louisville: Westminster John Knox, 1996), 317–26, at 318.

25. Brian Blount, *Then the Whisper Put on Flesh: New Testament Ethics in an African American Context* (Nashville: Abington Press, 2001), 93.

26. Frank Matera, *New Testament Ethics: The Legacies of Jesus and Paul* (Louisville: Westminster John Knox Press, 1996), 92. See additional comments by Richard Burridge, *Imitating Jesus: An Inclusive Approach to New Testament Ethics* (Grand Rapids, MI: Eerdmans, 2007), 291–93.

27. James F. Keenan, "Proposing Cardinal Virtues," *Theological Studies* 56, no. 4 (1995): 709–29; reprinted in Charles Curran and Richard McCormick, eds., *Readings in Moral Theology Number 11: The Historical Development of Fundamental Moral Theology in the United States* (New York: Paulist Press, 1999), 281–306; "Virtue Ethics and Sexual Ethics," *Louvain Studies* 30, no. 3 (2005): 183–203.

28. Burridge, *Imitating Jesus*, 33.

29. Burridge, *Imitating Jesus*, 61, 68.

30. Burridge, *Imitating Jesus*, 325–26.

31. Burridge, *Imitating Jesus*, 211–20.

32. Burridge, *Imitating Jesus*, 217.

33. Chan, *Doing Biblical Ethics in the Twenty-First Century*, 19.

34. Chan, *Doing Biblical Ethics in the Twenty-First Century*, 18–23. See Sandra M. Schneiders' works *The Revelatory Text: Interpreting the New Testament as Sacred Scripture* (Collegeville, MN: Liturgical Press, 1999) and *Written That You May Believe: Encountering Jesus in the Fourth Gospel* (New York: Crossroad, 2003).

35. Elisabeth Schüssler-Fiorenza, *In Memory of Her: A Feminist Theological Reconstruction of Christian Origins* (New York: Crossroad, 1983); *But She Said: Feminist Practices of Biblical Interpretation* (New York: Crossroad, 1994).

36. Phyllis Trible, *Texts of Terror: Literary-Feminist Readings of Biblical Narratives* (Philadelphia: Fortress Press, 1984); *God and the Rhetoric of Sexuality* (Philadelphia: Fortress Press, 1986).

37. Gina Hens-Piazza, *Nameless, Blameless and Without Shame: Two Cannibal Mothers Before a King* (Collegeville, MN: Liturgical Press, 2003).

38. Hens-Piazza, "Supporting Cast versus Supporting Caste: Reading the Old Testament as Praxis of Justice," in *The Bible and Catholic Theological Ethics*, ed. Yiu Sing Lúcás Chan, James F. Keenan, and Ronaldo Zacharias (Maryknoll, NY: Orbis, 2017), 109–20.

39. See, e.g., Patricia Sharbaugh, *Irrepressible Light: The Women of the New Testament* (Mahwah, NJ: Paulist Press, 2019).

40. Chan, *Doing Biblical Ethics in the Twenty-First Century*. Rasiah Sugirtharajah, *Asian Biblical Hermeneutics and Postcolonialism: Contesting the Interpretations* (Sheffield: Sheffield Academic Press, 1999); *The Bible and the Third World: The Precolonial, Colonial and Postcolonial Encounters* (New York: Cambridge University Press, 2001); *Postcolonial Criticism and Biblical Interpretation* (New York: Oxford University Press, 2002).

41. See George Griener and James F. Keenan, eds., *A Lúcás Chan Reader: Pioneering Essays on Biblical and Asian Theological Ethics* (Bangalore: Dharmarham, 2017).

CHAPTER TWO: MERCY

1. The assertion does not deny that many Christian teachers and pastors have viewed sexuality pessimistically, as we will see later.

2. Rudolf Bultmann, "Soma," in *Theology of the New Testament* (London: SCM, 1952), 1:192–203, at 192.

3. Robert Jewett, *Paul's Anthropological Terms* (Leiden: Brill, 1971), 1.

4. Gnosticism is a second-century heresy that maintained that the material world was made by an imperfect spirit and that the body was an unnecessary (and unworthy) appendage to the soul. Considering the body

as *soma* rather than *sarx* helped to keep Christianity from over-spiritualizing both reality and the human body.

5. Jewett, *Paul's Anthropological Terms*, 458.

6. Antoine Vergote, "The Body as Understood in Contemporary Thought and Biblical Categories," *Philosophy Today* 35 (1991): 93–105, at 96–97. See also Bultmann, "Soma," 192.

7. Brian Daley, "The Ripening of Salvation," *Communio* 17 (1990): 27–49, at 32; *The Hope of the Early Church* (New York: Cambridge University Press, 1991).

8. Gedaliahu Stroumsa, "*Caro salutis cardo*: Shaping the Person in Early Christian Thought," *History of Religions* 30 (1990): 25–50, at 25.

9. Stroumsa, "*Caro salutis cardo*," 35.

10. Stroumsa, "*Caro salutis cardo*," 39–40.

11. See Meeks, *The Origins of Christian Morality: The First Two Centuries* (New Haven: Yale University Press, 1993), 130–31; Vergote, "The Body as Understood," 95.

12. Stroumsa, "*Caro salutis cardo*," 33.

13. Stroumsa, "*Caro salutis cardo*," 44.

14. Peter Brown, "Late Antiquity," in *A History of Private Life*, ed. Paul Veyne (Cambridge, MA: Harvard University Press, 1987), 235–311, at 300.

15. Peter Brown, *The Body and Society: Men, Women, and Sexual Renunciation in Early Christianity* (New York: Columbia University Press, 1988), 437.

16. See, e.g., Efthalia Makris Walsh, "Wealthy and Impoverished Widows in the Writings of St. John Chrysostom," in *Wealth and Poverty in Early Church and Society*, ed. Susan Holman (Grand Rapids, MI: Baker Academic 2008), 176–86.

17. Brown, *Body and Society*, 259–84; 341–86.

18. Brown, *Body and Society*, 363.

19. Joyce Salisbury, *Church Fathers, Independent Virgins* (London: Verso, 1991).

20. Carolyn Osiek and Margaret MacDonald, *A Woman's Place: House Churches in Earliest Christianity* (Philadelphia: Fortress Press, 2005).

21. Elizabeth A. Clark, *Women in the Early Church* (Collegeville, MN: Liturgical Press, 1983).

22. Patricia Cox Miller, *Women in Early Christianity: Translations from Greek Texts* (Washington, DC: Catholic University of America Press, 2005).

23. Elizabeth A. Clark, *The Life of Melania the Younger: Introduction, Translation and Commentary* (New York: Edward Mellen Press, 1984). For more on the two Melanias, see the collection, Catherine M. Chin and

Caroline T. Schroeder, eds., *Melania: Early Christianity through the Life of One Family* (Oakland: University of California Press, 2017).

24. Mary Forman, *Praying with the Desert Mothers* (Collegeville, MN: Liturgical Press, 2005); Christine Valters Paintner, *Desert Fathers and Mothers: Early Christian Wisdom Sayings* (Woodstock, VT: Skylight Paths Publishing, 2012).

25. Gregory of Nyssa, *Vita Macrinae/Vie de Sainte Macrine*, text established and French trans. Pierre Maraval, Sources Chrétiennes 178 (Paris: Cerf, 1971).

26. See Joanne Turpin, "Macrina of Cappadocia," in *Women in Church History: 21 Stories for 21 Centuries* (Cincinnati: St. Anthony Messenger Press, 2007), 33–41, at 41. See Anne McGowan and Paul F. Bradshaw, eds., *The Pilgrimage of Egeria: A New Translation of the Itinerarium Egeriae with Introduction and Commentary* (Collegeville, MN: Liturgical Press, 2018).

27. Elizabeth Castelli, "Virginity and Its Meaning for Women's Sexuality in Early Christianity," *Journal of Feminist Studies of Religion* 2, no. 1 (1986): 61–88, at 63.

28. Kevin Madigan and Carolyn Osiek, *Ordained Women in the Early Church: A Documentary History* (Baltimore: Johns Hopkins University, 2003). See also Karen Torjesen, *When Women Were Priests: Women's Leadership in the Early Church and the Scandal of Their Subordination in the Rise of Christianity* (San Francisco: Harper, 1993); Gary Macy, *The Hidden History of Women's Ordination: Female Clergy in the Medieval West* (New York: Oxford University Press, 2008); Gary Macy, William T. Ditewig, Phyllis Zagano, *Women Deacons: Past, Present, Future* (Mahwah, NJ: Paulist Press, 2012).

29. Maureen Tilley, "Ordained Women in the Early Church: A Documentary History," *The Catholic Biblical Quarterly* 70, no. 1 (2008): 156–57, at 156.

30. Francine Cardman, "Acts of the Women Martyrs," *Anglican Theological Review* 70 (1989): 144–50, at 147. Turpin also treats Perpetua of Carthage in her *Women in Church History*, 16–24.

31. Cardman, "Acts of the Women Martyrs," 148.

32. Cardman, "Acts of the Women Martyrs," 150.

33. Meeks, *Origins of Christian Morality*, 104.

34. Meeks, *Origins of Christian Morality*, 104–9, at 104.

35. This information is culled from a variety of sources, esp. Théodore Koehler, "Miséricorde," in *Dictionnaire de spiritualité ascétique et mystique, doctrine et histoire*, ed. Marcel Viller (Paris: Beauchesne, 1980), 10:1313–28; Írenée Noye, "Miséricorde (Oeuvres de)," in Viller, *Dictionnaire*, 10:1328–50; J. M. Perrin, "Mercy, Works of," in *New Catholic Encyclopedia* (Washington, DC: Catholic University of America Press, 1967), 676–78.

36. Rodney Stark, *The Rise of Christianity: A Sociologist Reconsiders History* (Princeton: Princeton University Press, 1996), 147.

37. Stark, *Rise of Christianity*, 149–50.

38. Stark, *Rise of Christianity*, 156.

39. Stark, *Rise of Christianity*, 28–47. See also Marta Sordi, *The Christians and the Roman Empire* (Norman: University of Oklahoma Press, 1986).

40. Stark, *Rise of Christianity*, 161.

41. Stark, *Rise of Christianity*, 88.

42. Stark, *Rise of Christianity*, 212.

43. Peter Brown, *Through the Eye of a Needle: Wealth, the Fall of Rome, and the Making of Christianity in the West, 350–550 AD* (Princeton: Princeton University Press, 2012), 133.

44. Brown, *Through the Eye of a Needle*, 133.

45. Brown, *Through the Eye of a Needle*, 133.

46. Brown, *Through the Eye of a Needle*, 78.

47. Brown, *Through the Eye of a Needle*, 79.

48. Brown, *Through the Eye of a Needle*, 106.

49. Brown, *Through the Eye of a Needle*, 107–10.

50. Louis Vereecke, *Storia del Riposo Domenicale: Il Divieto delle 'opere servili nella domenica* (Rome: Alfonsianum University Press, 1973), 21–24.

51. Vereecke, *Storia del Riposo Domenicale*, 24–25.

52. Vereecke, *Storia del Riposo Domenicale*, 26–28.

53. Vereecke, *Storia del Riposo Domenicale*, 29–30.

54. Vereecke, *Storia del Riposo Domenicale*, 31–34.

55. Vereecke, *Storia del Riposo Domenicale*, 36.

56. John Mahoney, *The Making of Moral Theology: A Study of the Roman Catholic Tradition* (Oxford: Oxford University Press, 1987), 32.

57. James Brundage, *Law, Sex and Christian Society in Medieval Europe* (Chicago: University of Chicago Press, 1987), 9.

58. Pierre Payer, *The Bridling of Desire: Views of Sex in the Later Middle Ages* (Toronto: University of Toronto Press, 1993), 14.

59. Carla Ricci, *Mary Magdalene and Many Others: Women Who Followed Jesus* (Minneapolis: Fortress Press, 1994); Katherine Ludwig Jansen, *The Making of the Magdalen: Preaching and Popular Devotion in the Later Middle Ages* (Princeton: Princeton University Press, 2000).

60. Margaret Farley, "Sexual Ethics," in *Encyclopedia of Bioethics: Revised Edition*, ed. Warren Reich (New York: 1995), 5:2363–75, at 2367.

61. Brundage, *Law, Sex and Christian Society*, 70.

62. Louis Crompton, *Homosexuality and Civilization* (Cambridge, MA: Harvard University Press, 2003), 133–48.

63. Giovanni Cappelli, *Autoerotismo: Un problema morale nei primi secoli cristiani?* (Bologna: Edizioni Dehoniano, 1986).

64. Krister Stendahl, "The Apostle Paul and the Introspective Conscience of the West," *Harvard Theological Review* 56 (1963): 199–215.

65. Mahoney, *The Making of Moral Theology*, 48–57.

66. See interesting developments in Jennifer Herdt, *Putting on Virtue: The Legacy of the Splendid Vices* (Chicago: University of Chicago Press, 2008); James Wetzel, *Augustine and the Limits of Virtue* (New York: Cambridge University Press, 2008).

67. Alexander Flierl, *Die (Un-)Moralder Alltagslüge?! Wahrheit und Lüge im Alltagsethos aus Sicht der katholischen Moraltheologie*, Studien der Moraltheologie 32 (Muenster: 2005).

68. Lisa Sowle Cahill, *Love Your Enemies: Discipleship, Pacificism, and Just War Theory* (Minneapolis: Fortress Press, 1994), 55–80.

69. Lisa Sowle Cahill, *Sex, Gender and Christian Ethics* (Cambridge: Cambridge University Press, 1996), 121–65.

70. Mahoney, *The Making of Moral Theology*, 66.

71. On the other hand, see Willemien Otten, "Augustine on Marriage, Monasticism, and the Community of the Church," *Theological Studies* 59 (1998): 385–405.

72. Mahoney, *The Making of Moral Theology*, 58–67.

73. Cristina C. Traina, "Sex in the City of God," *Currents in Theology and Mission* 30, no. 1 (2003): 5–19.

74. Bernadette Brooten, "Nature, Law, and Custom in Augustine's *On the Good of Marriage*," in *Walk in the Ways of Wisdom: Essays in Honor of Elisabeth Schüssler Fiorenza*, ed. S. Matthews, C. B. Kittredge and M. Johnson-DeBaufre (Harrisburg, PA: Trinity Press, 2003), 181–93.

75. Margaret Miles, *Carnal Knowing: Female Nakedness and Religious Meaning in the West* (London: Vintage Press, 2006).

76. John T. Noonan Jr., *Contraception: A History of Its Treatment by the Catholic Theologians and Canonists* (Cambridge, MA: Harvard University Press, 1965), 130.

77. See, e.g., the classic study on self-love in Augustine, Oliver O'Donovan, *The Problem of Self-Love in Augustine* (New Haven: Yale University Press, 1980).

CHAPTER THREE: PATHWAYS TO HOLINESS

1. Louis Vereecke, CSsR, *De Guillaume d'Ockham à Saint Alphonse de Liguori. Etudes d'histoire de la théologie morale moderne 1300–1789* (Rome: Collegium S. Alfonsi de Urbe, 1986).

2. James F. Keenan, "John Mahoney's *The Making of Moral Theology*," in *The Oxford Handbook of Theological Ethics*, ed. Gilbert Meilaender

and William Werpehowski (Oxford: Oxford University Press, 2005), 503–19.

3. John Mahoney, *The Making of Moral Theology: A Study of the Roman Catholic Tradition* (New York: Oxford University Press, 1987), 1.

4. Mahoney, *Making of Moral Theology*, 28.

5. Mahoney, *Making of Moral Theology*, 28.

6. Mahoney, *Making of Moral Theology*, 38 and 45, respectively.

7. John Mahoney, *Seeking the Spirit: Essays in Moral and Pastoral Theology* (New York: Sheed and Ward, 1981).

8. Oliver O'Donovan locates Mahoney's book as belonging to the "genre of theological self-mystification—the most elegant and entertaining example of its kind. He has given his indictment with lucidity and irony….It is, in fact, a book all about the bad influences which 'conspired' to form Moral Theology" in his review, "The Making of Moral Theology," *Journal of Theological Studies* 39 (1988): 348–50, at 349. On the other hand, John Gallagher, author of *Time Past, Time Future: An Historical Study of Catholic Moral Theology* (New York: Paulist Press, 1989), objected to the fact that Mahoney was not more sin oriented. Gallagher believed that moral theology's sources result from the moral manuals of the seventeenth century and that what preceded them was not moral theology per se. Gallagher, "The Making of Moral Theology," *The Journal of Religion* 69 (1990): 279–80.

9. James Dallen, *The Reconciling Community: The Rite of Penance* (Collegeville, MN: Liturgical Press, 1986), 104.

10. Ceslas Spicq, *Théologie Morale du Nouveau Testament*, Tome II (Paris: Librairie Lecoffre, 1965), 688–744.

11. *Pace* Spicq, *hesed*, which is the fidelity of YHWH toward the people of YHWH meant that in that bond, the people were formed. Although imitation was not invoked, still, the people were very much formed to treat others as YHWH treated them.

12. Interestingly, throughout Italian cities we find churches dedicated to the *Most* Holy Trinity (Santissima Trinita), but in Florence, the title "Santissima" is not for the church of the Trinity, known there as simply "Santa Trinita," but rather for the church of the Annunciation, there called "Santissima Annuziata."

13. Charles Trinkaus, *In Our Image and Likeness: Humanity and Divinity in Italian Humanist Thought* (Notre Dame, IN: University of Notre Dame, 1995).

14. Ronaldo Zacharias, "Scripture and Sexual Ethics: From Absolute Trust and Systematic Suspicion to a Hermeneutics of Appreciation," in *The Bible and Catholic Theological Ethics*, ed. Lúcás Chan Yiu Sing, James F. Keenan, and Ronaldo Zacharias (Maryknoll, NY: Orbis, 2017), 273–86.

15. Louis Vereecke, "Storia della Teologia morale," *Nuovo dizionario di teologia morale* (Cinisello Balsamo: Edizioni Paoline, 1990), 1317.

16. Renzo Gerardi, *Storia della Morale: Interpretazioni teologiche dell'esperienza Cristiana* (Bologna: Edizioni Dehoniane Bologna, 2003), 109–11.

17. St. Ambrose, *On the Duties of the Clergy* (Savage, MN: Lighthouse Christian Publishing, 2013).

18. Ambrose, "*In Lucam* 5.51," in *Corpus Scriptorum Ecclesiasticorum Latinorum*, 32.4, ed. C. Schenkl (Vienna, 1937), 201, as quoted in Chan, *The Ten Commandments and the Beatitudes*, 164.

19. Gerardi, "La prima trattazione organica della morale cristiana in un'ottica practica," *Storia della Morale*, 134. See his full discussion, 132–37.

20. Servais Pinckaers, *Sources of Christian Ethics*, trans. Mary Thomas Noble (Washington, DC: Catholic University Press, 1995).

21. Augustine, *The Lord's Sermon on the Mount*, trans. John James Jepson (New York: Newman Press, 1948), §1. See also http://www.newadvent.org/fathers/16011.htm.

22. Augustine, *The Lord's Sermon on the Mount*, §1.

23. Chan, *Ten Commandments and Beatitudes*, 163–68.

24. Augustine, *The Lord's Sermon on the Mount*, §10.

25. Augustine, *The Lord's Sermon on the Mount*, §11.

26. Augustine, *The Lord's Sermon on the Mount*, §11.

27. Pinckaers, *Sources of Christian Ethics*, 145.

28. Pinckaers, *Sources of Christian Ethics*, 148.

29. On the Beatitudes, besides Chan's *Ten Commandments and the Beatitudes*, see Jeffrey P. Greenman, Timothy Larsen, and Stephen R Spencer, eds., *The Sermon on the Mount through the Ages* (Grand Rapids, MI: Brazos Press, 2007); Hans Dieter Betz, *The Sermon on the Mount* (Minneapolis: Fortress Press, 1995); W. Carter, *What Are They Saying About Matthew's Sermon on the Mount?* (New York: Paulist Press, 1994); Daniel J. Harrington, "The Sermon on the Mount—What Is It?" *Bible Today* 36, no. 6 (1998): 280–86; Joseph Kotva, *The Christian Case for Virtue Ethics* (Washington, DC: Georgetown University Press, 1996); Jan Lambrecht, *The Sermon on the Mount: Proclamation and Exhortation* (Wilmington, DE: Glazier, 1985); William Mattison, "The Beatitudes and Moral Theology: A Virtue Ethics Approach," *Nova et Vetera* 11, no. 3 (2013): 819–48; Allen Verhey, *The Great Reversal: Ethics and the New Testament* (Grand Rapids, MI: Eerdmans, 1984).

30. St. Gregory the Great, *Pastoral Care*, Ancient Christian Writers, trans. Henry Davis (New York: Paulist Press, 1978).

31. Gregory, *The Dialogues of St. Gregory the Great* (London: P. L. Warner, 1911).

32. St. Gregory the Great, *Morals on the Book of Job*, ed. Paul A. Böer (Lexington, KY: Veritatis Splendor Publications, 2012).

33. Lúcás Chan, *Biblical Ethics in the 21st Century: Developments, Emerging Consensus, and Future Directions* (Mahwah, NJ: Paulist Press, 2013); Lúcás Chan Yiu Sing, James Keenan, and Ronaldo Zacharias, eds., *The Bible and Catholic Theological Ethics.*

34. Gregory, *Morals on the Book of Job*, bk. 3, §§15–16, 1:117–18.

35. Gregory, *Morals on the Book of Job*, bk. 35, §§49, 651–52.

36. "In hoc quippe mundo humana anima quasi more navis est contra ictum fluminis conscendentis: uno in loco nequaquam stare permittitur, quia ad ima relabitur, nisi ad summa conetur. Gregory, *Reg. Past.* p. III, c. 34: ML 77, 118c.

37. "In via vitae non progredi regredi est." Bernard, *Serm II in festo. Purif.*, n. 3: ML 183, 369 C.

38. "In via Dei stare retrocedere est." Thomas attributed the quote to Bernard in *III Sen* d.29 a.8 qla2 1a. and to Gregory in the *Summa theologiae* II-II, q. 24, a. 6. ob3.

39. James Dallen, "Reconciliation, Sacrament of," in *New Dictionary of Sacramental Worship*, ed. Peter Fink (Collegeville, MN: Liturgical Press, 1991), 1052–64, at 1054.

40. Dallen, "Reconciliation, Sacrament of," 1055–57. See also Bernard Poschmann, *Penance and Anointing of the Sick* (New York: Herder and Herder, 1964).

41. Gary Anderson, *Sin: A History* (New Haven: Yale University, 2010).

42. John T. McNeill and Helen M. Gamer, eds., *Medieval Handbooks of Penance* (New York: Columbia University Press, 1990).

43. Hugh Connolly, *Irish Penitentials and Their Significance for the Sacrament of Penance Today* (Dublin: Four Courts Press, 1995), 17.

44. Connolly, *Irish Penitentials*, 14.

45. Dallen, "Reconciliation," 1056; see Connolly, *Irish Penitentials*, 18–20.

46. See, e.g., the "Penitential of Cummean," I. Of Gluttony 1, 13, 14; II. Of Fornication 1, 2, 3, 4, 5, 6, 17, 22, 23; III. Of Avarice 2. In McNeill, *Medieval Handbooks of Penance*, 100–110.

47. See, e.g., "Cummean," I. Of Gluttony 2, 3, 12; II. Of Fornication 8, 12, 13, 16; III. Of Avarice 1, 3, 16, 17, 18. In McNeill, *Medieval Handbooks of Penance*, 100–110.

48. McNeill, *Medieval Handbooks of Penance*, 100–102.

49. Dallen, *The Reconciling Community*, 139–203.

50. Kilian McDonnell, "The 'Summae confessorum' on the Integrity of Confession as Prolegomena for Luther and Trent," *Theological Studies* 54 (1993): 405–27, at 411.

51. Denziger-Schonmetzer, *Enchiridion Symbolorum*, 36th ed. (Freiburg: Herder, 1971), no. 812; hereafter cited as DS.

52. Henry Lea, *The History of Auricular Confession and Indulgences in the Latin Church* (Philadelphia: Lea Brothers, 1896), 1:230.

53. See Thomas Tentler, *Sin and Confession on the Eve of the Reformation* (Princeton: Princeton University Press, 1977).

54. Leonard Boyle makes clear that the Constitution of the Fourth Lateran Council, *Inter cetera*, explicitly allied the function of preaching and hearing confessions, in his *The Setting of the Summa Theologiae of Saint Thomas* (Toronto: Pontifical Institute of Medieval Studies, 1982), 1–4.

55. Leonard E. Boyle, *Pastoral Care, Clerical Education, and Canon Law, 1200–1400* (London: Variorum Reprints, 1981).

56. McDonnell, "The 'Summae confessorum,'" 122; regarding religious orders, he refers the reader to Thomas Tentler, *Sin and Confession on the Eve of the Reformation* (Princeton: Princeton University, 1977).

57. In addition to much of Boyle's *Pastoral Care*, see his "The Fourth Lateran Council and Manuals of Popular Theology," in *The Popular Literature of Medieval England*, ed. T. J. Heffernan (Knoxville: Univ. of Tennessee Press, 1985), 30–43.

58. Tentler, *Sin and Confession on the Eve of the Reformation*, 34–39; for his discussion on Luther's critique of the confessional see 352–63.

59. Angelus de Clavisio (Chivasso), *Summa confessorum* (Nuremberg: Anthony Koberger, 1492), "Interrogationes" cxlviii–clvi.

60. de Clavisio (Chivasso), *Summa confessorum*, cxlix.

61. de Clavisio (Chivasso), *Summa confessorum*, cxlviii.

62. de Clavisio (Chivasso), *Summa confessorum*, cxlix. In McDonnell.

63. Tentler, *Sin and Confession on the Eve of the Reformation*, 52.

64. The casuistry was purely about what was a committed sin, not about a failure to love, see Tentler, *Sin and Confession on the Eve of the Reformation*, 138–40.

65. Tentler, *Sin and Confession on the Eve of the Reformation*, 345, 346, 347, respectively. See also the debate, Tentler, "The Summa for Confessors as an Instrument of Social Control," in *The Pursuit of Holiness in Late Medieval and Renaissance Religion*, ed. Charles Trinkhaus and Heiko Oberman (Leiden: E. J. Brill, 1974), 103–25; "Response and Retractio," in Trinkhaus and Oberman, *The Pursuit of Holiness in Late Medieval and Renaissance Religion*, 131–37.

66. Part II: The Decalogue, "The Importance of the Instruction," in *The Catechism of the Council of Trent*, http://www.catholicapologetics.info/thechurch/catechism/TenCommandments.shtml.

67. Hildegard of Bingen, *Scivias* (New York: Paulist Press, 2007); see Elizabeth A. Dreyer, *Passsionate Spirituality: Hildegard of Bingen and Hadewijch of Brabant* (New York: Paulist Press, 2005); Dreyer, "Hildegard of Bingen," in *Accidental Theologians* (Cincinnati: Franciscan Media, 2014), 21–44; Barbara Newman, *Sister of Wisdom: St. Hildegard's Theology of the Feminine* (Berkeley: University of California Press, 1998); Newman, ed., *Voice of the Living Light: Hildegard of Bingen and Her World* (Berkeley: University of California Press, 1998).

68. Bernard McGinn, "The Human Person as Image of God: Eastern Christianity," in *Christian Spirituality: Origins to the Twelfth Century*, ed. Bernard McGinn, John Meyendorf, and Jean Leclercq, World Spirituality 16 (New York: Crossroad, 1985), 312–30, at 323. While the twelfth century marks the enormous systematic development of ascetical texts, a few appear earlier, e.g., Dhuoda's *Manual for My Son* (843) and Jonas of Orleans's treatise *Instruction of the Laity* (c. 828), see Jacques Fontaine, "The Practice of Christian Life: The Birth of the Laity," in McGinn, Meyendorf, and Leclercq, *Christian Spirituality*, 453–91.

69. Caroline Walker Bynum, "Did the Twelfth Century Discover the Individual?," in *Jesus as Mother: Studies in the Spirituality of the High Middle Ages* (Berkeley: University of California Press, 1984), 82–109, at 109.

70. Bynum, "Did the Twelfth Century Discover the Individual?," 86.

71. François Vandenbroucke, "Lay Spirituality in the Twelfth Century," in *History of Christian Spirituality* (London: Burns and Oates, 1968), 243–82. See also Thomas M. Osborne, *Love of Self and Love of God in Thirteenth-Century Ethics* (Notre Dame, IN: University of Notre Dame Press, 2005).

72. Bynum, "Did the Twelfth Century Discover the Individual?,"106.

73. Bynum, "Did the Twelfth Century Discover the Individual?,"106.

74. Thomas Aquinas, *Summa Theologiae*, II-II, q. 184, a. 1. See ad2, where Thomas states that perfection belongs to charity simply, the other virtues relatively.

75. Aquinas, *Summa Theologiae*, II-II, q. 186, a. 2c.

76. Aquinas, *Summa Theologiae*, II-II, q. 186, a. 1, ad4.

77. Aquinas, *Summa Theologiae*, II-II, q. 186, a. 3c.

78. Aquinas, *Summa Theologiae*, II-II, q. 184, a. 4c.

79. Giles Constable, *Three Studies in Medieval Religious and Social Thought* (New York: Cambridge University Press, 1995), 218.

80. Constable, *Three Studies*, 239.

81. See the claim in Robert Miola, *Early Modern Catholicism: An Anthropology of Primary Sources* (New York: Oxford University Press, 2007) 285; for much more detail, see Maximilian Von Habsburg, *Catholic and Protestant Translations of the* Imitatio Christi, *1425–1650: From Late Medieval Classic to Early Modern Bestseller* (New York: Routledge, 2016); William P. Anderson and Richard L. Diesslin, eds., *A Journey Through Christian Theology* (Philadelphia: Fortress Press, 2000), 98.

82. Thomas à Kempis, *Imitation of Christ*, Christian Classics Ethereal Library, bk. 1, chap. 20. http://www.ccel.org/ccel/kempis/imitation.i.html.

83. à Kempis, *Imitation of Christ*, bk. 1, chap. 1.

84. à Kempis, *Imitation of Christ*, bk. 1, chap. 1.

85. à Kempis, *Imitation of Christ*, bk. 1, chaps. 1, 17.

86. à Kempis, *Imitation of Christ*, bk. 1, chaps. 1, 20.

87. See Evan Howard, *A Guide to Christian Spiritual Formation: How Scripture, Spirit, Community, and Mission Shape Our Souls* (Ada, MI: Baker Academics, 2018), 91.

88. On Clare, see Michael Blastic, Wayne Hellmann, and Jay Hammond, eds., *The Writings of Clare of Assisi: Letters, Form of Life, Testament and Blessing*, Studies in Early Franciscan Sources (St. Bonaventure, NY: Franciscan Institute Publications, 2011); Turpin, "Clare of Assisi," in *Women in Church History: 21 Stories for 21 Centuries* (Cincinnati: St. Anthony Messenger Press, 2007), 116–27.

89. Caroline Walker Bynum, *Fragmentation and Redemption Essays on Gender and the Human Body in Medieval Religion* (New York: Zone Books, 1991), 153.

90. Catherine Mooney, *Gendered Voices: Medieval Saints and Their Interpreters* (Philadelphia: University of Pennsylvania Press, 1999), 66–67. Special thanks to Jacob Seet for pointing this out to me.

91. Teresa Berger, *Gender Differences and the Making of Liturgical History: Lifting a Veil on Liturgy's Past* (New York: Routledge, 2011), 66–67.

92. Caroline Bynum, *Holy Feast and Holy Fast: The Religious Significance of Food to Medieval Women* (Oakland: University of California Press, 1988).

93. Aquinas, *Summa Theologiae*, II-II, q. 180, a. 1c.

94. Aquinas, *Summa Theologiae*, II-II, q. 181, a. 1c.

95. Aquinas, *Summa Theologiae*, II-II, q. 182, a. 1c.

96. Aquinas, *Summa Theologiae*, II-II, q. 182, a. 1, ad3.

97. Aquinas, *Summa Theologiae*, II-II, q. 188, a. 6c.

98. Aquinas, *Summa Theologiae*, II-II, q. 188, a. 8c.

99. On Thomas's contributions to pathways to holiness, see Simon Tugwell, ed., *Albert and Thomas: Selected Writings* (New York: Paulist Press,

1988); Jean Pierre Torrell, OP, *Saint Thomas Aquinas, Volume 2: Spiritual Master* (Washington, DC: Catholic University of America Press, 2003).

100. See John O'Malley, *The First Jesuits* (Cambridge, MA: Harvard University Press, 1993), 192–98.

101. Charles Curran, "Roman Catholic Sexual Ethics: A Dissenting View," *Religion Online*, accessed December 9, 2021, https://www.religion-online.org/article/roman-catholic-sexual-ethics-a-dissenting-view/. This article originally appeared in *The Christian Century* (December 16, 1987): 1139–42. Very helpful in the history of church teaching on sexuality is Pierre Payer, *Sex and the Penitentials: The Development of a Sexual Code, 550–1150* (Toronto: Toronto University Press, 1984); *The Bridling of Desire: Views of Sex in the Later Middle Ages* (Toronto: University of Toronto Press, 1993); "Confession and the Study of Sex in the Middle Ages," in *Handbook of Medieval Sexuality*, ed. Vern L. Bullough and James A. Brundage (New York: Garland Publishing, 1996), 3–32.

102. See, e.g., Giovanni Cappelli, *Autoerotismo: Un problema-morale nei primi secoli cristiani?* (Bologna: Edizioni Dehoniano, 1986).

103. James A. Brundage, *Law, Sex, and Christian Society in Medieval Europe* (Chicago: University of Chicago Press, 1987), 9.

104. Jerome, *Against Jovinian*, 1.26, cited in David Hunter, ed., *Marriage and Sexuality in Early Christianity* (Minneapolis: Fortress Press, 2018), 28. See his chapter on Jerome, 153–64. For a fuller study, see his *Marriage, Celibacy, and Heresy in Ancient Christianity: The Jovinianist Controversy* (New York: Oxford University Press, 2007).

105. Louis Crompton, *Homosexuality and Civilization* (Cambridge, MA: Harvard University Press, 2003).

106. Jacqueline Murray, "Twice Marginal and Twice Invisible: Lesbians in the Middle Ages," in Bullough and Brundage, *Handbook of Medieval Sexuality*, 191–222.

107. Joyce Salisbury, "Gendered Sexuality," in Bullough and Brundage, *Handbook of Medieval Sexuality*, 33–50.

108. Murray, "Twice Marginal and Twice Invisible."

109. Ivo, *Opera Omnia* (Paris: Lavrentium Cottereau, 1647), in 9.106 and 9.110, respectively. See John T. Noonan Jr., who comments that Ivo's work is a milestone in *Contraception: A History of Its Treatment by the Catholic Theologians and Canonists* (Cambridge, MA: Harvard University Press, 1965), 172–73.

110. Noonan, *Contraception*, 224.

111. Peter Damien, *The Book of Gomorrah*, ed. Pierre Payer (Waterloo, ON: Wilfrid Laurier University Press, 1982), 29.

112. For more on Damien and his concern about monks, see Mark Jordan, *The Invention of Sodomy in Christian Theology* (Chicago: University of Chicago Press, 1997), 57–66.

113. Jordan, *Invention of Sodomy in Christian Theology*, 105.

114. Jordan, *Invention of Sodomy in Christian Theology*, 126.

115. Thomas Aquinas, *Summa Contra Gentiles*, III.122.

116. Thomas Aquinas, *Summa Theologiae*, II-II, q. 153, a. 3.

117. See Noonan, *Contraception*, 244–57; Josef Fuchs, *Die Sexualethik des heiligen Thomas von Aquin* (Cologne: J. P. Bachem, 1949); on semen itself as a preoccupation of Catholic moral teachers, see Hubertus Lutterbach, "Die Sexualtabus in den Bussbüchern," *Saeculum* 46 (1995): 216–48; *Sexualität im Mittelalter. Eine Kulturstudie anhand von Bussbüchern des 6. bis 12. Jahrhunderts* (Cologne: Böhlau Verlag, 1999).

118. Anthony Kosnick et al., *Human Sexuality: New Directions in American Catholic Thought* (New York: Paulist Press, 1977).

119. John Dedek, "Moral Absolutes in the Predecessors of St. Thomas," *Theological Studies* 38 (1977): 654–80; "Intrinsically Evil Acts: An Historical Study of the Mind of St. Thomas," *The Thomist* 43 (1979): 385–413; "Intrinsically Evil Acts: The Emergence of a Doctrine," *Recherches de theologie ancienne et medievale* 50 (1983): 191–226.

120. Lucius Iwejuru Ugorji, *The Principle of Double Effect: A Critical Appraisal of Its Traditional Understanding and Its Modern Reinterpretation* (Frankfurt Am Main: Peter Lang, 1985).

121. See Shaji George Kochuthara, *The Concept of Sexual Pleasure in the Catholic Moral Tradition* (Rome: Pontificia Università Gregoriana, 2007); Louis Vereecke, *De Guillaume d'Ockham à Saint Alphonse de Liguori: Études d'histoire de la théologie morale moderne, 1300–1787* (Rome: Alfonsianum University, 1986).

122. *The Catechism of the Council of Trent* (Charlotte, NC: TAN Books, 2009), §§ 338–55.

123. *Catechism of the Council of Trent*, §§ 431–39.

124. Patrick Boyle, *Parvitas Materiae in Sexto in Contemporary Catholic Thought* (Lanham, MD: University Press of America, 1987), 14–16.

125. John Connery, *Abortion: The Development of the Roman Catholic Perspective* (Chicago: Loyola University Press, 1977); John T. Noonan Jr., "An Almost Absolute Value in History," in *The Morality of Abortion*, ed. John T. Noonan Jr. (Cambridge, MA: Harvard University Press, 1970), 1–59.

126. As we saw in chap. 2, Alexander Flierl investigates the two differing trajectories throughout the tradition in his *Die (Un-)Moral der Alltagslüge?! Wahrheit und Lüge im Alltagsethos aus Sicht der katholischen Moraltheologie* (Münster 2005). Julia Fleming, "The Ethics of Lying in

Contemporary Moral Theology," *Louvain Studies* 24, no. 1 (1999): 57–71. Johann P. Sommerville argues that among seventeenth-century English Roman Catholic, Anglican, and Puritan writers there is greater similarity than previously acknowledged in their attempt to deal with equivocation in his "The 'New Art of Lying': Equivocation, Mental Reservation, and Casuistry," in *Conscience and Casuistry in Early Modern Europe*, ed. Edmund Leites (New York: Cambridge University Press, 1988), 159–84.

127. Between 1514 and 1518, eight Latin editions of the *Enchiridion* were printed. It was translated into English in 1519, German in 1520, Dutch in 1526, and Polish in 1535. The book was especially celebrated in Spain. See https://www.schillerinstitute.org/fid_91-96/952_erasmus.html.

128. Desiderius Erasmus, "Letter to Paul Voltz," in *Enchiridion Militis Christiani, Collected Works of Erasmus: Spiritualia*, ed. John O'Malley (Toronto: University of Toronto Press, 1988), 66:9. All subsequent citations from the *Enchiridion* are from this collection.

129. Enda McDonagh, *Doing the Truth: The Quest for Moral Theology* (Notre Dame, IN: University of Notre Dame Press, 1979), 15.

130. John O'Malley, "Introduction," vol. 66 of *Collected Works of Erasmus: Spiritualia*, ed. John O'Malley (Toronto: University of Toronto Press, 1988), xii.

131. John O'Malley, "Erasmus and Luther: Continuity and Discontinuity as Key to their Conflict," *The Sixteenth Century Journal* 5, no. 2 (1974): 47–65.

132. Quoted in Charles Fantazzi, "Introductory Note," in O'Malley, *Collected Works of Erasmus: Spiritualia*, 3.

133. O'Malley, "Introduction," in *Collected Works of Erasmus: Spiritualia*, 66:xli.

134. On vigilance in devotional literature, see R. Vernay, "Attention," in *Dictionnaire de spiritualité* I (Paris: Beauchesne Editor, 1937), 1058–77; on the scriptural roots to vigilance, see Joseph Plevnik, "1 Thess 5:1–11: Its Authenticity, Intention and Message," *Biblica* 60 (1979): 71–90.

135. Adolf von Harnack, *Militia Christi: die christliche Religion und der Soldatenstand in den ersten drei Jahrhunderten* (Tubingen: J. C. B. Mohr, 1905).

136. Johann Auer, "Militia Christi: Zur Geschichte eines christlichen Grundbildes," *Geist und Leben* 32 (1959): 340–351; Auer, "Militia Christi," *Lexikon für Theologie und Kirche*, 2nd ed. (1962) VII, 418–19.

137. Joseph de Guibert, *The Theology of the Spiritual Life* (New York: Sheed and Ward, 1953), 5.

138. See Constable, *Three Studies*, 146–49; see also Philip Sheldrake, *Images of Holiness: Explorations in Contemporary Spirituality* (London: Darton, Longman and Todd, 1987) who discusses the "spirituality of struggle." See

also Jean Leclerq's discussion of the "Christian Hero," in *History of Christian Spirituality*, 60–62.

139. See, e.g., Martin Thornton, *English Spirituality: An Outline of Ascetical Theology according to the English Pastoral Tradition* (London: SPCK, 1963), 215–17.

140. Thomas Aquinas, *Summa Theologiae*, I-II, q. 1, a. 3c.

141. See Adrien Demoustier, "L'originalité des 'Exercices spirituels,'" in *Les jésuites à l'âge baroque (1540–1640)*, ed. Luce Giard and Louis de Vaucelles (Grenoble: Jérôme Millon, 1996), 27–31.

142. Moshe Sluhovsky, "St. Ignatius of Loyola's 'Spiritual Exercises' and Their Contribution to Modern Introspective Subjectivity," *The Catholic Historical Review* 99, no. 4 (October 2013): 649–74, at 651.

143. O'Malley, *The First Jesuits*, 265.

144. O'Malley corrects and explains the more positive regard Ignatius had for Erasmus, *The First Jesuits*, 260–64. See also John Olin, *The Catholic Reformation: Savonarola to Ignatius Loyola; Reform in the Church 1495–1540* (New York: Harper and Row, 1969); Olin, "Erasmus and St. Ignatius Loyola," in *Six Essays on Erasmus* (New York: Fordham University Press, 1979), 75–92.

145. O'Malley, *The First Jesuits*, 4.

146. For more on the text and its influence, see O'Malley, *The First Jesuits*, 37–50; Robert E. McNally, "The Council of Trent, the Spiritual Exercises and the Catholic Reform," *Church History* 34, no. 1 (March 1965): 36–49.

147. Louis Puhl, *The Spiritual Exercises of Saint Ignatius: A New Translation Based on Studies in the Language of the Autograph* (Westminster, MD: The Newman Press, 1957), directives 97–98, pp. 44–45.

148. Puhl, *Spiritual Exercises of Saint Ignatius*, directive 234, p. 102.

149. See Ai Van Pham, "A Jesuit Accent for Contemporary Christian Ethics: A Study on the Relationship between Spirituality and Morality" (STD diss., Boston College, 2002).

150. O'Malley, *The First Jesuits*, 136–52.

151. Puhl, *Spiritual Exercises of Saint Ignatius*, directive 15, p. 6.

152. Puhl, *Spiritual Exercises of Saint Ignatius*, directive 53, p. 28.

153. O'Malley, *The First Jesuits*, 49.

154. Hugo Rahner, *Ignatius the Theologian* (London: Geoffrey Chapman, 1990).

CHAPTER FOUR: FROM THE TWELFTH TO THE SIXTEENTH CENTURY

1. Philipp W. Rosemann, *Peter Lombard* (New York: Oxford University Press, 2004), 24.

2. Rosemann, *Peter Lombard*, 24.

3. Marie-Dominique Chenu, "Masters of the Theological 'Science,'" in *Nature, Man, Society in the Twelfth Century: Essays on New Theological Perspectives in the Latin West* (Chicago: University of Chicago Press, 1968), 270–309, at 276.

4. Marcia L. Colish, *Medieval Foundations of the Western Intellectual Tradition 400–1400* (New Haven: Yale University Press, 1997), 175.

5. Colish, *Medieval Foundations*, 268–69.

6. Chenu, "Masters," 280.

7. Marcia L. Colish, *Peter Lombard* (Leiden: Brill, 1993), 91.

8. Although many consider Anselm of Canterbury (1033–1109) the father of Scholasticism, this chapter, like the book itself, is restricted to the history of theological ethics, whence Abelard is our point of departure since he is the first to work in the so-called field.

9. Betty Radice, ed. and trans., *The Letters of Abelard and Heloise* (New York: Penguin Books, 1974), 21.

10. Radice, *Letters of Abelard and Heloise*, 15.

11. Colish, *Medieval Foundations*, 275–77, at 276.

12. We will see more on nominalism at the end of this chapter and the beginning of the next.

13. Radice, *Letters of Abelard and Heloise*, 113–14.

14. Radice notes at 21, "This time he could hardly have made a worse decision."

15. John Marenbon, "Life, Milieu, and Intellectual Contexts," in *The Cambridge Companion to Abelard*, ed. Jeffrey E. Brower and Kevin Guilfoy (New York: Cambridge University Press, 2004), 13–44; see also his *The Philosophy of Peter Abelard* (New York: Cambridge University Press, 1997).

16. Roseman, *Peter Lombard*, 28.

17. Roseman, *Peter Lombard*, 27–28. On Hugh of St. Victor, see Boyd Taylor Coolman, *The Theology of Hugh of St. Victor: An Interpretation* (New York: Cambridge University Press, 2013); see also Steven Chase, *Contemplation and Compassion: The Victorine Tradition* (Maryknoll, NY: Orbis, 2003).

18. Roseman, *Peter Lombard*, 28–31.

19. Peter Abelard, *Ethical Writings: Ethics and Dialogue between a Philosopher, a Jew, and a Christian*, ed. and trans., Paul Vincent Spade (Indianapolis: Hackett Publishing Company, 1995); see Marilyn McCord Adams, "Introduction," in Abelard, *Ethical Writings*, 7–27.

20. The numbers refer to the paragraphs in the Spade edition of *The Ethics.*

21. Others do not emphasize this negative notion of consent; see, e.g., William Mann, "Ethics," in Brower and Guilfoy, *The Cambridge Companion to Abelard*, 279–309; Jean Porter, "Responsibility, Passion, and Sin: A Reassessment of Abelard's Ethics," *Journal of Religious Ethics* 28, no. 3 (September 2000): 367–94. I want to thank Xavier Montecel, a PhD student, who helped me to see that, for Abelard, consent is precisely a negative act.

22. I want to thank a student, Amanda Altobell, whose paper on Heloise introduced me to the work by Constant Mews and Barbara Newman.

23. Constant J. Mews, *Abelard and Heloise* (New York: Oxford University Press, 2005), 8.

24. Mews, *Abelard and Heloise*, 62.

25. Mews, *Abelard and Heloise*, 276.

26. Radice, *Letters of Abelard and Heloise*, 53.

27. Radice, *Letters of Abelard and Heloise*, 68.

28. Radice, *Letters of Abelard and Heloise*, 68.

29. Barbara Newman, "Authority, Authenticity and the Repression of Heloise," *Journal of Medieval and Renaissance Studies* 22 (1992): 121–57, at 148. Newman provides her own translation from *Historia Calamitatum*, ed. Jacques Monfrin (Paris: Vrin, 1959), 76.

30. Radice, *Letters of Abelard and Heloise*, 51–52.

31. Radice, *Letters of Abelard and Heloise*, 54.

32. Mews, *Abelard and Heloise*, 177. At 179, she notes that many of the philosopher's arguments parallel Heloise's.

33. Mews, *Abelard and Heloise*, 180.

34. Rosemann, *Peter Lombard*, 3.

35. G. R. Evans, *Mediaeval Commentaries on the Sentences of Peter Lombard: Current Research (Book 1)* (Leiden: Brill, 2002); Rosemann, *Mediaeval Commentaries on the Sentences of Peter Lombard (Book 2)* (Leiden: Brill, 2009).

36. Rosemann, *Peter Lombard*, 61.

37. Rosemann, *Peter Lombard*, 62. See also his *The Story of a Great Medieval Book: Peter Lombard's Sentences* (Toronto: Broadview, 2007).

38. Rosemann, *Peter Lombard*, 63–64.

39. Peter Lombard, *The Sentences, Book 4: On the Doctrine of Signs*, trans. Guiliano Silano (Toronto: Pontifical Institute of Medieval Studies, 2010).

40. Thomas Finn, "Sex and Marriage in the *Sentences* of Peter Lombard," *Theological Studies* 72, no. 1 (2011): 41–69.

41. Colish, *Medieval Foundations*, 284–85.

42. Twenty-five years ago I gave a lecture on ten worthy takeaways on Thomas Aquinas, at the invitation of Fergus Gordon Kerr (1931–) to the Dominican community at the University of Edinburgh. Subsequently it was published as "Ten Reasons Why Thomas Aquinas Is Important for Ethics Today," *New Blackfriars* 75 (1994): 354–63. That lecture serves as a foundation for these claims.

43. James A. Weisheipl, *Friar Thomas D'Aquino: His Life, Thoughts and Works*, 2nd ed. (Garden City, NY: Doubleday, 1983); Jean-Pierre Torrell, *Saint Thomas Aquinas: The Person and His Work* (Washington, DC: The Catholic University of America Press, 1996).

44. Leonard Boyle, *The Setting of the Summa Theologiae* (Toronto: PIMS, 1982).

45. Augustine, *De mor Eccl.* 2.13.

46. Augustine, *De Civ. Dei* 19.1.

47. Augustine, *De Civ. Dei* 19.1.

48. Augustine, *De Trin.* 13.3.

49. Augustine, *De Trin.* 13, 3, 4.

50. Augustine, *De doctr Christ* 1, 22.

51. Augustine, *De Civ. Dei* 19, 26.

52. Mark Jordan, *Teaching Bodies: Moral Formation in the Summa of Thomas Aquinas* (New York: Fordham University Press, 2016). Another insightful approach to the *Summa* is by reading Thomas through the lens of the four causes, see Nicholas Austin, *Aquinas on Virtue: A Causal Reading* (Washington, DC: Georgetown University Press, 2017).

53. Marie-Dominique Chenu, *Toward Understanding Saint Thomas* (Chicago: Henry Regnery, 1963).

54. Thomas Williams, "Saint Anselm," *Stanford Encyclopedia of Philosophy*, https://plato.stanford.edu/entries/anselm/.

55. James F. Keenan, "Can a Wrong Action Be Good? The Development of Theological Opinion on Erroneous Conscience," *Église et Théologie* 24 (1993): 205–19.

56. James Keenan, *Goodness and Rightness in Thomas Aquinas's Summa Theologiae* (Washington, DC: Georgetown University Press, 1992), 65–91.

57. Thomas Aquinas, *De virtutibus in communi*, *De caritate*, *De spe*, and *De virtutibus cardinalibus*.

58. Klaus Demmer, *Shaping the Moral Life: An Approach to Moral Theology* (Washington, DC: Georgetown University Press, 2000); *Living the Truth: A Theory of Action* (Washington, DC: Georgetown University Press, 2010).

59. Among Jean Porter's many contributions are *The Recovery of Virtue: The Relevance of Aquinas for Christian Ethics* (Louisville, KY: Westminster/John Knox, 1990); *Natural and Divine Law: Reclaiming the Tradition for Christian Ethics* (Grand Rapids, MI: Eerdmans, 1999); *Nature as Reason: A Thomistic Theory of the Natural Law* (Grand Rapids, MI: Eerdmans, 2004); *Justice as Virtue: A Thomistic Perspective* (Grand Rapids, MI: Eerdmans, 2016).

60. Augustine, *De Lib. Arb.* 2. 51.

61. Two further resources for understanding Thomas Aquinas better are the extraordinarily rich collection, Stephen Pope, ed., *The Ethics of Aquinas* (Washington, DC: Georgetown University Press, 2002) and the foundational introductory text, Jean-Pierre Torrell, *Saint Thomas Aquinas: The Person and His Work* (Washington, DC: Catholic University of America, 1996).

62. Odon Lottin, *Psychologie et morale aux XIIe et XIIIe siécles* (Gembloux, Belgium: J. Duculot), vol. I. 1942; II. 1948; III. 1949; IV. 1960. On Lottin, see Mary Jo Iozzio, *Self-determination and the Moral Act: A Study of the Contributions of Odon Lottin, O.S.B.* (Leuven: Peeters, 1995); Keenan, *A History of Catholic Moral Theology in the Twentieth Century: From Confessing Sins to Liberating Consciences* (New York: Continuum, 2010), 35–58.

63. John T. Noonan Jr., *The Church That Can and Cannot Change* (Notre Dame, IN: University of Notre Dame Press, 2005).

64. Thomas Williams, "John Duns Scotus," *Stanford Encyclopedia of Philosophy*. http://plato.stanford.edu/entries/duns-scotus/. On Scotus, see also William Frank, ed., *Duns Scotus on the Will and Morality* (Washington, DC: Catholic University of America Press, 1997); Thomas Williams, ed., *Cambridge Companion to Duns Scotus* (New York: Cambridge University Press, 2002).

65. On Ockham, see the controversial claims by Michael Allen Gillespie, *The Theological Origins of Modernity* (Chicago: University of Chicago Press, 2008).

66. On Ockham, see William of Ockham, *Quodlibetal Questions Volume 1* (New Haven: Yale University Press, 1991); Marilyn McCord Adams, *William Ockham*, 2 vols. (Notre Dame, IN: University of Notre Dame Press, 2nd rev. ed., 1989); Paul Vincent Spade, ed., *The Cambridge Companion to Ockham* (New York: Cambridge University Press, 1999); Rega Wood, *Ockham on the Virtues* (West Lafayette, IN: Purdue University Press, 1997).

67. On the eventual influence that Ockham would have on papal infallibility, see Brian Tierney, *Origins of Papal Infallibility, 1150–1350: A Study on the Concepts of Infallibility, Sovereignty and Tradition in the Middle Ages* (Leiden: Brill, 1997).

68. Paul Vincent Spade, "William of Ockham," *Stanford Encyclopedia of Philosophy*, http://plato.stanford.edu/entries/ockham/.

69. Guy Hamelin and Danilo Maia, "Nominalism and Semantics in Abelard and Ockham," *Logica Universalis* 9 (2015): 155–80.

70. See Servais Pinckaers, *Sources of Christian Ethics*, trans. Mary Thomas Noble (Washington, DC: Catholic University Press, 1995), 241–53. Pinckaers explained nominalism: "According to nominalism, only individual realities exist. They are unique in their singular existence. Universals are simply convenient labels, having no reality in themselves and only nominal value," at 272.

71. Marilyn McCord Adams, "The Structure of Ockham's Moral Theory," *The Context of Casuistry*, ed. James Keenan and Thomas Shannon (Washington, DC: Georgetown University Press, 1995), 25–52, at 25. She cites a variety of claimants. See also Thomas Shannon, "Method in Ethics: A Scotistic Contribution," in Keenan and Shannon, ed., *The Context of Casuistry*, 3–24.

72. See Wood, *Ockham on the Virtues*, 20–22.

CHAPTER FIVE: PATHWAYS TO MODERNITY I

1. John O'Malley, *Trent and All That: Renaming Catholicism in the Early Modern Era* (Cambridge, MA: Harvard University Press, 2000), 9. O'Malley first made the proposal in 1991, "Was Ignatius Loyola a Church Reformer? How to Look at Early Modern Catholicism," *Catholic Historical Review* 77 (1991): 177–93. See also John W. O'Malley, *Trent: What Happened at the Council* (Cambridge, MA: Harvard University Press, 2013); Kathleen M. Comerford and Hilmar B. Pabel, eds., *Early Modern Catholicism: Essays in Honour of John W. O'Malley, S.J.* (Toronto: University of Toronto Press, 2001).

2. O'Malley, *Trent and All That*, 143.

3. See James Keenan, "Casuistry," in *The Oxford Encyclopedia of the Reformation*, ed. Hans Hillerbrand (New York: Oxford University Press, 1996) I:272–74.

4. The distinction between high and low casuistry comes from Albert Jonsen and Stephen Toulmin, *The Abuse of Casuistry: A History of Moral Reasoning* (Berkeley: University of California Press, 1988), hereafter, *Abuse*.

5. John T. Noonan Jr., *Contraception: A History of Its Treatment by the Catholic Theologians and Canonists* (Cambridge, MA: Harvard University Press, 1965), 307.

6. On Martin's writings on sexuality, see Noonan, *Contraception*, 306–10; Shaji George Kochuthara, *The Concept of Sexual Pleasure in the Catholic Moral Tradition* (Rome: Editrice Pontificia Università Gregoriana, 2007), 232–36; Louis Vereecke, "Mariage et plaisir sexuel chez les théologiens de l'époque modern," in *De Guillaume d'Ockham à Saint Alphonse de Liguori: études d'histoire de la théologie morale modern, 1300–1787* (Rome: Collegium S. Alfonsi de Urbe, 1986), 531–52.

7. Francisco de Toledo, *Summa Casuum Conscientiae Sive De Instructione Sacerdotum, Libri Septem* (Constance: Apud Nicolaum Kalt, 1600).

8. See Keenan, "The Birth of Jesuit Casuistry: *Summa casuum conscientiae, sive de instructione sacerdotum, libri septem* by Francisco de Toledo (1532–1596)," in *The Mercurian Project: Forming Jesuit Culture, 1573–1580*, ed. Thomas M. McCoog (Rome: Institutum Historicum Societatis Iesu, 2004), 461–82.

9. John O'Malley, *The First Jesuits* (Cambridge, MA: Harvard University Press, 1993), 147.

10. Giancarlo Angelozzi, "Linsegnamento dei Casi di Coscienza nella Practica Educativa della Compagnia di Gesù," in *La 'Ratio Studiorum:' Modelli culturali e pratiche educative dei Gesuiti in Italia tra Cinque e Seicento*, ed. Gian Carlo Brizzi (Rome: Bulzoni Editore, 1981), 121–62.

11. Feliciano Cereceda, "Tolet, François," in *Dictionnaire de théologie catholique*, ed. Bernard Loth et Albert Michel (Paris: Letouzey et Ané, 1953–1972), XV:1223–25; "En el Cuarto Centenario del Nacimiento del P. Francisco Toledo," *Estudios eclesiásticos* 13 (1934): 90–108.

12. The translation is from John Noonan Jr., *The Scholastic Analysis of Usury* (Cambridge, MA: Harvard University Press, 1957), 137. The decretal reads: "Naviganti vel eunti ad nundinas certam mutuans pecuniae quantitatem pro eo, quod suscipit in se periculum, recepturus aliquid ultra sortem, usurarius est censendus." The statement is so surprising that Denzinger wonders whether the word *non* is omitted after "usurarius." Denzinger-Schoenmetzer, *Enchiridion Symbolorum Definitionum et Declarationum* (Rome: Herder, 1976), 269.

13. See Noonan, *Usury*, 133–53.

14. An analysis of this case appears in Louis Vereecke, "L'assurance maritime chez les théologiens des XVe et XVIe siècles," *Studia Moralia* 8 (1970): 347–85. See a discussion of Mair's casuistry in James Keenan, "The Casuistry of John Major, Nominalist Professor of Paris," in *The Context of Casuistry*, ed. James Keenan and Thomas Shannon (Washington, DC: Georgetown University Press, 1995), 85–102; hereafter, *Context*.

15. Precisely the argument of Thomas Kopfensteiner, "Science, Metaphor, and Casuistry," in *Context*, 207–20. See also Edward Long, *Conscience and Compromise: An Approach to Protestant Casuistry* (Philadelphia: Westminster Press, 1954).

16. "The Allen-Parsons Cases," in *Elizabethan Casuistry*, ed. Peter Holmes (London: Catholic Record Society, 1981), 63. Johann P. Sommerville argued for similarity among English Roman Catholic, Anglican, and Puritan writers in their attempt to deal with equivocation in "The 'New Art of Lying': Equivocation, Mental Reservation, and Casuistry," in *Conscience and Casuistry in Early Modern Europe*, ed. Edmund Leites (New York: Cambridge University Press, 1988) 159–84; hereafter, *Conscience*. About English Protestant casuistry see Kevin Kelly, *Conscience: Dictator or Guide? A Study in Seventeenth-Century English Protestant Moral Theology* (London: Geoffrey Chapman, 1967); Henry McAdoo, *The Structure of Caroline Moral Theology* (London: Longmans, 1949); Elliot Rose, *Cases of Conscience: Alternatives Open to Recusants and Puritans under Elizabeth I and James I* (New York: Cambridge University Press, 1975); Thomas Wood, *English Casuistical Divinity during the Seventeenth Century* (London: SPCK, 1952). More recently, Richard Miller, "Moral Sources, Ordinary Life, and Truth-Telling in Jeremy Taylor's Casuistry," in *Context*, 131–58.

17. Robert Persons, *The Christian Directory*, reprint of 1607 edition in *English Recusant Literature* series by vol. 41 (Menston, Yorkshire: Scholar Press, 1970), 3b. On Persons, see Francis Edwards, *Robert Persons* (St. Louis: Institute of Jesuit Sources, 1995); Joseph Crehan, *Fr. Persons, S.J.* (London: Burns and Oates, 1961), 84–96. On the extraordinary antipathy felt toward him, see Victor Houliston, "The Fabrication of the Myth of Father Parsons," *Recusant History* 22 (1974): 141–51; John Bossy, "The Heart of Robert Persons," in *The Reckoned Expense*, ed. Thomas McCoog (Woodbridge, England: Boydell Press, 1996), 141–58.

18. James F. Keenan, "Unexpected Consequences: A Jesuit and Puritan Book, Robert Persons's *Christian Directory*, and Its Relevance for Jesuit Spirituality Today," *Studies in the Spirituality of the Jesuits* 33, no. 2 (March 2001): 1–26; "Jesuit Casuistry or Jesuit Spirituality? The Roots of Seventeenth-Century British Puritan Practical Divinity," in *The Jesuits: Cultures, Sciences, and the Arts, 1540–1773*, ed. John O'Malley et al. (Toronto: Toronto University Press, 1999) 627–40; "Was William Perkins' *Whole Treatise of Cases of Conscience* Casuistry?: Hermeneutics and British Practical Divinity," in *Contexts of Conscience in Early Modern Europe: 1500–1700*, ed. Harald E. Braun and Edward Vallance (New York: Palgrave, 2004), 17–31.

19. Peter Milward, *Religious Controversies of the Elizabethan Age: A Survey of Printed Sources* (London: Scolar Press, 1977), 73–76.

20. A. W. Pollard and G. R. Redgrave, *A Short-Title Catalogue of Books Printed in England, Scotland, and Ireland: 1475–1640* (London: The Bibliographical Society, 1976), 2:217–18; L. Hicks, ed., *Letters and Memorials of Father Robert Parsons* (London: John Whitehead and Son, 1942), xliv.

21. Brad Gregory, "The True and Zealous Service of God: Robert Parsons, Edmund Bunny, and *The First Booke of the Christian Exercise*," *Journal of Ecclesiastical History* 45 (1994): 238–68, at 239.

22. Milward, *Religious Controversies*, 73–74; Helen White called it "incomparably the most popular book of spiritual guidance in sixteenth-century England" in *The Tudor Books of Saints and Martyrs* (Madison: University of Wisconsin Press, 1963), 205.

23. Edmund Bunny, *A Booke of Christian Exercise Appertaining to Resolution, That Is Shewing How That We Should Resolve Our Selves to Become Christians in Deed*, by R.P.; perused, and accompanied now with a treatise tending to pacification (London: N. Newton, 1585). See "Bunny, Edmund," in *The Dictionary of National Biography* (Oxford: Oxford University Press, 1973), 3:271–72; Nancy Lee Beaty, "Parsons, Bunny, and the Counter-Reformation 'Crafte,'" in *The Craft of Dying: A Study in the Literary Tradition of the Ars Moriendi in England* (New Haven: Yale University Press, 1970), 157–96.

24. Gregory, "The True and Zealous Service of God," 267.

25. Victor Houliston, "Why Robert Persons Would Not Be Pacified: Edmund Bunny's Theft of *The Book of Resolution*," in *Reckoned Expense: Edmund Campion and the Early English Jesuits: Essays in Celebration of the First Centenary of Campion Hall, Oxford (1896–1996)*, ed. Thomas McCoog (Rochester, NY: Boydell Press, 1996), 159–78.

26. Gregory, "The True and Zealous Service of God," 267.

27. Person's and Bunny's work was in turn adaptable. Emanuel Sonthom's *Gueldenes Kleinod der Kinder Gottes* (Frankfurt, 1612), one of the most famous books in the German Lutheran and Pietist tradition, is nothing more than a translation of Bunny's work. See the important discovery by Karl Josef Hoeltgen, "Die Loesung des alten Raetsels: Emanuel Sonthom, *Das Gueldene Kleinod* und das englische Original," *Anglia: Zeitschrift fuer Englische Philologie* 100 (1982): 357–72. For the influence of English devotional literature on seventeenth-century German piety, see Edgar McKenzie, ed., *A Catalog of British Devotional and Religious Books in German Translation from the Reformation to 1750* (Berlin: Walter de Gruyter, 1997).

28. This took particular expression in the warning in *The Spiritual Exercises of Saint Ignatius* that the director ought never get between the exercitant and the Lord and rather should permit the Creator to deal directly with the creature, and the creature directly with his Creator and Lord. Louis Puhl, *The Spiritual Exercises of Saint Ignatius: A New Translation Based*

on Studies in the Language of the Autograph (Westminster, MD: The Newman Press, 1957) directive 15, p. 6.

29. John O Malley, *The First Jesuits* (Cambridge, MA: Harvard University Press, 1993), 136–52.

30. On the evolution of casuistry in the confessional, see Miriam Turrini, *La coscienza e le leggi. Morale e diritto nei testi per la confessione della prima Età moderna* (Bologna: Società editrice il Mulino, 1991); Thomas Tentler, *Sin and Confession on the Eve of the Reformation* (Princeton: Princeton University Press, 1977).

31. Later, we will examine confraternities where laity, clergy, and religious gathered together for devotional practices of the corporal works of mercy.

32. On the unique role that circumstances played in confession, see Margaret Sampson, "Laxity and Liberty in Seventeenth-Century English Political Thought," *Conscience* 72–118, esp. 76, 96, 103, 116.

33. O'Malley, *The First Jesuits,* 136–52.

34. James F. Keenan, "The Return of Casuistry," *Theological Studies* 57 (1996): 123–29.

35. See the indispensable biography of John Mair, James K. Farge, "John Mair: An Historical Introduction," in *A Companion to the Theology of John Mair*, ed. John T. Slotemaker and Jeffrey C. Witt (Leiden: E. J. Brill, 2015), 13–22; also James K. Farge, *Biographical Register of Paris Doctors of Theology 1500–1536* (Toronto: Pontifical Institute of Mediaeval Studies, 1980), 305–9. Additionally, Alexander Broadie, "John Mair on the Writing of Theology," in Slotemaker and Witt, *A Companion to the Theology of John Mair*, 25–40.

36. See also J. H. Burns, "New Light on John Major," *The Innes Review* 5 (1954): 83–101; John Durkan, "John Major: After 400 Years," *The Innes Review* 1 (1950): 131–57; Aeneas Mackay, *Memoir of John Major of Haddington* (Edinburgh: Edinburgh University Press, 1892); Thomas Torrance, "La Philosophie et la théologie de Jean Mair ou Major (1469–1550)," *Archives de philosophie* 32 (1969): 531–47. On experience, particularly regarding sexual pleasure, Mair argues against Augustine and Huguccio, see Noonan, *Contraception*, 310–22; Louis Vereecke, "Mariage et plaisir sexuel chez les théologiens de l'époque moderne (1300–1789)," 245–66, and "Mariage et sexualité au déclin du Moyen-Âge," *La Vie spirituelle* 57 supp. (1961): 199–225.

37. Keenan, "John Mair's Moral Theology and Its Reception in the 16th Century," in Slotemaker and Witt, *A Companion to the Theology of John Mair*, 194–220.

38. From Mair's *Commentary of the Fourth Book of the Sentences*, quoted in Durkan, "John Major," 135.

39. Farge, "John Mair," 19.

40. Mair, *Commentary*, dist. 15, q. 31, case 15, fol. CIII.

41. Martha Nussbaum, "Aristotle on Human Nature and the Foundation of Ethics," in *World, Mind and Ethics: Essays on the Ethical Philosophy of Bernard Williams*, ed. J. E. Altham and Ross Harrison (Cambridge: Cambridge University Press), 86–131.

42. Albert Jonsen and Stephen Toulmin, *The Abuse of Casuistry: A History of Moral Reasoning* (Berkeley: University of California Press, 1988), 252; Yves Congar discusses the authority derived from the *quod* (the argument itself) and the *quo* (the authority figure who articulates the argument) in his important article "A Brief History of the Forms of the Magisterium and Its Relations with Scholars," in *The Magisterium and Morality*, Readings in Moral Theology 3, ed. Charles Curran and Richard McCormick (New York: Paulist Press, 1982), 314–31.

43. We should not imagine that casuistry was reckless. Julia Fleming argued just how painstakingly prudential casuists often were in making their arguments by studying the so-called prince of laxists, the seventeenth-century Spanish Cistercian Juan Caramuel (1606–82), in *Defending Probabilism: The Moral Theology of Juan Caramuel* (Washington, DC: Georgetown University Press, 2007).

44. Mair, *Commentary*, dist. 15, q. 36, fol. CVII. The case and its analysis appear in L. Vereecke, "La licéité du *cambium bursae* chez Jean Mair (1469–1550)," in *De Guillaume d'Ockham à Saint Alphonse de Liguori—Etudes d'histoire de la théologie morale moderne 1300–1787* (Rome: Alphonsianum University Press, 1986), 309–24.

45. See Noonan, *Usury*, 118–20, 126–28, 131–43, 250–59. The concept ought not to be confused with *damnum emergens* (loss occurring), which referred to an initial loss sustained by making the loan itself. This received theological approval before *lucrum cessans* (profit ceasing), which referred to a loss of that which could have been otherwise gained. Thomas Aquinas, e.g., condemned usury, *Summa theologiae* II–II, 78, 1, but permitted certain instances of *damnum emergens*, 78, 2, ad1. Later, as Noonan notes, Sts. Antoninus of Florence and Bernardino of Siena recognized the liceity of *lucrum cessans*, see his *Usury*, 115–26.

46. For more on this institution, see Keenan, "John Mair's Moral Theology," 201–4.

47. Keenan, "John Mair's Moral Theology," fol. CVII r.: "Respondetur quod casus est illicitus et modus sic vivendi est periculosus, inhonestus ab omni prudenti viro excutiendus."

48. Thomas Kuhn, *The Structure of Scientific Revolutions* (Chicago: University of Chicago Press, 1962).

49. See his *Commentary on the Fourth Book of the Sentences*, dist. 15, q. 49. The argument is recounted in Noonan, *Usury*, 211.

50. They do return in the late twentieth century; see John Dedek, *Titus and Bertha Ride Again* (New York: Sheed and Ward, 1974).

51. John Connery, "Discussion of Therapeutic Abortion (1500–1600)," in *Abortion: The Development of the Roman Catholic Perspective* (Chicago: Loyola Press, 1977), 124–41. See Marcia Sichol, "Women and the New Casuistry," *Thought* 67 (1992): 148–57; Lucinda Joy Peach, "Feminist Cautions about Casuistry: The Supreme Court's Abortion Decisions as Paradigms," *Policy Sciences* 27 (1994): 143–60.

52. See Sommerville above and, Keenan, "Mental Reservations," in *The Cambridge Encyclopedia of the Jesuits*, ed. Thomas Worcester (New York: Cambridge University Press, 2017), 513–14.

53. John Mahoney, *The Making of Moral Theology: A Study of the Roman Catholic Tradition* (New York: Oxford University Press, 1987), 180–84, 225–26, 240.

54. Servais Pinckaers, "Autonomie et heteronomie en morale selon S. Thomas d'Aquin," Carlos Josphat Pinto de Oliveira and Dietmar Mieth, eds., *Autonomie: Dimensions éthiques de la liberté* (Fribourg: University of Fribourg Press, 1978), 104–23; "La théologie morale à la période de la grande scholastique," *Nova et Vetera* 52 (1977): 118–31; "La theologie morale au declin du Moyen-Age: Le nominalisme," *Nova et Vetera* 52 (1977): 209–21. For a different read on Ockham, see Marilyn McCord Adams, "The Structure of Ockham's Moral Theory," *Context of Casuistry*, 25–51.

55. So argues Louis Vereecke, "Les éditions des oeuvres morales de Pierre de la Palu (+1342) a Paris au debut du XVIe siecle," *De Guillaume d'Ockham*, 133–48; Ricardo Villoslada, *La Universidad de Paris durante los estudios de Francisco de Vitoria, O.P.* (Rome: Gregorian University Press, 1938), 127–64. See also Heiko Oberman, *The Harvest of Medieval Theology, Gabriel Biel and Late Medieval Nominalism* (Cambridge, MA: Harvard University Press, 1967).

56. In his *Commentary on the Fourth Book of the Sentences* dist. 31, the only question, ad 2; see discussion in Louis Vereecke, "Mariage et sexualité au declin du moyen age," *De Guillaume d'Ockham*, 345–68.

57. Mair, *Quaestiones utilissimae in Quartum Sententiarum*, d. 31, art.1., fol. 204b.

58. See Vereecke, "Mariage et sexualité au déclin du moyen âge," 345–68.

59. Noonan, *Contraception*, 310–22. See also Vereecke, "Mariage et sexualité au déclin du Moyen âge," 199–225. On the topic itself as well as Mair's significant contributions, see Shaji George Kochuthara, *Towards a Theology of Sexual Pleasure: Continuity and Development in the Theology of*

Sexual Pleasure in the Catholic Moral Tradition (Saarbrücken: LAP Lambert Academic Publishing, 2011).

60. Jonsen and Toulmin, "The Roots of Casuistry in Antiquity," in *The Abuse of Casuistry*, 47–74.

61. See Keenan, "Distinguishing Charity as Goodness and Prudence as Rightness," *The Thomist* 56 (1992): 407–26; *Goodness and Rightness in Thomas Aquinas's Summa Theologiae* (Washington, DC: Georgetown University Press, 1992). See also Daniel Nelson, *The Priority of Prudence* (University Park: Penn State University Press, 1992).

62. See John Treloar, "Moral Virtue and the Demise of Prudence in the Thought of Francis Suárez," *American Catholic Philosophical Quarterly* 65 (1991): 387–405.

63. *Commentary on the Fourth Book of the Sentences*, dist. 31, art. 1, fol. 204.

64. Peter Holmes, ed., *Caroline Casuistry: The Cases of Conscience of Fr Thomas Southwell, SJ*, Catholic Record Society Publications 84 (Rochester, NY: The Boydell Press, 2012), 50.

65. Holmes, *Caroline Casuistry*, 51.

66. Jonsen and Toulmin, "Roots of Casuistry," 18, emphasis in text.

67. "Giovanni Major sembra l'ultimo scolastico." Louis Vereecke, *Storia della teologia morale dal XIV al XVI secolo* (Rome: Accademia Alfonsiana, 1979), 122.

68. John Durkan, "The Cultural Background in Sixteenth-Century Scotland," in *Essays on the Scottish Reformation, 1513–1625*, ed. David Roberts (Glasgow: Johns, Burns, and Sons, 1962), 281.

69. Brian Tierney, *The Idea of Natural Rights* (Atlanta: Scholars Press, 1997), 240.

70. Bartolomé de las Casas, *In Defense of the Indians*, trans. and ed. Stafford Poole (DeKalb: Northern Illinois University Press, 1992).

71. De las Casas, *In Defense of the Indians*, 326.

72. De las Casas, *In Defense of the Indians*, 329.

73. John T. Noonan Jr., "If John Major Were an Indian," in *A Church That Can and Cannot Change* (Notre Dame, IN: University of Notre Dame Press, 2005), 68–77.

74. *Commentary on the Fourth Book of the Sentences*, dist. 31, art. 1, fol. 204b.

75. Noonan, *Contraception*, 311. See also Vereecke, "Mariage et plaisir sexuel."

76. John Bossy, "Seven Sins into Ten Commandments," *Conscience*, 214–34.

77. Louis Pascoe, *Jean Gerson: Principles of Church Reform* (Leiden: Brill, 1973); D. Catherine Brown, *Pastor and Laity in the Theology of Jean*

Gerson (New York: Cambridge University Press, 1987). See also on Gerson, F. Dominic Longo, *Spiritual Grammar: Genre and the Saintly Subject in Islam and Christianity* (New York: Fordham University Press, 2019).

78. See Yiu Sing Lúcás Chan's excellent summary, "The Decalogue in History," in his *The Ten Commandments and the Beatitudes: Biblical Studies and Ethics for Real Life* (New York: Rowman and Littlefield, 2012), 23–31; also James F. Keenan, "The Decalogue and the Moral Manual Tradition: From Trent to Vatican II," in *The Decalogue and Its Cultural Influence*, ed. Dominik Markl (Sheffield: Phoenix Press, 2013), 214–29; Sigrid Müller, "Die Bedeutung des Dekalogs für die Entwicklung der neuzeitlichen Moraltheologie im Zeichen der Kasuistik," in *Gliederungssysteme Angewandter Ethik. Ein Handbuch. Nach einem Projekt von Wilhelm Korff*, ed. Markus Vogt (Vienna: Herder, 2016), 256–83.

79. Martin Luther, *The Large Catechism of Martin Luther* (Philadelphia: Fortress Press, 1959), 35.

80. Luther, *The Large Catechism*, 44.

81. Luther, *The Large Catechism*, 15.

82. Martin Luther, *Small Catechism* (Minneapolis: Augsburg Publishing, 1929), 83. He begins each commandment's explanation with the same remark: "We should fear and love God so that...."

83. John Calvin, *Catechismus* (Pittsburgh: Battles, 1972).

84. John Calvin, *Institutes of the Christian Religion* (Grand Rapids, MI: Wm. B. Eerdmans, 1949), 1:447. See Bossy, "Seven Sins into Ten Commandments," 216.

85. *Catechism of the Council of Trent for Parish Priests* (New York: Herder, 1934), 357–58.

86. See, e.g., Thomas Tentler, *Sin and Confession on the Eve of the Reformation* (Princeton: Princeton University Press, 1977).

87. Thomas Slater, *A Manual of Moral Theology*, 2nd ed., 2 vols. (New York: Benziger Brothers, 1908), 1:60–61. Slater's position confirms the long-standing affirmation that an act made in good but erroneous conscience remained good. See James Keenan, "Can a Wrong Action Be Good? The Development of Theological Opinion on Erroneous Conscience," *Église et Théologie* 24 (1993): 205–19; Brian Johnstone, "Erroneous Conscience in *Veritatis Splendor* and the Theological Tradition," in *The Splendor of Accuracy* , ed. Joseph Selling and Jan Jans (Grand Rapids, MI: Eerdmans, 1994): 114–35; Werner Wolbert, "Problems Concerning Erroneous Conscience," *Studia theologica* 50 (1996): 162–75; Josef Fuchs, "Was heisst 'Irriges Gewissen,'" in *Fur eine menschliche Moral* (Freiburg: Herder, 1997): 54–64; Gerald Gleeson, "Conscience and Conversion," *Australian EJournal of Theology* 1, no. 1 (August 2003).

88. See Fleming, *Defending Probabilism*; Mahoney provided superb material on probabilism, *The Making of Moral Theology*, 135–56. Jonsen and Toulmin, *The Abuse of Casuistry*, 229–66; Louis Vereecke, *De Guillaume d'Ockham à Saint Alphonse de Liguori*; Keenan, "Probabilism," in Worcester, *The Cambridge Encyclopedia of the Jesuits*, 650–52. For an extensive consideration, see Robert Maryks, *Saint Cicero and the Jesuits: The Influence of the Liberal Arts on the Adoption of Moral Probabilism (Catholic Christendom, 1300–1700)* (New York: Routledge, 2008). More recently, see Rudolf Schuessler, *The Debate on Probable Opinions in the Scholastic Tradition* (Leiden: Brill, 2019).

89. Slater, *A Manual*, 70.

90. Slater, *A Manual*, 72.

91. Jean-Pascal Gay, *Jesuit Civil Wars: Theology, Politics and Government under Tirso González (1687–1705)* (Farnham: Ashgate Publishers, 2012); see Mahoney, *The Making of Moral Theology*, 141–42.

92. James F. Keenan, "Can a Wrong Action Be Good? The Development of Theological Opinion on Erroneous Conscience," *Église et Théologie* 24 (1993): 205–19.

93. See Keenan, *A History of Catholic Moral Theology in the Twentieth Century*, 9–35.

94. Blaise Pascal, *Provincial Letters* (London: Wipf and Stock Publishers, 1997).

95. Francisco de Toledo, *Summa casuum conscientiae sive De instructione sacerdotum, libri septem* (Konstanz: Nicolaus Kalt, 1600).

96. J. Ignacio Tellechea Idígoras, "Censura inédita del Padre Francisco Toledo, S.J., sobre el catecismo del arzobispo Carranza: Cotejo con la de Melchor Cano," *Revista Española de Teología* 29 (1969): 3–35; see O'Malley, *The First Jesuits*, 317–20.

97. John T. Noonan Jr., *The Scholastic Analysis of Usury* (Cambridge, MA: Harvard University Press, 1957) 206–21, at 214.

98. O'Malley, *The First Jesuits*, 147.

99. Giancarlo Angelozzi, "L'insegnamento dei Casi di Coscienza nella pratica educativa della Compagnia di Gesù," in *La "ratio studiorum": Modelli culturali e pratiche educative dei Gesuiti in Italia tra Cinque e Seicento*, ed. Gian Carlo Brizzi (Rome: Bulzoni, 1981), 121–62.

100. Feliciano Cereceda, "Tolet, François," in *Dictionnaire de théologie catholique*, ed. Bernard Loth and Albert Michel (Paris: Letouzey et Ané, 1953–72), 15:1223–25; "En el cuarto centenario del nacimiento del P. Francisco Toledo," *Estudios eclestiásticos* 13 (1934): 90–108.

101. See James F. Keenan, "Was William Perkins' *Whole Treatise of Cases of Conscience* Casuistry?: Hermeneutics and British Practical Divinity," in *Con-*

texts of Conscience in Early Modern Europe: 1500–1700, ed. Harald E. Braun and Edward Vallance (New York: Palgrave, 2004), 17–31.

102. Toledo, *Summa*, fol. 1.

103. Toledo, *Summa*, fol. 5.

104. Toledo, *Summa*, fol. 463.

105. Toledo, *Summa*, fol. 344.

106. Considerable work has been done on the work of another, slightly later Jesuit Casuist, Leonardus Lessius. See Toon van Houdt, "Money, Time, and Labour: Leonardus Lessius and the Ethics of Lending and Interest Taking," *Ethical Perspectives* 2 (1995): 18–22; "Tradition and Renewal in Late Scholastic Economic Thought: The Case of Leonardus Lessius (1554–1623)," *Journal of Medieval and Early Modern Studies* 28 (1998): 51–75; with Martin Stone "Probabilism and Its Methods: Leonardus Lessius and His Contribution to the Development of Jesuit Casuistry," *Ephemerides Theologicae Lovanienses* 75 (1999): 359–94.

107. Toledo, *Summa*, fol. 428.

108. Albert Jonsen, "The Confessor as Experienced Physician: Casuistry and Clinical Ethics," in *Religious Methods and Resources in Bioethics*, ed. P. F. Camenisch (Dordrecht: Kluwer Academics, 1994).

109. On the two forms of casuistry, see James F. Keenan, "Applying the Seventeenth-Century Casuistry of Accommodation to HIV Prevention," *Theological Studies* 60 (1999): 492–512. On the development of the tradition of these summaries, see John Thomas Noonan, "Development in Moral Doctrine," in *Context*, 188–204; Thomas Kopfensteiner, "Science, Metaphor and Moral Casuistry," in *Context*, 207–20.

110. See Noonan, "Abortion and the Catholic Church: A Summary History," *The American Journal of Jurisprudence* 12, no. 1 (1967): 85–131; Connery, "Discussion of Therapeutic Abortion (1500–1600)."

111. Joseph Mangan, "An Historical Analysis of the Principle of Double Effect," *Theological Studies* 10 (1949): 41–61.

112. Josef Ghoos, "L'Acte à double effet: Étude de théologie positive," *Ephemerides theologicae lovanienses* 27 (1951): 30–52. See James F. Keenan, "The Function of the Principle of Double Effect," *Theological Studies* 54 (1993): 294–315. See also Nancy M. Rourke, "Where Is the Wrong?: A Comparison of Two Accounts of the Principle of Double Effect," *Irish Theological Quarterly* 76, no. 2 (2011): 150–63. On recent hesitancy on Ghoos' work, see José Rojas, "Double Effect and John of St. Thomas: A Review of Jozef Ghoos' Historical Analysis," *Ephemerides theologicae Lovanienses* 93, no. 1 (2017): 29–50.

113. See John Dedek, "Moral Absolutes in the Predecessors of St. Thomas," *Theological Studies* 38 (1977): 654–80; "Intrinsically Evil Acts: An Historical Study of the Mind of St. Thomas," *The Thomist* 43 (1979):

385–413; "Intrinsically Evil Acts: The Emergence of a Doctrine," *Recherches de théologie ancienne et médiévale* 50 (1983): 191–226.

114. Rightly, Bruno Schueller argued that the first condition of the principle of double effect is the foundation for the second and third, i.e., the intrinsically wrong activity cannot be engaged as object of activity (first condition), as intention (second condition), or as material cause (third condition). Thus, the principle applies only to those cases where the object, the intention, and the cause each approximates but is distinguishable from acting, intending, or causing an intrinsically wrong action. These instances are few, Schueller concludes, and therefore the principle has narrow application. See Bruno Schueller, "The Double Effect in Catholic Thought: A Reevaluation," in *Doing Evil to Achieve Good*, ed. Richard McCormick and Paul Ramsey (Chicago: Loyola University Press, 1978): 165–91. See also Lucius Ugorji, *The Principle of Double Effect* (Frankfurt am Main: Peter Lang, 1985); Peter Knauer, "The Hermeneutic Function of the Principle of Double-Effect," in *Readings in Moral Theology, No. 1*, ed. Charles Curran and Richard McCormick (New York: Paulist Press, 1979), 1–39; Joseph Selling, "The Problem of Reinterpreting the Principle of Double Effect," *Louvain Studies* 8 (1980): 47–62; Haig Katchadourian, "Is the Principle of Double Effect Morally Acceptable?" *International Philosophical Quarterly* 27 (1988): 21–30; Keenan, "Taking Aim at the Principle of Double Effect: Reply to Khatchadourian," *International Philosophical Quarterly* 28 (1988): 201–5; "The Function of the Principle of Double Effect," *Theological Studies* 54 (1993): 294–315.

CHAPTER SIX: PATHWAYS TO MODERNITY II

1. Christopher Black, *Italian Confraternities in the Sixteenth Century* (New York: Cambridge University Press, 1989); Nicholas Terpstra, *Lay Confraternities and Civic Religion in Renaissance Bologna* (Cambridge, UK: Cambridge University Press, 1995); Terpstra, *Cultures of Charity: Women, Politics, and the Reform of Poor Relief in Renaissance Italy* (Cambridge, MA: Harvard University Press, 2013). That these confraternities were not without their own problems, see Terpstra's *Lost Girls: Sex and Death in Renaissance Florence* (Baltimore: Johns Hopkins University Press, 2012).

2. This information is culled from a variety of sources, especially Théodore Koehler, "Miséricorde," in *Dictionnaire de spiritualité ascétique et mystique, doctrine et histoire*, ed. Marcel Viller (Paris: Beauchesne, 1980), 10:1313–28; Irenée Noye, "Miséricorde (Oeuvres de)," in Viller, *Dictionnaire*, 10:1328–50; J. M. Perrin, "Mercy, Works of," in *New Catholic Encyclopedia* (Washington, DC: Catholic University of America Press, 1967), 676–78.

3. See Timothy Miller and John Nesbitt, *Walking Corpses: Leprosy in Byzantium and the Medieval West* (Ithaca, NY: Cornell University Press, 2014).

4. Bruce M. Rothschild, "History of Syphilis," *Clinical Infectious Diseases* 40, no. 10 (2005): 1454–63.

5. Daniela Solfaroli Camillocci, *I devoti della carità. Le confraternite del Divino Amore nell'Italia del primo Cinquecento*, vol. 98. (Naples: Città del Sole 2002); Mario Fois, "La Risposta confraternale alle Emergenze sanitarie e sociali della prima metà del Cinquecento Romano. Le Confraternite del Divino Amore e di S. Girolamo della Carità," *Archivum Historiae Pontificiae* 41 (2003): 83–107.

6. Clement, *First Epistle*, New Advent.org, accessed December 21, 2021, http://www.newadvent.org/fathers/1010.htm.

7. James William Brodman, *Ransoming Captives in Crusader Spain: The Order of Merced on the Medieval Spanish Frontier* (Philadelphia: University of Pennsylvania Press, 1986).

8. John O'Malley, *The First Jesuits* (Cambridge, MA: Harvard University Press, 1993), 167–78.

9. See Black on the imprisoned in *Italian Confraternities*, 213–33.

10. Six hundred years later, Sister Helen Prejean provides the same support in her accompaniment of those who are sentenced to death for capital crimes: she attends their executions, telling them to look on her face and see the face of Christ. She details her work in her beautiful book *Dead Man Walking* (New York: Vintage Press, 1994).

11. Nicholas Terpstra, Adriano Prosperi, and Stefania Pastore, eds., *Faith's Boundaries: Laity and Clergy in Early Modern Confraternities* (Turnhout: Brepols, 2013). See also Konrad Eisenbichler, ed., *A Companion to Medieval and Early Modern Confraternities* (New York: Brill, 2019).

12. Christopher Minster, "Biography of Antonio de Montesinos, Defender of Indigenous Rights: A Voice Crying in the Wilderness," ThoughtCo.com, updated August 20, 2019, https://www.thoughtco.com/antonio-de-montesinos-2136370.

13. A superb collection of essays establishes the extraordinary impact the sermon had in launching the ethical critique of the *encomienda* system: Silke Jansen and Irene M. Weis, eds., *Fray Antonio de Montesino y su tiempo* (Madrid: Iberoamericana, Vervuert, 2017). For an equally superb account of the conquest, see Luis N. Rivera, *A Violent Evangelism: The Political and Religious Conquest of the Americas* (Louisville, KY: Westminster/John Knox Press, 1992).

14. George Sanderlin, ed., *Witness: Writing of Bartolomé de Las Casas* (Maryknoll, NY: Orbis, 1993), 66–67.

15. Francesco Compagnoni, OP, and Helen Alford, OP, eds., *Preaching Justice: Dominican Contributions to Social Ethics in the Twentieth Century* (Dublin: Dominican Publications, 2007).

16. Renzo Gerardi, *Storia della Morale: Interpretazioni teologiche dell'esperienza Cristiana* (Bologna: Edizioni Dehoniane Bologna, 2003), 326–28.

17. For his theological development, see Anthony Pagden's helpful "Introduction," in Francisco de Vitoria, *Political Writings*, ed. Anthony Pagden and Jeremy Lawrance (New York: Cambridge University Press, 1992), xiii–xxx.

18. Vitoria, *Political Writings*, xiv. See Lu Ann Homza, "Erasmus as Hero, or Heretic? Spanish Humanism and the Valladolid Assembly of 1527," *Renaissance Quarterly* 50, no. 1 (Spring 1997): 78–118.

19. Vitoria, *Political Writings*, xiv.

20. For more on Vitoria's teaching style, see Ricardo Villoslada, *La Universidad de París durante los estudios de Francisco de Vitoria, O.P.* (Rome: Gregorian University Press, 1938); Francisco De Vitoria, OP, *On Homicide & Commentary on Summa theologiae IIa–IIae Q. 64 (Thomas Aquinas)*, ed. and trans. John P. Doyle (Milwaukee: Marquette University Press, 1997), 11–14.

21. Andreas Wagner, "Francisco de Vitoria," *Great Christian Jurists in Spanish History*, ed. Rafael Domingo and Javier Martínez-Torrón (New York: Cambridge University Press, 2018), 84–97.

22. Wagner, "Francisco de Vitoria," 86.

23. Wagner, "Francisco de Vitoria," 86.

24. Vitoria, "On Dietary Laws, or Self-Restraint," Q.1 a.4, p. 225.

25. Brian Tierney, *The Idea of Natural Rights: Studies on Natural Rights, Natural Law and Church Law 1150–1625* (Atlanta: Scholars Press, 1997), 259–72, at 260.

26. Tierney, *Idea of Natural Rights*, 272. See also Roger Ruston, *Human Rights and the Image of God* (London: SCM Press, 2004), 99–115. For a somewhat different claim about Vitoria's articulation of rights, see Bernard V. Brady, "An Analysis of the Use of Rights Language in Pre-Modern Thought," *Thomist* 57, no. 1 (1993): 97–122.

27. Gerardi, *Storia della Morale*, 328–30, at 329.

28. Wagner, "Francisco de Vitoria," 87–88.

29. Anthony Pagden, "The School of Salamanca, the Requerimiento, and the Papal Donation of Alexander VI," *Republics of Letters* 5, no. 3 (2017), https://arcade.stanford.edu/rofl/school-salamanca-requerimiento-and-papal-donation-alexander-vi.

30. On the *requerimiento* that demanded such authority, Ruston, *Human Rights*, 72–76.

31. Grégoire Catta, "Francisco de Vitoria's Moral Cosmopolitanism and Contemporary Catholic Social Teaching," *Journal of the Society of Christian Ethics* 36, no. 2 (2016): 63–78, at 66.

32. Gustavo Gozzi, *Rights and Civilizations: A History and Philosophy of International Law* (New York: Cambridge University Press, 2019), 3–7, at 6. See also James Brown Scott, *The Spanish Origin of International Law: Lectures on Francisco de Vitoria (1480–1546) and Francisco Suárez (1548–1617)* (Washington, DC: Georgetown University Press, 1928).

33. Thomas Aquinas, *Summa Theologiae*, I.-II., q. 91, a. 2c.

34. Vitoria, "On Civil Power," Q.3 a.4, p. 40.

35. For more on *ius gentium*, see Vitoria, "On the American Indians," xv–xvi, xxv–xxviii; Catta, "Vitoria's Moral Cosmopolitanism," 66–69.

36. Vitoria, "On the Law of War," Q.3 a.6, p. 321.

37. Ruston, *Human Rights*, 76.

38. Wagner, "Francisco de Vitoria," 93–98, at 93; Marcia Sichol, *The Making of a Nuclear Peace: The Task of Today's Just War Theorists* (Washington, DC: Georgetown University Press, 1990), 68–72; Steven P. Lee, *Ethics and War* (New York: Cambridge University Press, 2012), 85–93, 152–56; Michael A. Newton and Larry May, *Proportionality in International Law* (New York: Oxford University Press, 2014), 75–77.

39. Gregory Reichberg, Henryk Syse, and Endre Begby, eds., *The Ethics of War: Classic and Contemporary Readings* (Malden, MA: Blackwell Publishing, 2006), 288.

40. Vitoria, "On the Power of the Church I," Q.5 a.3, p. 88. See Vitoria's two *relectiones* "On the Power of the Church I" (1532) and "On the Power of the Church II" (1533), in Vitoria, 47–108 and 109–51, respectively. It should be noted that the pope had recourse when temporal rulers overstepped their responsibilities and caused their subjects a loss of spiritual goods; he could contest the legitimacy of such a "temporal" law, see "On the Power of the Church I" Q.5 a.6, pp. 90–1. See also xxii–xxiii.

41. Vitoria, "On the Power of the Church I," Q.5 a.2, P., 85.

42. Ruston, *Human Rights*, 76–77.

43. Vitoria, Letter to Miguel de Arcos, OP, September 1534, in Vitoria, "On the Power of the Church I," 331–33, at 331.

44. Vitoria, Letter to Miguel de Arcos, OP, 332.

45. Vitoria, Letter to Miguel de Arcos, OP, 333.

46. Vitoria, "On the American Indians," xxiv.

47. Vitoria, "On the American Indians," Introduction, 238.

48. Vitoria, "On the American Indians," Introduction, 238.

49. Vitoria, "On the American Indians," Introduction, Q.1 a.1, p. 239.

50. Vitoria, "On the American Indians," Introduction, 240.

51. Vitoria, "On the American Indians," Introduction, a.4, p. 246.

52. Vitoria, "On the American Indians," Introduction, a.6, p. 250.

53. Vitoria, "On the American Indians," Introduction, Q.1 conclusion, p. 250–51.

54. Vitoria, "On the American Indians," Introduction, Q.2 a.2, p. 260.

55. Vitoria, "On the American Indians," Introduction, Q.2 aa.1–7, pp. 251–77.

56. Vitoria, "On the American Indians," Introduction, Q.2 a.4, p. 271.

57. Vitoria, "On the American Indians," Introduction, Q.3 a.1, p. 282.

58. See Ruston, *Human Rights*, 80–98.

59. Vitoria, "On the American Indians," Introduction, Q.3 a.5, p. 288.

60. See James Brown Scott, *The Catholic Conception of International Law* (Clark, NJ: The Law Book Exchange, Ltd., 2007); William Bain, "Vitoria: The Law of War, Saving the Innocent, and the Image of God," *From Just and Unjust Military Intervention: European Thinkers from Vitoria to Mill*, ed. Stefano Recchia and Jennifer Welsh (New York: Cambridge University Press, 2013), 70–95; Peter Hipold, "R2P and Humanitarian Intervention in a Historical Perspective," *The Responsibility to Protect* (New York: Brill, 2015), 60–122; Beatriz Salamanca, "Early Modern Controversies of Mobility within the Spanish Empire: Francisco de Vitoria and the Peaceful Right to Travel," *Tropos* 3, no. 1 (2015).

61. Although we are interested in his position here in intervening to protect those threatened with human sacrifice and cannibalism, Vitoria also raised other questions in the *relectio* about food and certain obligations regarding eating that later shaped teachings on end-of-life issues in health care. See Julia Fleming, "'When Meats Are Like Medicine': Vitoria and Lessius on the Role of Food in the Duty to Preserve Life," *Theological Studies* 69, no. 1 (2008): 99–115.

62. Vitoria, "On Dietary Laws," Q.1 a.4, p. 225.

63. Vitoria, "On Dietary Laws," Q.1 a.5, p. 225.

64. Vitoria, "On Dietary Laws," 226.

65. Vitoria, "On Dietary Laws," 226.

66. Vitoria, "On Dietary Laws," 227.

67. Vitoria, "On Dietary Laws," 227.

68. Vitoria, "On Dietary Laws," 229.

69. Wagner, "Francisco de Vitoria," 90.

70. Francisco Suárez, Thomas Pink, Gwladys L. Williams, and Henry Davis, eds., *Selections from Three Works: A Treatise on Laws and God the Lawgiver; A Defence of the Catholic and Apostolic Faith; A Work on the Three Theological Virtues: Faith, Hope, and Charity* (Indianapolis: Liberty Fund, 2015); Henrik Lagerlund, "Francisco Suárez," *Great Christian Jurists*, 210–25; Benjamin Hill and Henrik Lagerlund, *The Philosophy of Franciso Suárez*

(New York: Oxford University Press, 2015); Elisabeth Rain Kincaid, "'Sharers in the Divine Image': Francisco Suárez and the Justification of Female Political Authority," *Political Theology* 19, no. 4 (March 2018): 331–48; Kincaid, "Settling Law: Suárez's Theory of Custom for Contemporary Contexts," *Francisco Suárez (1548–1616): Jesuits and the Complexities of Modernity*, ed. R. A. Maryks and J. A. Senent de Frutos (Leiden: Brill, 2019), 178–201; Kincaid, "Christianity's Defense against Tyrants," *America*, August 17, 2020, https://www.americamagazine.org/politics-society/2020/07/17/christianitys-defense-against-tyrants.

71. Ruston, *Human Rights*, 133.

72. Ruston lists these as the results from the Valladolid (1550–51) debate, *Human Rights*, 153–54.

73. With the exception of Ruston, whose work is effectively a comparison of the two Spaniards with John Locke, most editors and authors focus on either one of these two figures singularly, without noticing the other. An exception is Lawrence Clayton, *Bartolomé de las Casas: A Biography* (New York: Cambridge University Press, 2012).

74. David Orique, "Bartolomé de las Casas: A Brief Outline of His Life and Labor," accessed December 22, 2021, http://www.lascasas.org/manissues.htm. See Charles H. Lippy, Robert Choquette, and Stafford Poole, *Christianity Comes to the Americas: 1492–1776* (New York: Paragon House, 1992).

75. Orique, "Bartolomé de las Casas."

76. Orique, "Bartolomé de las Casas."

77. Ruston, *Human Rights*, 123.

78. Bartolomé de las Casas, *The Only Way*, ed. Helen Rand Parish, trans. Francis Patrick Sullivan, SJ (New York: Paulist Press, 1992).

79. Ruston, *Human Rights*, 128. Ruston takes the account from a report by Antonio de Remesal found in Enrique Ruiz Maldonado, "Bartolomé de las Casas y la justicia en Indias," *Ciencia Tomista* 101 (1974): 351–410, at 371.

80. See Henry Raup Wagner and Helen Rand Parish, *The Life and Writings of Bartolomé de Las Casas* (Albuquerque: University of New Mexico Press, 1967), 98–100. This and other sources were found in the extraordinarily well done Wikipedia entry, "Bartolomé de las Casas," at https://en.wikipedia.org/wiki/Bartolom%C3%A9_de_las_Casas#cite_note-53.

81. Pope Paul III, *Sublimus Dei: On the Enslavement and Evangelization of Indians*, May 29, 1537, https://www.papalencyclicals.net/Paul03/p3subli.htm.

82. Ruston, *Human Rights*, 129–31.

83. Bartolomé de las Casas, *A Short Account of the Destruction of the Indies*, trans. Nigel Griffin (New York: Penguin Classics, 1999). See the

free Project Guttenberg ebook: http://www.gutenberg.org/cache/epub/20321/pg20321-images.html.

84. Wagner and Parish, *Bartolomé de Las Casas*, 109–13.

85. Ruston, *Human Rights*, 133.

86. Ruston, *Human Rights*, 137.

87. David Orique, *To Heaven or to Hell: Bartolomé de Las Casas's Confesionario* (University Park: Penn State University Press, 2018); and "On Confessions: Bartolomé de Las Casas," in *Political Dissent: A Global Reader*, ed. Derrick Malone-France (Lanham, MD: Lexington Books, 2012), 75–86.

88. Clayton, *Bartolomé de las Casas*, 135–39, at 135; see his "Bartolomé de las Casas and the African Slave Trade," *History Compass* 7, no. 6 (2009): 1526–41.

89. Clayton, *Bartolomé de las Casas*, 136.

90. Clayton, *Bartolomé de las Casas*, 420–28; See Helen Parish, *The Only Way*, Addendum III: "Las Casas' Condemnation of African Slavery," 201–8 (204–8 have the texts from The History of the Indies); Gustavo Gutiérrez, *Las Casas: In Search of the Poor of Jesus Christ*, trans. Richard Barr (Maryknoll, NY: Orbis, 1993), 319.

91. Ruston, *Human Rights*, 153.

92. Aristotle, *The Politics*, trans. B. Jowett (Oxford: Clarendon Press, 1885), bk. 1, https://oll.libertyfund.org/titles/aristotle-the-politics-vol-1--5.

93. Ruston, *Human Rights*, 145. See Lewis Hanke, *All Mankind Is One: A Study of the Disputation between Bartolomé de Las Casas and Juan Ginés de Sepúlveda in 1550 on the Intellectual and Religious Capacity of the American Indian* (DeKalb: Northern Illinois University Press, 1994).

94. See Bartolomé de Las Casas, *In Defense of the Indians*, trans. Stafford Poole (DeKalb: Northern Illinois University Press, 1992), "Summary of Sepúlveda's Positions," 11–16; see also Ruston, *Human Rights*, 145.

95. See de Las Casas, *In Defense of the Indians*.

96. Ruston, *Human Rights*, 147.

97. Ruston, *Human Rights*, 153–54.

98. See Francis Patrick Sullivan, *Indian Freedom: The Cause of Bartolomé de las Casas (1484–1566); A Reader* (Kansas City, MO: Sheed and Ward, 1995).

CHAPTER SEVEN: REFORMING MORAL THEOLOGY

1. Robert Maryks and Jonathan Wright, eds., *Jesuit Survival and Restoration: A Global History (1773–1900)* (Leiden: Brill, 2014).

2. Pope Francis has illustrated his affinity to St. Alphonsus, see his *Message to Mark the 150th Anniversary of the Proclamation of St. Alphonsus Maria de Liguori Doctor Ecclesiae*, March 23, 2021, https://www.vatican.va/content/francesco/en/messages/pont-messages/2021/documents/papa-francesco_20210323_messaggio-santalfonso.html.

3. In Naples, Maria Lorenza Longo (1463–1542) helped Ettore Vernazza establish the Incurabili hospital in Naples and was particularly successful in serving the needs of sex workers afflicted by the disease. See Marco Luchetti, "Maria Lorenza Longo and the birth of the "Incurabili" Hospital in Naples," *Hektoen International: A Journal of Medical Humanities* (Summer 2010), https://hekint.org/2019/09/03/maria-lorenza-longo-and-the-birth-of-the-incurabili-hospital-in-naples/.

4. Frederick M. Jones, ed., *Alphonsus de Liguori: Selected Writings* (Mahwah, NJ: Paulist Press, 1999), 17.

5. Giovanni Romeo, *Aspettando il boia: condannati a morte, confortatori e inquisitori nella Napoli della Controriforma*, vol. 54 (Florence: Sansoni, 1993). See also "Confraternita dei Bianchi: Sede presso Ospedale Incurabili," accessed December 22, 2021, https://ospedaleincurabili.jimdofree.com/religiose-santi-beati-e-laici/confraternita-dei-bianchi/.

6. Alphonsus Liguori, "Advice for Priests Who Minister to Those Condemned to Death," in Jones, *Alphonsus de Liguori*, 330–36. Liguori also wrote an important manual in the tradition of the art of dying, known as the *ars moriendi*, where one lives a Christian life by preparing for a Christian death: Alphonsus Liguori, *Preparation for Death* (Rockford, IL: TAN Books and Publishers, 1982).

7. Liguori is not the first to author such a manual. Much has been written on its prototype, the late-fifteenth-century *Bologna Comforters' Manual*, used by the Bolognese confraternity of *Santa Maria della Morte*, but shared with other confraternities throughout the peninsula, including Ravenna, Ferrara, Padua, and Genoa. See Nicholas Terpstra, "The Bologna Comforter's Manual: Comforting by the Books: Editorial Notes on *The Bologna Comforters' Manual* Book 1," in *The Art of Executing Well: Rituals of Execution in Renaissance Italy*, ed. Nicholas Terpstra (Kirksville, MO: Truman State University Press, 2008), 183–292; Nicholas Terpstra, "Piety and Punishment: The Lay Conforteria and Civic Justice in Sixteenth-Century Bologna," *Sixteenth Century Journal* 22, no. 4 (1991): 679–94; Adriano Prosperi, *Crime and Forgiveness: Christianizing Execution in Medieval Europe* (Cambridge, MA: Harvard University Press, 2020). Special thanks to Shaun Slusarski for introducing me to this text.

8. Communion had been generally taken once during Easter time, following the Easter duty requirement that was promulgated in the early thirteenth century. From the thirteenth century, religious leaders like St.

Catherine of Siena saw the importance of more frequent communion as a way of receiving sacramental nourishment to grow in following Christ. In the sixteenth century, St. Ignatius similarly argued in its favor. Even in the eighteenth century this was considered a valid proposal though not the common practice that it has become.

9. Jones, *Alphonsus de Liguori*, 24.

10. François Genet, *Théologie Morale Ou Résolution Des Cas De Conscience Selon L'ecriture Sainte, Les Canons Et Les Saints Pères: Par L'ordre De Mgr L'évêque De Grenoble* (Charleston: Nabu Press, 2011); James R. Pollock, SJ, *François Genet: The Man and His Methodology* (Rome: Università Gregoriana, 1984).

11. Louis Vereecke, "Évolution de la théologie morale du Concile de Trente à s. Alphonse de Liguori," *Studia Moralia* 25, no.1 (1987): 7–27.

12. Renzo Gerardi, *Storia della morale: Interpretazioni teologiche dell'esperienza cristiana: periodi e correnti, autori e opere* (Bologna: EDB, 2003), 388.

13. Jones, *Alphonsus de Liguori*, 22.

14. Frederick M. Jones, *Alphonsus de Liguori: The Saint of Bourbon Naples, 1696–1787* (Westminster, MD: Christian Classics, 1992), 67.

15. Marciano Vidal, "La 'praxis': rasgo característico de la moral alfonsiana y reto a la teología moral actual," *Studia Moralia* 25, no. 2 (1987): 299–326, at 320. See also Marciano Vidal, *Frente al rigorismo moral, benignidad pastoral, Alfonso de Liguori (1696–1787)* (Madrid: El Perpetuo Socorro, 1986).

16. Vidal, "La 'praxis,'" 323–25. For his part, Bernhard Häring, CSsR, makes a similar point about the law of the spirit evident in the work of Liguori, in "Vita in Christo: Il 'Si' riconoscente alle legge dello Spirito," *Studia Moralia* 25, no. 2 (1987): 279–99.

17. Salvino Raponi, "Attualizzazione del pensiero di s. Alfonso sopratutto in merito all'attività pastorale a carattere popolare e alla chiamata di tutti alla santità," *Studia Moralia* 25, no. 2 (1987): 327–58.

18. From Alphonsus, as reported in Théodule Rey-Mermet, *Moral Choices: The Moral Theology of Saint Alphonsus Liguori* (Liguori, MO: Liguori Press, 1998), 103; and from Antonio Maria Tannoia, *Della vita ed Istituto del Ven. Servo di Dio Alfonso M. Liguori* (Naples: Materdomini, 1982), 3:153.

19. Rey-Mermet, *Moral Choices*, 103.

20. Rey-Mermet, *Moral Choices*, 102.

21. Rey-Mermet, *Moral Choices*, 97.

22. Rey-Mermet, *Moral Choices*, 67. See Alfonso Amarante, "La misericordia in Sant'Alfonso Maria de Liguori," *Studia Moralia, Supplemento* 7, 54, no.1 (2016): 15–32.

23. Jones, *Alphonsus de Liguori*, 26.

24. Sabatino Majorano, "La teologia morale nell'insieme del pensiero alfonsiano," *Studia Moralia* 25, no. 1 (1987): 79–103, at 103.

25. Domenico Capone, "La 'theologia morallis' di S. Alfonso: Prudenzialità nella scienza casistica per la prudenza nella coscienza," *Studia Morale* 25, no. 1 (1987): 27–78; see also Alfonso Vincenzo Amarante, "Prudenza E Prudenzialità in S. Alfonso: Lettura Con Domenico Capone CSsR," *Studia Moralia* 43, no. 2 (2005): 469–92.

26. See Alfonso Amarante, "Pastoralità come criterio morale," *Studia Moralia* 53, no. 1 (2015): 37–59.

27. St. Alphonsus, *Conscience: Writings from Moral Theology*, ed. and trans. Raphael Gallagher (Liguori, MO: Liguori Press, 2019), xix–xx (hereafter, Gallagher, *Conscience*).

28. Rey-Mermet, *Moral Choices*, 44.

29. Rey-Mermet, *Moral Choices*, 45–47.

30. Gallagher, *Conscience*, 3. For Redemptorist writings on conscience, see Marian Nalepa and Terence Kennedy, eds., *La Coscienza morale oggi* (Rome: Editiones Academicae Alphonsianae, 1987).

31. Gallagher, *Conscience*, 4.

32. Gallagher, *Conscience*, 5.

33. Gallagher, *Conscience*, 190–91.

34. Gallagher, *Conscience*, 164–65.

35. Gallagher, *Conscience*, xviii.

36. Gallagher, *Conscience*, 62.

37. Gallagher, *Conscience*, 61–160.

38. In 1762, Alphonsus was ordained the bishop of Sant'Agata dei Goti, a position he tried to avoid, see Jones, *Liguori: The Saint of Bourbon Naples*, 357–486.

39. Raphael Gallagher, "The Systematization of Alphonsus' Moral Theology through the Manuals," *Studia Moralia* 25, no. 2 (1987): 247–78.

40. Michael Moran, "The Writings of Francis Patrick Kenrick, Archbishop of Baltimore (1797–1863)," *Records of the American Catholic Historical Society of Philadelphia* 41, no. 3 (1930): 230–62, at 245.

41. Charles E. Curran, *Catholic Moral Theology in the United States: A History* (Washington, DC: Georgetown University Press, 2008), 13–17.

42. Gallagher, "The Systematization of Alphonsus' Moral Theology," 276–77.

43. Gallagher, "The Systematization of Alphonsus' Moral Theology," 276.

44. John W. O'Malley, *The Jesuits: A History from Ignatius to the Present* (Lanham, MD: Rowman and Littlefield, 2014), 64–65.

45. O'Malley, *Jesuits: A History*, 51.

46. O'Malley, *Jesuits: A History*, 66.

47. O'Malley, *Jesuits: A History*, 67–68.

48. O'Malley, *Jesuits: A History*, 69–70.

49. On Pascal, See Albert Jonsen and Stephen Toulmin, *The Abuse of Casuistry: A History of Moral Reasoning* (Berkeley: University of California Press, 1988), 231–78.

50. O'Malley, *Jesuits: A History*, 71–73.

51. O'Malley, *Jesuits: A History*, 48.

52. Martín Morales, "Violencia y misión en la antigua provincia del Paraguay," *Studia Missionalia* 60 (2011): 235–55; Casiano Néstor Carvallo, "La Victoria Misionera de Mbororé, *Historia y Arqueología Marítima*, http://www.histarmar.com.ar/InfHistorica-2/Mbororе-Victoria.htm.

53. Andrés Ignacio Prieto, "Paraguay Missions ("Reductions"), in *The Cambridge Encyclopedia of the Jesuits*, ed. Thomas Worcester (New York: Cambridge University Press, 2017), 586–88; Philip Caraman, *The Lost Paradise: An Account of the Jesuits in Paraguay (1607–1768)* (London: Sidgwick and Jackson, 1975).

54. Tamar Herzog, "Guaranis and Jesuits: Bordering the Spanish and the Portuguese Empires," *ReVista: Harvard Review of Latin America*, March 29, 2015, https://revista.drclas.harvard.edu/book/guaranis-and-jesuits.

55. O'Malley, *Jesuits: A History*, 80.

56. O'Malley, *Jesuits: A History*, 75–81; Jonathan Wright, "Suppression," in Worcester, *The Cambridge Encyclopedia of the Jesuits*, 767–69; Jeffrey D. Burson and Jonathan Wright, *The Jesuit Suppression in Global Context: Causes, Events, and Consequences* (New York: Cambridge University Press, 2015); Paul Shore, "The Years of Jesuit Suppression, 1773–1814: Survival, Setbacks, and Transformation," *Brill Research Perspectives in Jesuit Studies* (December 2020): 1–117, https://doi.org/10.1163/25897454-12340005. See also Robert Scully, "The Suppression of the Society of Jesus: A Perfect Storm in the Age of the Enlightenment," *Studies in the Spirituality of the Jesuits* 45, no. 2 (September 2013).

57. O'Malley, *Jesuits: A History*, 86.

58. Jonathan Wright, "The Suppression and Restoration," in *The Cambridge Companion to the Jesuits*, ed. Thomas Worcester (Cambridge: Cambridge University Press, 2008), 263–77; Thomas Worcester, "A Restored Society or a New Society of Jesus," in *Jesuit Survival and Restoration: A Global History 1773–1900* , ed. Robert Maryks and Jonathan Wright (Leiden: Brill, 2014), 13–33.

59. O'Malley, *Jesuits: A History*, 89.

60. O'Malley, *Jesuits: A History*, 90.

61. Oliver P. Rafferty, ed., *George Tyrrell and Catholic Modernism* (Dublin: Four Courts Press, 2010); "George Tyrrell and Catholic Mod-

ernism," *Thinking Faith* (July 6, 2009), https://www.thinkingfaith.org/articles/20090706_1.htm; Anthony M. Maher, *The Forgotten Jesuit of Catholic Modernism: George Tyrrell's Prophetic Theology* (Minneapolis: Fortress Press, 2017).

62. David G. Schultenover, "Luis Martín García, the Jesuit General of the Modernist Crisis (1892–1906): On Historical Criticism," *The Catholic Historical Review* 89, no. 3 (July 2003): 434–63.

63. Bernhard Knorn, "Jesuits in Systematic Theology: A Historiographical Essay," Jesuit Historiography Online (January 2017), https://referenceworks.brillonline.com/entries/jesuit-historiography-online/jesuits-in-systematic-theology-a-historiographical-essay-COM_196256.

64. Curran, *Catholic Moral Theology in the United States*, 7. Gerardi makes the same assessment in *Storia della Morale*, 415.

65. Raphael Gallagher, "The Moral Method of St. Alphonsus in the Light of the 'Vindiciae' Controversy," *Spicilegium Historicum Congregatinis SS.mi Redemptoris* 45 (1997): 331–49. See Gerardi, *Storia della morale*, 413–15.

66. Gerardi, *Storia della morale*, 414.

67. Aloysius Sabetti, *Compendium theologiae moralis*, 7th ed. (New York: Pustet, 1892).

68. Curran, *Catholic Moral Theology in the United States*, 17.

69. Curran, *Catholic Moral Theology in the United States*, 21.

70. See Gerardi, *Storia della morale*, 399–404.

71. Much of the work on the manualists appears in greater depth in an earlier work by me, *A History of Catholic Moral Theology in the Twentieth Century: From Confessing Sins to Liberating Consciences* (New York: Continuum, 2010), see 9–34, 111–40.

72. Congregation for the Doctrine of the Faith, *Considerations Regarding Proposals to Give Legal Recognition to Unions between Homosexual Persons*, Vatican City, July 31, 2003, https://www.vatican.va/roman_curia/congregations/cfaith/documents/rc_con_cfaith_doc_20030731_homosexual-unions_en.html.

73. James Alison, "Yes, But Is It True?" accessed December 22, 2021, http://jamesalison.com/yes-but-is-it-true/.

74. Thomas Slater, *A Manual of Moral Theology for English-speaking Countries* (London: Benziger Brothers, 1906).

75. Thomas Slater, *De justitia et jure* (London: Burns and Oates, 1898); *Principia theologiae moralis* (London: Burns and Oates, 1902); *Cases of Conscience for English-speaking Countries* (New York: Benziger, 1911–12); *Questions of Morality* (New York: Benziger, 1915); *A Short History of Moral Theology* (New York: Benziger, 1909); *Religion and Human Interests* (New York: Benziger, 1918); *The Morals of Today* (New York: Benziger, 1920); *The Foundation of True Morality* (New York: Benziger, 1920); *Christ and*

Evolution (London: Burns, Oates & Washbourne, 1923); *Points of Church Law, Mysticism, and Morality* (New York: P. J. Kennedy, 1924); *Back to Theology* (New York: Benziger, 1925).

76. Slater, *Manual of Moral Theology*, 6.

77. Slater, *Manual of Moral Theology*, 5–6.

78. Slater, *Manual of Moral Theology*, 6.

79. As we have seen throughout from the sixteenth century onward, the seventh commandment always commanded more attention than any in both the casuist and manualist traditions.

80. See Mark Jordan, *The Invention of Sodomy in Christian Theology* (Chicago: University of Chicago Press, 1997).

81. Slater, *Manual of Moral Theology*, 18.

82. Slater, *Manual of Moral Theology*, 53.

83. Slater, *Manual of Moral Theology*, 60.

84. Slater, *Manual of Moral Theology*, 60–61. Slater's position confirms the long-standing affirmation that an act made in good but erroneous conscience remains good. See James Keenan, "Can a Wrong Action Be Good? The Development of Theological Opinion on Erroneous Conscience," *Église et Théologie* 24 (1993): 205–19; Brian Johnstone, "Erroneous Conscience in *Veritatis Splendor* and the Theological Tradition," in *The Splendor of Accuracy*, ed. Joseph Selling and Jan Jans (Grand Rapids, MI: Eerdmans, 1994), 114–35; Werner Wolbert, "Problems Concerning Erroneous Conscience," *Studia theologica* 50 (1996): 162–75; Josef Fuchs, "Was heisst Irriges 'Gewissen,'" in *Für eine menschliche Moral* (Freiburg: Herder, 1997), 54–64.

85. Slater, *Manual of Moral Theology*, 70.

86. Slater, *Manual of Moral Theology*, 274.

87. Slater, *Manual of Moral Theology*, 275–76.

88. Slater, *Manual of Moral Theology*, 276–77.

89. Slater, *Manual of Moral Theology*, 277–81, at 279.

90. Slater, *Manual of Moral Theology*, 288.

91. See Lucius Iwejuru Ugorji, *The Principle of Double Effect: A Critical Appraisal of Its Traditional Understanding and Its Modern Reinterpretation* (Frankfurt Am Main: Peter Lang, 1985).

92. Slater, *Manual of Moral Theology*, 302.

93. Slater, *Manual of Moral Theology*, 303.

94. Slater, *Manual of Moral Theology*, 304.

95. Slater, *Manual of Moral Theology*, 308–9.

96. John Connery, *Abortion: The Development of the Roman Catholic Perspective* (Chicago: Loyola University Press, 1977); John T. Noonan Jr., "An Almost Absolute Value in History," in *The Morality of Abortion:*

Legal and Historical Perspectives (Cambridge, MA: Harvard University Press, 1970).

97. Slater, *Manual of Moral Theology*, 314–15.

98. Patrick Boyle, *Parvitas Materiae in Sexto in Contemporary Catholic Thought* (Lanham, MD: University Press of America, 1987); James Brundage, *Law, Sex and Christian Society in Medieval Europe* (Chicago: University of Chicago Press, 1987).

99. Slater, *Manual of Moral Theology*, 330–34. See also Giovanni Cappelli, *Autoerotismo: Un problema morale nei primi secoli cristiani?* (Bologna: Edizioni Dehoniano, 1986). Hubertus Lutterbach, "Die Sexualtabus in den Bussbüchern," *Saeculum* 46 (1995): 216–48.

100. "Periodica de re canonica," https://www.unigre.it/en/research-and-publications/periodicals/periodica-de-re-canonica/our-history/.

101. Gerald Kelly, "The Duty of Using Artificial Means of Preserving Life," *Theological Studies* 11, no. 2 (1950): 203–20, at 220; *Medico-Moral Problems* (St. Louis: The Catholic Health Association of The United States and Canada, 1958).

102. John Ford, "The Morality of Obliteration Bombing," *Theological Studies* 5, no. 3 (1944): 261–309.

103. Oliver Morgan, "'Chemical Comforting' and the Theology of John C. Ford, SJ: Classic Answers to a Contemporary Problem," *Journal of Ministry in Addiction and Recovery* 6, no. 1 (1999): 29–66.

104. John Ford and Gerald Kelly, *Contemporary Moral Theology I: Questions in Fundamental Moral Theology I* (Westminster, MD: Newman Press, 1964) and *Contemporary Moral Theology II: Marriage Questions* (Westminster, MD: Newman Press, 1964).

105. Ford and Kelly, *Contemporary Moral Theology I*, 20–21.

106. Henry Davis, *Moral and Pastoral Theology*, 4th ed. 4 vols. (New York: Sheed and Ward, 1943).

107. Davis, *Moral and Pastoral Theology*, 1:ix.

108. Davis, *Moral and Pastoral Theology*, 355.

109. Davis, *Moral and Pastoral Theology*, 355–56.

110. Slater, *Manual of Moral Theology*, 79.

111. Davis, *Moral and Pastoral Theology*, 1:67–78. See, e.g., how the Jesuit Bartholomew Kiely, a professor at the Gregorian University, argued that even if the hierarchy was wrong in its teaching on a matter, still that would be better than promoting a moral chaos that would result from the irresponsible presumption that each person could reason on her own, in his "The Impracticality of Proportionalism," *Gregorianum* 66 (1985): 655–86; for his seminal work, see *Psychology and Moral Theology: Lines of Convergence* (Rome: Gregorian University Press, 1980).

112. Ford and Kelly, *Contemporary Moral Theology I*, 174–351.

113. Pope Pius XI, *Casti Connubii* (December 31, 1930), http://www.vatican.va/content/pius-xi/en/encyclicals/documents/hf_p-xi_enc_19301231_casti-connubii.html. Paragraphs 56 and 95 refer to the changed teachings by other churches; noteworthy is the Church of England's Lambeth conference in the summer of 1930, which was recognized by very different readers of the encyclical; see Margaret Sanger, "Birth Control Advances: A Reply to the Pope," https://proquest.libguides.com/historyvault/sanger; John Kippley, "Casti Connubii: 60 Years Later," *Homiletic and Pastoral Review*, June 1991, https://www.ewtn.com/catholicism/library/casti-connubii-60-years-later-11227.

114. Keenan, *A History*, 9–34.

115. Pope Leo XIII, *Rerum Novarum* (May 15, 1951), http://www.vatican.va/content/leo-xiii/en/encyclicals/documents/hf_l-xiii_enc_15051891_rerum-novarum.html.

116. Similarly, major social ethicists and theologians like Oswald von Nell-Breuning (1890–1991) and John Courtney Murray (1904–67) published and developed this field throughout the first seventy years of the twentieth century, see Keenan, "Making Sense of Eighty Years of Theological Ethics," *Theological Studies* 80, no.1 (2019): 148–68.

117. Heribert Jone, *Moral Theology* (Westminster, MD: Newman Press, 1945).

118. Jone, *Moral Theology* (Charlotte, NC: Tan Books, 2009).

119. Stephen Schloesser, "Against Forgetting: Memory, History, Vatican II," *Theological Studies* 67, no. 2 (2006): 275–314.

120. Charles E. Curran, *Catholic Moral Theology in the United States* (Washington, DC: Georgetown University Press, 2008), 6; Giuseppe Angelini and Ambrogio Valsecchi, *Disegno Storico della teologia morale* (Bologna: Edizione Dehoniane, 1972), 128–30.

121. See Gerardi, *Storia della morale*, 431–32.

122. Richard Schaefer, "A Critique of Everyday Reason: Johann Michael Sailer and the Catholic Enlightenment in Germany," *Intellectual History Review* 30, no. 4 (2020): 653–71, at 659; Johann Michael Sailer, *Vernunftlehre für Menschen wie sie sind, d.i. Anleitung zur Erkenntniß und Liebe der Wahrheit* (Munich: Strobel, 1795), at 24.

123. Kathleen A. Cahalan, *Formed in the Image of Christ: The Sacramental-Moral Theology of Bernard Häring, C.Ss.R* (Collegeville, MN: Liturgical Press, 2004), 19.

124. Johann Baptist von Hirscher, *Die Christliche Moral als Lehre von der Verwirklichung des Göttlichen Reiches in der Menschheit* (Tübingen: H. Laupp, 1835).

125. Donald J. Dietrich, "Priests and Political Thought: Theology and Reform in Central Europe, 1845–1855," *Catholic Historical Review* 72, no. 4 (October 1985): 519–46, at 523–24.

126. Dietrich, "Priests and Political Thought," 544.

127. Dietrich, "Priests and Political Thought," 546.

128. Franz Xaver Linsenmann, *Lehrbuch der Moraltheologie* (Freiburg im Breisgau: Herder, 1878).

129. Gerardi, *Storia della morale*, 437–38.

130. James Megivern, *The Death Penalty: An Historical and Theological Survey* (New York: Paulist Press, 1997), 248–52. See Linsenmann, *Lehrbuch der Moraltheologie*, 471–82. See also Gerhard Gloege, *Die Todesstrafe als Theologisches Problem* (Berlin: Springer, 1966).

131. Shaji George Kochuthara, *Towards a Theology of Sexual Pleasure: Continuity and Development in the Theology of Sexual Pleasure in the Catholic Moral Tradition* (Düsseldorf: Lambert, 2011), 245.

132. See, e.g., Schaefer, "Political Theology and Nineteenth-Century Catholicism," *Nineteenth Century Contexts* 36, no. 3 (2014): 269–85. See also Stuart Chalmers, "Fritz Tillmann, Discipleship and the Renewal of Moral Theology," in *Irish Theological Quarterly* 86–84 (2021) that raises up not only Hirscher and Linsenmann, but also several manualists who seek to improve their tradition by a better incorporation of the virtues.

133. Much of my work on Tillmann, Gilleman, Lottin, and Häring appears in greater depth in *A History*, 35–110.

134. Fritz Tillmann, *Die Idee der Nachfolge Christi* (Dusseldorf: Patmos, 1934).

135. Karl-Heinz Kleber, *Historia Docet: Zur Geschichte der Moraltheologie* Studien der Moraltheologie 15 (Münster: LIT Verlag, 2005), 89.

136. Fritz Tillmann, *Der Meister Ruft* (Düsseldorf: Patmos Verlag, 1937); *The Master Calls: A Handbook of Morals for the Layman* (Baltimore: Helicon Press, 1960), 4–5.

137. Gérard Gilleman, *Le primat de la charité en théologie morale: essai méthodologique* (Paris: Desclée de Brouwer, 1952). Gilleman, *The Primacy of Charity in Moral Theology* (Westminster, MD: Newman Press, 1959).

138. Odon Lottin, *Psychologie et morale aux XIIe et XIIIe siècles* (Gembloux, Belgium: J. Duculot), vol. I, 1942; II, 1948; III, 1949; IV, 1960 (hereafter, *Psychologie et morale*).

139. For a superb introduction, see Mary Jo Iozzio, *Self-determination and the Moral Act: A Study of the Contributions of Odon Lottin, O.S.B.* (Leuven: Peeters Publishing, 1995).

140. Odon Lottin, *Principes de Morale* (Louvain: Abbaye du Mont César, 1946).

141. Odon Lottin, *Morale Fondamentale* (Tournai, Belgium: 1954).

142. Lottin, *Morale Fondamentale*, 23–25. He entitles this section, "Causes de l'inferiorité actuelle de la théologie morale."

143. Lottin, *Morale Fondamentale*, 297–339.

144. Lottin, *Morale Fondamentale*, 54 ff.

145. Lottin, *Au Coeur de la Morale Chrétienne* (Tournai: Declees, 1957), 6.

146. Bernard Häring, *My Witness for the Church* (Mahwah, NJ: Paulist Press, 1992), 19.

147. Häring, *My Witness*, 132.

148. Bernard Häring, *Embattled Witness: Memories of a Time of War* (New York: Seabury Press, 1976).

149. Häring, *Embattled Witness*, 23–24.

150. Häring, *Das Gesetz Christi* (Freiburg: Verlag Wewel, 1954); *The Law of Christ* (Paramus, NJ: Newman Press, 1961).

151. Häring, *Law of Christ*, vii.

152. James F. Keenan, "Bernard Häring's Influence on American Catholic Moral Theology," *Journal of Moral Theology* 1, no. 1 (2012): 23–42.

153. Keenan, *A History*, 59–110.

154. Curran, *Catholic Moral Theology in the U.S.* (Washington, DC: Georgetown University Press, 2008), 59.

155. Curran, *Catholic Moral Theology in the U.S.*, 63–82.

156. Eric Genilo, *John Cuthbert Ford: Moral Theologian at the End of the Manualist Era* (Washington, DC: Georgetown University Press, 2007).

157. Ford and Kelly, *Contemporary Moral Theology I*, 111. They refer to a radio address by Pope Pius XII, "De Conscientia Christiana in Iuvenibus Recte Efformanda," *Acta Apostolica Sedis*, 44 (12–28 April 1952), 271.

158. John Ford and Gerald Kelly, "Notes on Moral Theology, 1953," *Theological Studies* 15, no. 1 (1954): 52–102, at 53; see also Gerald Kelly, "Current Theology: Notes on Moral Theology, 1952," *Theological Studies* 14, no. 1 (1953): 31–72.

159. John Farraher, "Notes on Moral Theology," *Theological Studies* 21, no. 4 (1960): 581–625, at 581.

160. W. van der Marck, OP, "Vruchtbaarheidsregeling: poging tot antwoord op een nog open vraag," *Tijdsckrift voor théologie* 3 (1963): 378–413; L. Janssens, "Morale conjugale et progestogènes," *Ephemerides theologicae Lovanienses* 39 (October–December 1963): 787–826. Lynch, "Current Theology: Notes on Moral Theology," *Theological Studies* 25, no. 2 (1964): 232–53, at 246.

161. Daniel Callahan, "Authority and the Theologian," *Commonweal*, June 5, 1964, 319–23.

162. David Kelly, *The Emergence of Roman Catholic Medical Ethics in North America* (New York: The Edwin Mellen Press, 1979), 231.

163. While I provide much greater depth on Vatican II in *A History*, 95–110, more recently I was invited to write further on it in "The Renewal of Moral Theology," in *Cambridge Companion to Vatican II*, ed. Richard Gaillardetz (New York: Cambridge University Press, 2020), 318–37. These more recent insights very much animate these pages.

164. "Decree on the Training of Priests, *Optatam Totius*, October 28, 1965," in *Vatican Council II: Constitutions, Decrees, Declarations*, ed. Austin Flannery (Northport, NY: Costello Publications, 1996), 365–84, at 376–77 (hereafter, *Vatican Council II*).

165. Josef Fuchs, "Theologia moralis perficienda: votum Concilii Vaticani II," *Periodica de re morali, canonica, litugica*," 55 (1966): 499–548. In English, "Moral Theology according to Vatican II," *Human Values and Christian Morality* (Dublin: Gill and Macmillan, 1970), 1–55.

166. Fuchs, "Moral Theology," 2.

167. Fuchs, "Moral Theology," 3.

168. Fuchs, "Moral Theology," 20.

169. Fuchs, "Moral Theology," 3.

170. Richard Gula, *Reason Informed by Faith* (New York: Paulist Press, 1989), 29.

171. Kenneth Melchin, "Revisionists, Deontologists, and the Structure of Moral Understanding," *Theological Studies* 51, no. 3 (1990): 389–426.

172. Janssens developed a personalist ethics within a profoundly social/relational context, the notion of the fundamental option as well as the distinction between ontic and moral goodness and evil. See Joseph A. Selling, *Personalist Morals: Essays in Honor of Professor Louis Janssens* (Leuven: Leuven University Press, 1988). As I argue in *A History* (141–96), Janssens and Fuchs very much provided the platforms for all that would follow in moral theology. Although his own theology was deeply indebted to the transcendental Thomism of Karl Rahner, Fuchs esteemed Janssens. As a student of Fuchs, I remember that on my first visit to his office he had a photo of him and Janssens sitting together on a couch; it was their first time meeting and the only photo on his desk.

173. Charles Curran, "Bernard Häring: A Moral Theologian Whose Soul Matched His Scholarship," *National Catholic Reporter* 34, no. 34 (July 17, 1998): 11.

174. Joseph Selling, "*Gaudium et Spes*: A Manifesto for Contemporary Moral Theology," in *Vatican II and Its Legacy*, ed. M. Lamberigts and L. Kenis (Leuven: Peter, 2002), 145–62.

175. Philippe Bordeyne, *L'Homme et son angoisse: La Théologie Morale de "Gaudium et Spes"* (Paris: Cerf, 2004).

176. See, e.g., Häring, *Law of Christ*, I: 135–89.

177. "Pastoral Constitution on the Church in the Modern World, *Gaudium et Spes*, December 7, 1965," *Vatican Council II*, 163–82, at 178.

178. John O'Malley, *What Happened at Vatican II* (Cambridge, MA: Harvard University Press, 2008), 308–9.

179. "Declaration on Religious Liberty, *Dignitatis Humanae*, December 7, 1965," *Vatican Council II*, 551–68, at 551.

180. Josef Fuchs, ed., *Das Gewissen* (Düsseldorf: Patmos Verlag, 1979); Marian Nalepa and Terence Kennedy, eds., *La Coscienza morale oggi* (Rome: Editiones Academicae Alphonsianae, 1987); Charles E. Curran, ed., *Readings in Moral Theology No. 14: Conscience* (Mahwah, NJ: Paulist Press, 2004).

181. Eric D'Arcy, *Conscience and Its Right to Freedom* (London: Sheed and Ward, 1961); Linda Hogan, *Confronting the Truth: Conscience in the Catholic Tradition* (Mahwah, NJ: Paulist Press, 2001); Kevin Kelly, *Conscience: Dictator or Guide* (London: Geoffrey Chapman, 1967); Anne Patrick, *Liberating Consciences* (New York: Continuum, 1997); Osamu Takeuchi, *Conscience and Personality* (Chiba, Japan: Kyoyusha, 2003); Paul Valadier, *Éloge de la conscience* (Paris: Seuil, 1994).

182. See the discussion on his influence below.

183. Clearly the most important study of the preconciliar debate is Ambrogio Valsecchi, *Controversy: The Birth Control Debate 1958–1968* (Cleveland: Corpus Books, 1968).

184. Mark S. Massa, *The Structures of Theological Revolutions: How the Fight over Birth Control Transformed American Catholicism* (New York: Oxford University Press, 2018), 56–60.

185. O'Malley, *What Happened at Vatican II*, 284–89; Jan Grootaers and Jan Jans, *La régulation des naissances à Vatican II: Une semaine de crise* (Leuven: Peeters, 2002).

186. Josef Fuchs, *Natural Law: A Theological Investigation* (New York: Sheed and Ward, 1965) 12; *Lex Naturae. Zur Theologie des Naturrechts* (Düsseldorf: Patmos, 1955).

187. Mark Graham, *Josef Fuchs on Natural Law* (Washington, DC: Georgetown University Press, 2002); Keenan, "Josef Fuchs and the Question of Moral Objectivity in Roman Catholic Ethical Reasoning," *Religious Studies Review* 24, no. 3 (1998): 253–58; Keenan, "Josef Fuchs at Eighty," *Irish Theological Quarterly* 59, no. 3 (1993): 204–10; Keenan, "Champion of Conscience," *America*, April 4, 2005, 6, https://www.americamagazine.org/issue/526/other-things/champion-conscience.

188. Keenan, *A History*, 120–34.

189. The majority report was never published, although copies of it can be found through a variety of sources. See here, the document: http://www.ldysinger.com/@magist/1963_Paul6/068_hum_vitae/majority%20report.pdf.

190. See Genilo, *John Cuthbert Ford*, 63–65.

191. See Keenan, *A History*, 111–40.

192. John Horgan, *Humanae vitae and the Bishops* (Dublin: Irish University Press, 1972).

193. On Curran, see Keenan, *A History*, 96–104, 147–50; James J. Walter, Timothy O'Connell, and Thomas Shannon, eds., *A Call to Fidelity: On the Moral Theology of Charles E. Curran* (Washington, DC: Georgetown University Press, 2002); Massa, *The Structure of Theological Revolutions*, 79–105. On McCormick, see Keenan, "Making Sense of Eighty Years of Theological Ethics." On the entire impact of *Humanae Vitae*, see Keenan, *A History*, 141–72.

194. Cardinal John Henry Newman, "An Essay on the Development of Christian Doctrine," in *Conscience, Consensus, and the Development of Doctrine*, ed. James Gaffney (New York: Doubleday, 1992), 38–385.

195. Newman, "An Essay on the Development of Christian Doctrine," 33.

196. Gerard H. McCarren, "Development of Doctrine," in *The Cambridge Companion to John Henry Newman*, ed. Ian Ker and Terrence Merigan (Cambridge: Cambridge University Press, 2009), 118–36, at 121.

197. John W. O'Malley, "Does Church Teaching Change: The Development of Doctrine at Trent, Vatican I, and Vatican II," *Commonweal*, July 31, 2019, https://www.commonwealmagazine.org/does-church-teaching-change.

198. Yves Congar, *The Meaning of the Tradition* (San Francisco: Ignatius Press, 2004).

199. Bernard Lonergan, "Christ as Subject: A Reply," *Gregorianum* 40, no. 2 (1959): 242–70; reprinted in Frederick Crowe, *Collection* (New York: Herder, 1967), 153–84, and *The Subject* (Milwaukee: Marquette University, 1968).

200. Lonergan, "Dehellenization of Dogma," *Theological Studies* 28, no. 2 (1967): 336–51 (reprinted in William Ryan and Bernard Tyrrell, eds., *A Second Collection* [Philadelphia: Westminster Press, 1975], 11–32); "Transition from A Classicist World View to Historical Mindedness," *A Second Collection*, 1–9; "Theology in its New Context," *A Second Collection*, 55–67.

201. Phil Keane, "The Objective Moral Order," *Theological Studies* 43, no. 4 (1982): 260–78; Kenneth Melchin, *History, Ethics and Emergent*

Probability: Ethics, Society and History in the Work of Bernard Lonergan (Lanham, MD.: University Press of America, 1987); Richard Gula, *Reason Informed by Faith: Foundations of Moral Theology* (New York: Paulist Press, 1989), 25–41; Thomas Kopfensteiner, "Historical Epistemology," *Heythrop Journal* 33, no. 1 (1992): 45–60; Mark Miller, *Living Ethically in Christ: Is Christian Ethics Unique?* (New York: Peter Lang, 1999).

202. Joseph Fletcher, *Situation Ethics: The New Morality* (Philadelphia: Westminster Press, 1966).

203. "In hoc quippe mundo humana anima quasi more navis est contra ictum fluminis conscendentis: uno in loco nequaquam stare permittitur, quia ad ima relabitur, nisi ad summa conetur." Gregory, *Reg. Past.* p. III, c. 34: ML 77, 118c.

204. "In via vitae non progredi regredi est." Bernard, *Serm. II in festo Purif.*, n. 3: ML 183, 369 C.

205. "In via Dei stare retrocedere est." Thomas attributes this quote to Bernard in *In III Sen.* d29, a8, qla2, 1a, and to Gregory in ST II–II, q. 24, a. 6, ob. 3.

206. Klaus Demmer, *Living the Truth: A Theory of Action* (Washington, DC: Georgetown University Press, 2010); Keenan, "Remembering Klaus Demmer," *Commonweal*, July 24, 2014.

207. Josef Fuchs, "Innovative Morality," *Moral Demands and Personal Obligations* (Washington, DC: Georgetown University Press, 1993), 114–19.

208. Klaus Demmer, "Die autonome Moral: Eine Anfrage an die Denkform," in *Fundamente der theologischen Ethik: Bilanz und Neuansatze*, ed. Adrian Holderegger (Freiburg: Herder, 1996), 261–76.

209. Marciano Vidal, "Progress in the Moral Tradition," *Catholic Ethicists on HIV/AIDS Prevention*, 257–70.

210. Jean-Marie Aubert, "Morale et Casuistique," *Recherches de Science Religieuses* 68 (1980): 167–204.

211. Demmer, "Erwägungen über den Segen der Kasuistik," *Gregorianum* 63, no. 1 (1982): 133–40.

212. Thomas R. Kopfensteiner, "Science, Metaphor, and Moral Casuistry," in *The Context of Casuistry*, ed. James F. Keenan, SJ, and Thomas A. Shannon (Washington, DC: Georgetown University Press, 1995), 207–20.

213. John T. Noonan Jr., "Development in Moral Doctrine," in Keenan and Shannon, *The Context of Casuistry*, 188–204; *The Church That Can and Cannot Change* (Notre Dame, IN: University of Notre Dame Press, 2005).

CHAPTER EIGHT: MORAL AGENCY FOR A GLOBAL THEOLOGICAL ETHICS

1. Canon law (588 §1–3) defines religious institutes as either lay or clerical according to whether the specific institute functions through the authority and exercise of sacred orders. Still today, women religious orders are defined as lay.

2. Charles E. Curran, "Margaret A. Farley," in *Diverse Voices in Modern US Moral Theology* (Washington, DC: Georgetown University Press, 2018), 129–50. For an introduction to Gustafson, see his *Moral Discernment in the Christian Life: Essays in Theological Ethics* (Louisville, KY: Westminster John Knox, 2007).

3. Joan Glisky, IHM, "Sister Mary Emil Penet, IHM: Founder of the Sister Formation Project," *Catholic Education* 9, no. 3 (March 2006): 360–77.

4. Mark Latkovic, "William May: Moral Theologian, *sentire cum Ecclesia*," *Linacre Quarterly* 82, no. 3 (2015): 191–92.

5. Curran, "Lisa Sowle Cahill," in *Diverse Voices in Modern US Moral Theology*, 151–76.

6. Curran, "Germain G. Grisez," in *Diverse Voices in Modern US Moral Theology*, 85–106; Matthew Bunson, "In Memoriam: Germain Grisez, Great Defender of *Humanae Vitae* (1929–2018)," *National Catholic Register*, February 2, 2018.

7. Sr. Vimala Chenginimattam, CMC, "Gender Perspectives in India," in *Moral Theology in India Today*, ed. Shaji George Kochuthara (Bangalore: Dharmaram Publications, 2013), 417–41; "Emerging Voices," in *Building Bridges in Sarajevo: The Plenary Papers of Sarajevo 2018*, ed. Kristin Heyer, James F. Keenan, and Andrea Vicini (Maryknoll, NY: Orbis, 2019), 28–31.

8. Eight women were funded through cooperation with Catholic Theological Ethics in the World Church (CTEWC), see the account, James Keenan, "Introduction," in *Catholic Theological Ethics Past, Present, and Future: The Trento Conference* (Maryknoll, NY: Orbis, 2011), 3–4; see also Margaret Ssebunya's account of her studies, "Emerging Voices," in Keenan, *Catholic Theological Ethics Past, Present, and Future*, 35–39.

9. Sr. Anne Nasimiyu-Wasike, LSOSF, "Christology and an African Woman's Experience," in *Jesus in African Christianity: Experimentation and Diversity in African Christology*, ed. J.N.K. Mugambi and Laurenti Magesa

(Nairobi: Initiatives, 1989), 123–35, and in Robert J. Schreiter, ed., *Faces of Jesus in Africa* (Maryknoll, NY: Orbis, 1991), 70–81.

10. Sr. Anne Nasimiyu-Wasike, LSOSF, "Christianity and the African Rituals of Birth and Naming" and "Polygamy: A Feminist Critique," in *The Will to Arise: Women, Tradition, and the Church in Africa*, ed. Mercy A. Oduyoye and Musimbi R. A. Kanyoro (Maryknoll, NY: Orbis, 1992), 40–53, 101–18, respectively.

11. Sr. Anne Nasimiyu-Wasike, LSOSF, "The Missing Voices of Women," in Keenan, *Catholic Theological Ethics Past, Present, and Future*, 107–15.

12. Sr. Anne Nasimiyu-Wasike, LSOSF, "Is Mutuality Possible: An African Response," *Missiology: An International Review* 29.1 (January 2001): 45–53, at 46.

13. Sr. Anne Nasimiyu-Wasike, LSOSF, "Education of Women Religious in Africa: A Moral Right," *Asian Horizons* 12, no. 1 (March 2018): 22–36.

14. The volume was edited by Shaji George Kochuthara, "Moral Right for the Education of Religious Women," *Asian Horizons* 12, no. 1: 3–6. Chenginimattam also contributed to the volume, "Daughter of the Church to Doctor of the Church: St Teresa of Avila; A Role Model for Women Religious," *Asian Horizons* 12, no. 1: 129–46.

15. Emily Reimer-Barry, "In Gratitude for the Life and Witness of Sr. Anne Nasimiyu-Wasike, LSOSF," *Catholic Moral Theology*, February 27, 2018, https://catholicmoraltheology.com/in-gratitude-for-the-life-and-witness-of-sister-anne-nasimiyu-wasike-lsosf/; James Keenan, "Agency and the Moral Right to an Education for Women Religious," *Asian Horizons* 12, no. 1 (2018): 7–21.

16. Nhu Y Lan Tran, "Isolated Voices," in Heyer, Keenan, and Vicini, *Building Bridges in Sarajevo*, 43–46.

17. Zorica Maros, "Isolated Voices," in Heyer, Keenan, and Vicini, *Building Bridges in Sarajevo*, 40–43.

18. The list is not complete, I am sure. I welcome any information that augments this account, but by naming the new ethicists, hopefully, we can appreciate how significantly they changed the field. See Mary Ann Hinsdale, "Who Are the "Begats?" or "Women Theologians Shaping Women Theologians," *Journal of Feminist Studies in Religion* 33, no. 1 (2017): 91–106. This essay is part of a section, *Women in American Catholic Theology Fifty Years after Vatican II*, see Jessica Coblentz, "Introduction," 87–89.

19. See, e.g., Vimala Chenginimattam, CMC, "Through Her Eyes: The Role of Women Theological Ethicists in Terms of the Future Development of Moral Theology," in *Doing Catholic Theological Ethics in a Cross*

Cultural and Interreligious Asian Context, ed. Yiu Sing Lúcás Chan, James F. Keenan, and Shaji George Kochuthara (Bangalore: Dharmaram Press, 2016), 305–11; Teresia Hinga, "Remembering and Honoring Professor Sr. Anne Nasimiyu Wasike: A Concerned, Socially Engaged and (not so) Little Sr. of St. Francis," CTEWC, July 1, 2018, https://catholicethics.com/forum/remembering-and-honoring-professor-sr-anne-nasimiyu-wasike-a-concerned-socially-engaged-and-not-so-little-sr-of-st-francis/.

20. M. Carmel McEnroy, *Guests in Their Own House: The Women of Vatican II* (Eugene, OR: Wipf & Stock, 2011); see earlier Mary Luke Tobin, "Women in the Church: Vatican II and After," *Ecumenical Review* 37, no. 3 (1985): 295–305.

21. Catherine LaCugna, "Catholic Women as Ministers and Theologians," *America* 167, no. 10 (October 10, 1992): 238–48.

22. Cardinal Franjo Šeper, "Sacred Congregation for the Doctrine of the Faith: Declaration," December 15, 1979, https://www.vatican.va/roman_curia/congregations/cfaith/documents/rc_con_cfaith_doc_19791215_christi-ecclesia_en.html; Roger Haight, "Hans Küng, Influential Vatican II Theologian Censured by John Paul II, Dies at 93," *America*, April 6, 2021, https://www.americamagazine.org/faith/2021/04/06/hans-kung-death-obituary-vatican-ii-240394.

23. See the recollection of one of the former priests so disciplined, William C. Birdsall, "Last Word: A Brush of the Butterfly's Wing," *Commonweal*, November 17, 2016, https://www.commonwealmagazine.org/last-word-brush-butterfly%E2%80%99s-wing; on the discipline, "Vatican Rules Against Priests Who Disagreed on an Encyclical," *New York Times*, April 30, 1971, https://www.nytimes.com/1971/04/30/archives/vatican-rules-against-priests-who-disagreed-on-an-encyclical.html.

24. Cardinal Joseph Ratzinger, "Letter to Father Charles Curran" (July 25, 1986), http://www.vatican.va/roman_curia/congregations/cfaith/documents/rc_con_cfaith_doc_19860725_carlo-curran_en.html.

25. On the proceedings against Curran, see Charles E. Curran, *Loyal Dissent: Memoir of a Catholic Theologian* (Washington, DC: Georgetown University Press, 2007); earlier Curran provided copies of the exchange between him and the Congregation in *Faithful Dissent* (Kansas City: Sheed and Ward, 1986); see also the account by Richard McCormick, "L'Affaire Curran," in *The Critical Calling: Reflections on Moral Dilemmas since Vatican II* (Washington, DC: Georgetown University Press, 1989), 111–30. Notably, on the recent death of Hans Küng, Curran recounted how Küng visited Curran to support him in the isolating effects of the investigation, see Charles E. Curran, "Charles Curran Remembers Hans Küng," *National Catholic Reporter*, August 9, 2021, https://www.ncronline.org/news/people/charles-curran-remembers-hans-kung.

26. Charles E. Curran and Robert E. Hunt, *Dissent in and for the Church* (Kansas City: Sheed and Ward, 1969); Curran, ed., *Contraception: Authority and Dissent* (New York: Herder and Herder, 1969); Curran and Richard McCormick, eds., *Dissent in the Church: Readings in Moral Theology No. 6* (Mahwah NJ: Paulist Press, 1987); Hans Küng and Jürgen Moltmann, eds., *The Right to Dissent, Concilium* 158, no. 8 (1982).

27. Richard McCormick, "Chill Factor in Contemporary Moral Theology," in *The Critical Calling*, 71–94.

28. Benedict M. Ashley, "The Chill Factor in Moral Theology," *The Linacre Quarterly* 57, no. 4 (1980): 67–77.

29. See Bradford Hinze, "A Decade of Disciplining Theologians," *Horizons* 37, no. 1 (2010): 92–126. See also Richard Gaillardetz, ed., *When the Magisterium Intervenes: The Magisterium and Theologians in Today's Church* (Collegeville, MN: Liturgical Press, 2012).

30. Margaret Farley, *Just Love: A Framework for Christian Sexual Ethics* (New York: Continuum, 2006).

31. "Notification on the Book *Just Love: A Framework for Christian Sexual Ethics* by Sr. Margaret A. Farley, RSM" (June 4, 2012), https://www.vatican.va/roman_curia/congregations/cfaith/documents/rc_con_cfaith_doc_20120330_nota-farley_en.html.

32. I conclude my *History of Catholic Moral Theology in the Twentieth Century* with a summary of Farley's work as an emblematic indication of how justice now enters into the heart of theological ethics, 221–22.

33. Grawemeyer Award in Religion, Louisville Seminary, accessed May 20, 2021, https://www.lpts.edu/friends/grawemeyer/.

34. "Response to the Vatican's Notification Regarding Just Love: A Framework for Christian Sexual Ethics," *Prnewswire*, June 4, 2012, https://www.prnewswire.com/news-releases/response-to-vaticans-notification-regarding-just-love-a-framework-for-christian-sexual-ethics-156956095.html.

35. Antonio Autiero, "The Human Being between Polis and Ekklesia," *Studia Liturgica* 38, no. 1 (2008): 17–30, at 24.

36. Tobias Winright, "L'Affaire Farley and the Ongoing Chill in Contemporary Moral Theology," *Catholic Moral Theology*, June 4, 2012, https://catholicmoraltheology.com/laffaire-farley-and-the-ongoing-chill-factor-in-contemporary-moral-theology/.

37. "Academics React to Move against Farley's Book," *National Catholic Reporter*, June 4, 2012, https://www.ncronline.org/news/vatican/academics-react-vatican-move-against-farley-book.

38. Charles E. Curran, "Moral Theology in the United States 1966–1985," in *Sixty Years of Moral Theology* (Mahwah, NJ: Paulist Press, 2020), 141–162, at 153–54.

39. University of Notre Dame, "The Idea of the University" (July 23, 1967), http://archives.nd.edu/episodes/visitors/lol/idea.htm.

40. Curran, "Moral Theology in the United States," 156.

41. "Academics React to Move against Farley's Book."

42. Todd A. Salzman and Michael G. Lawler, *The Sexual Person: Toward a Renewed Catholic Anthropology* (Washington, DC: Georgetown University Press, 2008); United States Conference of Catholic Bishops, Committee on Doctrine, "Inadequacies in the Theological Methodology and Conclusions of *The Sexual Person: Toward a Renewed Catholic Anthropology* by Todd A. Salzman and Michael G. Lawler," September 15, 2010.

43. Todd A. Salzman and Michael G. Lawler, "Magisterium, Theologians, and the Need for Dialogue," *Horizons* 46, no. 1 (2019): 79–112, at 79. They refer explicitly to the work, Bradford Hinze, *Practices of Dialogue in the Roman Catholic Church: Aims and Obstacles, Lessons and Laments* (New York: Continuum, 2006).

44. For example, from just the United States, see Lisa Sowle Cahill, *Between the Sexes: Foundations for a Christian Ethics of Sexuality* (New York: Paulist Press, 1985); *Sex, Gender and Christian Ethics* (New York: Cambridge University Press, 1996); Florence Caffrey Bourg, *Where Two or Three Are Gathered: Christian Families as Domestic Churches* (Notre Dame, IN: University of Notre Dame Press, 2004); David Matzko McCarthy, *Sex and Love in the Home: A Theology of the Household* (London: SCM, 2004); Julie Hanlon Rubio, *Family Ethics* (Washington, DC: Georgetown University Press, 2010); Charles Curran and Julie Hanlon Rubio, eds., *Marriage: Readings in Moral Theology Number 15* (Mahwah, NJ: Paulist Press, 2009); Jason King and Julie Hanlon Rubio, eds., *Sex, Love, and Families: Catholic Perspectives* (Collegeville, MN: Liturgical Press, 2020).

45. Charles Curran, "Catholic Social and Sexual Teaching: A Methodological Comparison," *Theology Today* 45, no. 4 (1988): 425–40.

46. Lisa Sowle Cahill, *Between the Sexes.*

47. Cahill, "Sexual Ethics: A Feminist Biblical Perspective," *Interpretation* 49, no. 1 (1995): 5–16.

48. Lisa Sowle Cahill, *Women and Sexuality* (New York: Paulist Press, 1992), 78.

49. Lisa Sowle Cahill, *Sex, Gender and Christian Ethics*, 110.

50. See also Lisa Sowle Cahill, "Community and Universals: A Misplaced Debate in Christian Ethics," *Annual of the Society of Christian Ethics* 18 (1998): 3–12.

51. Lisa Sowle Cahill, *Family: A Christian Social Perspective* (Minneapolis: Fortress Press, 2000); "Feminist Theology, Catholicism, and the Family," in *Full of Hope: Critical Social Perspectives on Theology*, ed. Magdala Thompson (Mahwah, NJ: Paulist Press, 2003).

52. Lisa Sowle Cahill, "Marriage: Developments in Catholic Theology and Ethics," *Theological Studies* 64, no. 1 (2003): 78–105; "Equality in Marriage; The Biblical Challenge," in *Marriage in the Catholic Tradition: Scripture, Tradition, and Experience*, ed. Todd A. Salzman, Thomas M. Kelly, and John J. O'Keefe (New York: Crossroad, 2004), 66–75.

53. Lisa Sowle Cahill, "On Being a Catholic Feminist" (Bannan Center for Jesuit Education, Santa Clara University, 2003).

54. Lisa Sowle Cahill, "Catholic Sexual Ethics and the Dignity of the Person: A Double Message," *Theological Studies* 50, no. 1 (1989): 120–50; "Feminist Ethics," *Theological Studies* 51, no. 1 (1990): 49–64.

55. Cahill, *Bioethics and the Common Good* (Milwaukee: Marquette University Press, 2003).

56. Cahill, ed., *Genetics, Theology, Ethics*; "Bioethics," *Theological Studies* 67, no. 1 (2006): 120–42; "Bioethics, Relationships, and Participation in the Common Good," in *Health and Human Flourishing: Religion, Medicine and Moral Anthropology*, ed. Carol Taylor and Roberto Dell'Oro (Washington, DC: Georgetown University Press, 2006); "AIDS, Justice and the Common Good," in *Catholic Ethicists on HIV/AIDS Prevention* (hereafter as *CEHP*), ed. James Keenan, assisted by Lisa Sowle Cahill, Jon Fuller, and Kevin Kelly (New York: Continuum, 2000), 282–93; "Realigning Catholic Priorities: Bioethics and the Common Good," *America*, September 13, 2004, 11–13; "Women's Health and Human Flourishing," in *Women's Health Issues*, ed. Elio Sgreccia (Rome: Societa Editrice Universo, 2003), 93–103; "Bioethics, Theology, and Social Change," *Journal of Religious Ethics* 31, no. 3 (2003): 363–98; "Biotech and Justice: Catching Up with the Real World Order," *Hastings Center Report* 34, no. 4 (2003): 33–44.

57. Lisa Sowle Cahill, *Theological Bioethics: Participation, Justice and Change* (Washington, DC: Georgetown University Press, 2005).

58. Lisa Sowle Cahill, "Moral Theology: From Evolutionary to Revolutionary Change," in *Catholic Theological Ethics in the World Church: The Plenary Papers from the First Cross-Cultural Conference on Catholic Theological Ethics* (hereafter, *CTEWC*) (New York: Continuum, 2007), 221–227, at 223.

59. Cahill, "Moral Theology: From Evolutionary to Revolutionary Change," 225.

60. An indispensable resource is Kenneth Himes, *Modern Catholic Social Teaching* (Washington, DC: Georgetown University Press, 2005).

61. Edward Vacek, *Love, Human and Divine: The Heart of Christian Ethics* (Washington, DC: Georgetown University Press, 1994); Timothy Jackson, *The Priority of Love: Christian Charity and Social Justice* (Princeton: Princeton University Press, 2003).

62. James Keenan, "The Problem with Thomas Aquinas's Concept of Sin," *Heythrop Journal* 35 (1994): 401–20.

63. Pope Francis, *Fratelli Tutti* (October 3, 2020), http://www.vatican.va/content/francesco/en/encyclicals/documents/papa-francesco_20201003_enciclica-fratelli-tutti.html.

64. Pope John Paul II, *Salvifici Doloris* (February 11, 1984), http://www.vatican.va/content/john-paul-ii/en/apost_letters/1984/documents/hf_jp-ii_apl_11021984_salvifici-doloris.html.

65. Gustavo Gutiérrez, *A Theology of Liberation: History, Politics, Salvation* (Maryknoll, NY: Orbis, 1971).

66. Gustavo Gutiérrez, "Option for the Poor," in *Mysterium Liberationis: Fundamental Concepts of Liberation Theology*, ed. Ignacio Ellacuría and Jon Sobrino (Maryknoll, NY: Orbis, 1993), 235–50; James Nickoloff, ed., *Gustavo Gutiérrez: Essential Writings* (Maryknoll, NY: Orbis, 1996).

67. Recent work on these structures is significant, see Daniel Daly, *Structures of Virtue and Vice* (Washington, DC: Georgetown University Press, 2021); Daniel Finn, ed., *Moral Agency within Social Structures and Culture: A Primer on Critical Realism for Christian Ethics* (Washington, DC: Georgetown University Press, 2020).

68. Gustavo Gutiérrez, *On Job: God Talk and the Suffering of the Innocent* (Maryknoll, NY: Orbis, 1987).

69. Gustavo Gutiérrez, *Las Casas: In Search of the Poor of Jesus Christ* (Maryknoll, NY: Orbis, 1993); see Helen Rand Parish, María Concepta Maciel, and Gustavo Gutiérrez, *Bartolomé de las Casas: Liberation of the Oppressed* (Berkeley: University of California Press, 1984).

70. Leonardo Boff and Clodovis Boff, *Introducing Liberation Theology* (Maryknoll, NY: Orbis, 1987); Leonardo Boff, *Jesus Christ Liberator: A Critical Christology for Our Times* (Maryknoll, NY: Orbis, 1978); *Liberating Grace* (Maryknoll, NY: Orbis, 1979); Clodovis Boff, "Epistemology and Method of the Theology of Liberation," in Ellacuría and Sobrino, *Mysterium Liberationis*, 57–84.

71. Enrique Dussel, *Ethics and the Theology of Liberation* (Maryknoll, NY: Orbis, 1978); *The History of the Church in Latin America: Colonialism to Liberation (1492–1979)* (Grand Rapids, MI: Eerdmans, 1981); *Etica de la liberacion en la edad de la globalizacion y la exclusion* (Madrid: Trotta, 1998); Roberto Goizueta, *Liberation Method and Dialogue: Enrique Dussel and North American Theological Discourse* (Atlanta: Scholar's Press, 1987).

72. Jon Sobrino, "Theology in a Suffering World," in *The Principle of Mercy* (Maryknoll, NY: Orbis, 1994), 27–46. Stephen Pope, ed., *Hope and Solidarity: Jon Sobrino's Challenge to Christian Theology* (Maryknoll, NY: Orbis, 2008).

73. Jon Sobrino, *Christology at the Crossroads* (Maryknoll, NY: Orbis, 1976); *Jesus the Liberator: A Historical-Theological Reading of Jesus of Nazareth* (Maryknoll, NY: Orbis, 1993).

74. Jon Sobrino, "The Central Position of the Reign of God in Liberation Theology," in Ellacuría and Sobrino, *Mysterium Liberationis*, 350–487; "Systematic Christology: Jesus Christ, the Absolute Mediator of the Reign of God," 440–61; Sobrino, *No Salvation Outside the Poor: Prophetic-Utopian Essays* (Maryknoll, NY: Orbis, 2008).

75. Jon Sobrino, "Spirituality and the Following of Jesus," in Ellacuría and Sobrino, *Mysterium Liberationis*, 677–701.

76. Edward Schillebeeckx, *Christ* (New York: Seabury Press, 1980), 675.

77. Schillebeeckx, *Christ*, 725.

78. Schillebeeckx, *Christ*, 724–25.

79. Schillebeeckx, *Christ*, 728.

80. Mary Catherine Hilkert, *Speaking with Authority* (Mahwah, NJ: Paulist Press, 2001), 126.

81. See also Kathleen McManus, *Unbroken Communion: The Place and Meaning of Suffering in the Theology of Edward Schillebeeckx* (New York: Rowman and Littlefield, 2003); Robin Ryan, *God and the Mystery of Human Suffering: A Theological Conversation across the Ages* (Mahwah, NJ: Paulist Press, 2011).

82. Johann Baptist Metz, *Poverty of the Spirit* (New York: Paulist Press, 1968).

83. Dorothee Sölle, *Suffering* (Philadelphia: Fortress Press, 1975).

84. Robert Gascoigne, "Suffering and Theological Ethics: Intimidation and Hope," in *CTEWC*, 163–66, at 163.

85. Laurenti Magesa, "Locating the Church among the Wretched of the Earth," in *CTEWC* 49–56, at 50. See Peter Kanyandago, ed., *Marginalized Africa: An International Perspective* (Nairobi: Paulines Publications Africa, 2002).

86. Ronaldo Zacharias, "Dreaming of a New Moral Theology for Brazil," in *CTEWC*, 116–23, at 117.

87. Vimal Tirimanna, "Globalization Needs to Count Human Persons," in *CTEWC*, 245–52, at 246.

88. Antonio Autiero, "On the Ecclesial Vocation of the Moral Theologian: Some Significant Shifts of Emphasis," in *The Catholic Ethicist in the Local Church*, ed. Antonio Autiero and Laurenti Magesa (Maryknoll, NY: Orbis, 2018), 94–107, at 102.

89. Kenneth Himes, "Catholic Social Teaching That Is Both Local and Universal," in Autiero and Magesa, *The Catholic Ethicist*, 66–78, at 67.

90. George Kodithottam, "Justice as Healing: Reflections on the Understanding of Justice, Based on an Indian Experience of Criminal Justice Delivery in a Rural Non-Christian Community," in Autiero and Magesa, *The Catholic Ethicist*, 212–21; Mary Jo Iozzio, "Counting the Uncounted: A Theo-Ethical Imperative for the Theological Ethicist in Raising a Challenge to the Widespread and Unrecognized Practices of Exclusion," in *The Catholic Ethicist*, 247–258. For a fine portrait of the contemporary ethicist, see Lindsay Marcellus, "The Emerging Vocation of the Moral Theologian: Commonalities across Contexts," in Autiero and Magesa, *The Catholic Ethicist*, 293–311.

91. James Keenan, *A History of Catholic Moral Theology in the Twentieth Century: From Confessing Sins to Liberating Consciences* (New York: Continuum, 2010), 197–99.

92. Marciano Vidal, "La preferencia por el pobre, criterio de moral," *Studia Moralia* 20, no. 2 (1982): 277–304; *Feminismo y ética. Cómo "feminizar" la moral* (Madrid: PPC, 2000).

93. Enda McDonagh, *Immersed in Mystery: Enroute to Theology* (Dublin: Veritas, 2007), 43; see also *Gift and Call: Towards a Christian Theology of Morality* (Dublin: Gill and Macmillan, 1975); *Doing the Truth: The Quest for Moral Theology* (Notre Dame, IN: University of Notre Dame Press, 1979); *Vulnerable to the Holy: In Faith, Morality and Art* (Dublin: St. Columba's, 2004); "The Good News in Moral Theology, of Hospitality, Healing, and Hope," in *Moral Theology for the Twenty-First Century*, 80–86; "The Reign of God: Signposts for Catholic Theology," in *CEHP*, 317–23.

94. Kevin Kelly, *New Directions in Moral Theology* (London: Geoffrey Chapman, 1992); *New Directions in Sexual Morality: Moral Theology and the Challenge of AIDS* (London: Geoffrey Chapman, 1998); *From a Parish Base* (London: Darton, Longman and Todd, 1999); "A Moral Theologian Faces the New Millennium in a Time of AIDS," in *CEHP*, 324–32.

95. Enrico Chiavacci, *Dal dominio alla pace. Scritti sulla globalizzazione* (Molfetta: La Meridiana, 1993); "Globalization and Justice: New Horizons for Moral Theology," in *CTEWC*, 239–44.

96. Antonio Autiero, *Das Fremde, das Andere und das Selbst: Provokationen an die theologische Ethik* (Münster: Antrittsvorlesung, 1993).

97. Antonio Autiero, "L'etica di fronte alla malattia. Il paradigma della AIDS," in *La Coscienza Morale Oggi*, ed. Marian Nalepa and Terrence Kennedy (Rome: Edacalf, 1987), 599–615; "Anthropologische und ethische Überlegungen zum Thema AIDS," in *Prüfsteine medizinischer Ethik*, ed. H. R. Zielinski (Grevenbroich: AMEG, 1988), 51–85; "Quale etica per una sessualitá al positivo?" in *AIDS e assistenza domiciliare. Esperienze a confronto*, ed. A. Cargnel (Rome: Sedac, 1995), 291–97; "AIDS. Quale sfida per l'etica?," *Rivista di teologia morale* 80 (1988): 13–19. See also "L'etica

della salute. Tra diritti negati e dovere di solidarietá," *Global Bioethics* 3 (1993): 157–63.

98. Antonio Autiero, "Essere nel mondo. Ecologia dei bisogni," in *Corso di morale*, vol. 2, ed. Tullo Goffi and G. Piana (Brescia: Queriniana, 1983), 97–125; "Ambiti e prospettive dell'etica medica," *Studia moralia* 2 (1983): 405–15; "Le sfide etiche del III millennio: il paradigma dell'ecologia," *Problemi di Bioetica* 7 (1990): 39–49; "Esiste un'etica ambientale?" in *Diritto pubblico dell'ambiente*, ed. V. Domenicelli (Padua: CEDAM, 1996), 7–27; "Etiche per la sostenibilità," in *Per la sostenibilitá: Etica ambientale e antropologia*, ed. Simone Morandini (Padua: Gregoriana, 2007), 111–19.

99. James Keenan, "Prophetic Pragmatism and Descending to Matters of Detail," *Theological Studies* 79, no. 1 (2018): 128–45.

100. Albert R. Jonsen and Stephen Toulmin, *The Abuse of Casuistry: A History of Moral Reasoning* (Berkeley: University of California Press, 1988).

101. See also Malcolm Gladwell's work on this in *Revisionist History*, "The Standard Case" (July 18, 2019); "Dr. Rock's Taxonomy" (July 25, 2019); and "Descending into the Particular" (August 1, 2019), https://podcasts.apple.com/us/podcast/id1119389968.

102. Edmund Leites, *Conscience and Casuistry in Early Modern Europe* (New York: Cambridge University Press, 1988); James Keenan and Thomas Shannon, eds., *The Context of Casuistry* (Washington, DC: Georgetown University Press, 1995); Keenan, "The Return of Casuistry," *Theological Studies* 57, no. 1 (1996): 123–39.

103. James Keenan, "Making a Case for Casuistry: AIDS and Its Ethical Challenges," in *Hva er Kasuistikk?: Om moralsk laering og refleksjon i tilknytning til forbilder og eksempler*, ed. Jon Wetlesen (Oslo: Oslo University Press, 1998), 163–86; "Applying the Seventeenth Century Casuistry of Accommodation to HIV Prevention," *Theological Studies* 60, no. 3 (1999): 492–512.

104. Carlo Ginzburg with Lucio Biasiori, eds., *A Historical Approach to Casuistry: Norms and Exceptions in a Comparative Perspective* (London: Bloomsbury Academic, 2020).

105. Christiana Z. Peppard and Andrea Vicini, eds., *Just Sustainability: Technology, Ecology and Resource Extraction* (Maryknoll, NY: Orbis, 2015). See their respective work in the field: Peppard, *Just Water: Theology, Ethics, and the Global Water Crisis* (Maryknoll, NY: Orbis, 2014); Vicini, "New Insights in Environmental and Sustainable Ethics," *Asian Horizons: Dharmaram Journal of Theology* 6, no. 2 (2012): 309–28.

106. John Sniegocki, "The Political Economy of Sustainability," in Peppard and Vicini, *Just Sustainability*, 57–68.

107. Mark Graham, "The Unsavory Gamble of Industrial Agriculture," in Peppard and Vicini, *Just Sustainability*, 105–16.

108. Teresia Hinga, "Of Empty Granaries, Stolen Harvests, and the Weapon of Grain: Applied Ethics in Search of Sustainable Food Security," in Peppard and Vicini, *Just Sustainability*, 94–104.

109. Jacquineau Azétsop, "Health Systems Challenges, National HIV/AIDS Response, and Public Health Policy in Chad: Ethical and Efficiency Requirements for Sustainable Health Systems," in Peppard and Vicini, *Just Sustainability*, 131–44.

110. Peter Knox, "Sustainable Mining in South Africa: A Concept in Search of a Theory," in Peppard and Vicini, *Just Sustainability*, 117–31.

111. Ann Marie Mealey, "Feminism and Ecology," in Peppard and Vicini, *Just Sustainability*, 182–93.

112. Nancy M. Rourke, "A Catholic Virtues Ecology," in Peppard and Vicini, *Just Sustainability*, 194–204.

113. Christine Firer Hinze, "Unleashing Catholicism's Stranded Assets in the Fight for Just Sustainability," in Peppard and Vicini, *Just Sustainability*, 205–22.

114. Daniel R. DiLeo, "Fostering Just Sustainability through Ignatian Spirituality," in Peppard and Vicini, *Just Sustainability*, 250–58.

115. For more foundational material on each of the continents, see my *A History of Catholic Moral Theology in the Twentieth Century*, 197–240.

116. Marciano Vidal, "Is Morality Based on Autonomy Compatible with the Ethics of Liberation?" in *Ethics of Liberation or the Liberation of Ethics*, ed. Dietmar Mieth and Jacques Pohier (London: T and T Clark, 1984), 80–86; Dietmar Mieth, "Autonomy or Liberation—Two Paradigms of Christian Ethics?" in Meith and Pohier, *Ethics of Liberation or the Liberation of Ethics*, 87–93.

117. Tony Mifsud, *Moral de Discernimento* (Santiago de Chile: San Pablo, 1987); *Ethos Cotidiano: Un Proceso de discernimento* (Santiago de Chile: Universidad Alberto Hurtado, 2006); "The Development of a Liberation Ethic in the Documents of the Church since Vatican II," in Mieth and Pohier, *Ethics of Liberation*, 48–53.

118. Francisco Moreno Rejón, *Salvar la Vida de los Pobres: Aportes a la Teología Moral* (Lima: CEPA 1986); *Moral Theology from the Poor: Moral Challenges of the Theology of Liberation* (Quezon City: Claretian Press, 1988); "Fundamental Moral Theology in the Theology of Liberation," in Ellacuría and Sobrino, *Mysterium Liberationis*, 210–21; "Seeking the Kingdom and Its Justice: the Development of the Ethic of Liberation," in Mieth and Pohier, *Ethics of Liberation*, 35–41.

119. Antonio Moser and Bernardino Leers, *Moral Theology: Dead Ends and Alternatives* (Maryknoll, NY: Orbis, 1990); Antonio Moser, "The

Representation of God in the Ethic of Liberation," in Mieth and Pohier, *Ethics of Liberation*, 42–47.

120. Rogue Junges, *Evento Cristo e Ação Humana. Temas fundamentais da Ética teológica* (São Leopoldo: Unisinos, 2001).

121. Marcio Fabri dos Anjos, "Teología de la Liberación," in *Diccionario Latinoamericano de Bioética*, ed. Juan Carlos Tealdi (Bogota: UNESCO, 2008), 12–14; "Challenges of Pluralism to Moral Theology," *CTEWC* 228–36; "Power and Vulnerability: A Contribution of Developing Countries to the Ethical Debate on Genetics," in *Genetics, Theology, and Ethics: An Interdisciplinary Conversation*, ed. Lisa Sowle Cahill (New York: Crossroad, 2005), 137–57; "Bioética em perspectiva de libertação," in *Bioética: poder e justiça*, ed. Volnei Garrafa and Leo Pessini (São Paulo: SBB & Loyola & S. Camilo, 2003), 455–65; "Power, Ethics and the Poor in Human Genetic Research," in *The Ethics of Genetic Engineering*, ed. Lisa Sowle Cahill and Maureen Junker Kenny (Maryknoll, NY: Orbis, 1998), 73–82; "Medical Ethics in the Developing World: A Liberation Theology Perspective," *Journal of Medicine and Philosophy* 21, no. 6 (1996): 629–37.

122. Ivone Gebara, "Option for the Poor as an Option for Poor Women," in *Women, Work, and Poverty*, ed. Elisabeth Schüssler Fiorenza (Maryknoll, NY: Orbis, 1987), 110–17; "Women Doing Theology in Latin America," in *Through Her Eyes: Women's Theology from Latin America*, ed. Elsa Tamez (Maryknoll, NY: Orbis, 1989), 37–48; "Women and Spirituality: A Latin American Perspective," *The Way* 38, no. 3 (1998): 240–51; *As incômodas filhas de Eva na Igreja da América Latina*, 2nd ed. (São Paulo: Paulinas, 1990); *Longing for Running Water: Ecofeminism and Liberation* (Minneapolis: Fortress Press, 1999); *Out of the Depths: Women's Experience of Evil and Salvation* (Minneapolis: Augsburg-Fortress, 2002).

123. Ivone Gebara and Maria Clara Bingemer, *A mulher faz Teologia* (Petrópolis: Vozes, 1986); "Mary," in Ellacuría and Sobrino, *Mysterium Liberationis*, 482–96; *Mary: Mother of God, Mother of the Poor* (Eugene, OR: Wipf & Stock, 2004).

124. Maria Clara Bingemer, *Latin American Theology: Roots and Branches* (Maryknoll, NY: Orbis, 2016); *Cuerpo de mujer y experiência de Dios. Sentir y experimentar a Dios de un modo femenino* (Buenos Aires: San Benito, 2007); *Simone Weil: la fuerza y la debilidad del amor* (Pamplona: Verbo Divino, 2009).

125. Ana María Trepedino and Margarida L. Ribeiro Brandao, "Women and the Theology of Liberation," in Ellacuría and Sobrino, *Mysterium Liberationis*, 221–31.

126. Ana María Bidegain, "Women and the Theology of Liberation," in Tamez, *Through Her Eyes*, 15–36.

127. María Pilar Aquino, *Our Cry For Life: Feminist Theology from Latin America* (Maryknoll, NY: Orbis, 1993); "Women's Contribution to Theology in Latin America," in *Feminist Ethics and the Catholic Moral Tradition*, ed. Charles Curran, Margaret Farley, Richard McCormick (Mahwah, NJ: Paulist Press, 1996), 90–119 (hereafter, *Feminist Ethics*); with Elsa Tamez, *Teología Feminista Latinoamericana* (Quito: Ediciones Abya-Yala, 1998); with Roberto Goizueta, ed., *Theology: Expanding the Borders* (Mystic, CT: Twenty-Third Publications, 1998); with Daisy L. Machado and Jeanette Rodríguez, eds., *A Reader in Latina Feminist Theology: Religion and Justice* (Austin: University of Texas Press, 2002).

128. Ada María Isasi-Díaz, "Defining our *Proyecto Histórico*: *Mujerista* Strategies for Liberation," Curran, Farley, and McCormick, *Feminist Ethics*, 120–35, at 121; *En la Lucha—In the Struggle: A Hispanic Women's Liberation Theology* (Minneapolis: Augsburg Fortress, 1993, 2003); *La Lucha Continues* (Maryknoll, NY: Orbis, 2004). See Curran, "Ada María Isasi-Díaz," in *Diverse Voices*, 177–96.

129. Two very different works, with the same title cover the events from Medellín to Puebla: Alfonso Lopez Trujillo, *De Medellín a Puebla* (Madrid: Editorial Católica, 1980); Enrique Dussel, *De Medellín a Puebla: Una década de sangre y esperanza, 1968–1979* (Madrid: Edicol, 1979); see also Paul Sigmund, "The Birth of Liberation Theology: Medellín and Beyond," "The Battle of Puebla," *Liberation Theology at the Crossroads* (New York: Oxford University Press, 1990), 28–39, 93–107.

130. See Jon Sobrino, *The Principle of Mercy: Taking the Crucified People from the Cross* (Maryknoll, NY: Orbis, 1994); *Witnesses to the Kingdom: The Martyrs of El Salvador and the Crucified Peoples* (Maryknoll, NY: Orbis, 2003).

131. Cardinal Joseph Ratzinger, "Instruction on Certain Aspects of the *Theology of Liberation*," August 6, 1984, http://www.vatican.va/roman_curia/congregations/cfaith/documents/rc_con_cfaith_doc_19840806_theology-liberation_en.html.

132. Cardinal Joseph Ratzinger, "Instruction on *Christian Freedom and Liberation*," March 22, 1986, http://www.vatican.va/roman_curia/congregations/cfaith/documents/rc_con_cfaith_doc_19860322_freedom-liberation_en.html.

133. Congregation for the Doctrine of the Faith, "Notification on the Book *Church: Charism and Power; Essay on Militant Ecclesiology* by Father Leonardo Boff, O.F.M.," March 11, 1985, *AAS* 77 (1985): 756–62.

134. Congregation for the Doctrine of the Faith, "Notification on the works of Father Jon Sobrino SJ," November 26, 2006, http://www.vatican.va/roman_curia/congregations/cfaith/documents/rc_con_cfaith_doc_20061126_notification-sobrino_en.html.

135. Emilce Cuda, ed., *Hacia una Ética de Participación y Esperanza: Congreso LatinoAmericano de Ética Teológica* (Bogotá: Javeriana University, 2017).

136. Dávila, "Discussing Racial Justice in Light of 2016: Black Lives Matter, a Trump Presidency, and the Continued Struggle for Racial Justice," *Journal of Religious Ethics* 45, no. 4 (2017): 761–92; "Public Theology as Bridge Building," *Horizons* (Spring 2017): 367–73.

137. Mawuto R. Afan, "The Main 'Building Sites' of Ethics in West Africa," in *CTEWC*, 39–48.

138. Engelbert Mveng, "Impoverishment and Liberation: A Theological Approach for Africa and the Third World," in *Paths of African Theology*, ed. Rosino Gibellini (Maryknoll, NY: Orbis, 1994), 154–63; *Théologie, Libération et Cultures Africaines: Dialogue sur l'anthropologie Négro-africaine* (Yaoundé, Cameroon: Présence Africaine, 1996); "La théologie africaine de la libération," *Theologies of the Third World: Convergences and Differences* 219 (1988): 31–51.

139. Laurenti Magesa, "Locating the Church among the Wretched of the Earth," in *CTEWC*, 49–56, at 50.

140. Meinrad Hebga, "Engelbert Mveng: A Pioneer of African Theology," in *African Theology in the 21st Century: The Contribution of the Pioneers*, ed. Bénézet Bujo and Juvénqal Ilunga Muya (Nairobi: Paulines Publications, 2003), 39–46 (hereafter, *African Theology 1*); Yvon Elenga, *Père Engelbert Mveng SJ: un pionnier. Recueil d'hommages à l'occasion du dixième anniversaire de sa mort* (Kinshasa: Editions Loyola-Canisius, 2005).

141. Y. Assogba, *Jean-Marc Ela: Le sociologue et théologien africain en boubou* (Paris: L'Harmattan, 1999).

142. See above, *African Theology 1.*

143. Emmanuel Ntakarutimana, "Msgr. Tharcisse Tshibangu: Champion of an 'African-coloured' Theology," in *African Theology 1*, 47–63.

144. This debate appeared in "Débat sur la 'Théologie Africaine,'" *Revue du Clergé Africain* 15 (1960): 333–52; reprinted in *African Theology 1*, 183–99.

145. Bujo, "Introduction to the Tshibangu and Vanneste Debate," *African Theology 1*, 179–82.

146. Placide Tempels, *La Philosophie Bantoue* (Elisabethville, Congo: Louvania, 1945); *Bantu Philosophy* (Paris: Présence Africaine, 1959).

147. John Mbiti, *African Religion and Philosophy* (New York: Praeger Publishers, 1969).

148. John Mbiti, *Concepts of God in Africa* (London: SPCK, 1970).

149. John Mbiti, *Love and Marriage in Africa* (London: Longman, 1973).

150. John Mbiti, *Introduction to African Religion* (Oxford: Heinemann International Literature and Texts, 1975).

151. Patrick Watchege, "Charles Nyamiti: The Vibrant Pioneer of African Inculturated Theology," in *African Theology: The Contribution of the Pioneers*, vol. 2 (Nairobi: Paulines Edition, 2006), 149–62 (hereafter, *African Theology 2*); Mika Vähäkangas, *In Search of Foundations for African Catholicism: Charles Nyamiti's Theological Methodology* (Leiden: Brill, 1999).

152. Charles Nyamiti, "African Christologies Today," in *Faces of Jesus in Africa*, ed. Robert Schreiter (Maryknoll, NY: Orbis, 1991), 3–23; *Some Contemporary Models of African Ecclesiology: A Critical Assessment in the Light of Biblical and Church Teaching* (Nairobi: CUEA Publications, 2007); *Jesus Christ, the Ancestor of Humankind: An Essay on African Christology* (Nairobi: CUEA Publications, 2006).

153. Peter Schineller, *A Handbook on Inculturation* (Mahwah, NJ: Paulist Press, 1990); Alward Shorter, *Toward a Theology of Inculturation* (Maryknoll, NY: Orbis, 1995).

154. Bénézet Bujo, *African Christian Morality at the Age of Inculturation* (Nairobi: St. Paul, 1990); *African Theology in Its Social Context* (Maryknoll, NY: Orbis, 1992); Michael Kirwen, ed., *African Cultural Knowledge: Themes and Embedded Beliefs* (Nairobi: MIAS Books, 2005).

155. Juvénal Ilunga Muya, "Bénézet Bujo: The Awakening of a Systematic and Authentically African Thought," *African Theology 1*, 107–49, at 130–31.

156. Bénézet Bujo, *Moralautonomie und Normenfindung bei Thomas von Aquin* (Vienna: Schöningh, 1979).

157. Bénézet Bujo, *The Ethical Dimension of Community: The African Model and the Dialogue between North and South* (Nairobi: St. Paul, 1997), 15–89; Elochukwu E. Uzukwu, *A Listening Church: Autonomy and Communion in African Churches* (Maryknoll, NY: Orbis, 1996); William O'Neill, "African Moral Theology," *Theological Studies* 62, no. 1 (2001): 122–39.

158. Bénézet Bujo, *Foundations of an African Ethic: Beyond the Universal Claims of Western Morality* (New York: Crossroad, 2001), 185–86.

159. Paulinus Ikechukwu Odozor raises critical questions about Bujo's approach to inculturation in "An African Moral Theology of Inculturation," *Theological Studies* 69, no. 3 (2008): 583–609.

160. Laurenti Magesa, "Recognizing the Reality of African Religion in Tanzania," in *CEHP*, 76–84.

161. Emmanuel Katongole, "AIDS, Africa, and the 'Age of Miraculous Medicine,'" in *Applied Ethics in the World Church: The Padua Conference*, ed. Linda Hogan (Maryknoll, NY: Orbis, 2008), 137–46; *A Future for Africa: Critical Essays in Christian Social Imagination* (Scranton: University of Scranton Press, 2005).

162. Bénézet Bujo and Michael Czerny, *AIDS in Africa: Theological Reflections* (Nairobi: Paulines Publications, 2007).

163. Peter Kanyandago, "Is God African? Theological Reflections on the AIDS Scourge," in *Challenges and Prospects of the Church in Africa*, ed. N. W. Ndung'u and P. N. Mwaura (Nairobi: Paulines Publications Africa, 2005), 145–59; Peter Kanyandago, ed., *The Cries of the Poor: Questions and Responses for African Christianity* (Kisubi, Uganda: Marianum Press Ltd, 2002).

164. Paul Chummar, "HIV/AIDS in Africa: A Task for an Inculturated Theological Ethics," in Hogan, *Applied Ethics*, 155–62; Agbonkhianmeghe Orobator, "Ethics of HIV/AIDS Prevention: Paradigms of a New Discourse from an African Perspective," in Hogan, *Applied Ethics*, 147–54.

165. Michael Czerny, ed., *AIDS and the Church in Africa* (Nairobi: Paulines Publications, 2005).

166. Paterne-Auxence Mombé, *Rays of Hope: Managing HIV and AIDS in Africa* (Nairobi: Paulines, 2003, 2008).

167. Ghislain Tshikendwa Matadi, *Suffering, Belief, Hope: The Wisdom of Job for an AIDS-Stricken Africa* (Nairobi: Paulines Publications, 2008).

168. Peter Knox, *AIDS, Ancestors and Salvation: Local Beliefs in Christian Ministry to the Sick* (Nairobi: Paulines Publications, 2008).

169. Paterne A. Mombé, Agbonkhianmeghe E. Orobator, and Dannielle Vela, eds., *AIDS, 30 Years Down the Line...Faith-Based Reflections about the Epidemic in Africa* (Nairobi: Paulines Publications, 2012).

170. Jean-Marc Ela, *Le Cri de l'homme africain* (Paris: Harmattan, 1980); "La Foi des pauvres en acte," *Telema* 35 (July–September 1983): 45–72; *Ma foi d'africain* (Paris: Karthala, 1985); *Afrique, l'irruption des Pauvres* (Paris: Harmattan, 2000); *African Cry* (Eugene, OR: Wipf & Stock, 2005); Bénézet Bujo, "Jean Marc Ela: Champion of a Theology Under the Trees," in *African Theology 2*, 182–214.

171. Jean-Marc Ela, "Christianity and Liberation in Africa," in Gibellini, *Paths of African Theology*, 143–44.

172. Aquiline Tarimo and William O'Neill, "What San Salvador Says to Nairobi: The Liberation Ethics of Ignacio Ellacuría," in *The Love That Produces Hope: The Thought of Ignacio Ellacuría*, ed. Burke and Robert Lassalle-Klein (Collegeville, MN: Liturgical Press, 2006), 237–49. See also Tarimo, *Human Rights, Cultural Differences, and the Church in Africa* (Morogoro, Tanzania: Salvatorian Institute of Philosophy and Theology, 2004); *Applied Ethics and Africa's Social Reconstruction* (Nairobi: Acton Publishers, 2005); "Globalization and African Economic Reforms," in Hogan, *Applied Ethics*, 32–38.

173. Teresia Hinga, "Between Colonialism and Inculturation, Feminist Theologies in Africa," *The Power of Naming: A Concilium Reader in*

Feminist Liberation Theology, ed. Elisabeth Schüssler Fiorenza (Maryknoll, NY: Orbis, 1996), 36–45; "Jesus Christ and the Liberation of Women in Africa," in *The Will to Arise: Women, Tradition, and the Church in Africa*, ed. Mercy Amba Oduyoye and Musimbi R. A. Kanyoro (Maryknoll, NY: Orbis, 2001), 183–95; "Becoming Better Samaritans: Gender, Catholic Social Teaching and the Quest for Alternative Models of Doing Social Justice in Africa," in Hogan, *Applied Ethics*, 85–97.

174. Mercy Amba Oduyoye, *Daughters of Anowa: African Women and Patriarchy* (Maryknoll, NY: Orbis, 1995); Oduyoye, "Feminist Theology in an African Perspective," in Gibellini, *Paths of African Theology*, 166–81; *Introducing African Women's Theology* (Cleveland: Pilgrim Press, 2001).

175. Anne Nasimiyu-Wasike, "Christianity and the African Rituals of Birth and Naming" and "Polygamy: A Feminist Critique," in Oduyoye and Kanyoro, *The Will to Arise*, 40–53, 101–18; Anne Nasimiyu-Wasike, "Christology and an African Woman's Experience," in Schreiter, *Faces of Jesus in Africa*, 70–84.

176. For the relationship between the two, see Emmanuel Martey, *African Theology: Inculturation and Liberation* (Maryknoll, NY: Orbis, 1994).

177. Laurenti Magesa, "Christ the Liberator and Africa Today," in Schreiter, *Faces of Jesus in Africa*, 151–63; Richard Rwiza, "Laurenti Magesa: An African Liberation Theologian," in *African Theology 2*, 231–58.

178. Laurenti Magesa, *African Religion: The Moral Traditions of Abundant Life* (Maryknoll, NY: Orbis, 1997); see subsequently his *What Is Not Sacred: African Spirituality* (Maryknoll, NY: Orbis, 2013).

179. John Mary Waliggo, "African Christology in a Situation of Suffering," in Schreiter, *Faces of Jesus in Africa*, 164–80.

180. John Mary Waliggo, ed., *Inculturation: Its Meaning and Urgency* (Kampala: St. Paul Publications, 1986).

181. John Mary Waliggo, "Inculturation in the Age of Globalization," in *Challenges to Theology in Africa Today: Challenges to Theology in Africa Today*, ed. Patrick Ryan (Nairobi: CUEA Publications, 2002), 95–113; Peter Kanyadago, "John Mary Waliggo: The Theology of John Mary Waliggo," in *African Theology 2*, 215–30.

182. John Mary Waliggo, "A Woman Confronts Social Stigma in Uganda," in *CEHP*, 48–56.

183. John Mary Waliggo, "'The Synod of Hope' at a Time of Crisis in Africa," in *The African Synod: Documents, Reflections, Perspectives*, ed. Maura Browne (Maryknoll, NY: Orbis, 1996), 199–210; see also Sébastien Muyengo Mulombe, "Authenticity and Credibility: Moral Challenges after the African Synod," in *CTEWC*, 57–62; Aylward Shorter, *Christianity and the African Imagination after the Synod Resources for Inculturation* (Nairobi: Paulines Publications, 1998).

184. Agbonkhianmeghe E. Orobator, *From Crisis to Kairos: The Mission of the Church in the Time of HIV/AIDS, Refugees and Poverty* (Nairobi: Paulines Publications, 2005).

185. Agbonkhianmeghe E. Orobator, "Ethics of HIV/AIDS Prevention." For the work of such women, see Margaret Farley, "Partnership in Hope: Gender, Faith, and Responses to HIV/AIDS in Africa," *Journal of Feminist Studies in Religion* 20, no. 1 (2004): 133–48.

186. Agbonkhianmeghe E. Orobator, *The Church as Family: African Ecclesiology in Its Social Context* (Nairobi: Paulines Publications, 2000).

187. Agbonkhianmeghe E. Orobator, *Theology Brewed in an African Pot* (Maryknoll, NY: Orbis, 2008).

188. Elias Opongo and Agbonkhianmeghe Orobator, *Faith Doing Justice: A Manual for Social Analysis, Catholic Social Teachings and Social Justice* (Nairobi: Paulines Africa Publications, 2007).

189. Richard N. Rwiza, *Formation of Christian Conscience in Modern Africa* (Nairobi: Paulines Edition, 2001); Anozie Onyema, *The Moral Significance of African Traditional Religion for Christian Conscience* (Port Harcourt, Nigeria: Lynno Nigeria Coy, 2004).

190. Agbonkhianmeghe E. Orobator, *Religion and Faith in Africa: Confessions of an Animist* (Maryknoll, NY: Orbis, 2018).

191. Karl H. Peschke, *Christian Ethics: Moral Theology in the Light of Vatican II*, vol. 1: *General Moral Theology* (Bangalore: Theological Publications in India, 1991), and *Christian Ethics: Moral Theology in the Light of Vatican II*, vol. 2: *Special Moral Theology* (Bangalore: Theological Publications in India, 1992).

192. Soosai Arokiasamy, *Social Sin: Its Challenges to Christian Life* (Bangalore: Claretian Publications, 1991).

193. Gali Bali, "Rev. Fr. Soosai Arokiasamy, S.J.: Man of the Church," *Vidyajyoti Journal of Theological Reflection* 66 (2002): 567–73, at 570–71. See Arokiasamy, "Traditional Theology and People's Theology: Tasks and Prospects," *Jeevadhara* 136 (1993): 309–18.

194. Soosai Arokiasamy, "Sarvodaya through Antodaya: The Liberation of the Poor in the Contextualization of Morals," *Vidyajyoti Journal of Theological Reflection* 51, no. 11 (November 1987): 545–64; Xavier Ilango, "Morality from a Dalit Perspective," *Jeevadhara* 28, no. 168 (November 1998): 426–40.

195. John Chathanatt, *Gandhi and Gutiérrez: Two Paradigms of Liberative Transformation* (New Delhi: Decent Publishers, 2004).

196. John Chathanatt, "Reclaiming our Vintage Values: This Hour of the Economic History of India," *Jeevadhara* 26, no. 156 (November 1996): 435–56; "An Ethical Analysis of Globalization from an Indian Perspective," in Hogan, *Applied Ethics*, 21–31.

197. Soosai Arokiasamy, "Human Rights: Collective, Societal and Liberational Perspectives," *Jeevadhara* 21 (January 1991): 53–62; John Chathanatt, "Human Rights: A Historical Overview," *Vidyajyoti Journal of Theological Reflection* 31 (February 2001): 11–122.

198. Clement Campos, "Doing Christian Ethics in India's World of Cultural Complexity and Social Inequality," in *CTEWC*, 82–90; "A Catholic Hospital in India Is Asked to Cooperate with an HIV Prevention Program," in *CEHP*, 199–210.

199. Campos, "Doing Christian Ethics in India's World of Cultural Complexity and Social Inequality," in *CTEWC* 84; Keenan, "Clement Campos Bridge-Builder Par Excellence," in *Combining Moral Truth with Pastoral Compassion: The Papers and Articles of Rev. Dr. Clement Campos, C.Ss.R.*, ed. Assisi Saldanha (Bangalore: Redemptorist Publications, 2019). Soosai Arokiasamy, "Liberation Ethics of Ecology," *Jeevadhara* 18, no. 103 (1988): 32–39.

200. Agnes Brazal, "Globalization and Catholic Theological Ethics: A Southeast Asian Perspective," in *CTEWC*, 74–82.

201. Fausto Gomez, "Globalization: Ethical and Christian Perspective," *Religious Life Asia* 3, no. 2 (April–June 2001): 45–63; see Dominador Bombongan Jr., "From Dependency to Globalization: A Changed Context for Liberation Theology," *Hapag* 1, no. 2 (2004): 33–63.

202. Fausto Gomez, "The Holy Eucharist and Commitment to Justice and Solidarity," *Philippiniana Sacra* 22, no. 66 (September–December 1987): 403–20.

203. Fausto Gomez, "St. Thomas Aquinas: Justice, Property and the Poor," *Philippiniana Sacra* 30, no. 89 (May–August 1995): 251–76.

204. Ronaldo Tuazon, "Narrating Christian Ethics from the Margins," *Hapág* 4 (2007): 27–60.

205. Ma. Christina Astorga, "Culture, Religion, and Moral Vision: A Theological Discourse on the Filipino People Power Revolution of 1986," *Theological Studies* 67, no. 3 (2006): 567–601.

206. Agnes Brazal and Andrea Lizares Si, eds., *Body and Sexuality* (Quezon City: Ateneo de Manila, 2007).

207. Ma. Christina Astorga, "The Feminization of AIDS in the Philippines," in *Calling for Justice throughout the World: Catholic Women Theologians on the HIV/AIDS Pandemic*, ed. Mary Jo Iozzio with Mary Doyle Roche and Elsie Miranda (New York: Continuum, 2009), 157–66.

208. Agnes Brazal and Daniel Pilario, "Disciplines, Interdisciplinarity, and Theology," *Hapág* 4 (2007): 5–25.

209. Agnes Brazal, "Information, Sex Education, and Church Intervention in Public Policy in the Philippines," in Iozzio, Roche, and Miranda, *Calling for Justice throughout the World*, 61–67.

210. Osamu Takeuchi, *Conscience and Personality: A New Understanding of Conscience and Its Inculturation in Japanese Moral Theology* (Chiba, Japan: Kyoyusha, 2003).

211. Haruko K. Okano, *Die Stellung Der Frau Im Shinto* (Wiesbaden: Otto Harrassowitz, 1976).

212. Haruko K. Okano, "Moral Responsibility in the Japanese Context: A Perspective from Feminist Theology," in *Für die Freiheit verantwortlich: Festschrift fur Karl-Wilhelm Merks zum 65. Geburtstag*, ed. Jan Jans (Freiburg: Herder, 2004), 162–69, at 167, 168, respectively.

213. Yiu Sing Lúcás Chan, *Biblical Ethics in the 21st Century: Developments, Emerging Consensus, and Future Directions* (Mahwah, NJ: Paulist Press, 2013).

214. Yiu Sing Lúcás Chan, *The Ten Commandments and the Beatitudes: Biblical Studies and Ethics for Real Life* (Lanham, MD: Rowman and Littlefield, 2012).

215. Yiu Sing Lúcás Chan, "Boaz as a Model of Hospitality for Community Rebuilding in the Postexilic Period and the Modern World," *Budhi* 10, no. 1 (2006): 21–46; "The Hebrew Bible and the Discourse on Migration: A Reflection on the Virtue of Hospitality in the Book of Ruth," *Asian Horizons* 8, no. 4 (2014): 665–79; see James Keenan, "Hospitality: Interpreting Lúcás Chan's Work through a Timely, Biblical Virtue from the Book of Ruth," in *Bridging Scripture and Moral Theology: Essays in Dialogue with Yiu Sing Lúcás Chan, S.J.*, ed. Michael Cover, John Thiede, and Joshua Burns (Lanham, MD: Lexington Books, 2019), 3–22.

216. Lúcás Chan, "The Bible and Theological Ethics: 3D," *Theological Studies* 75, no. 1 (2014): 112–28.

217. Lúcás Chan and James Keenan, "Bridging Christian Ethics and Confucianism through Virtue Ethics," *Chinese Cross Currents* 5, no. 3 (2007): 74–85; Yiu Sing Lúcás Chan, "As West Meets East: Reading Xunzi's A Discussion of Rites through the Lens of Contemporary Western Ritual Theories," in *"Ahme nach, was du vollziehst": Positionsbestimmungen zum Verhältnis von Liturgie und Ethik*, ed. Martin Stuflesser and Stephan Winter (Regensburg: Friedrich Pustet, 2009), 101–20.

218. Yiu Sing Lúcás Chan, "Bridging Christian and Confucian Ethics: Is the Bridge Adequately Catholic and Asian," *Asian Christian Review* 5, no. 1 (2011): 49–73.

219. Yiu Sing Lúcás Chan, James F. Keenan, and Ronaldo Zacharias, eds., *The Bible and Catholic Theological Ethics* (Maryknoll, NY: Orbis, 2017).

220. Yiu Sing Lúcás Chan, James F. Keenan, and Shaji George Kochuthara, eds., *Doing Asian Theological Ethics in a Cross-Cultural and an Interreligious Context* (Bengaluru: Dharmaram Publications, 2016).

221. See George Griener and James Keenan, eds., *A Lúcás Chan Reader: Pioneering Essays on Biblical and Asian Theological Ethics* (Bengaluru: Dharmarham, 2017); Michael Cover, John Thiede, and Joshua Burns, eds., *Bridging Scripture and Moral Theology: Essays in Dialogue with Yiu Sing Lúcás Chan, S.J.*; George Griener, "Remembering Lúcás Chan Yiu-Sing," *America*, May 24, 2015, https://www.americamagazine.org/content/all-things/remembering-lucas-chan-yiu-sing; Joshua McElwee, "Pioneering Theologian in Biblical Ethics Dies at 46," *National Catholic Reporter*, May 22, 2015, https://www.ncronline.org/news/people/pioneering-asian-theologian-biblical-ethics-dies-46.

222. Cardinal Oswald Gracias, "Doing Catholic Theological Ethics in a Cross-Cultural and Inter-Religious Asian Context," in Chan, Keenan, and Kochuthara, *Doing Asian Theological Ethics*, 153–60; Clement Campos, "Rooting Christian Ethics in an Encounter with Contextual Resources," in Chan, Keenan, and Kochuthara, *Doing Asian Theological Ethics*, 34–46; Mathew Illathuparampil, "Doing Catholic Theological Ethics in Multi-Religious India," in Chan, Keenan, and Kochuthara, *Doing Asian Theological Ethics*, 168–80.

223. Stanislaus Alla, "*Hindutva @ 90* and the Challenge of Engaging Hinduism," in Chan, Keenan, and Kochuthara, *Doing Asian Theological Ethics*, 83–96; Morris Antonysamy, "Patriarchy, Rape and Brutality: Exploring the Roots of Sexual Violence against Women in India," in Chan, Keenan, and Kochuthara, *Doing Asian Theological Ethics*, 140–51; John Karuvelil, "Structural Legitimization of Dehumanization in India," in Chan, Keenan, and Kochuthara, *Doing Asian Theological Ethics*, 124–39.

224. John Crasta, "The Chotanagpur Tribes as Agents of Environmental Redemption in the Context of the Current Ethical Debate on the Ecological Crisis," in Chan, Keenan, and Kochuthara, *Doing Asian Theological Ethics*, 223–36; Vimala Chenginimattam, "Through Her Eyes," in Chan, Keenan, and Kochuthara, *Doing Asian Theological Ethics*, 305–11.

225. Jose Mario Francisco, "Context in Doing Moral Theology: East Asian Considerations," in Chan, Keenan, and Kochuthara, *Doing Asian Theological Ethics*, 59–72; Anthonette Collado Mendoza, "*Whose Is the Land?* Land Grabbing within the Development Enterprise in Asia," in Chan, Keenan, and Kochuthara, *Doing Asian Theological Ethics*, 111–23; Eric Marcelo Genilo, "Church Power and the Reproductive Health Debate in the Philippines," in Chan, Keenan, and Kochuthara, *Doing Asian Theological Ethics*, 277–90; Christina A. Astorga, "The Triple Cries of Poor, Women, and the Earth: Interlocking Oppressions in the Christian Context," in Chan, Keenan, and Kochuthara, *Doing Asian Theological Ethics*, 250–62.

226. Mary Yuen, "Cross-Cultural Solidarity in the Pro-democratic Umbrella Movement of Hong Kong," in Chan, Keenan, and Kochuthara, *Doing Asian Theological Ethics*, 97–110; Sharon Bong, "A God by Any Other Name," in Chan, Keenan, and Kochuthara, *Doing Asian Theological Ethics*, 181–93; Maurice Nyunt Wai, "Being a Theological Ethicist in a Politically Challenging Environment," in Chan, Keenan, and Kochuthara, *Doing Asian Theological Ethics*, 312–20.

227. Besides Astorga, Karuvelil, and Chenginimattam above, see Bernhard Kieser, "Beyond the Maid Trade: Indonesia Labour Migrants and their Communicative Practice," in Chan, Keenan, and Kochuthara, *Doing Asian Theological Ethics*, 263–75.

228. Joseph Goh, "'Why Is It Wrong?': Conceptualisations of Gay-Wrongdoing and Sexual Ethics among Gay-Identifying Malaysian men," in Chan, Keenan, and Kochuthara, *Doing Asian Theological Ethics*, 347–60. See his *Living Out Sexuality and Faith: Body Admissions of Malaysian Gay and Bisexual Men* (London: Routledge, 2017) and *Becoming a Malaysian Trans Man: Gender, Society, Body and Faith* (London: Palgrave Macmillan, 2020); see also Goh, Sharon Bong, and Thaatchaayini Kananatu, eds., *Gender and Sexuality Justice in Asia: Finding Resolutions through Conflicts* (New York: Springer, 2020). On intersectionality, see Leslie McCall, "The Complexity of Intersectionality," *Signs* 30, no. 3 (2005): 1771–1801; Nancy J. Ramsay, "Intersectionality: A Model for Addressing the Complexity of Oppression and Privilege," *Pastoral Psychology* 63, no. 4 (2014): 453–69.

229. Shaji George Kochuthara, "Ongoing Renewal of Moral Theology in India," *Asian Horizons* 9, no. 1 (2015): 197–214.

230. Yiu Sing Lúcás Chan, "Doing Catholic Theological Ethics: Some Reflections on the Asian Scenario," in *Moral Theology in India Today: The DVK National Workshop on Moral Theology*, ed. Shaji George Kochuthara (Bangalore: Dharmaram Publications, 2013), 101–21.

231. Shaji Kochuthara, "Editorial: *Amoris Laetitia*," *Asian Horizons* 10, no. 1 (2017): 3–8.

232. Shaji Kochuthara, "Biblical Theology: Asian Contribution" *Asian Horizons* 13, no. 3 (September 2019).

233. Juan José Tamayo, "Reception of the Theology of Liberation," in Ellacuría and Sobrino, *Mysterium Liberationis*, 33–56.

234. Penny Lernoux, *Cry of the People* (Garden City: Doubleday, 1980).

235. Arthur McGovern, *Liberation Theology and Its Critics: Toward an Assessment* (Maryknoll, NY: Orbis, 1989).

236. Thomas Schubeck, *Liberation Ethics* (Minneapolis: Augsburg, 1993); "Ethics and Liberation Theology," *Theological Studies* 56, no. 1 (1995): 107–58.

237. Alfred Hennelly, *Theology for a Liberating Church: The New Praxis of Freedom* (Washington, DC: Georgetown University Press, 1988); *Liberation Theology: A Documentary History* (Maryknoll, NY: Orbis 1990); *Liberation Theologies: The Global Pursuit of Justice* (New London, CT: Twenty-Third Publications, 1995).

238. Roger Haight, *An Alternative Vision: An Introduction to Liberation Theology* (New York: Paulist Press, 1989).

239. Dean Brackley, *Divine Revolution: Salvation and Liberation in Catholic Thought* (Eugene, OR: Wipf and Stock, 2004). Brackley coauthored with Schubeck, "Moral Theology in Latin America," *Theological Studies* 63, no. 1 (2002): 123–38.

240. Kevin Burke, *The Ground Beneath the Cross: The Theology of Ignacio Ellacuría* (Washington, DC: Georgetown University Press, 2004); Burke and Robert Lassalle-Klein, *The Love That Produces Hope: The Thought of Ignacio Ellacuría* (Collegeville, MN: Liturgical Press, 2006); Michael Lee, *Bearing the Weight of Salvation: The Soteriology of Ignacio Ellacuría* (New York: Crossroad, 2009).

241. Kenneth Himes, "Liberation Theology and Catholic Social Teaching," *Hope and Solidarity*, 228–41.

242. Gregory Baum, "Structures of Sin," in *The Logic of Solidarity: Commentaries on Pope John Paul II's Encyclical "On Social Concern,"* ed. Gregory Baum and Robert Ellsberg (Maryknoll, NY: Orbis, 1989), 110–17.

243. Peter Henriot, "The Concept of Social Sin," *Catholic Mind* (1973): 38–53; Kenneth Himes, "Social Sin and the Role of the Individual," *Annual of the Society of Christian Ethics* (1986): 183–213; Mark O'Keefe, *What Are They Saying About Social Sin?* (Mahwah, NJ: Paulist Press, 1990); Margaret Pfiel, "Doctrinal Implications of Magisterial Use of the Language of Social Sin," *Louvain Studies* 27, no. 2 (2002): 132–52, at 152.

244. Donal Dorr, *Option for the Poor: A Hundred Years of Vatican Social Teaching* (Maryknoll, NY: Orbis, 1983).

245. United States Conference of Catholic Bishops, *The Challenge of Peace: God's Promise and Our Response* (May 3, 1983), https://www.usccb.org/issues-and-action/human-life-and-dignity/war-and-peace/nuclear-weapons/upload/statement-the-challenge-of-peace-1983-05-03.pdf.

246. Thomas Nairn, ed., *The Seamless Garment: Writings on the Consistent Ethic of Life* (Maryknoll, NY: Orbis, 2008).

247. United States Conference of Catholic Bishops, *Economic Justice for All*, November 13, 1986; https://www.usccb.org/upload/economic_justice_for_all.pdf.

248. David Hollenbach, *Claims in Conflict: Retrieving and Renewing the Catholic Human Rights Tradition* (New York: Paulist Press 1979); *Nuclear Ethics: A Christian Moral Argument* (New York: Paulist Press, 1983); *The*

Common Good and Christian Ethics (New York: Cambridge University Press, 2002); *Justice, Peace, and Human Rights: American Catholic Social Ethics in a Pluralistic World* (New York: Crossroad, 1988); *The Global Face of Public Faith: Politics, Human Rights, and Christian Faith* (Washington, DC: Georgetown University Press, 2003).

249. David Hollenbach, ed., *Refugee Rights: Ethics, Advocacy, and Africa* (Washington, DC: Georgetown University Press, 2008).

250. David Hollenbach, "Catholic Ethics in a World Church: A U.S. View," in *CTEWC*, 140–146.

251. James Cone, *Black Theology and Black Power* (Maryknoll, NY: Orbis, 1969, 1987).

252. James Cone, *A Black Theology of Liberation* (Maryknoll, NY: Orbis, 1970).

253. James Cone, *The God of the Oppressed* (Maryknoll, NY: Orbis, 1987).

254. James Cone, *The Cross and the Lynching Tree* (Maryknoll, NY: Orbis, 2013).

255. Bryan N. Massingale, "Breaking Barriers: Review of *The Cross and the Lynching Tree*," *America*, July 1, 2014, https://epublications.marquette.edu/cgi/viewcontent.cgi?article=1430&context=theo_fac.

256. M. Shawn Copeland, "Critical Theologies for the Liberation of Women," in *The Power of Naming*, ed. Elisabeth Schüssler Fiorenza (Maryknoll, NY: Orbis, 1996), 141–51.

257. M. Shawn Copeland, "Black Political Theologies," in *The Blackwell Companion to Political Theology*, ed. Peter Scott and William Cavanaugh (Oxford: Blackwell Publishers, 2003), 271–87; "Doing Black Catholic Theology: Rhythm, Structure, and Aesthetics," *Chicago Studies* 42, no. 2 (Summer 2003): 127–41; "Tradition and the Traditions of African American Catholicism," *Theological Studies* 61, no. 4 (2000): 632–71; "Method in Emerging Black Catholic Theology," in *Taking Down Our Harps*, ed. Diana Hayes and Cyprian Davis (Maryknoll, NY: Orbis, 1998), 120–44. See also Jamie Phelps, "Inculturating Jesus," in Hayes and Davis, *Taking Down Our Harps*, 67–101; Phelps, "Communion Ecclesiology and Black Liberation Theology," *Theological Studies* 61, no. 4 (2000): 672–99.

258. M. Shawn Copeland, "The Interaction of Racism, Sexism and Classism in Women's Exploitation," in *Women, Work, and Poverty*, ed. Elisabeth Schüssler Fiorenza (Maryknoll, NY: Orbis, 1987), 19–27.

259. M. Shawn Copeland, "The Church Is Marked by Suffering," in *The Many Marks of the Church*, ed. William Madges and Michael J. Daley (New London, CT: Twenty-Third Publications, 2006), 212–16; Copeland, "'Wading Through Many Sorrows': Toward a Theology of Suffering in a Womanist Perspective," in *Feminist Ethics and the Catholic Moral Tradition*,

ed. Charles Curran, Margaret Farley, and Richard McCormick (Mahwah, NJ: Paulist Press, 1996), 136–63.

260. M. Shawn Copeland, *Enfleshing Freedom: Body, Race, and Being* (Minneapolis: Fortress Press, 2008).

261. M. Shawn Copeland with LaReine-Marie Mosely and Albert J. Raboteau, eds., *Uncommon Faithfulness: The Black Catholic Experience* (Maryknoll, NY: Orbis, 2009); *Knowing Christ Crucified: The Witness of African American Religious Experience* (Maryknoll, NY: Orbis, 2018).

262. M. Shawn Copeland, "White Supremacy and the Anti-Black Logics in the Making of U.S. Catholicism," in *Anti-Blackness and Christian Ethics*, ed. Vincent Lloyd and Andrew Prevot (Maryknoll, NY: Orbis, 2017), 61–75.

263. Bryan Massingale, *The Social Dimensions of Sin and Reconciliation in the Theologies of James Cone and Gustavo Gutiérrez* (Rome: Academina Alphonsiana, 1991).

264. Bryan Massingale, "Ethical Reflection upon Environmental Racism in the Light of Catholic Social Teaching," in *The Challenge of Global Stewardship: Roman Catholic Response*, ed. Todd David Whitmore and Maura Ryan (Notre Dame, IN: University of Notre Dame Press, 1997).

265. Bryan Massingale, "The African American Experience and U.S. Roman Catholic Ethics: Strangers and Aliens No Longer?" in Phelps, *Black and Catholic: The Challenge and Gift of Black Folk; Contributions of African American Experience and Thought to Catholic Theology* (Milwaukee, WI: Marquette University Pr, 1998), 79–101.

266. Michael Fahey, "From the Editor's Desk," *Theological Studies* 61, no. 4 (2000): 603.

267. James Cone, "Black Liberation Theology and Black Catholics: A Critical Conversation," *Theological Studies* 61, no. 4 (2000): 731–47.

268. Bryan Massingale, "James Cone and Recent Catholic Episcopal Teaching on Racism," *Theological Studies* 61, no. 4 (2000): 700–730.

269. Bryan Massingale, *Racial Justice and the Catholic Church* (Maryknoll, NY: Orbis, 2010). See also his *Poverty and Racism: Overlapping Threats to the Common Good* (Washington, DC: Catholic Charities USA, 2008); "The Scandal of Poverty: 'Cultural Indifference' and the Option for the Poor Post-Katrina," *Journal of Religion and Society* Supplement Series 4 (2008): 55–72; "Racial Reconciliation in Christian Ethics: Toward Starting a Conversation," *Journal of the Black Catholic Theological Symposium* 2 (2008): 31–57; "Has the Silence Been Broken? Catholic Theological Ethics and Racial Justice," *Theological Studies* 75, no. 1 (2014): 133–35.

270. Elisabeth Schüssler Fiorenza, "Feminist Theology as a Critical Theology of Liberation," *Theological Studies* 36 (1975): 605–26; "Discipleship and Patriarchy," *Feminist Ethics*, 33–65; *In Memory of Her:*

A Feminist Theological Reconstruction of Christian Origins (New York: Crossroad, 1992).

271. Margaret Farley, "Feminist Ethics," *Feminist Ethics*, 5–10; "A Feminist Respect of Persons, *Feminist Ethics*, 164–83.

272. Susan Ross, "Feminist Theology: A Review of Literature," *Feminist Ethics*, 11–31; Lisa Sowle Cahill, "Feminist Ethics, Differences, and Common Ground," *Feminist Ethics*, 184–205; Barbara Andolsen, "Whose Sexuality? Whose Tradition? Women, Experience, and Roman Catholic Sexual Ethics," *Feminist Ethics*, 207–39.

273. See Rosemary Radford Ruether, *Sexism and God Talk* (Boston: Beacon, 1983); Anne Carr, *Transforming Grace: Christian Tradition and Women's Experience* (San Francisco: Harper and Row, 1988); Sandra Schneiders, *Beyond Patching: Faith and Feminism in the Catholic Church* (Mahwah, NJ: Paulist Press, 1991); Elisabeth Johnson, *She Who Is: The Mystery of God in Feminist Discourse* (New York: Crossroad, 1992).

274. Christine Gudorf, *The Body Sex and Pleasure* (Cleveland: Pilgrim Press, 1994); Patricia Beattie Jung, ed., *Sexual Diversity and Catholicism: Toward the Development of Moral Theology* (Collegeville, MN: Liturgical Press, 2001); Aline Kalbian, *Sexing the Church: Gender, Power, and Ethics in Contemporary Catholicism* (Bloomington: Indiana University Press, 2005).

275. Anne Patrick, "Toward Renewing 'The Life and Culture of Fallen Man': *Gaudium et Spes* as Catalyst for Catholic Feminist Theology," *Feminist Ethics*, 483–510; Christine Firer Hinze, "Social and Economic Ethics," *Theological Studies* 70, no. 1 (2009): 159–76; Firer Hinze, "Bridge Discourse on Wage Justice: Roman Catholic and Feminist Perspectives on the Family Living Wage," *Feminist Ethics*, 511–40; Mary Elsbernd, "Social Ethics," *Theological Studies* 66, no. 1 (2005): 137–58; Elsbernd and Reimund Bieringer, *When Love Is Not Enough: A Theo-Ethic of Justice* (Collegeville, MN: Liturgical Press, 2002).

276. Maura Ryan, "Health and Human Rights," *Theological Studies* 69, no. 1 (2008): 144–63; "Beyond a Western Bioethics?" *Theological Studies* 65, no. 1 (2004): 158–78; "The Argument for Unlimited Procreative Liberty: A Feminist Critique," *Feminist Ethics*, 383–401.

277. Mary Jo Iozzio, *Calling for Justice Throughout the World.*

278. Christine Gudorf and Regina Wolfe, eds., *Ethics and World Religions: Cross-Cultural Case Studies* (Maryknoll, NY: Orbis, 1999).

279. See James Keenan, ed., *CEHP* published later also in the Philippines and Brazil.

280. For accounts, see James Keenan, "Introduction," in *CTEWC*, 1–6; Linda Hogan, "Cross Cultural Conversations," in *Applied Ethics in the World Church: The Padua Conference* (Maryknoll, NY: Orbis, 2008), 1–11.

281. Agnes Brazal, Aloysius Cartagenas, Eric Genilo, and James Keenan, eds., *Transformative Theological Ethics: East Asian Contexts* (Quezon City: Ateneo de Manila University Press, 2010).

282. James Keenan, ed., *Catholic Theological Ethics, Past, Present, and Future: The Trento Conference* (Maryknoll, NY: Orbis, 2011); Keenan, "What Happened at Trento 2010?" *Theological Studies* 72, no. 1 (2011): 131–49.

283. Kristin Heyer, James Keenan, and Andrea Vicini, eds., *Building Bridges in Sarajevo: The Plenary Papers of Sarajevo 2018* (Maryknoll, NY: Orbis, 2019).

284. Linda Hogan and Agbonkhianmeghe Orobator, eds., *Feminist Catholic Theological Ethics: Conversations in the World Church* (Maryknoll, NY: Orbis, 2014); Agnes Brazal and Maria Theresa Dávila, eds, *Living With(out) Borders: Catholic Theological Ethics on the Migrations of Peoples* (Maryknoll, NY: Orbis, 2016); James Keenan and Mark McGreevy, *Street Homelessness and Catholic Theological Ethics* (Maryknoll, NY: Orbis, 2019).

285. Kristin Heyer and Linda Hogan, "Beyond the Northern Paradigm: Catholic Theological Ethics in Global Perspective," *Journal of the Society of Christian Ethics* 39, no. 1 (Spring/Summer 2019): 21–38, https://doi.org/10.5840/jsce20193251. James Keenan, "Pursuing Ethics by Building Bridges Beyond the Northern Paradigm," *Religions* 10, no. 8 (2019): 490; https://doi.org/10.3390/rel10080490.

286. "Who We Are," Catholic Theological Ethics in the World Church, accessed May 20, 2021, https://catholicethics.com/who-we-are/.

287. Shirmohammad Davoodvand, Abbas Abbaszadeh, Fazlollah Ahmadi, "Patient Advocacy from the Clinical Nurses' Viewpoint: A Qualitative Study," *Journal of Medical Ethics and History of Medicine* 9, no. 5 (June 11, 2016), https://www.ncbi.nlm.nih.gov/pmc/articles/PMC4958925/.

288. Pope Francis, *Amoris Laetitia* (March 19, 2016), no. 311, https://w2.vatican.va/content/dam/francesco/pdf/apost_exhortations/documents/papa-francesco_esortazione-ap_20160319_amoris-laetitia_en.pdf.

289. Conor M. Kelly, "The Role of the Moral Theologian in the Church: A Proposal in Light of *Amoris Laetitia*," *Theological Studies* 77, no. 4 (2016): 922–48.

Index